FAILURE IN BRITISH GOVERNMENT

The Politics of the Poll Tax

p. 226

Cover back panel: clockwise from top left-hand corner: Margaret Thatcher, Nicholas Ridley, Kenneth Baker, Michael Heseltine, Michael Howard, Chris Patten, Patrick Jenkin, William Whitelaw, William Waldegrave.

FAILURE IN BRITISH GOVERNMENT

The Politics of the Poll Tax

DAVID BUTLER
Nuffield College, Oxford

ANDREW ADONIS
Financial Times

TONY TRAVERS
London School of Economics

OXFORD UNIVERSITY PRESS
1994

Oxford University Press, Walton Street, Oxford OX2 6DP

Oxford New York
Athens Auckland Bangkok Bombay
Calcutta Cape Town Dar es Salaam Delhi
Florence Hong Kong Istanbul Karachi
Kuala Lumpur Madras Madrid Melbourne
Mexico City Nairobi Paris Singapore
Taipei Tokyo Toronto
and associated companies in
Berlin Ibadan

Oxford is a trade mark of Oxford University Press

Published in the United States
by Oxford University Press Inc., New York

British Library Cataloguing in Publication Data

Data available

Library of Congress Cataloging in Publication Data
Butler, David, 1924–
Failure in British government : the politics of the poll tax /
David Butler, Andrew Adonis, Tony Travers.
Includes bibliographical references and index.
1. Poll tax—Great Britain—History. 2. Great Britian—Politics
and government—20th century. I. Adonis, Andrew, 1963–
II. Travers, Tony. III. Title.
HJ4935.G7B87 1994 336.2'5'0941—dc20 94–17140
ISBN 0-19-827875-6 (cloth)
ISBN 0-19-827876-4 (pbk.)

1 3 5 7 9 10 8 6 4 2

Set by Hope Services (Abingdon) Ltd.
Printed in Great Britain
on acid-free paper by
Biddles Ltd
Guildford & King's Lynn

ACKNOWLEDGEMENTS

This book was written with the help of many people. We interviewed most of the principal actors in the events we describe in these pages and many of them were kind enough to comment on parts of our manuscript. Since anonymity was often a condition, we leave them all unnamed, but we are deeply grateful to them. Material cited in the text without references is largely derived from our interviews and comments received.

We owe an institutional debt to Nuffield College, to the London School of Economics, and to the *Financial Times* for much technical help, and to our many friends in these bodies who have assisted us with argument and information. We are particularly grateful to Vernon Bogdanor, Roger Bright, Peter Dickson, Richard Harbord, George Jones, James Kellas, Anthony Mayer, Peter Riddell, and Conrad Russell who read drafts. Hazel Johnstone and Elaine Herman provided invaluable help with word-processing. The responsibility for what follows is entirely ours.

January 1994   D.B.
                                                                          A.A.
                                                                          T.T.

CONTENTS

List of Figures   viii

List of Tables   ix

List of Cartoons   x

1. Introduction   1

PART I THE RISE AND FALL OF THE POLL TAX

2. Prologue, 1377–1984   11

3. Gestation, 1984–1985   41

4. Birth, 1985–1986   70

5. Enactment, 1986–1988   88

6. Implementation, 1988–1990   126

7. Collapse 1990–1994   154

PART II THE POLL TAX AND BRITISH GOVERNMENT

8. Cabinet   187

9. Civil Service   206

10. Parliament   224

11. Public Opinion   246

12. Local Government   265

13. Questions   286

14. Conclusion   302

Appendix 1. Chronology   307

Appendix 2. Key People and Events   313

Appendix 3. Gains and losses by household type
              and income level (1981 Green Paper)   314

Bibliography   316

Index   325

LIST OF FIGURES

5.1 1986 Green Paper: gainers and losers from a community
    charge (1986)   92
11.1 National Newspapers, Poll Tax Coverage (January
    1986–April 1990)   264

LIST OF TABLES

1.1 Key statistics, 1984–1992   6
6.1 Scotland's poll tax levels, 1989–1990   133
7.1 Per cent change in Conservative vote, 1986–1990   162
10.1 Conservative poll tax rebels   236
11.1 Polls on fairness of poll tax   260
11.2 Verdicts on poll tax   260
12.1 Local government finance and manpower, 1900–1980   269

LIST OF CARTOONS

'It's Your Money *We* Want'   16

Mrs Thatcher's Motor Car   57

Mrs Thatcher as Lion-Tamer   112

Lord Whitelaw as Raleigh   124

Poll Tax Christmas Card   135

Mrs Thatcher as Nelson   153

Monkeys Typing   157

Wandsworth and Westminster   161

Three Kings   208

Mutiny on the Flagship   237

Mastermind   278

Poll Tax Hydra   294

Can't Pay, Won't Pay   299

Cartoons reproduced by kind permission of the artists.

1

INTRODUCTION

> It was fundamentally flawed and politically incredible. I guess it was the single most unpopular policy any government has introduced since the War.
>
> Chris Patten, Environment Secretary 1989–90[1]

The poll tax affair is unique. Modern British history offers no comparable instance of a government putting a single piece of legislation so prominently in the forefront of its programme, forcefully implementing it, and then ignominiously abandoning it in the course of a single parliament. The story of the poll tax is fascinating in itself, with its interplay of personalities and institutions, with its muddles and high drama. It was the high-water mark of Thatcherism, and has much to say about that phenomenon. Yet it also provides a classic case-study in contemporary British government and politics, throwing new light on almost every part of the system. An ingenious but flawed initiative of the first importance was allowed to go ahead unchecked, despite all the supposed safeguards and filters of the policy-making and legislative processes. Despite the legendary resources of the British State and law-abiding nature of its people, it proved virtually impossible to implement, mobilizing popular resistance to a degree unprecedented since the General Strike of 1926. And it ended with the dethronement of its sponsor, Margaret Thatcher, the strongest Prime Minister to hold office in Britain since Winston Churchill in the Second World War.

In the pages that follow, we try to tell, in an authoritative

[1] Letter to the authors, Nov. 1993.

way, the story of the poll tax from its origins in the early 1980s to its abandonment in 1991.

The Falklands War, although a military triumph, was the result of a policy disaster. It cost the United Kingdom 1,031 casualties and £350m. in operational costs. The government set up a committee under Lord Franks to discover whether anyone was to blame and whether any lessons were to be learnt. Local disasters, involving train crashes or child abuse, invariably precipitate elaborate enquiries. The poll tax, an aborted policy which, on a modest estimate, cost the country at least £1.5bn. (or over £20bn. if transfers from national taxation are included) and which came close to undermining the whole structure of local government, provoked no such official post-mortem. John Major's government plainly wanted to bury the issue. Even the opposition saw little mileage in pursuing it. This book in a modest way seeks to fill the gap, exploring how the poll tax came about and why it went wrong.

In his memoirs Kenneth Baker claims that the poll tax, as introduced in 1990, was a fundamentally different animal to that created by him in the Department of the Environment in 1985. 'The painful and voracious creature which emerged as the poll tax was not the proposal put forward in my original 1986 Green Paper,' he insists.[2] While not endorsing his account in all particulars, we accept that the 1990 poll tax as introduced was indeed very different from the one envisaged in 1985. But that serves to beg the important questions: how and why? How did it come to be so badly botched in execution? And why did the processes of government prove unable to prevent the mangling? These subsidiary questions pose a further challenge to explain the failure of checks and balances, within and beyond the executive machine.

The first half of the book is a chronicle of the rise and fall of the poll tax. It is a saga that embraces almost every major aspect of the political system: prime-ministerial power; cabinet structure and working; ministerial styles and interrelations; parliamentary processes and efficiency; the role of the civil service; the influence of pressure groups and public opinion; the status

---

[2] Kenneth Baker, *The Turbulent Years* (1993), 138.

and functions of local government; the Union with Scotland; party structures and their ability to shape policy; and, overshadowing all the rest, the very essence of political leadership in Britain. A glance at any formal textbook on British government will show that, among all the conventional divisions of the subject, foreign affairs and defence stand out as the only ones which could not be illustrated by the poll tax story. Even Europe and the monarchy have a place. The neglect, bordering on contempt, for wider European practice in local government and local taxation exhibited by the authors of the poll tax is a telling commentary on Britain's rapport with its continental neighbours in the 1980s; while publicity about the exemption of the Queen from poll tax, and the tax treatment of the royal household, presaged the sustained controversy of the early 1990s over the role and privileges of the royal family.

Accordingly, in the second half of the book we have ventured to turn our study of this one episode into a more wide-ranging essay on the practice and institutions of British government. As with any case-study, we face the problem of representativeness. We are dealing in this book with a unique and shattering event: since the rise of democracy in Britain, few first-order policy initiatives have gone through such a turbulent passage. Perhaps only successive proposals for the government of Ireland, sprawling across the decades since Gladstone's first Home Rule Bill of 1886, compare with it. That very fact justifies the book. It renders the need for an authoritative account compelling. And it makes the lessons to be learnt significant. For with an unwritten Constitution, under which government is conducted largely by custom and practice, the rules of the game are ultimately determined in moments of crisis; only then do the dynamics of the system become fully apparent, enabling politicians to discover whether assumptions and conventions are indeed sacred, as they find out what the political class and public opinion will let them get away with. We do not suppose that the poll tax episode has—or will have—any exact parallel. But we have no doubt that it has left an indelible mark on the British Constitution, and that an examination of what happened can flood light on the way that British government works.

INTRODUCTION

Almost everyone now agrees with Chris Patten, the man charged with introducing the poll tax in England and Wales, that it was 'fundamentally flawed and politically incredible'. It has been repudiated by most of its sponsors. In all our discussions with policy-makers and politicians, which included most of those most intimately involved with the poll tax, the number now prepared to defend it could be counted on the fingers of one hand. Many claimed that they never even supported it at the time; others told us that its design and implementation were so badly botched that abolition was essential, or at least inevitable. Yet it was a policy passed into law after protracted examination by capable politicians and experienced civil servants. It was, of course, opposed by many at the time. But it is not enough to observe that a combination of experts, opposition parties, local government, pressure groups, and protracted parliamentary and public debate failed to halt or modify the reform. Their impotence flowed, in large measure, from their failure to appreciate the extent of its flaws and their inability to offer a convincing alternative vision of the function and funding of local government to the one set out by the Thatcher government.

What went wrong? Are we to blame particular individuals? Or the mood of the time? Or the working of the system? Certainly, the system failed, and the pages that follow offer a devastating critique of the failure. But we have to ask whether it was indeed a fundamentally erroneous policy or whether, with more skilful handling and slower introduction, it might have succeeded. The goal claimed for it, the establishment of really accountable local government, was laudable. Was its achievement frustrated by the headlong start of the tax, full-blown, in 1990, coinciding with the onset of high interest rates and a faltering economy? If in 1987 Nicholas Ridley had not abandoned the staging of its introduction, might not the whole package have proved acceptable? Would it have worked if Nigel Lawson had provided larger Treasury grants, reducing the level of the tax? Or was it, as Chris Patten believes, doomed to fail however it was introduced? The concluding chapters address those questions.

4

Few of those involved come well out of this story. Among leading Conservatives, Nigel Lawson and Michael Heseltine have the cleanest slate. Their opposition to the policy is well documented. Others, who were silent at the time, claim to have been sceptical throughout. But there is no doubt of the enthusiasm of Kenneth Baker and William Waldegrave and some of their civil servants and outside advisers. How important in their deliberations was a sycophantic eagerness to satisfy Mrs Thatcher's well-known desire to end the rating system, and how important were genuine convictions that a great social advance could be achieved by giving every citizen some financial involvement in the level of local government expenditure? Pure politics mixed with a serious experiment in social engineering.

At the outset, however, we need to set the scene. The bare statistics of the period are set out in Table 1.1. The poll tax belongs to what might be termed the 'third wave' of Thatcherism.[3] Mrs Thatcher had come to power in 1979 in the wake of a seemingly disastrous economic and political decade— from Heath's U-turn and the first oil crisis to the IMF visit and the Winter of Discontent. The initial three years of the Thatcher administration—the 'first wave'—were characterized by soaring unemployment and inflation; the prime minister's overriding impulse was a determination not to succumb to the economic and industrial pressures that had destroyed her predecessors. In 1982 the tide turned. Victory in the Falklands brightened the national mood and transformed Mrs Thatcher's standing. The Conservative triumph in the 1983 election was followed by an unmistakable economic recovery and the successful confrontation with Arthur Scargill's miners. In this 'second wave' it was not all plain sailing, but the self-confidence engendered in Mrs Thatcher and her colleagues by the Falklands, by the 'economic miracle', and by their 1983 and 1987 election victories gave the government a greater sense of authority and command than any since Attlee's post-war

[3] See Peter Riddell, *The Thatcher Era and its Legacy* (1991) and Hugo Young, *One of Us* (1993), for compelling single-volume studies of the Thatcher government.

Table 1.1 *Key statistics, 1984–1992*

	Real personal disposable income 1985=100	Year on year inflation %+	Unemployment %	Gross domestic product 1985= 100	Days lost in strikes (000's)	Average party % MORI polls		
						Con.	Lab.	Lib/SDP
1984	97	3.3	11.1	96	27 335	41	38	20
1985	100	4.6	11.3	100	6 380	36	35	24
1986	104	2.4	11.6	104	1 921	37	38	27
1987	108	4.1	10.0	109	3 393	45	34	27
1988	114	6.5	8.1	114	3 699	46	39	12
1989	119	6.4	6.3	116	3 428	40	44	10
1990	125	9.0	5.8	117	1 905	36	49	10
1991	123	4.2	8.0	114	761	40	42	14
1992	125	1.5	9.8	113	528	39	41	16

administration. Privatization, liberalization, and an assault on the institutions of the corporate State were its hallmarks. The government lost by-elections and was periodically behind in the polls. But secure with a landslide majority and a divided and demoralized opposition, Mrs Thatcher met public hostility with undisguised disdain, supremely confident of her capacity to rally support in the only polls that mattered. The 1987 election was the first since 1935—which led to Neville Chamberlain's government—to give a second landslide in a row to the same party.

The precedent ought not to have been encouraging. 1987 ushered in a 'third wave', devoted above all to an increasingly erratic assault on those deemed by the Prime Minister—often in defiance of ardent Thatcherites—to be obstacles to the triumph of Thatcherism. In one sense, it was hubris. By 1987, local government was the only national institution with sufficient power to challenge either the authority or—at a deeper level—the ideology of the Thatcher government. The trade unions were prostrate. Jacques Delors was still a new boy in Brussels. The Berlin Wall had yet to collapse. The professions were introspective, fighting to defend their privileges from

radical assault. The Church of England had fired its last shot—
Faith in the City—and exhibited its impotence and internal
divisions in the process. The universities had done the same
when Oxford, in an extraordinary pantomime, first proposed,
then refused, to award an honorary degree to the Prime
Minister.

Almost alone, local government stood out. The red flag
wavers—Derek Hatton's Liverpool, Ted Knight's Lambeth—
were the most egregious provocation. But they were part of a
wider opposition ascendancy in local government. Hit by successive mid-term revolts in local elections, by 1985 the Tories
were weaker in local government than they had been for a generation. The May 1985 county elections, coinciding with the
key stages in the evolution of the poll tax, took them to a new
nadir. It was hardly surprising that Mrs Thatcher thought
'something must be done' about local government. Her long-
standing hostility to the rates was well known to the ministers
and officials around her; and fresh from her victory in abolishing Ken Livingstone's Greater London Council, she and they
were by now inured to the sound and fury that inevitably
issued from the local authorities themselves. The poll tax followed. A party which had come to power on a wave of revul-
sion against Labour's incapacity to govern almost perished
through the chaos caused by its own dogmatic approach to the
challenge of government.

However, the politics of Thatcherism is only one of the long-
term perspectives required to set the poll tax in context. The
urge to take radical measures to deal with a recalcitrant local
government reflected, in acute form, a tension between central
and local government endemic in Britain's modern political history. Operating within a unitary state with strong local traditions but an unwritten Constitution changeable at will by a
simple parliamentary majority, central–local relations in Britain
have often been fraught. In the past Westminster has relied on
local authorities to deliver ambitious social policies like public
health in the 1920s or large-scale council housing in the 1950s.
But for governments intent, instead, on rolling back social
spending, or slowing its growth, local 'autonomy' has been a

persistent irritant. The more determined the government, the more irritating the autonomy; and none has been more determined than Mrs Thatcher's.

There is, emphatically, nothing new to the central–local dichotomy in British politics exemplified by the poll tax crisis.[4] But until the 1980s the system had always managed to jog along, a tribute to the robustness of the structure created by the great late-Victorian local government statutes of 1888, 1894, and 1899.[5] Under Mrs Thatcher, relations between central and local government suffered a virtual breakdown. The poll tax was the bitter fruit of that breakdown; digesting it was one of the most traumatic experiences of modern British history.

[4] The most influential of recent studies on the theme are: James Bulpitt, *Territory and Power in the United Kingdom* (1983); William Miller, *Irrelevant Elections? The Quality of Local Democracy in Britain* (1988); R. A. W. Rhodes, *The National World of Local Government* (1986); M. Loughlin, D. Gelfand, and K. Young, *Half a Century of Municipal Decline 1935–1985* (1985); Tony Travers, *The Politics of Local Government Finance* (1986); and Patrick Dunleavy, *Urban Political Analysis* (1980).

[5] Ken Young, 'Rationale, Structure, Finance', in S. J. Bailey and R. Paddison, *The Reform of Local Government Finance in Britain* (1988), 7.

PART I

THE RISE AND FALL OF THE POLL TAX

2

PROLOGUE, 1377–1984

> The subjects of every state ought to contribute to the
> support of the government, as nearly as possible, in pro-
> portion to their respective abilities; that is, in proportion
> to the revenue which they respectively enjoy under the
> protection of the state.
>
> Adam Smith, *The Wealth of Nations* (1778)

Three concerted attempts have been made to levy a flat-rate
poll tax in England in the last six hundred years. Two were
introduced within a short period in the fourteenth century; the
third was levied by Mrs Thatcher's government in the late
twentieth. All were abject failures, collapsing amid widespread
evasion and near-universal discontent. The Peasants' Revolt of
1381 produced the greatest absolute level of civil disobedience.
But relative to the standards of the day, the backlash in 1990
was not far behind.

The fourteenth-century poll taxes were levied under Richard
II in 1377 and 1380. The 1377 tax was set at the rate of one
groat (four pence) per adult throughout the country. The 1380
tax was set at the far higher rate of one shilling. According to
the *Oxford History of England*:

in 1380, beyond a vague stipulation that the rich ought to help the
poor, no provision was made for grading. . . . The result was gross
unfairness in the incidence of the tax. In villages where there was a
resident man of means, his poorer neighbours were dependent on his
generosity; in others . . . the poorest labourer might find himself com-
pelled to pay two shillings for himself and his wife. Most objection-
able of all was the conduct of the collectors. A poll tax, being based
on something in the nature of a census, necessitated inquiries into per-

sonal circumstances which could hardly fail to provoke resentment; and the officials were not delicate in their methods.

The result was evasion on a large scale. If we were to take the poll tax returns as our evidence we should have to deduce a fall of one-third in the adult population between 1377 and 1381.[1]

The parallels with 1990 are clear. In virtually every aspect, including the redistribution of the tax burden, administration problems, a reduction in the registered population, and the encouragement of civil disturbances, the 1990 community charge followed a pattern set by its 1380 predecessor. The popular reaction succeeded in repealing the tax on both occasions.

Once it was clear that the yield of the 1380 poll tax would fall well short of what had been expected, officials were appointed by parliament to improve collection. The observation in the *Oxford History* that they were 'not delicate in their methods' is unduly delicate. The age exemption for children worked on the principle that girls were exempt if they were virgin. A certain John Legge, Serjeant-at-Law, insisted on ascertaining this by physical examinations conducted in public. When the peasants revolted the following year, Serjeant Legge was executed on Tower Hill.[2] Yet despite the efforts of Legge and his fellow officials, the collection rate remained abysmal.[3]

The civil disturbances triggered off by the 1380 poll tax are familiar to schoolchildren. The gathering of local people in East Anglia and Kent, culminating in Wat Tyler's march on London in the summer of 1381, constitute the 'Peasants' Revolt'. Poll tax was not the only reason for the uprising, but it was a single issue focusing other discontents, notably failures in the administration of the law and oppression by landlords.[4] The leaders of the revolt were executed, but their achievements were con-

---

[1] M. McKisack, *The Fourteenth Century* (1959), 406–7.

[2] Earl Russell reminded the House of Lords of the events in his speech on the second reading of the 1988 Bill to enact the poll tax. *HL Debs.*, 9 May 1988, col. 901.

[3] C. Oman, *The Great Revolt of 1381* (1906), 29.

[4] C. Dyer, 'The Social and Economic Background to the Rural Revolt of 1381', in R. H. Hilton and T. H. Aston (eds.), *The English Rising of 1381* (1984), 42.

siderable. 'The Peasants' Revolt was the most successful of all movements of resistance to the demands of the crown, and served to ensure that the system of direct lay taxation remained essentially unchanged until the sixteenth century.'[5] Poll tax arrears were written off by parliament later in 1381. Sir Richard Waldegrave, Speaker of the House of Commons, who had himself been a poll tax commissioner in Essex, blamed the failure of the tax on 'dishonest, greedy and violent officials'.[6] His descendant, William Waldegrave, was to be a chief instigator of the next flat-rate poll tax 600 years later.

Succeeding generations regarded the 1381 poll tax as an object lesson in how not to tax. However, by the seventeenth century the collective memory had dimmed sufficiently for parliament to attempt a succession of graduated poll taxes. (Graduated poll taxes had also been levied in the fourteenth century.) Charles I's Long Parliament, faced with an Irish rebellion in 1641, decided to levy a poll tax to fund the army. The Commons 'considered a proposal for a poll tax, apparently on the ground that they could think of nothing else'.[7] (A similar process of elimination led to the 1990 tax.) The levy approved by the Commons was steeply graduated by social status, ranging from £100 for a duke down to 6d. for every person over 16 who was not in receipt of alms. There was a sliding scale for bishops, esquires and gentlemen. Catholics were to pay double.[8]

The 1641 tax was imposed without a census of population or a register of taxpayers. As in 1381, the yield fell well short of expectations. People undervalued themselves socially to reduce their tax bill. 'The graduated assessment, based on men's assessment of their own status, was designed to tax snobbery, but the desire to avoid taxation appeared to be even stronger than the desire for social climbing.'[9] 'Distresses' were imposed on non-payers in the form of goods or livestock, but evasion

---

[5] J. A. Tuck, 'Nobles, Commons and the Great Revolt of 1381', in Hilton and Aston, *English Rising*, 205.

[6] Ibid.

[7] C. Russell, 'England's Last Poll Tax', *History Today* (1987). [8] Ibid.

[9] C. Russell, *The Fall of the British Monarchies* (1991), 336.

was again widespread and the collection alarmingly slow. Debts mounted up. Worse still, debts were increased by interest charges caused by borrowing to anticipate money which was late.[10] Thomas Smith, secretary to the Earl of Northumberland, believed the tax would yield 'a million at least', but by the end of August 1641 only £54,064 had come in.[11]

Cromwell's Commonwealth levied no poll taxes. But the forty years after the Restoration in 1660 saw a succession of poll taxes, all graduated. Most of them were levied in time of war and appear to have been paid grudgingly. The last was in 1698. It was replaced by a land tax which raised more than three times the amount with less disturbance. By now, the moral of poll taxes was clear to all: either they were flat rate and produced riot or rebellion, or else they were graduated and the yield was severely disappointing.

Mrs Thatcher, as a proponent of traditional education, should perhaps have read the history of the poll tax. Problems associated with the major poll taxes of 1381 and 1641 were precise predictors of the difficulties encountered in 1990.

RATING DISCONTENT

Taxation has never been popular, and property rates are no exception. The wealthier subjects of Elizabeth I were as aggrieved by their property taxes as the subjects of the second Elizabeth four centuries later. Nor is there anything new in Tory fears of overspending by left-wing councils. Late-Victorian Conservatives were deeply worried that the introduction of democratic local government would yield councils with working-class majorities determined to soak the rich. Lord Salisbury, whose 1888 County Council Act made the biggest stride towards the modern system, called it 'leaving the cat in charge of the cream jug'.[12]

Salisbury recoiled from blatantly anti-democratic measures, such as extra votes or council seats for larger ratepayers, as

[10] Russell, 'England's Last Poll Tax'.
[11] Russell, *Fall of the British Monarchies*, 336.
[12] A. L. Kennedy, *Salisbury* (1953), 199.

likely to be counter-productive. Nor did he seek to replace the rates with a more regressive tax. Instead he tightly constrained local authority powers on the one hand; and on the other he did his best to make local government 'safe' by keeping it in the hands of the respectable, propertied classes.[13] Aristocratic grandees dominated county government until the interwar years, sometimes beyond. But elected city authorities, particularly in London, soon came to be dominated by variable combinations of 'Liberals', 'progressives', and 'socialists', committed to expensive schemes of municipal improvement. The outcry from the propetied classes was deafening. As the Association for the Protection of Property Owners put it in a widely circulated pamphlet in 1905:

The community is exploited for the benefit of one class, who did not contribute directly to the rates at all. It is impossible for the more substantial ratepayers to obtain fair representation on the local authorities in many parts of London and they have practically become victims to an organised system of plunder.[14]

If rates were an abiding grievance, the sharp expansion of local government responsibilities in the post-1918 decades ensured that resentment remained as fierce as ever.[15] Charged by Salisbury with the drains, dustbins and 'local improvement', by the 1960s councils were responsible for education at all levels, for housing near a third of Britain's population, and for providing it with a plethora of expensive social services. By now health and public utilities had been taken away, but housing and education left local councils the agents of more than a fifth of public spending. Substantial extra funding came from the centre; but, apart from user-charges, all that had to be funded locally fell on the rates. The abolition of the ratepayers'

[13] A. Adonis, *Making Aristocracy Work: The Peerage and the Political System in Britain 1884–1914* (1993), esp. 186–95.

[14] A. Offer, *Property and Politics 1870–1914: Landownership, Law, Ideology and Urban Development in England* (1981), 302–3.

[15] See P. G. Richards, 'The Recent History of Local Fiscal Reform', in S. J. Bailey and R. Paddison, *The Reform of Local Government Finance in Britain* (1988), 25–41.

A London County Council Election Poster 1907

franchise after the Second World War made the relationship between the vote and payment for local services more tenuous than ever.

In 1955 Frank Turnbull, Under-Secretary at the Treasury, wondered on paper whether a per capita tax falling (with some exceptions) on all citizens, as an addition to the rates, would 'touch the pockets of irresponsible voters'.[16] Disquiet about the fairness of the rating system, particularly the rumpus caused by the English revaluation of 1963, led the Macmillan government to appoint the Allen Committee 'to assess the impact of rates on households in different income groups and in different parts of Great Britain'.[17] Its report, published after Labour had taken office under Harold Wilson, showed beyond argument that rates were regressive. Rates amounted to about 8 per cent of the very lowest incomes but less than 2 per cent of the highest incomes.[18] Evidence was cited which would be repeated *ad nauseam* twenty years later as part of the justification for the introduction of a poll tax. The committee received much evidence from the public 'that rates ought to have some relation to the services enjoyed by the individual ratepayer. Retired people without children of school age complain that the greater part of the rates they pay is spent on the education of other people's children.'[19]

The idea that rates should relate to services provided for particular taxpayers was not new. Before the First World War, it was widely believed that they did in fact do so. In 1912 Edwin Cannan wrote: 'it happens in practice that the nearest possible approximation to local rating according to ability and the nearest possible approximation of local rating according to benefit are one and the same thing, namely the rating of persons in respect of fixed property in the district.'[20] Cannan argued that local government services were provided largely for the benefit

[16] Forthcoming book by Charles Raab on local government finance in the 1950s.

[17] Cmnd. 2582. Secretary of State for Scotland and Minister of Housing and Local Government, 1965, p. iv.

[18] Ibid., 141.

[19] Ibid., 48.

[20] E. Cannan, *History of Local Rates in England* (1912), 17.

of owners of property in proportion to the property owned, and property-owners were likely to be able to pay in proportion to the value of their property. In reality, it is unlikely that this was the case even then. But the imposition of major housing and welfare responsibilities on local government massively increased the extent to which some ratepayers paid for services from which they did not benefit directly.[21] And the system of central grants, funded out of national taxation, further confused any possible link between rates and spending. By the 1960s complaints at the unfairness of the system were regularly voiced by Tory activists at party conferences. The relationship between taxes paid and services received was now tenuous in the extreme.

Regardless of theoretical debates about the fairness of rating and the accountability of local government, by the early 1960s rates had clearly become unacceptably onerous for people on lower incomes. With hindsight, the Allen Committee clearly pointed towards the political debates of the 1980s about who should pay for local authority services. The committee argued that rates were 'certainly regressive in their impact on one-person and two-person households'.[22] As a result, the Labour government which inherited the report decided to introduce a system of rate rebates; in addition, by increasing central grants, it reduced the overall rise in rates from year to year.[23]

As Richard Crossman's diaries testify, the 1966 proposals for bigger grants and rate rebates were little more than a short-term reaction to the unpopularity of rates.[24] The Labour government realized there were serious difficulties with the local taxation system, but found no better way of reacting than to disguise the problem with additional central government cash. More positively, Crossman argued that, within the then existing

[21] R. Jackman, 'Local Government Finance', in M. Loughlin, M. D. Gelfand and K. Young (eds.), *Half a Century of Municipal Decline 1935–1985* (1985), 153.

[22] Cmnd. 2582. Secretary of State for Scotland and Minister of Housing and Local Government, 1965, para. 347.

[23] Cmnd. 2923. Minister of Housing and Local Government, 1966, paras. 11–12.

[24] R. Crossman, *The Diaries of a Cabinet Minister* (1975), i. 251, 303.

structure of local government, there was no possibility of a new and fairer local tax to replace the rates.[25] Whether Labour would have introduced a new local tax in the wake of a structural reform is a matter of conjecture; certainly, the Redcliffe-Maud Commission, appointed by Crossman to review local authority structures, was a sufficient excuse for delay. In the process, the last best chance for consensual reform was lost: at a time when far-reaching institutional reform was all the rage, and increases in public expenditure and taxation were accepted by the electorate as never before or since, the government left well alone.

The report of the Redcliffe-Maud Commission, published in 1969, proposed a sharp reduction in the number of councils in England.[26] First Labour and then, after their 1970 victory, the Tories, published their reactions.[27] The new Conservative government decided to move ahead to a system which, although it cut the number of local authorities from over 1,500 to about 500, was significantly different from the one outlined by Redcliffe-Maud. One of the constants of post-war local government reform is the repudiation by governments of both parties of the advice of expert independent committees which they themselves had appointed.

In its report, the Redcliffe-Maud Commission expressed concern that the new local government structure should be supported by an adequate financial system with sufficient revenues of its own. Without financial reforms, local government would be 'cramped and handicapped as a self-governing institution'.[28] The report noted shrewdly:

Since the present local government system took shape at the end of the last century many new taxes have come into being, most of them more productive, progressive and elastic than local government's sole tax, the rates. All of these new taxes have been appropriated by central government.[29]

[25] Cmnd. 2923, para. 5.

[26] Lord Redcliffe-Maud (Chairman) *Report of the Royal Commission on Local Government in England* (1969), *Cmnd. 4040*, paras. 1–5.

[27] *Cmnd. 4276* and *Cmnd. 4584*.

[28] Redcliffe-Maud, para. 527.   [29] Ibid., para. 524.

However, local authority finance was beyond the terms of reference of the Commission, and it was left to a wholly separate exercise to examine the funding of the new structure of local government.

1971: A STAB AT RATING REFORM

Having proposed its new structure for local authorities, the Heath government set up a review of funding. It did so partly in response to pressure from constituency associations, and partly for completeness. As on virtually all previous and future occasions, the financing of local government was examined separately from its structure and functions.

The review led to Peter Walker's Green Paper of 1971. No proposals were made for a new local tax. A number of possible reforms to local government finance were outlined, though these had to be 'set against the Government's electoral pledge to reduce and reform taxation'.[30] As for the rating system: 'Rates have considerable merits as a tax. But they have their defects too. Their effect on individual ratepayers in some cases bears little relationship to ability to pay. The yield does not have the buoyancy required to keep pace with the growth of services.'[31]

The 1971 Green Paper noted another problem with the rates: the large number of people who had earnings but who made no direct contribution to local tax revenue. 'It is pointed out for example that a family which includes several wage earners can nevertheless pay the same rates as the single old-age pensioner who lives next door.'[32] The spectre of the single pensioner living cheek by jowl with multiple wage-earners, which was to dominate the 1980s poll tax debate, thus made its first appearance in an official document. The Green Paper argued that earning non-householders did, in fact, contribute towards local government through their payments of national taxes, which were used, in part, to fund government grants to councils. It went on: 'The proposal most frequently canvassed for making

[30] Cmnd. 4741, Dept. of the Environment, 1971, para. 6.
[31] Ibid., para. 11. [32] Ibid., para. 2.64.

the earning non-householder pay more is that the householder should be surcharged by way of an addition to his rate bill of a proportionate or fixed amount from each earner.'[33]

However, the idea of such a surcharge—a ratepayers' poll tax—was quickly dismissed. It would be 'a big administrative task'.[34] In addition,

the size of the surcharge would have to be arbitrary, but a proportionate levy of more than 20 per cent of the rate bill for each additional earner would be difficult to defend. On this basis, the yield would add no more than about 2 per cent to the total rate bill. About the same yield would be obtained from a fixed levy or poll tax for each earner.

Thus the words 'poll tax' did appear in the 1971 consultative document, but only in an appendix which dismissed the idea out of hand.

No local tax reform was introduced to accompany the structural reforms which took place in 1974 (England and Wales) and 1975 (Scotland). Despite the Redcliffe-Maud Commission's warning that local government would be cramped and handicapped without financial reforms, the Heath government did not change the rating system. By the time it left office, the tide for reform had turned. The 1973 oil shock, and the inflation and industrial strife which followed it, poisoned the environment. It was never to be as favourable again.

So great had been the rise in council spending that by the mid-1970s central government grants were accounting for about 60 per cent of local income. Rates now raised just 40 per cent of each pound spent, with domestic rates making up about half of the total (i.e. twenty pence in the pound). By the time that rebates had been taken into account, some authorities were receiving as little as 10 per cent of their income directly from household ratepayers. Disenchantment with local taxation, exacerbated by the concentration of spending on social provision, gave a powerful stimulus to the development of policy in the Conservative party in the latter half of the 1970s. But the Tories were not alone: the events of 1973 to 1976 had just as great an impact on Labour politics. The 1973 English

[33] Ibid., para. 2.66. [34] Ibid., para. 2.68.

revaluation—the third since the war—substantially redistributed local tax burdens, and structural reorganization in 1974 was accompanied by very large rate increases (30 per cent on average). The resulting outcry led Wilson's Labour government to introduce short-term help for domestic ratepayers.[35] The major rate increases of 1974–5 also stimulated Anthony Crosland, Labour's new Environment Secretary, to set up a committee, chaired by Frank Layfield, to review the whole subject of local government finance. The backdrop was bleak: a national budgetary crisis which led to major cuts in public spending. In 1975 Crosland famously told local authorities: 'the party's over'.[36]

ABOLISH THE RATES?

Meanwhile, the Conservative party's manifesto for the October 1974 general election promised the abolition of domestic rates. This commitment, and a somewhat weaker one in the 1979 manifesto, stoked up pressure from the party's activists, and a hard core of back-benchers, to abandon the rates. The 1974 commitment was made by Mrs Thatcher, in her role as the Conservative party's environment spokesman. It was not her idea; it was the result of Edward Heath's attempt to bolster Tory support among home-owners. Mrs Thatcher herself had no idea how she was supposed to replace the rates.[37] (She was also required to make another, even more dramatic, promise to limit the mortgage rate to no more than 9.5 per cent.) Labour avoided such bold gestures, simply pointing to Layfield's work in progress—though not with high expectations of a permanent solution to what were by now seen as the intractable problems of local government finance.[38]

Layfield's report, published in 1976, remains the definitive analysis of the problems of modern local authority finance. It

[35] N. Hepworth, *The Finance of Local Government* (1976), 101.

[36] The remark was made at a civic luncheon in Manchester, 9 May 1975.

[37] M. Thatcher, *The Downing Street Years* (1993), 644.

[38] A. Alexander, 'Structure, Centralisation and the Position of Local Government', in M. Loughlin, M. D. Gelfand, and K. Young, *Half a Century of Municipal Decline*, 67.

concluded that 'the main responsibility for local expenditure and taxation should be placed either upon the government or upon local authorities'. Of the two it believed the first—local responsibility—was far and away the more preferable. 'There is a strongly held view amongst us that the only way to sustain a vital local democracy is to enlarge the share of local taxation in total local revenue,' it argued, concluding that the best available instrument for the purpose was a local income tax.[39]

Layfield presented Westminster with a straight choice: a financial system which would enhance local democracy or one which would make it clear that central government was to be held to account. The poll tax received short shrift. During the early weeks of Layfield's work, between August and October 1974, the possibility of a poll tax—as an add-on for earning non-householders—was listed among a range of options to be considered. But it was rapidly rejected as a serious contender to replace or supplement the rates.[40] The words 'poll tax' do not appear in the report itself, though the possibility of 'a fixed sum per head' does feature in the context of the problem of the earning non-householder.[41]

The Department of the Environment had discussed a 'poll tax on earning non-householders' in its evidence to the committee[42] and it also produced a table about the financial impact of the move to a poll tax of this kind. The Layfield Committee went back to the arguments about earning non-householders which had previously been examined in the 1971 Green Paper, but it noted that such a flat-rate tax 'would be regressive as between contributors'.[43] Moreover, the 'complications and costs' of administration would be out of proportion to the likely yield and it would be 'difficult to prevent widespread evasion'.[44] There would be insufficient gain in accountability to justify a fixed sum per head for earning non-householders.

[39] *Report of the Committee of Enquiry into Local Government Finance* (1976), 300–1. Cmnd. 6453.

[40] Interview with Professor George Jones, a member of the Layfield Committee.

[41] Cmnd. 6453, 163.   [42] Ibid., App. 1, 124.   [43] Ibid., 163.

[44] Ibid., 164.

The government responded to Layfield in 1977 with a thin and lacklustre Green Paper. By now the Environment Secretary was Peter Shore, notoriously more conservative than Crosland. He rejected Layfield's view that responsibility for local authority spending and taxation should be clearly located either with central or local government. 'The disadvantages of both the centralist and localist approaches are clear', concluded the Green Paper weakly, 'and the Government do not think there is a case for the adoption of either.'[45] In considering possible new sources of local revenue, the government rejected the abolition of rates, citing constitutional objections to doing so. 'To abolish rates and add the burden to national taxation would mean the end of local taxation. A significant source of local income is necessary to preserve local democracy.'[46] In the light of Norman Lamont's decision in his 1991 budget to switch part of the burden of local taxation to value added tax, raising the rate to 17.5 per cent, the Green Paper's observation that 'if the burden of domestic rates was transferred to VAT, the standard rate would be 14 per cent',[47] appears modest indeed.

The issue of earning non-householders, which had led the Department of the Environment to discuss the possibility of a 'poll tax', was dismissed in summary fashion: 'Although earning non-householders do not pay rates directly, all who pay national taxes contribute indirectly to the large part of local spending met by Government grant.'[48] A poll tax was not mentioned by the Green Paper in a section on 'Other Sources of Local Revenue'. Instead, the consultative document's key proposals were (i) to move to capital valuation for domestic rates and (ii) to replace the 'needs' and 'resources' elements of the rate support grant with a single 'unitary' grant. Interestingly, given the failure to soften the financial blow of the new community charge bills in 1990, the government acknowledged the need to provide for phasing in the effects of the move to the new basis of valuation. 'In the more extreme cases . . . permanent arrangements may be made to mitigate the effects of the change.'[49] By 1977 Labour

[45] Cmnd. 6813, Dept. of the Environment, 1977, para. 2.8.
[46] Ibid., para. 6.3   [47] Ibid., para. 6.3.   [48] Ibid., para. 6.6.
[49] Ibid., para. 6.19.

had no parliamentary majority, and could enact neither capital valuation of rates nor a unitary grant. The direct consequences of the 1977 Green Paper and of Layfield were therefore minimal.

The Conservatives, now under Mrs Thatcher's leadership, were also considering local government finance. Mrs Thatcher's views on the rates are well known—'manifestly unfair and unConservative . . . a tax on improving one's home', as she puts it briskly in her memoirs.[50] In 1975, a policy group, chaired by Keith Speed, was set up to examine the rates and possible reforms. The group included Charles Morrison, who was to become one of the community charge's most active opponents within the parliamentary party, and John Grugeon, leader of Kent County Council, who became a strong public opponent of the rates during the early 1980s. Mrs Thatcher made it clear to Speed that she supported a local sales tax as a replacement for domestic rates. However, the group decided that none of the proposed replacements was credible, and the 1979 manifesto commitment on the subject—'cutting income tax must take priority for the time being over abolition of the domestic rating system'[51]—was deliberately intended to row back from the 1974 pledge.

The 1979 manifesto also committed the Tories to reducing public expenditure. During the election campaign, the Conservatives made it clear that major areas of public spending, particularly health, and law and order, would be protected from any real reductions. By implication, reductions would have to be made in provision such as housing, education, and social services if the overall objective of reduced spending were to be achieved. Local government, as the main provider of the latter group of services, would have to make economies.[52]

1979 AND ALL THAT

From the outset, the Thatcher government was determined to reduced local authority spending, as an essential part of its

[50] Thatcher, *Downing Street Years*, 644.
[51] Conservative Party Manifesto, 1979, 14.
[52] T. Travers, *The Politics of Local Government Finance* (1986), 80.

strategy to cut the State down to size and reduce taxation. At this stage, antipathy to local government as such was not particularly evident. Local government had been colonized by the Tories in opposition. Michael Heseltine, appointed as Environment Secretary by Mrs Thatcher to shake up the sleepy Department of the Environment and make it less the advocate for town halls in Whitehall, was far from instinctively hostile to local authorities and their leaders, as he was to show on Merseyside in the wake of the 1981 Toxteth riots. Rather, he saw overblown local spending as symptomatic of the managerial weakness bedevilling government as a whole, central and local. As he put in his 1986 tract *Where There's a Will*: 'In 1979 the pattern of local government had two peculiarities of special interest to me. More councils were under Tory control than ever before; and more people than ever before were employed by local government.'[53]

None the less, Heseltine's inheritance was stark, and he had nothing to offer but further cuts. Labour had cut back the level of grant support to local government from 66.5 to 61 per cent of expenditure. Growth in real current spending had virtually stopped between 1976 and 1979. On taking office, Heseltine immediately announced plans to reduce spending. Local authority spending in 1979–80 was to be cut by 1 per cent in real terms below the level of the previous year. Central grants to local government were to be cut by £300m. in the current financial year, 1979–80. At a meeting with local authority leaders on 31 July, Heseltine announced that spending plans for 1980–1 would be 1 per cent lower in real terms than the revised plan for 1979–80. Within three months of taking office, he had cut spending for 1980–1 by 5.5 per cent in real terms below the level projected by the outgoing Labour government.

To add insult to injury, Heseltine also made it clear that he would take action against local authorities which did not heed the new stringency. Addressing a local authority associations conference in Scarborough in September 1979, he warned that no government, 'of whatever party', would or could tolerate

[53] M. Heseltine, *Where There's a Will* (1990 edn.), 40.

local authorities pursuing their own ends regardless of the expressed views of the government. In November, he announced his intention to take powers to curb 'overspenders'.

The new government was on the move against local authorities. Over the next few years, successive initiatives were pursued in an attempt to reduce local government spending. First came 'transitional arrangements' to penalize authorities which were deemed overspenders in 1980–1. Grant was reduced for such authorities. Then, in 1981, there followed a new 'block grant' replacing the 'needs' and the 'resources' elements of the rate support grant. This block grant was precisely the same one which had been proposed (though called 'unitary grant') by Peter Shore in the 1977 Green Paper. Block grant included an in-built penalty for authorities which spent above a government-determined estimate of their need to spend (called 'grant-related expenditure'). After that came a system of 'targets' and 'penalties', superimposed on grant during 1981–2 to reinforce the effect of block grant.

The government toyed with the idea of going over the heads of councils entirely, and obliging them to hold referendums before committing themselves to extra spending. In 1981 Labour-controlled Coventry held a referendum offering the city's electorate a choice between more services or lower rates. The result was a handsome victory for lower rates. The outcome led Heseltine and Mrs Thatcher to draw up plans compelling councils to hold referendums before proceeding with spending judged 'excessive' by Whitehall.[54] Had they done so, the history of local government in the following decade might have been radically different; but the proposal, in Mrs Thatcher's words, 'drew howls of protest from local authorities and the Tory back-benchers whom they so easily influenced', and was abandoned.[55]

[54] Richards, 'Recent History of Local Fiscal Reform', 25–41.

[55] Thatcher, *Downing Street Years*, 644. Mrs Thatcher resurrected the idea at the height of the poll tax crisis, when she proposed to a cabinet committee that tight spending limits be imposed on all councils, from which they would be excused only if they held a local referendum. Kenneth Baker dismisses it as a 'one-person campaign', and it got nowhere. See Baker, *Turbulent Years* (1993), 137.

The government backed up overall cuts in local authority grants with penalties aimed at particular councils. Expecting rates increases to make councillors unpopular with their electorates, ministers anticipated that councils would cut spending to match cuts in grant. In the event, they failed to do so. Local elections in 1980 and 1981 led to heavy losses for the Conservatives, with Labour taking control of town and county halls. New Labour administrations came to power committed to increase local spending. The struggle between central and local government intensified.

Real current expenditure by local authorities fell slightly in 1980–1 and 1981–2, but it started to rise thereafter. Meanwhile, central government grant fell from 61 per cent of income in 1979–80 to 53 per cent in 1982–3.[56] Against a background of deep recession and unemployment topping three million, the rate rises were keenly felt. Political reaction to the rates was intensified by the large increases imposed in 1981 by authorities which moved from Conservative to Labour control in the local elections. The Greater London Council, which levied a large supplementary (i.e. mid-year) rate during 1981 to fund its cheap fares policy, produced the greatest reaction.[57]

Labour's success in the 1981 Greater London Council election had caused a political sensation. Labour fought against Sir Horace Cutler's Tory administration with the impeccably moderate Andrew McIntosh as leader. Less than twenty-four hours after their victory, the new Labour group summarily replaced McIntosh with Ken Livingstone, previously a little-known Camden council left-winger. This coup, vividly symbolizing not just the divorce between the Tories and local government, but the rise of the municipal left at the expense of old-style Labour 'managers', gave a sharp edge to the politics of local government. In his memoirs, Kenneth Baker pointedly quotes a post-election declaration by Livingstone:

No one will be in any doubt that the GLC is now a campaigning organ and a bastion of power for the Labour movement. Part of our

[56] Travers, *Politics of Local Government Finance*, Table App. 9 and 13.
[57] J. Carvel, *Citizen Ken* (1984), 116–18.

task is to sustain a holding operation until such time as the Tory government can be brought down and replaced by a left-wing Labour government.[58]

Nor was the GLC a case apart. In the other metropolitan counties the Conservatives lost still more decisively, dropping from 380 seats in 1977 to 122 in 1981. That was on top of the 1980 district elections which saw Conservative representation halved in the seats up for election. In Downing Street and at the Department of the Environment, local government was becoming the enemy.

The large rates increases of 1980 and 1981 fuelled pressure within the Conservative Party to take action on the 1974 commitment to abolish domestic rates. Sir Hugh Fraser's Rating System (Abolition) Bill, introduced under the 10-minute rule in December 1981, gained support from Tory MPs of all shades of opinion, including Peter Temple-Morris, Patrick Cormack, and Sydney Chapman on the left, and Teddy Taylor and James Pawsey on the right. While the Bill's sponsors had no alternative in mind, their activities highlighted the Tory rank-and-file's growing frustration with the *status quo*.

POLL TAX IN THE SHADOWS

The government's response was to publish a Green Paper entitled *Alternatives to Domestic Rates*. It covered much the same ground as the 1971 Green Paper and the Layfield Committee: Peter Walker even teased Michael Heseltine that he was just copying his work of ten years earlier. There was, however, one crucial difference, little noticed at the time. One of the major 'alternatives' to rates considered in 1981 had not been examined in 1971 or 1976. This novelty was the poll tax.

The 1981 Green Paper considered four possible local taxes: local income tax (LIT), local sales tax, property taxes, and poll tax. Unlike 1971, when the words 'poll tax' were mentioned only in the context of a tiny levy on earning non-householders, or 1976, when Layfield failed even to mention a poll tax, the

[58] Baker, *Turbulent Years*, 99.

29

1981 Green Paper elevated the poll tax to a co-equal status with the three hardy annuals of LIT, sales tax, and property taxes.

How, in the space of five years, had the unthinkable become the co-equal? The question is not easy to answer. There is no evidence that either Margaret Thatcher or Michael Heseltine personally encouraged such a reform. Mrs Thatcher had favoured a sales tax during the Conservatives' period in opposition up to 1979. Heseltine, among the least ideologically driven of ministers, had shown no interest in a poll tax, and opposed it on every occasion it surfaced.

In early 1980 the Conservative Political Centre published a pamphlet, by John Heddle, Tory MP for Mid-Staffordshire, which discussed a poll tax as a possible alternative to the rates. Noting the 'persistent arguments' which had been put forward in the past in support of a poll tax, Heddle cited it as a 'means whereby earning non-householders can make a direct contribution to the cost of local services'.[59] However, Heddle went on to list the problems: a poll tax would be regressive, unrelated to the receipt of services or ability to pay, difficult to administer, and would be unlikely to produce much revenue. Heddle concluded by remarking: 'one is driven back to the conclusion that local property tax is the least unsuitable form of taxation available to local authorities.'[60]

There had, however, been one authoritative examination of poll tax in the period between the Conservatives' assumption of office and the publication of the Green Paper in December 1981. In 1980, three free-market academics at the London School of Economics, Christopher Foster, Richard Jackman, and Morris Perlman, produced a thoroughgoing analysis of the economics of local government. Their book, *Local Government Finance in a Unitary State*, included a section on poll tax which, at first glance, appeared relatively encouraging:

In the literature of public finance, the superior economic efficiency of a poll tax above other taxes is based on its not being a disincentive to

[59] J. Heddle, *The Great Rate Debate* (1980), 20.
[60] Ibid., 21.

work since its incidence is independent of how much work is done or income earned, and it does not distort how income is spent.[61]

Later in the book, the authors criticized the poll tax on the grounds that 'it offends against common perceptions of equity while [it is] not as efficient as a specific charge,'[62] but they clearly regarded it as a respectable option. The 1990 poll tax, of course, was to be dressed up as just such a 'specific charge'— the 'community charge'.

While there is no evidence that the work of Foster and his colleagues led directly to poll tax appearing in the 1981 Green Paper, there is little doubt that by raising the idea in such an academically respectable source, the authors helped pitch it into the debate about the future of local government finance. Christopher Foster had worked closely with D.o.E. officials during the late 1970s; his views had been noted by key officials in the D.o.E.'s local government finance directorate, not least by Terry Heiser, the department's permanent secretary after 1984 who was behind the invitation to Foster to serve as an assessor to the key departmental 'studies' team which produced the poll tax a year later.[63]

Public discussion of poll tax before the publication of the 1981 Green Paper occurred at the conference of the Rating and Valuation Association in Torquay, where the leader of Kent County Council, Sir John Grugeon, advocated a poll tax on the grounds that it would be highly visible and would improve accountability. Grugeon, a senior local government Tory, had been influential in various Conservative policy groups during the 1970s, including Keith Speed's committee mentioned earlier. He repeated his support for a poll tax in a letter to the *Financial Times* in November 1981.[64]

Alongside Foster and Grugeon, right-wing think-tanks were also thinking the unthinkable. As yet none of them had

[61] C. Foster, R. Jackman, and M. Perlman, *Local Government Finance in a Unitary State* (1980), 220.

[62] Ibid., 233.

[63] M. Crick, and A. van Klaveren, 'Poll Tax: Mrs Thatcher's Greatest Blunder', *Contemporary Record* (Winter 1991), 412.

[64] *Financial Times*, 26 Nov. 1981.

published any reports advocating a move to poll tax. However, one of the doyens of the think-tank world, Madsen Pirie, wrote an article in the *Daily Mail* during October 1981 which proposed a per capita tax. This piece appeared just as civil servants were preparing the final drafts of the Green Paper. The stimulus for the article was a previous discussion at St Andrews University between Pirie and Douglas Mason, a lecturer in the economics department and leader of the Tories on Kirckaldy council. Mason was to become a proselytizer for the poll tax. The *Daily Mail* article, sketchy though it was, gave the right a glimmering of a policy and confirmed the Department of the Environment in its readiness to treat the idea as politically respectable, in Tory circles, at least.

The civil servants who wrote the 1981 Green Paper say they only included the poll tax for the sake of completeness and never remotely considered it a serious runner. On one account, when the tax was discussed, the review group broke out into laughter. 'Try collecting that in Brixton,' said one official. Nevertheless, the poll tax was now *an* option. The influence of Foster, Grugeon, and the Adam Smith Institute had got it that far. The 1981 Green Paper included another tell-tale sign for those attempting to read the runes. The non-earning householder, who had featured in earlier reports, now appeared right at the start. The opening lines of the paper noted

dissatisfaction with the way in which local people contributed to the cost of local services through the present system of domestic rates. Some domestic ratepayers believe that they pay too large a share of that cost, pointing out that other local people who are not householders are not required to pay rates at all.[65]

However, the 1981 Green Paper discussed the poll tax with little enthusiasm. It was genuinely a *green* paper, in the sense that the government was offering a number of possible ways of financing local authorities without any preordained favourite. The Green Paper discussed ways in which domestic rates might be improved and set out three alternative ways of raising local income: local income tax, sales tax, and poll tax.

[65] Cmnd. 8449, Dept. of the Environment, 1981.

The paper proceeded to assess each of the four possible local taxes against a number of criteria—practicability; fairness; accountability; ease of administration; implications for other taxes; financial control; and suitability for all tiers of local government. To be *practicable*, the tax had to be capable of a substantial, reasonably distributed, and predictable yield. *Fairness* meant that a system of local tax 'which is to command wide public support must be seen to be broadly fair' and must therefore 'create a link between the receipt of services and a payment for such provision'. It must be seen to be fair between people in different areas with similar circumstances and must take account of individuals' capacity to pay. *Accountability* would be achieved by a tax which was perceptible and which as far as possible would be paid directly by as many people as possible who benefited from services provided by the local authority. Unacceptable *collection costs* had to be avoided. *Implications for other taxes* had to be kept to a minimum by any local tax, particularly if central and local government were sharing a tax-base. To achieve *financial control*, the local tax would have to produce a predictable yield, preferably without a buoyant tax-base. Finally, it was essential that whatever local tax were used, *every tier* of local government, including parishes, should be able to use it.

Poll tax, according to the government, could, in principle, be levied in a number of different ways. 'For example, it could be levied on every adult, every elector or every person with income.'[66] Thus the link was made between the concerns expressed in previous official documents about earning non-householders and the reality of a proper poll tax on all adults. Examining poll tax in the context of the government's criteria, it scored well on some and badly on others. Possible non-administrative advantages were held to include the fact that poll tax would be very perceptible, would allow close financial control, and could be made suitable for all tiers of local government. However, in a long section on practicability, the Green Paper presciently listed all the dreadful administrative problems which eventually overtook the community charge in the years

[66] Ibid., para 7.2.

following its introduction. Furthermore, it was noted that administrative costs would probably be higher than for rates.

Tellingly, there was no attempt to measure poll tax against the fairness criterion. But the implications of a number of tables and charts published at the back of the Green Paper were unmistakable. This little-publicized research showed (though in a way which looked innocuous) how households would gain and lose because of the move from domestic rates to a poll tax. Thus, for example, a single adult would gain out of the move to poll tax. Such a person on average earnings in England was shown as being better off (i.e. paying less local tax) by an amount equivalent to 1.4 per cent of their net income (over 2 per cent in London). On the other hand, a household with three or more earning adults in England would lose an amount equivalent to 1.2 per cent of their net income.[67] (See Appendix 3.)

While such gains and losses may appear small in percentage terms, the scale of losses for an average-income three-adult household would be relatively large in absolute cash terms because the small percentage would be applied to a relatively large earnings total. By 1990, three average-earners would have taken home between £30,000 and £40,000: an extra 1.2 per cent off their net income meant an extra tax bill of £360 or more. The gains and losses predicted in the 1981 Green Paper came to pass with the 1989–90 reforms in Scotland, England, and Wales. The political reaction to such a redistribution of burden was to play a major part in destroying the poll tax.

The overall tone of the Green Paper was unambiguous. None of the taxes on offer, notably local income tax, local sales tax, or poll tax, was sufficiently robust and effective to replace domestic property rates. 'None of them is easy—no tax is popular,' it concluded. Nevertheless, the intention was to move forward to a system which would remedy the shortcomings of the domestic rating system as quickly as possible. At the very least, the back-benches had been temporarily pacified and the evil day when reform would take place had been pushed off into the future.[68]

[67] Cmnd. 8449, Dept. of the Environment, 1981, 77–8.
[68] Travers, *Politics of Local Government Finance*, 113.

In retrospect, it is extraordinary that such an effective poll tax demolition job should have been overridden within three years by those—including many of the same people—who produced the poll tax. The 1981 Green Paper was not even the last word in the same vein: a parliamentary committee, and yet another government consultation paper, were to say the same thing. There was, however, one significant omen. When the draft of the Green Paper came back to Michael Heseltine's office from No. 10, the following remark was scrawled in the prime-ministerial hand next to a passage on rising local spending: 'I will not tolerate failure in this area.'

Almost immediately after publication of the Heseltine Green Paper, in December 1981, the newly established Environment Committee of the House of Commons decided to use it as the basis for an enquiry of its own. Again, pressure came from Tory back-benchers, who formed the majority: Labour members opposed an enquiry, but the Tories insisted.[69] Evidence was sought from all the leading bodies concerned with local government. The Department of the Environment supplied evidence about responses to the Green Paper which indicated that, out of 1,124 submissions, support for retention of a reformed rating system was almost the same as for abolition of the rates.[70] However, detailed consideration of the evidence shows that the overwhelming majority of those who opposed the rates were private individuals, whereas official organizations and local authorities were equally strongly in favour of retention.

In written and oral evidence, the Department of the Environment took great care to avoid giving the impression that poll tax was either a good or a bad thing. Under questioning from the committee, Tom King, the Minister of State for Local Government, and D.o.E. Under-Secretary Terry Heiser played a straight bat. In response to a question about the costs of using poll tax as a top-up to the rates, Terry Heiser volunteered:

If we start from the perceived unfairness of domestic rates and a perception that a number of people do not pay directly towards the cost

[69] G. Drewry, (ed.), *The New Select Committees* (2nd edn., 1989), 155.
[70] Environment Com. (1981–2), iii. 26.

of services, one of the gains of Poll Tax would be that such people would be seen to pay something; but there would be an administrative cost.[71]

Note the highly conditional wording. Officials took pains to distance themselves even from the simple and widespread accusation that some people were receiving services while paying no local tax. In its written evidence, the D.o.E. was able to provide no overseas evidence of poll taxes in operation at other than very low levels (i.e. under £10 per head). Indeed, it suggested that poll taxes were gradually dying out.

The Environment Committee was also highly sceptical of a poll tax. Tory MPs such as Robin Squire, Norman Miscampbell, and Fergus Montgomery probed on questions about unfairness, evasion, and the lack of foreign evidence. They were rarely satisfied. Squire, an Essex MP but the antithesis of Essex Man, was, between 1986 and 1990, to become one of the poll tax's most consistent opponents. However, the poll tax did get a hearing in some respectable guises before the committee. Christopher Foster, one of the earlier-mentioned authors of the 1980 book *Local Government Finance in a Unitary State*, which had considered the poll tax seriously, argued in his written evidence that poll tax was within his 'inner circle' of serious contenders to fund local government. It would, he argued, have some great advantages: it was probably no more costly to administer than the rates; its yield was predictable; it was at least as visible as rates; and it entailed no problems of equalization. Regressiveness was 'possibly not practically important' since changes in income tax thresholds and other taxation could be made to offset any regressive impact.[72] Foster aired doubts about a poll tax, but they were somewhat perverse, notably his fear that since the more affluent tended to make disproportionate use of local services, they would thus have an incentive to lobby for higher spending once a poll tax had been introduced. However, Foster stressed that the poll tax would be right only as a partial replacement for the rates. He was more cautious

---

[71] Environment Com., ii. 218 (italics added).   [72] Ibid., ii. 76–7.

still in his oral evidence to the committee, saying that he was 'not very enamoured of a poll tax'.[73]

In its report, published just as the Falklands were being retaken in July 1982, the Environment Committee rejected poll tax outright:

The Committee acknowledges that a Poll Tax would have some limited merit as a supplementary tax but is persuaded by the much greater weight of evidence to the contrary and recommends strongly that a Poll Tax, even at a low level, should not be introduced.[74]

And that was that. A prolonged period of official silence greeted the report. In the real world of central–local relations, the war over expenditure was all-absorbing. The Treasury, led by Leon Brittan, Chief Secretary, continued to put immense pressure on the D.o.E. to bring down local authority spending. Each year, in the Treasury's view, local authorities were 'overspending' by a significant margin. Brittan's role in pushing hard for greater control over local government finance was important in generating the political pressure which achieved action.[75] A cabinet committee was set up on 16 June 1982 to consider local government expenditure, rates, structure, and transport.[76] The committee, chaired by William Whitelaw, then Home Secretary, included Leon Brittan and ministers from the departments with local government responsibilities.

The Whitelaw committee considered, *inter alia*, the abolition of the Greater London Council and the six metropolitan county councils. In July 1982, Brittan declared publicly that 'overspending will soon force any government to take further steps in the direction of central control'. A subcommittee of officials was set up, chaired by Terry Heiser, then deputy secretary at D.o.E., including among its members David Heigham, the D.o.E.'s chief economic adviser, Richard Jameson, accountant-general at the Department of Education and Science, and two Treasury officials, Robert Culpin and Paula Diggle. It came up with the idea of rate limitation, though not without protest

[73] Ibid., ii. 83.   [74] Ibid., i. p. xxiii.
[75] G. Jones, and J. Stewart, *The Case for Local Government* (1983) ch. 7.
[76] *The Economist*, 16 Mar. 1985.

from the spending departments. Most ministers on the cabinet committee were hostile to the idea: Michael Heseltine and his deputy Tom King believed that rate-capping would be complicated and unconstitutional. The Treasury, led by Leon Brittan, kept up their pressure for tough action. Environment department officials and ministers came close to despair. Even the Attorney-General, Sir Michael Havers, was called in for advice.

The subcommittee reported to the full cabinet on 17 January 1983 proposing small changes in rates policy, consultation between local authorities and business ratepayers, and the abolition of the metropolitan counties. This relatively limited package was a victory for the cautious D.o.E. line. But it was promptly rejected by Mrs Thatcher. If rates could not be abolished, she wanted a foolproof system of limiting local authority spending. Tom King, by now Environment Secretary (Michael Heseltine had moved to defence), was sent away to produce one: he set Heiser to the task, and by the start of May 1983, a rate limitation scheme was forthcoming, despite deep reservations inside the D.o.E. about its long-term feasibility. Tom King had the consolation that capping might at least make it possible to envisage dropping the cumbersome system of targets and penalties introduced the previous year.

On 9 May, Mrs Thatcher called a general election. Three days later, the cabinet considered Heiser's 'selective' and 'general' schemes of rate limitation. These schemes, plus the abolition of the GLC and the metropolitan counties, were rushed into the Conservative manifesto. Given the constitutional implications of capping local taxation for the first time and of the abolition of seven major city-wide authorities, this was an extraordinarily short and ill-considered process. Ministers reportedly felt 'bounced' into the commitments, but the manifesto deliberately included no commitment to abolish, or even to review, the rating system itself.

The government's reasons for keeping the rates were detailed in a White Paper entitled *Rates*, published in August 1983, soon after the Conservatives' landslide election victory. Patrick Jenkin had succeeded Tom King as Environment Secretary. Jenkin, who lost out to Nigel Lawson in the contest to succeed

Sir Geoffrey Howe as chancellor, had more the air of a permanent secretary *manqué* than of a streetwise politician. But in this
first review he qualified on both counts. *Rates* once again
rehearsed the arguments for and against a number of possible
local taxes, including poll tax. But the result of the governmen-
t's search had been conclusive: rates had to stay. The reasoning
for keeping rates is worth quoting at length, given that precisely one year later, the same government was to embark on a
review which would abandon the rates in favour of the poll tax.
The White Paper explained:

It was clear from the response to the [1981] Green Paper and from
the evidence given to the Environment Committee that no consensus
can be found for an alternative local tax to replace domestic rates. The
Government recognise that rates are far from being an ideal or popular tax. But they do have advantages. They are highly perceptible to
ratepayers and they promote accountability. They are well understood,
cheap to collect and very difficult to evade. They act as an incentive to
the most efficient use of property. . . . The Government have concluded . . . that rates should remain for the foreseeable future the
main source of local revenue for local government.[77]

Mrs Thatcher's government was not renowned for seeking consensus. However, when faced with the widely understood political difficulties of replacing domestic rates, the failure to achieve
any widespread agreement on a new local tax proved an attractive excuse for inaction. In the light of the later political reaction to the 1984–5 Scottish rating revaluation, and to the
subsequent introduction of the poll tax, such caution was fully
justified.

Legislation to cap the rates was duly introduced. As Environment Secretary, Patrick Jenkin conceded that there were constitutional implications arising from such a reform. Nevertheless,
the demands of economic management and the need to protect
ratepayers overrode these theoretical niceties. Senior Conservatives, including the former prime minister Edward Heath and
the ex-Environment Secretary Geoffrey Rippon, as well as
William Benyon and Anthony Beaumont-Dark, spoke out

[77] Cmnd. 9008, Dept. of the Environment, 1983, 14.

strongly against the new powers. But with a landslide majority, such 'wet' opposition counted for nothing. The Rates Act was passed in the summer of 1984 and rate limitation was imposed for the first time in the 1985–6 financial year.

As late as 1983, therefore, rates were seen as an unavoidable fact of life. The 1981 Green Paper, in common with the 1977 and 1971 Green Papers, had led to no new local tax. A 1983 White Paper envisaged rates surviving 'for the foreseeable future'. If Mrs Thatcher's self-styled radical administration, pressed by a Conservative party which hated property taxes, could not find a workable alternative to the rates, who could?

3

GESTATION, 1984–1985

> Much was made of the little old lady in the large house
> left to her by her husband, but living on a modest capital
> or pension. One can only say that any little old lady living
> in a large house during the champagne and marijuana
> housing market of middle-period Margaret Thatcher need
> have done only one thing: sell it for a grotesque, untaxed
> capital gain before going to live in a smaller house and
> pay much less in rates. To say this, however, is to be tire-
> somely rational.
>
> Edward Pearce, *Machiavelli's Children* (1993)

By the summer of 1984, the local government situation was
becoming desperate for Patrick Jenkin. Ken Livingstone badly
worsted Jenkin in his skilful 'Say No to No Say' campaign to
save the Greater London Council. The House of Lords deep-
ened the Environment Secretary's humiliation by wreaking
havoc with his plans to abolish the GLC before the arrangements were in place for the transfer of its responsibilities. And
barely a fortnight after that blow, in mid-July Jenkin was further damaged by his financial settlement with Liverpool, which
was widely seen as a victory for the Militant-dominated council.
'Liverpool millions, Jenkin nil', ran the headline in the normally staid *Economist*.[1] It went on to predict a 'full scale rebellion' in 1985. 'The lesson that will be drawn by councils on Mr
Jenkin's rate-capping list is that the government can be faced
down.'

That is precisely the lesson that was drawn by hard-left
Labour authorities. Creative accounting was spreading fast.

[1] *The Economist*, 14 July 1984.

Department of the Environment officials and local authority treasurers alike were coming to believe that the system of local finance, notably the machinery for determining government grants, was collapsing under the strain of new legislation, particularly the cumbersome regime of 'targets and penalties'.

Kenneth Baker, appointed local government minister under Jenkin in the autumn, describes the department (with a touch of self-interest) as in a 'very demoralised state' on his arrival. Its ministers and officials 'didn't believe that it could actually win anything'.[2] This acute pessimism was underlined by an authoritative report from the Audit Commission lambasting the whole system of block grants.[3] The commission, a creation of Michael Heseltine's first stint as Environment Secretary, was under the direction of John Banham, a self-confessed 'loose cannon' recruited from the consultants McKinsey's, who was to go on to become director-general of the CBI and then, in 1991, to chair the Local Government Commission. As a government-appointed body whose primary objective was to improve local authority economy and efficiency, it was viewed with some suspicion by local government. A report laying bare the baroque deficiencies of block grant, showing how the government was itself impeding local authority economy, efficiency, and effectiveness, was an ideal opportunity for the commission to demonstrate its independence.

The publication of the report in late August 1984 produced a classic 'dog bites master' reaction from the media. Despite some reservations about the detail, local government leaders loved it.

By law, the Audit Commission had to consult the Department of the Environment on the contents of the report, so the department's local government finance officials were well apprised that Banham was about to fire a blunderbuss at the grant system. During the spring and summer of 1984 senior D.o.E. civil servants had several meetings with Audit Commission staff and consultants. Back at their headquarters in Marsham Street, Terry Heiser and his colleagues responsible

[2] Kenneth Baker, *The Turbulent Years* (1993), 98.
[3] *The Impact on Local Authorities' Economy, Efficiency and Effectiveness of the Block Grant Distribution*, Audit Commission, 1984.

for local finance were strengthened in their belief that the grant system would have to be overhauled. As early as April 1984 the D.o.E. had accepted a request from the local authority associations for discussions about the future of targets and penalties.

In considering an overhaul, Terry Heiser's private view was that the existing controls on local government spending were unsustainable. Even with rate-capping superimposed on the expenditure targets, which were in turn superimposed on the block grant system, local authority spending was still increasing. Legal challenges by some councils against their targets penalties were proving costly and troublesome.[4] The government had already lost a case brought by Camden, challenging its grant decisions. Other such cases were being prepared.

D.o.E. officials were keenly aware of other political pressures influencing the Whitehall debate about local government. Patrick Jenkin was fighting for political survival. It was not just the GLC and Liverpool that were producing weekly crises: housing policy, the use of capital receipts from council house sales, and the (as yet unreformed) rate support grant were providing continuous difficulties. Jenkin had announced on 24 July that he intended to cap the rates of eighteen authorities in England in 1985–6. Sixteen of the eighteen were Labour-controlled. Many of these councils started to consider plans for non-compliance with the capping legislation. Leading Labour councillors in London and other urban centres called for illegal action to thwart capping. The confusion which had been created during the spring and summer of 1984 when Liverpool had failed to set a rate was cited as justification for the 'no rate' option. A number of Labour councillors took the view that such a policy would bring pressure to bear on the government to drop capping. There was speculation in the press that the D.o.E. would seek further legislation to deal with the problems created if one or more authorities were to refuse to set a rate.

Local government was only one of the battlegrounds across which Mrs Thatcher's government was confronting the militant left in the summer and autumn of 1984. While Jenkin was

[4] M. Grant, *Rate Capping and the Law* (1984), 13–23.

struggling to hold off Derek Hatton and Ken Livingstone, who had succeeded in league with the House of Lords in prolonging the GLC's life until the spring of 1986, Mrs Thatcher was engaged in mortal combat with Arthur Scargill's miners. For a year from March 1984, pithead violence, intransigent negotiations, and bitter public recriminations led the news night by night.[5] Ultimately these battles divided and weakened the Labour movement, not the government; but in the summer of 1984, the crucial starting-date for the poll tax as a serious policy, such an outcome was far from assured. In Mrs Thatcher's mind—and many of her supporters'—Scargill, Hatton, and Livingstone were all from the same stable, harboured by trade union and local government sanctuaries which it was the mission of Thatcherism to destroy. The unions were her immediate priority; but none of her ministers, least of all the beleaguered Jenkin, could mistake her views on the town hall barons.

TOWARDS ANOTHER REVIEW

The chaotic state of the grant system, coupled with apparent anarchy in some parts of local government, led senior D.o.E. officials to the conclusion, during the spring and summer of 1984, that there should be a detailed review of the grant system. An internal seminar held at the Environment Department during the summer concluded, in the words of a civil servant who went on to become a member of the team which created the poll tax, that 'the grant system was falling to bits'. Patrick Jenkin, whose early career had been at the Bar, recognized the legal danger signals in the capping regime and had no difficulty in accepting the need for such a review. Furthermore, Jenkin was facing a Tory conference in October at which he would almost certainly, from the motions submitted, have to deal with loud demands for further action on the rates. Given his recent humiliations at the hands of Hatton and Livingstone, Jenkin was desperate to find something with which to appease

[5] See M. Adeney and J. Lloyd, *The Miners' Strike 1984–5* (1986).

the party faithful. He knew how well a continuation of the *status quo* plus a bit more capping was likely to go down at the Brighton conference.

On Sunday 2 September Mrs Thatcher summoned the beleaguered Jenkin, and a few colleagues, to a lunch at Chequers to discuss the forthcoming conference. The others present included John Biffen, Nicholas Ridley, and John Gummer, the Tory Party Chairman. As the gathering moved to the drawing-room for coffee, Jenkin proposed another review of the local government finance system.[6] Gummer, who shared Jenkin's fears about the mood of the party activists, gave him strong support.[7] Mrs Thatcher was not immediately convinced: she had already been through the hoops twice, with the 1981 Green Paper and 1983 White Paper, and feared to raise 'expectations that we could not meet'. But, by the end of the afternoon, she had given Jenkin permission to undertake 'studies of the most serious inequities and deficiencies of the present system'. If this sounded tentative, it was; but another meeting at Chequers, held after the party conference, on 28 October, to explain the complexities of the grant system to the Prime Minister, left her 'more convinced than ever of the fundamental absurdities of the present system'.

What Jenkin had in fact done, between these two Chequers meetings, was to light a small fire in the middle of a parched forest. For a year or so, the flames were controllable; within three years they had consumed the entire preceding system of local authority taxation; another three years on, they helped destroy the Prime Minister who ignited them.

It is worth pausing to consider what might have happened in the autumn of 1984. There was nothing inevitable about reform. Indeed, there was initially little cabinet enthusiasm for a review. Even after it had been approved by the cabinet, it might have been sidelined with a few junior D.o.E. officials under the control of one of the department's lacklustre second-rank ministers.

[6] M. Crick and A. van Klaveren 'Poll Tax: Mrs Thatcher's Greatest Blunder', *Contemporary Record*, (Winter 1991) 401.

[7] M. Thatcher, *The Downing Street Years* (1993), 646, from which most of the rest of the paragraph is also drawn.

Even in the hands of senior civil servants and dynamic ministers, it might have concentrated on local authority structure, drawing back from a belt-and-braces reform of local authority finance, especially given the failure of all earlier attempts to find a realistic alternative to the rates. It might have returned to the earlier idea of local referendums. At this early point, it was envisaged that the 'studies' would cover both the funding and structure of local government, as well as its electoral arrangements, so there were several alternative avenues. Furthermore, the political imperative might have weakened, with the party conference over and the GLC *brouhaha* finally drawing to a close.

None of those things happened. Ken Livingstone kept his campaign alive, masterly to the end. The studies were accepted by the cabinet; an exceptionally able team was set up in the Department of the Environment; intellectually powerful and ambitious ministers took charge; and a glittering array of external 'assessors' was appointed to assist the government insiders. Although it had started modestly as an attempt to sort out the grant system, a massive sledgehammer was now brought to bear on a medium-sized nut. Moreover, the political imperative behind the review, far from weakening, was sharply reinforced by a wholly unanticipated development—a political storm in Scotland over the rating revaluation. The studies would have taken place without the Scottish revaluation; but the Scottish controversy gave them a greater urgency, and transformed the climate in which they were to be received by Mrs Thatcher and senior ministers outside the Marsham Street home of the D.o.E..

THE WALDEGRAVE–BAKER 'STUDIES'

Patrick Jenkin announced the 'studies' at the Conservative party conference at Brighton, the day before the Grand Hotel was devastated by an IRA bomb. Back at Marsham Street, a team of officials was put together. While the department was used to undertaking tasks in groups of this kind, the new team was unusual in several respects. The intellectual calibre of those recruited was out of the ordinary. The involvement of an official from the Treasury was exceptional. And the relationship between ministers and civil servants on the review was far less formal than was usual.

Although Terry Heiser was in overall control of the operation, day-to-day responsibility for heading up the review was given to Anthony Mayer, an assistant secretary. As effective head of the review, Mayer reported directly to ministers—unusually for an official of such a relatively junior rank. Mayer was told by Heiser that he could have anyone he wanted in this team. Those selected were, in the words of one close to the review, 'the brightest selection of people ever gathered' to consider local government reform, though an outsider who had contact with them describes them as 'highly educated barrow boys'. They included several other D.o.E. officials, notably Roger Bright, John Smith, and David Lewis. The latter two were talented economists with expertise in local government finance. Two officials were brought in from outside D.o.E.. Jill Rutter, seconded from the Treasury, was a high-flyer who knew and liked the other members of the review team and was keen to take a break from the Treasury. Don Brereton, drawn from the Department of Health and Social Security, had been Jenkin's private secretary when he was Social Services Secretary in the early 1980s. Heiser's Under-Secretary, Peter Owen, who had (together with Heiser) pushed for a review of the grant system, was later added to the team, and eventually took charge of the 'studies'.

Ministerial control over the studies passed from Patrick Jenkin to two junior ministers: Kenneth Baker (Minister of State) and William Waldegrave (parliamentary under-secretary). Jenkin was still weighed down by the GLC abolition and had already told Baker he did not expect to stay in the government long;[8] he was happy to let his junior ministers make the running. Their motivation can only be speculated upon. Certainly, both were exceptionally ambitious, even by the standards of modern Tory politics. The complex subject-matter and

[8] Baker, *Turbulent Years*, 98.

apparent impossibility of finding a solution appealed to William Waldegrave, who believed himself to be one of the cleverest members of the government. Once they had identified the target, both he and Baker were anxious to 'deliver' a solution, and in the process to erase their ungainly 'wet' reputations. In both cases the reputation owed more to close associations with Edward Heath than to any particular policy stance: Baker's formidable presentational skills had no marked ideological bent, while in *The Binding of Leviathan* (1978) Waldegrave had already signed up to much of the Thatcherite agenda. Yet they both had spurs to earn to become 'One of Us', and knew it.

Intellect was bound up with ambition at ministerial and official levels. Waldegrave became the effective ministerial leader of the studies, with Mayer taking control of the civil service team. Both men had worked—though not at the same time—at the Central Policy Review Staff (CPRS), the so-called 'think-tank', under Lord Rothschild. Heiser pushed for experts from outside the Department to be involved as 'assessors' for the studies. Four such assessors were approached and operated as advisers to the studies from November 1984 until August 1985.

At Mrs Thatcher's suggestion, Waldegrave asked Lord Rothschild to become one of the assessors.[9] A millionaire scientist and scion of the banking family, Rothschild was the ultimate Establishment figure: versatile, charming, giving the appearance of effortlessness. He was joined by three other assessors. One was a personal friend, Leonard Hoffmann, a QC who had served on the royal commission on gambling which Rothschild had chaired in the late 1970s. Hoffmann was an assessor only until March 1985, when he was appointed a judge. Waldegrave also asked a retired Glasgow university academic, Tom Wilson, to join the group; he had known Wilson at All Souls in 1974, and was one of a group of Conservative MPs who had been advised by Wilson in the early 1980s. None of Rothschild, Wilson, or Hoffman had any expert knowledge of local government finance. They were simply clever men who

[9] Thatcher, *Downing Street Years*, 646.

48

were linked by their acquaintance with Waldegrave and/or each other. Hoffmann saw himself as a barrister providing a client with disinterested advice; both Waldegrave and Mayer had worked at the CPRS under Lord Rothschild. Moreover, none of them knew much about local government. The CPRS's major report on local government in 1977 had been researched and published after Rothschild had left the think-tank. Nigel Lawson believed it to be 'a fatal invitation':

Rothschild prided himself on having no political judgment: he was above that sort of thing. Unfortunately, William Waldegrave seemed to consider it an advantage that Rothschild would examine the issue with a mind uncluttered by political preconceptions.[10]

However, the fourth assessor was a different character altogether, invited at the behest of Terry Heiser. Christopher Foster was one of the authors of *Local Government Finance in a Unitary State*, the book mentioned earlier as a likely source for the poll tax's inclusion in the 1981 Green Paper.[11] Alone of the assessors, Foster was fully conversant with the complexities of local authority finance in general, and the possibilities of a poll tax in particular. He had lectured in economics at the LSE, been an adviser on local authority finance to the 1974–9 Labour government, served as director of the Centre for Environmental Studies (a D.o.E.-funded think-tank which researched local government), and was, by 1984, a director of Coopers and Lybrand, the accountancy firm, working on the consultancy side. One of those rare birds able to prosper in academe and the business world alike, Foster sent Waldegrave a copy of his *Local Government Finance in a Unitary State* soon after the latter had been appointed a minister at the D.o.E.. Ministers and civil servants at the D.o.E. were well acquainted with Foster and his local government work. Jenkin, too, knew him as one of the team of advisers who had helped him devise the regulatory system for British Telecom when, as Secretary of State for Trade and Industry, he had embarked on the privatization of BT.

The key ministers and officials involved in the studies team

---

[10] N. Lawson, *The View from No. 11* (1992), 570.   [11] See p. 30.

were linked by friendship and had worked together in the past. Baker and Waldegrave had served together in Edward Heath's private office following the February 1974 general election. Waldegrave had been a member of Rothschild's 'think-tank' during the 1970s. Indeed, he had once been engaged to Rothschild's daughter, and the two were extremely close. Rothschild was a friend of Lenny Hoffmann, whom he asked to be appointed as an assessor. Rothschild was also head of the Central Policy Review Staff when Anthony Mayer had been seconded there; Mayer left the civil service to work at Rothschild's bank at the end of 1985. Waldegrave had worked on a pamphlet with Tom Wilson, and the two had known each other at All Souls, Oxford. Terry Heiser, who instigated the studies in 1984, was a personal friend of Mayer, Roger Bright, Jill Rutter, and Peter Owen. Christopher Foster had helped Heiser at D.o.E. during the late-1970s. The team—apart from the assessors—worked in harmony: ministers and officials even played bridge together.[12] The sense of camaraderie, even of mission, was unusually strong for a departmental policy review.

WORK BEGINS

The civil servants, headed by Mayer, started their work in early October 1984. Terry Heiser had given them six months to sort out local government finance, though at this early point, their brief included both finance and structure. Their terms of reference were to review local government with the aim of increasing accountability. Mayer, with long experience of local authority finance, was well acquainted with the limited options available.

The team moved at breakneck speed. This was no old-style committee or commission where the great and the good pored over widely collected evidence for months or years. As if to stress the break with previous ways of working, no effort was made to talk to Sir Frank Layfield, chairman of the departmental committee which reviewed local authority finance between

---

[12] Crick and van Klaveren, 'Poll Tax', 404.

1974 and 1976. Few people in Britain had a better grasp of the issues involved, but Layfield's advice was deliberately not sought.

In the first days of the team's work, William Waldegrave led brainstorming sessions, after which papers would be produced on topics selected for more detailed examination. The officials trawled back through the 1981 papers, some of which had been written by team members themselves. The work was separated into a number of distinct topics, including local taxation, the grant system, non-domestic rates, and the structure of local government. The assessors did not attend the early meetings, but were in some cases asked for detailed assistance with the topics under consideration.

Two ideas guided the studies team from the outset. The first was that if local electors knew the true cost to them of their local authority, they would seek to influence its spending decisions through the ballot-box—and generally in a downwards direction. All the team members believed that the combination of an excessively complicated grant system and a two-tier structure of local government left local electors in the dark when it came to ascribing responsibility for rate increases. The Audit Commission had noted in its report on block grant that authorities were, in effect, playing the grant system for financial advantage.[13] The need for improved accountability soon became an article of faith within the review.

The second guiding idea was equally simple, and led directly to the poll tax. Those who voted for local government were different from those who paid for it: if all electors received a tax bill, accountability would work properly. Until then it was bound to be defective. Again, the back-up statistics were compelling. Of every pound spent by local authorities, roughly 50p was funded by central government through the—flawed—grant system. Of the 50p financed locally, 25p was paid by business ratepayers (mostly by companies which, of course, had no vote). Thus, only about 25p in the pound was paid by household ratepayers. Of the 25p contributed by householders, about 5p

[13] Audit Commission, 1985, 18.

was paid by the government through rebates. Thus, only about 20p was, on average, directly paid by domestic ratepayers for a pound's worth of spending. 'The tax base was too narrow and the burden of rates fell on too few shoulders,' concluded Baker.[14]

Looked at another way, of the 40 million electors in Britain, only about 18 million-odd were billed as ratepayers. Because of rebates, some 3½ to 4 million households received full or partial rebates. Therefore, perhaps as few as 14 million people paid rates out of 40 million. In many Labour-controlled inner-city areas, the proportions were even more skewed: businesses were in some cases paying 75 per cent or more of all rates, while over half of domestic ratepayers were on rebates. Moreover, several of Labour's inner-city authorities were in the hands of radical left-wingers who were intent on waging a bitter war with the government over a wide range of political issues, notably rate-capping. One of those involved in the studies noted that there was 'growing anarchy' in local government at this time, and also 'minimal incentive in many local authorities voluntarily to keep down spending or rates because someone else would pick up most of the tab'.

The issue of non-householders, who benefited from local services while making no direct local tax contribution, had been raised before. The 1971 Green Paper, the Layfield Committee, and the 1981 Green Paper all mentioned the perceived unfairness of the rates with regard to earning non-householders and non-earning householders. Placing them at the forefront of their minds, Baker and Waldegrave persuaded themselves that a fundamental injustice was at stake, the eradication of which required abolition of the rates. Typically it took the form of the 'little old lady', or 'widow', living next door to a household of several wage-earners, where both households paid the same rates bill.

It is hard to exaggerate the political potency of the 'little old ladies' to the poll tax debate. As a beleaguered minority, they excited the anguish of everyone involved in the review; and

---

[14] Baker, *Turbulent Years*, 116.

as an image in the minds of Tory politicians, they usurped rational thinking on the subject of the pros and cons of different taxes, and the capacity of rebates to iron out flagrant anomalies. Almost every Tory politician—and several officials—we encountered invoked for us the spectre of the widow (always a widow, usually aged) living next door to the family of father and several earning sons (always sons, often strapping). Significantly, the tale of two neighbours appears almost identically in the memoirs of both Mrs Thatcher and Kenneth Baker. Mrs Thatcher writes, apropos her mailbag:

I witnessed a chorus of complaints from people living alone—widows for example—who consumed far less of local authority services than the large family next door with several working sons, but who were expected to pay the same rates bills.[15]

As for Baker:

An elderly widow on a limited income could find herself paying the same high rates as a similar house next door where there were three wage-earners who could easily share the cost between them.[16]

Were Tories being deluged by letters from elderly widows unable to pay their rate bills, or was it a convenient, tear-jerking justification for a change decided upon for other reasons? In reality, probably neither the one nor the other. Undoubtedly there *was* a constituency of aggrieved pensioners, many of them widows, who faced large rates bills for family homes, and whose savings made them ineligible for rebates. Some of them doubtless wrote to their MPs, pointing the finger next door, though our questions to Tory MPs about constituency correspondence have not revealed an abundance of such letters. Of far greater significance, it appears, was the fact that Tory constituency executives were disproportionately composed of such people—pensioners, particularly *single* pensioners, who never ceased to complain about their rates bills. When Tory MPs said they were subject to 'strong

---

[15] Thatcher, *Downing Street Years*, 644.
[16] Baker, *Turbulent Years*, 115.

constituency pressure' to 'do something about the rates', further questioning usually ascertained that the pressure came most strongly from their constituency parties, particularly at social and other events involving the older members. At no point, whether in the review or in the parliamentary debates, were any figures produced about the number of hard-pressed pensioners unable to claim rebates which would make their rates bills manageable. Nor does it appear that anyone—not even Mrs Thatcher and Kenneth Baker—ever attempted to procure any.

One of the studies team's assessors had long been concerned with the distortions caused by the grant system, by non-domestic rate contributions, and by non-ratepaying voters. Christopher Foster had commented as early as 1977 on the unacceptability of the then open-ended grant system, and had advocated arrangements which penalized high-spenders.[17] (It was precisely such a system which, by 1984, was in a mess.) Then, in 1982, Foster, writing with Richard Jackman, advocated setting an authority's grant entitlement each year, once and for all. At the same time, non-domestic rates should be set nationally at a uniform level across the country.[18] They argued that a grant fixed irrevocably at the start of the financial year would end the practice of grant allocations to individual councils changing radically within a financial year, with perverse incentives built into the system. Fixing non-domestic rates nationally would remove the possibility that councillors could exploit local business ratepayers. Thus, if grant *and* business rate income were fixed by central government at the start of the financial year, the full impact of marginal changes in local authority spending changes would fall on the local tax. Accountability of local authorities to their electors would be radically improved: such would be the 'gearing' of increases in spending to increases in local tax on the smaller local tax-base, it would be possible to remove rate-capping and the target system.

[17] Foster, 'Central Government's Response to the Layfield Committee', paper given at the 1977 CIPFA Conference, 10–12.
[18] C. D. Foster, and R. Jackman, (1982), 'Accountability and Control of Local Spending' in *Public Money*, 2/2.

These proposals proved so appealing that the review team picked them up almost at once, and the 1982 Foster–Jackman proposals were precisely those adopted by the team at a relatively early point in their deliberations. So the first part of the final set of proposals was in place well before Christmas 1984.

The poll tax was slower in coming. It had its first outing in November 1984 during a visit to Scottish Office civil servants. As we shall soon see, Scotland was perceived by Scottish Office ministers to be seething with discontent against the rates. When raised by the review team with Scottish Office officials, the poll tax 'fell on extremely stony ground', in the words of one member.

None the less, it was becoming increasingly attractive to the review group. Its members all knew how few local tax options were available. Nothing had changed since 1981: the possibilities remained local income tax (LIT), local sales tax, property tax, and poll tax. It was almost immediately clear that local income tax was a dead duck. Mrs Thatcher was dedicated to cutting income tax: it was inconceivable that she would accept the imposition of perhaps 5p on the basic tax rate, particularly if it gave the hated local authorities greater fiscal freedom. The Treasury would also fight LIT to the death. When it had been considered in 1981, only George Younger had supported it. Also, few people would pay LIT in areas where there was high unemployment, i.e. the same inner city authorities that were piling it on the rates. From the start, LIT was consigned to the dustbin. As Kenneth Baker put it: 'I was not in favour of giving Labour City Councils the immense power of a redistributive tax: that would be one way of establishing a Labour Chancellor of the Exchequer in town halls'.[19]

Of course, that argument was just as applicable to property rates. Rates were, according to a civil servant on the team, 'beyond the terms of reference of the studies'. But even if their abolition was not predetermined, it was soon clear from ministers that they would survive only if nothing better could be found.

[19] Baker, *Turbulent Years*, 118.

Local sales tax had been supported by Mrs Thatcher in opposition in the 1970s. But the disadvantages so cogently argued against sales tax in the 1981 Green Paper still held good. Britain was too small a country for authority-to-authority variations in local sales tax: the public would 'border-hop' to buy their goods in low-tax areas, which could lead to substantial distortions in business location. 'If London had one level [of sales tax] and Surrey had another then you could envisage butter being smuggled over Epsom Downs,' quipped Kenneth Baker.[20]

That left poll tax. By a process of elimination, poll tax came to occupy the review in November and December 1984 as a possible local government tax. At this point, a per capita tax was considered only as a supplement to the rates. Between December and March it moved from being a supplement to being a possible replacement. The staging is important. From discussions with officials on the review, it seems highly unlikely that at the outset it would have been treated seriously by civil servants as a full replacement for the rates; but having adjusted to the idea of it as a *supplement*, it was fairly easy to envisage it as a tax able to bear the weight of all *additional* spending. From there, it was a relatively short step, in intellectual terms at least, to accepting it as the sole local authority tax.

The short logical steps did not stop there. As soon as the poll tax got to the stage of being accepted as a tax at all, the administrative and accountability arguments against having the rates running alongside militated strongly in favour of straight substitution. And once it was accepted that substitution was the aim, the same arguments were deployed first to reduce, then to abolish, the transitional period when the two taxes would run in tandem. 'Obfuscation' was a word much in vogue in the review. A system of rates plus poll tax would obfuscate accountability. So would dual running. So would exemptions for the poor. It was to take three years and three Environment Secretaries to get from the first step to the last, with successive ministers making what appeared to them to be the next, small, logical move.

[20] Baker, *Turbulent Years*, 117.

But why was the poll tax ever treated seriously even as a supplement? It was a process of elimination, coupled with a powerful motivation to find an alternative to the rates, and Rothschild and Waldegrave's capacity to think the unthinkable. Christopher Foster played a key role in the process. 'He did not propose it as a solution particularly vehemently: it was simply that when the other options were ruled out one by one, Foster would explain how a per capita tax was perfectly workable.'[21] The wider political background also needs to be appreciated. It was not just the battles with the hard left: by the mid-1980s, the government was accustomed to pioneering radical reforms which proved unpopular at first but soon defied the critics and gained general acceptance. Privatization is a case in point; in that field, ironically, none was stronger for defying public opinion than Nigel Lawson. In his memoirs he writes:

In advance of every significant privatisation, public opinion was invariably hostile to the idea, and there was no way in which it could be won round except by the Government going ahead and doing it. Then

---

[21] Crick and van Klaveren, 'Poll Tax', 403.

THE RISE AND FALL OF THE POLL TAX

when the scare stories which had been so luridly peddled by the Opposition . . . were proved to be unfounded, the private sector status of the industry concerned became accepted as a fact of life.[22]

Most of the ministers involved thought it would be the same with the poll tax.

The motives of those who instigated the reform varied considerably. Senior officials at the Department of the Environment, supported by Jenkin, were hoping that they could sort out local government finance in general, and end the crisis over 'targets and penalties' in particular. Kenneth Baker and William Waldegrave wanted a solution to the rates problem which would convince Mrs Thatcher that they were 'one of us'. The external assessors, none of them dedicated Thatcherites, were genuinely seeking to bring their disinterested advice to bear on the process: in so far as they had any personal or professional motives (Foster was knighted in 1986), they were tied up with being 'useful' to ministers, not in producing the poll tax in particular. Team members—young officials from D.o.E., the Treasury, and DHSS operating outside traditional civil service conventions—clearly relished the intellectual challenge of being able to brainstorm, with all the status and freedom which that offered civil service high-flyers. Indeed, one member of the team saw the exercise as Waldegrave re-creating a think-tank akin to the old Central Policy Review Staff.

By Christmas 1984, then, the modest 'studies' which Terry Heiser and Peter Owen had argued for during the summer had taken on a life of their own. One close to the team claims that Heiser and Owen were 'left behind by the monster they had created'. Further brainstorming sessions and meetings between ministers and the team, supplemented by papers from the external assessors, led to the evolution of a range of options between November 1984 and January 1985. In just twelve weeks the team concluded:

(i) that the promotion of accountability of local authorities to their electorates was the overriding issue;

---

[22] Lawson, *View from No. 11*, 201.

(ii) that the full marginal effect of changes in a council's spending should fall on local taxpayers;

(iii) that many local electors were, unfairly, making no direct contribution towards the cost of local services;

These conclusions were closely related to the ministerial preoccupations described earlier. By late January 1985, three clear policies had emerged. First, there was the Foster–Jackman proposal that the non-domestic rate should become a national tax, set by the government, and assigned to local authorities; and that grant would be fixed before the start of the financial year to ensure that the full marginal effect of council spending decisions fell on local taxpayers. Second, there was a poll tax as a supplement to the rates, which appeared to offer a promising way of promoting accountability. Third, there was the creation of unitary authorities and a more transparent grant system, also intended to promote accountability.

To consolidate progress, a seminar was organized for 3 February 1985 at the Capital Hotel in Knightsbridge, central London. Appropriately enough, the D.o.E. officials who attended had to get away early from the farewell lunch for their retiring permanent secretary, Sir George Moseley, who was succeeded by Terry Heiser. All the leading lights were present: Jenkin, Baker, Waldegrave, Rothschild, Foster, Wilson, Hoffmann, Heiser, Owen, Mayer, Bright, and Rutter. Michael Ancram, George Younger's deputy at the Scottish Office, also attended. The Scottish Office was by now becoming keenly interested in the studies, as the controversy surrounding the rating revaluation north of the border continued unabated.

For the first time, extensive use was made of visual aids, with a slide presentation by Mayer and Bright. Rothschild was strongly convinced of the importance of good presentation: at the CPRS he insisted that his staff 'stood before Ministers with screen, slides, and pointer, and took them through the cases that the CPRS wanted to put across'.[23] Slide shows were to become a regular feature of official and ministerial efforts to sell

[23] T. Blackstone and W. Plowden, *Inside the Think Tank* (1990), 50.

their ideas about the reform of local government finance. Kenneth Baker prided himself on being a good ad-man, with a flair for presentation.

If the team leaders were convinced of the need for effective oral and visual presentation, they were less enthusiastic about written material. No papers were circulated in advance of the Capital Hotel meeting. It was feared that they would leak. Several of those who attended, particularly Tom Wilson and Leonard Hoffmann, had no advance warning of where the studies were leading. When they sat in a stuffy hotel room on that mid-winter Sunday afternoon, the evident momentum towards a per capita tax and 'marginality'—the principle that the full impact of council spending decisions should fall on local taxpayers—came as a surprise to them.

The thrust of the presentation at the Capital Hotel was that the marginal tax burden should fall on the whole electorate. No final decision about the move to a poll tax was made at this point. Even if the idea was becoming irresistible, it was not yet inevitable that poll tax would be the only local tax. Ministers and officials could see different ways of incorporating a per capita tax. It could, for example, have been an add-on to the rates bill to reflect the number of adults (possibly only those with incomes) in the household. It could have been added on to the rates bill to fund that part of a council's spending which was in excess of a government-set bench-mark. A third option was to levy a per capita charge on each household weighted by the value of the property occupied. A fourth idea, increasingly favoured by the team as the weeks went on, was to introduce a poll tax alongside a modernized property tax. Spending would be divided between different kinds of services, with poll tax funding 'people-related' provisions such as education and personal social services, while the property tax funded 'property-related' provisions such as fire services, roads, and waste collection. However, the team accepted that a rating revaluation was politically unacceptable, and it followed that any modernized property tax would have had to be on a new basis, preferably the total floorspace of each home.

The conviction that a rating revaluation would be a non-starter was founded on the experience of the revaluation in Scotland, which was proceeding in tandem with the review in London. Panic in the Scottish Office and beyond at the political impact of the revaluation provided critical momentum to the poll tax in the spring of 1985. We must therefore leave Waldegrave and his colleagues for a while and move north of the border.

THE SCOTTISH REVALUATION REBELLION

Conservative activists had long hated the rates, north and south of the border. But for as long as increases in rates bills could be kept down, and a redistribution of the rates burden harmful to middle-class Tory voters could be avoided, rates reform was an issue that could be left alone. Periodic denunciation of the status quo by Tory leaders was enough, coupled with wringing-of-hands at the impossibility of finding a workable alternative.

In England the background rumbling, though getting louder, never broke into a full-scale storm. A revaluation of all rated property might have caused an eruption, given the relative increase in the value of property in the south-east since the previous valuation in 1973. But Michael Heseltine avoided the storm by the simple expedient of deferring a revaluation in England and Wales *sine die*. 'We've got this problem,' Heseltine is said to have prefaced a conversation with Mrs Thatcher about the question of an English revaluation after the Tories took office in 1979. 'There's no problem,' she countered swiftly. 'We're not doing it.'

In Scotland, however, the option of 'not doing it' was not on. Until 1985, Margaret Thatcher's Scottish Secretary was the diffident but determined George Younger, a Winchester-educated Scot from a prominent Tory family. Despite a lack of ideological zest, Younger's no-nonsense manner and old world courtesy appealed to Mrs Thatcher—a relationship similar to that she had with Lord Carrington, her first Foreign Secretary. Ignorant of Scottish politics, she gave Younger a fairly free rein north of the border. None the less, on the question of local government finance his freedom of manœuvre was far less than Heseltine's, since by statute a revaluation had to take place every five years unless parliament voted explicitly to defer the revaluation. The last revaluation had taken place in 1978; the next was due in 1983. With an election imminent, Younger postponed the revaluation. But, as he put it, 'after the one post-ponement, we were simply running out of excuses and had to go ahead in 1984.'

The 1984–5 revaluation in Scotland was the trigger for an outburst of bitter hostility to the rates north of the border. So far as the government was concerned, the hostility was medi-ated mostly through the Scottish Conservative party—which, by now pushed back into its suburban and rural heartlands, served to magnify and distort it. The previous revaluation had taken place under a Labour government, and its net effect was a mar-ginal shift in the rates burden away from residential property and towards industry, minimizing the repercussions inside the Conservative party. There was no such defence in 1985. The revaluation was authorized by a Tory Scottish Secretary; the main losers were middle-class home-owners—in other words, Scottish Tory voters; and the failure to put in place either an effective phasing scheme for losers, or a generous scheme of transitional relief, increased the backlash.

In global terms, the revaluation was hardly seismic. The rate-able values of Scottish households rose by about 260 per cent, industrial values by about 170 per cent, commercial values somewhere between the two. After the revaluation the average Scottish domestic rates bill was still only £406. The share of total rateable values ascribed to householders increased from about 37 to 42 per cent—in effect a 14 per cent increase before inflation, council spending decisions, and adjustments to gov-ernment grant. However, with all three of those forces pressing rate demands sharply upwards in 1985, householders were faced with huge relative increases in rates bills, particularly in areas (i.e. most of the cities) with Labour councils. Edinburgh house-holders, for example, had to cope with a rates increase of 40 per cent between 1985 and 1986; in Barnton, the city's most affluent suburb, the rates bill for a large, four-bedroomed detached bungalow rose from £1,600 to £2,347.[24] Again, it was the elderly pensioners who called the tune. The affluent south Edinburgh district of Morningside, part of the constituency of Michael Ancram, the junior Scottish Office minister with responsibility for local government, was reputed to have a higher proportion of elderly, single ladies than anywhere in Scotland. As a senior Scottish office official of the time put it: 'the basis of the poll tax was the old ladies of Morningside living in six-bedroomed family houses who had no children at home and only had their bins emptied once a week.'

The Scottish Office failed to foresee the effects of the redistribution, and was 'taken completely by surprise', according to one close observer. George Younger was widely blamed, not least by Mrs Thatcher.[25] In fact, it was only in November 1984 that the first indications of the trend of the revaluation came through from the assessors. In an attempt to forestall the impact, Younger ended industrial derating; it was not until February 1985 that the full impact became clear with the publication of the revised valuations. 'The rates assessors kept their cards close to their chests,' insists a minister at the time. 'We simply didn't know until February what the full impact would be, by when it was too late to ensure immediate phasing or other relief.'

Local Tory associations 'went berserk', in the words of one MP. Yet far from dampening down the protest, senior Tories stoked it up, notably Sir James Goold, the Tories' abrasive Scottish chairman, appointed by Mrs Thatcher, who made alarmist public statements. Goold even waved his own revaluation form at one interviewer. Younger and Ancram summoned Goold to London for a dressing-down, not omitting to point out to him that in his own case he had confused his new rateable value with the far less extra he would actually have to pay once the rate poundage had been set (a common confusion fuelling the protest). Goold backtracked a few steps in public,[26] but the damage had already been done. Mrs Thatcher had been

---

[24] *The Economist* 2 Mar 85; *Sunday Times*, 1 April 1990.

[25] Thatcher, *Downing Street Years*, 647; Baker, *Turbulent Years*, 115–16.

[26] *Scotsman*, 25 Feb. 1985.

briefed privately by Goold in mid-February, and at the end of the month she held a meeting to discuss the situation. 'Scottish ministers, businessmen and Tory supporters began with one voice to call for an immediate end to the rating system,' she recalls.[27]

The political impact of the Scottish furore was further heightened a month later with a visit by William Whitelaw, Mrs Thatcher's long-suffering deputy, to the affluent Glasgow suburb of Bearsden. Bearsden was the first parliamentary seat Whitelaw had fought in the 1950s; he was the constituency association's honorary president and put in regular appearances on its golf-courses. It was home from home. But when he spoke to a largely Tory audience in the constituency, he was persistently heckled about the revaluation. On his own account, it was his second worst reception by a Tory audience in his entire career (the worst being the 1981 Tory conference as Home Secretary), and he was severely shaken. Bearsden Tories paid the bulk of their rates to Labour-controlled Strathclyde regional council, dominated by socialist Glasgow. This made the revaluation truly a 'double whammy': they faced increases in absolute terms, and the redistribution of the domestic rates burden away from city centres and towards the suburbs made them, so they thought, still more vulnerable to 'robbery' by the Glasgow Labour party.

To cap it all, in the same week as Whitelaw's visit to Bearsden Labour won a safe Tory regional council seat comprising a quarter of George Younger's highly marginal Ayr constituency. Younger recalled: 'Following Willie's visit there was a right royal rumpus. Mrs Thatcher was keenly aware of what would happen if her old ladies in Finchley suddenly found themselves facing a ten-times increase in their rates bills.'[28] Note, again, the 'old ladies'.

What Younger and Whitelaw wanted was a replacement for the rates. And they wanted it in March 1985, just as Waldegrave's review team had come up with what it regarded as a viable alternative. The congruence of the two developments

---

[27] Thatcher, *Downing Street Years*, 47.   [28] *Sunday Times*, 1 April 1990.

was to drive the poll tax over its first major hurdle—prime-ministerial approval.

FROM THE CAPITAL HOTEL TO CHEQUERS

Scotland was not, however, the only external 'shock' pushing Mrs Thatcher to embrace the poll tax. During the early months of 1985 councillors in many of the highest-profile Labour authorities in the country were settling down to defy the government. Nine of the eighteen councils capped for 1985-6 failed to set their annual rate by the end of April 1985, well beyond the start of the financial year. By 31 May Camden, Lambeth, and Liverpool had still not set a rate. In the end, Lambeth and Liverpool set their rates so late that the district auditor served notice that financial losses had been incurred because of the delay. Councillors from the two authorities—led by 'Red Ted' Knight—were eventually disqualified and surcharged as a result of their actions.[29] The legal challenges occurred well after the decision for the poll tax had been taken; but the acrimony was fully evident by March.

However, getting the infant per capita charge of the Capital Hotel into a full-blown poll tax was a considerable task. It was not achieved without sharp disagreements emerging between the team and its advisers. Eight weeks elapsed between the presentation of the team's work at the Capital Hotel on 3 February and the next, crucial, point in the genesis of the 1990 poll tax: an all-day meeting with Mrs Thatcher at Chequers on 31 March.

There was little disagreement at the Capital Hotel about the broad thrust of the team's conclusions: the grant system needed reform and more people should contribute towards the costs of local services. Soon after the Capital Hotel meeting the studies team firmly opted for a poll tax, either as part of or as the whole of a new tax, as the only serious way forward. The team's work now turned to the various options for the tax, the

[29] T. Travers, *The Politics of Local Government Finance* (1986), 164-71.

practical difficulties involved, and the question of whether it should be a supplement or replacement.

The team soon concluded that the 'mixed tax' options were administratively awkward and incomprehensible to the electorate. So the prime aim of clear accountability would not be achieved. William Waldegrave was the first to be fully convinced that a simple poll tax was the best answer.

By early March a full-fledged poll tax, to be known as the 'personal charge' or 'resident's charge' had emerged. The nomenclature was important, as the reformers were increasingly leaning intellectually towards the notion of making all adults pay a 'charge' for their local services. Accountability would thus be strengthened by a direct relationship between payment and the receipt of services. At this stage it was envisaged that the charge would come in at a low level—about £50—and run alongside rates for a period of up to ten years.[30] It was not even clear to all members of the review that the poll tax would completely replace the rates at the end of that period.

At this critical juncture the assessors were marginalized from the review. Rothschild, Hoffmann, Wilson, and Foster had all been at the Capital Hotel, but—apart from one further, fruitless, meeting in August—they were consulted only individually after that. That was probably because of the four of them, two were more or less opposed to the poll tax, and a third (Rothschild) at best lukewarm in favour. Only Christopher Foster appears to have been fully on board,[31] providing the intellectual justification for the poll tax and the new grant arrangements as a way of improving accountability by ensuring that everyone paid towards the full marginal cost of a council's spending. Victor Rothschild blew hot and cold. Tom Wilson was highly sceptical, and seriously considered resigning as an assessor once the idea of a per capita tax emerged as the key outcome of the team's work. Leonard Hoffmann shared many of Wilson's concerns about poll tax. He wrote a detailed opin-

[30] Baker, *Turbulent Years*, 119.
[31] After the Chequers meeting Foster tried hard to persuade Lawson of the virtues of the poll tax. See Ch. 4 below.

ion, which Lord Rothschild had published and circulated—in neat red covers—in early March.

Hoffmann's decision to write a detailed paper on the issues at stake was wholly consistent with the view he had of his involvement in the process. Refusing to be swept up in the self-generating enthusiasm of the studies team, he regarded the government as a client to be advised and warned. Remarkably, given that he had no local government background, his paper succeeded in predicting most of the consequences of the poll tax. He accepted the government's premiss that accountability was the key to making local authority finance work. He also accepted that differences between local authorities' expenditure needs should be taken into account by the grant system, but that the use of complicated formulae to assess the rate support grant undermined accountability and in reality provided largely arbitrary levels of funding designed to tackle social deprivation. Cruder measures of deprivation, assessing needs in terms of a flat-rate payment per head, would probably be just as fair overall, and bolster accountability. Every pound of spending above the basic, standard, level would then fall on local domestic taxpayers.

However, when it came to the local tax which was to bear the burden, Hoffman could see no alternative to the rates that was not open to still more serious failings. A poll tax, he argued, would

require wholly new administrative machinery and will undoubtedly be more difficult to collect than rates. Its principal advantage is that it will be paid by rich and poor alike, thereby increasing accountability. On the other hand, this advantage will be bought at the cost of greater administrative costs and the unpopularity bound to be caused by the introduction of an overtly regressive tax.

The advice could not have been clearer: poll tax was a non-starter.

Incredibly, Victor Rothschild circulated Hoffmann's paper to some, though not all, of the ministers and those directly involved in the studies team. It is not clear what criteria Rothschild used in deciding who should receive it. Tom

Wilson, a fellow assessor, was not sent a copy, perhaps because his own opposition was by now overt. Even more remarkably, Patrick Jenkin, who was still Environment Secretary, never saw the paper, though the officials in the team did so. The team prepared a brief about it for Baker and Waldegrave. Mrs Thatcher was sent a copy, and wrote to Rothschild describing it as 'most lucid', which Hoffmann took to mean that she did not agree with its arguments. Hoffmann now believes that the document should have been more forceful, rather than simply providing a wet blanket at a time when the review team was becoming more and more strongly committed to poll tax. As for Rothschild, his precise views remain an enigma. He was not entirely happy with the poll tax, but if he sympathized with his friend Hoffmann's objections, he did not put his name to the dissenting paper, or to any other. He may not even have said the same thing to different people: certainly, those involved recollect him as for and against in almost equal numbers.[32]

In any event, by now the studies team was not to be deflected. Patrick Jenkin arranged with the prime minister to present the team's findings at the end of March, and preparation for this meeting became all-absorbing. New and improved slides were made up. Baker and Waldegrave talked to Jenkin about how they should get their message across to Mrs Thatcher, who was notoriously impatient when dealing with proposals for new policy. Waldegrave, Rothschild, and Heiser went to the Cabinet Office to practise in front of Sir Robert Armstrong, the Cabinet Secretary. The officials also took care to prepare the arguments and materials necessary to put on a good show for the cabinet. The presentation on 31 March would be the first that any member of the cabinet—with the exception of Patrick Jenkin—had seen of the studies.

A few days before the 31 March meeting, an event took place almost as important as the presentation itself. Willie Whitelaw, fresh from Bearsden, saw Mrs Thatcher and told her something

[32] For what it is worth, shortly before his death in 1990 Rothschild told Kenneth Rose, his biographer, that Mrs Thatcher was 'going around saying that "Victor devised the poll tax"'. He assured Rose that in fact he had supported a local income tax. Crick and van Klaveren, 'Poll Tax', 408.

had to be done urgently to tackle the rates. Whitelaw's intervention, signifying as it did the readiness of the 'solid mass' in
the cabinet and party to line up behind reform, registered with
Mrs Thatcher's highly sensitive political antennae. The only
commentator to realize this at the time was Peter Riddell of the
Financial Times, who wrote that at a ministerial meeting on 25
March Whitelaw 'shocked' colleagues with his report on of the
strength of feeling in Scotland on the issue, describing his
three-day Bearsden visit as 'one of the most uncomfortable
political experiences of my life'.[33] Riddell believed Whitelaw's
intervention was a 'key influence on the prime minister's decision to order quicker decision-making about the rating system
reform in Britain'. But even he did not realize how close the
decisions were to being made.

[33] *Financial Times*, 28 Mar. 1985.

4

BIRTH, 1985–1986

It was a colossal error of judgement on her part to seek to
turn a form of taxation which had been notorious
throughout the ages into the flagship of her Government.
Yet it is quite untrue to say that her Cabinet colleagues
were 'bounced' into accepting it.
          Nigel Lawson, *The View from No. 11* (1992)

For a first-rank policy with far-reaching ramifications, the poll
tax had a remarkably short pregnancy: little more than a month,
to be precise. But it would be quite wrong to suggest—as did
many a Tory in the wake of Mrs Thatcher's downfall—that the
birth was attended only by Mrs Thatcher and a few select par-
tisans. On the contrary, virtually the entire cabinet approved
the idea well before it came up for formal cabinet endorsement
in January 1986.

Nearly half of the cabinet went to the Chequers meeting on
Sunday, 31 March 1985 at which, in Mrs Thatcher's words,
'the community charge was born'.[1] In addition to the Prime
Minister, there was Lord Whitelaw, Patrick Jenkin, George
Younger, Nicholas Edwards (Welsh Secretary), Douglas Hurd
(Northern Ireland Secretary), Leon Brittan (Home Secretary),
Peter Rees (Chief Secretary to the Treasury), and Lord Young
(Minister without Portfolio). The party chairman, John
Gummer and the junior Scottish Office minister, Michael
Ancram, were also there. Kenneth Baker and William
Waldegrave presented the findings of their team. Other than
the Cabinet Office secretariat, only three civil servants and one
assessor were present. Lord Rothschild was the assessor. Terry

---

[1] M. Thatcher, *The Downing Street Years* (1993), 648.

Heiser and Anthony Mayer were on hand to provide technical information and answer questions. Barry Hart, a junior D.o.E. official, was present to operate the visual aids.

There were three notable absentees from Chequers. The first was the Chancellor of the Exchequer, Nigel Lawson. In his autobiography, Lawson explained, in characteristic terms:

> I was of course invited. I never liked giving up a Sunday in this way, and having been assured that this was simply a preliminary discussion at which no decisions would be taken, I foolishly decided not to go and to send Peter Rees, then my Chief Secretary, in my place. Before leaving for the weekend, I briefed him to register my firm opposition to a poll tax, and gave him the arguments to use.[2]

Lawson had not been approached by the team or its ministers at any time before Chequers. Jill Rutter, as a middle-ranking Treasury official in the team, was presumably giving her colleagues some idea of the way things were progressing, but there had, by the end of March, been no direct discussion with the chancellor about the proposed reforms.

The second absentee, at least as significant in stature, had not even been invited—namely local government. Neither at Chequers, nor at any of the preceding review meetings, were any local authority representatives present. In the case of the Labour-dominated local authority associations, the failure to consult might be understandable, given the context. In the case of Tory leaders of local authorities, it was more bizarre. And the absence of a single senior local authority treasurer, past or present, can only be described as wilful negligence. 'It didn't seem at all odd to us not to have any local government people there,' said one of those involved. 'After all, they were the problem.' But a senior Treasury official drew a parallel with tax changes piloted by his department, where the Inland Revenue or other relevant agencies would be engaged from the outset, acting as a firm practical check on wilder ideas and making clear the financial 'cushion' needed to ensure successful implementation.

The third absentee was the Adam Smith Institute, or any

[2] N. Lawson, *The View from No. 11* (1992), 571.

other right-wing pressure group. In terms of the decisions taken in March 1985, pressure from Whitelaw, Younger, and the ministers at the Department of the Environment for an alternative to the rates was far more important than the overtly ideological attachment to the poll tax coming from the likes of Michael Forsyth, then an obscure back-bencher, let alone from Douglas Mason, the St Andrews economist whose Adam Smith Institute pamphlet setting out the detailed case for a poll tax did not appear until *after* the Chequers meeting.[3] Mason worked as a part-time adviser to Allan Stewart, industry minister at the Scottish Office. But he spoke to no other senior Scottish Tories besides Stewart, and in March he had 'no idea' that the tide had turned decisively towards the poll tax. It was not until a Sunday TV interview by George Younger in the late summer that he knew for sure.[4]

That, however, is not to say that the pro-poll-tax lobby was unimportant, still less that the motivation of Whitelaw and the others was unideological. All the ministers involved agreed on the same overriding priority: to reduce the rates burden on Tory supporters quickly, and to do so without increasing income tax. The poll tax appeared an ideal vehicle for the job, and the fact that it did so owed much to the popularization of the idea in Tory circles by the ASI and others. In the 1981 Heseltine review, George Younger is known to have favoured a local income tax; Mrs Thatcher had earlier favoured a local sales tax; by 1985 they both readily went along with the poll tax.

THE CHEQUERS MEETING

Kenneth Baker opened the Chequers meeting with a detailed exposition of the inadequacies of the existing system of local

[3] *Revising the Rating System* (ASI, 1985). Forsyth's pamphlet, *The Case for a Poll Tax* (Conservative Research Centre, 1985), drafted by Mason, appeared a few weeks later still.

[4] Douglas Mason next hit the headlines in June 1989 with an Adam Smith Institute plan to uproot Hong Kong and move its people to the remote west coast of Scotland as a solution to the problem of what to do with the colony post-1997. 'A colony the size of Hong Kong would scarcely be noticed,' he wrote. As yet (1994) he has not succeeded in matching the poll tax triumph with a remarkable departure in colonial policy.

government finance. The arguments are by now familiar: local elections were ineffective mechanisms for ensuring accountability; large numbers of single pensioners were living next door to multiple earners; rates were unfair because only a majority paid them; worse still, the overall system of local authority finance did not provide a pound-for-pound relationship between changes in spending and changes in local taxation. As a result of the failings of the system, many people could vote for services for which they did not pay. There were unfairnesses as between individuals and areas. Local government spending had risen inexorably. Colour slides, with numerous tables and pie-charts, were used for illustration, and the chairs in the Chequers drawing room were arranged theatre-style for better viewing. As with the earlier Capital Hotel meeting, no papers were circulated before or at the meeting.

Following Baker's presentation, William Waldegrave moved on to the team's proposed reforms. The package would, he said, right the wrongs which Baker had so effectively highlighted. The first key element in the package was to ensure that, in future, the full marginal cost of a council's spending fell on local taxpayers—the Foster–Jackman 1982 critique described in Chapter 3.[5] Central grant to local government would be set and fixed before the start of the financial year. Non-domestic rates would be set by central government and allocated to councils by formula.

The second of Waldegrave's proposals was for a new 'city grant' to direct the greater part of the resources needed for equalization between authorities. Third came a recommendation to improve accountability by a single tier of unitary authorities and annual local elections.

The poll tax was the fourth proposal. As presented by Waldegrave, the plan was that domestic rates should be replaced by a combination of a modernized property tax and a poll tax, with the poll tax gradually taking an increased share. It was estimated that an average poll tax of £140 per adult would have been necessary fully to replace domestic rates. (The actual

[5] See p. 54.

figure for England in 1990 was to be £360.) There would be rebates for the poor, but not paid in such a way as to shield any local taxpayer from the marginal effect of council spending decisions. Waldegrave finished his exposition with carefully chosen words suggested by Patrick Jenkin: 'and so, Prime Minister, you will have fulfilled your promise to abolish the rates'.[6]

After Baker and Waldegrave had laid out the results of their team's efforts, Michael Ancram, who had arrived late with George Younger because of a plane delay, added his view about the importance of the reform for Scotland, following the disastrous revaluation. In fact this was the first time that either Ancram or George Younger had seen the review team's ideas in detail. Although officials from the Scottish and Welsh offices had been consulted by Mayer and his colleagues, they played virtually no role in the development of the plans. When Ancram had said his piece Younger chipped in: 'all my political life I have been waiting for this'.[7]

Many of those present at Chequers remember that Waldegrave was the most enthusiastic supporter of the poll tax. Indeed 'he hardened up the people element [i.e. the poll tax] during the presentation to Mrs T', according to one observer. What had been created, and what clearly appealed to Waldegrave, was a theoretically elegant way of ensuring that every adult made a direct contribution towards the cost of each marginal pound of council spending.

A lengthy discussion followed the presentations, during which the only official present from the studies team was Mayer. The proposal to move to single-tier authorities was rejected outright: 'we could not do everything at once,' says Mrs Thatcher.[8] Annual local elections were 'put on the back-burner',[9] from which they never subsequently shifted. But on the funding proposals, the package received prime ministerial

[6] K. Baker, *The Turbulent Years* (1993), 122; M. Crick and A. van Klaveren, 'Poll Tax: Mrs Thatcher's Greatest Blunder', *Contemporary Record* (Winter 1991), 409.

[7] Baker, *Turbulent Years*, 122.　　　[8] Thatcher, *Downing Street Years*, 649.

[9] Baker, *Turbulent Years*, 123.

endorsement, and vocal or tacit support from almost everyone else present. Peter Rees, singing from his master's hymn-sheet, politely laid out the Treasury's opposition to anything resembling a poll tax; indeed, he said, the Treasury could see little wrong with the rates. Leon Brittan raised the question of civil liberties, queried the issue of the register for the tax, and worried that it might be seen as a tax on voting. The question of administrative costs was also discussed, to which the D.o.E.'s reply was that the new tax would cost more to collect than rates, but not a 'great amount' more. But one of the D.o.E. ministers said it was easily collectable, and at the end of what one of those present describes as a 'triumphal and historic day', Mrs Thatcher was enthusiastic. Waldegrave and his colleagues were congratulated by the Prime Minister and invited to develop their ideas into a full-fledged scheme.

However historic in retrospect, there was still nothing inevitable about the poll tax after the Chequers meeting. The proposal had yet to go through the cabinet process, and the Chancellor of the Exchequer had yet to have his say. But the idea of a poll tax—now increasingly referred to as the 'resident's charge'—as a straightforward replacement for domestic rates had gained powerful prime ministerial support. There was no effective opposition from any of the ministers present at Chequers. The poll tax moved from being an option to being the most likely way forward. The momentum was becoming irresistible: the degree to which that was so is evident from internal Whitehall memos of dissent, written only weeks after Chequers, which take the form of proposals to mitigate the worst effects of the tax.

Mrs Thatcher had not, as is widely believed (even by Patrick Jenkin on the evidence of his advice to Waldegrave about the closing remarks of his Chequers presentation), been obsessed by her government's failure to abolish domestic rates. Her 1974 promise to abolish the rates was made at the behest of Edward Heath. Between 1974 and 1979 she leaned in favour of a local sales tax to replace the rates, and the Tories' 1979 manifesto was deliberately worded to sideline the issue.[10] The 1983

[10] See Ch. 2.

manifesto included no commitment to abolish rates, merely to cap the rates of high-spenders. As late as September 1984 Patrick Jenkin had had to convince her that a review of local government finance was worth the time and effort. She hated the rates, and jumped at the chance to get rid of them. But she had no inclination to leap into a void, or to run huge risks. On the basis of the Baker–Waldegrave presentation, and the support of Whitelaw and Younger, she confidently believed she was doing neither.

At Chequers Mrs Thatcher was convinced by the work of Baker, Waldegrave, and their quasi-think-tank that a workable replacement for the rates had, finally, been found. The radical nature of the proposals appealed to her. She had been *converted*; and with the zeal of a convert, her pragmatic cynicism about the impossibility of abolishing the rates was replaced with an equally strong belief that something could be done. As late as mid-May the *Guardian* was reporting that 'the debate [within the cabinet] over a poll tax as a partial replacement for the present system is likely to be bitter'.[11] In reality, the debate within government was practically over by the end of the Chequers meeting on 31 March. The bitterness was to come in implementing the decision.

NIGEL LAWSON ATTACKS THE POLL TAX

By the dawn of April Fools' Day 1985, then, the poll tax had gathered powerful momentum. It did not, however, gather Nigel Lawson. Having given Peter Rees his marching orders, the Chancellor was taken aback to read, over his leisurely breakfast on the day of the Chequers meeting, an article in the *Sunday Times* entitled 'POLL TAX PLAN TO EASE RATES'. The article suggested that a poll tax of £120 per adult would be introduced as a replacement for a large part of the rates. Business rates would be capped, and the package of reforms would be likely to form part of the next Conservative election manifesto. Lawson describes the upshot:

[11] *Guardian*, 11 May 1985.

Once I found out from Peter Rees what had happened at the Chequers meeting I was horrified . . . it was clear to me that the idea of replacing domestic rates with a poll tax would be a political disaster. I asked William Waldegrave to come round and see me privately at Number 11 and told him as much. He noted my dissent but defended his ideas vigorously, apparently confident that there was considerable Prime Ministerial momentum behind them. This prompted me to explain the political dangers as I saw them to Margaret directly at one of our regular bilaterals. She played down the advanced state of the discussion, assuring me that I would be a member of the Cabinet committee responsible for the reform of local finance and that I could lay all my objections before it.[12]

Lawson accordingly set to work on a counterblast to the Baker–Waldegrave plans, hoping to sink the poll tax in the first cabinet committee on the subject scheduled for late May. Forewarned, ministers at the Department of the Environment sent Christopher Foster to No. 11 in an attempt to moderate the Chancellor's open opposition. Foster knew Lawson well from earlier privatization work, but his foray was entirely fruitless. 'I was totally unpersuaded,' Lawson recalled in a 1993 Channel 4 interview:

I have great respect for Chris Foster's judgement but I think on this it was totally mistaken, but it's not surprising because he's an economist and my objection was essentially a political objection.

In his memorandum[13] Lawson accepted some parts of the Chequers package, such as the nationalization of the non-domestic rate. But his hostility to the poll tax was absolute. Drawing extensively on the study team's own poll tax exemplifications, which had been circulated to the cabinet committee in a 'specification report' for the new tax—the first paper on the poll tax to be circulated to anyone outside the studies team—he claimed that the impact of the proposed tax would be 'horrifying':

A pensioner couple in Inner London could find themselves paying 22 per cent of their net income in poll tax, whereas a better-off couple in

[12] Lawson, *View from No. 11*, 572.
[13] Part of the memo is printed, and the rest summarized, in Lawson, *View from No. 11*, 573–5.

the suburbs would pay only 1 per cent. We should be forced to give so many exemptions and concessions (inevitably to the benefit of high-spending authorities in Inner London) that the flat-rate poll tax would rapidly become a surrogate income tax. That is what a 'graduated residents' charge' is.

Furthermore, Lawson argued, phasing in the poll tax would be 'hideous', and councils would use the reform to 'bump up' their spending. In short, he concluded, the new tax would be 'unworkable and politically catastrophic'.

Lawson went on to spell out his alternative proposal for reform: a reformed rating system. He wanted rates to be based on bands of capital value, as they were to be under the council tax that succeeded the poll tax. Confronting head-on the now-legendary problem of single pensioners—'the most deeply felt injustice of the rating system,' he conceded—Lawson proposed a fixed percentage reduction for pensioners living alone. Finally, he proposed to transfer a large part of education funding from local to central government, with a consequent cut in grants to councils.

That much was stated. Unstated, but critical to Lawson's outlook, was his fear that Baker and Waldegrave were in the throes of undermining his ambitious programme of reform of personal taxation, which was to culminate in his 1988 budget simplifying the income tax structure and cutting the top rate to 40p. The poll tax would be a highly perceptible direct tax, offsetting the effect of his income tax changes in reducing the direct tax burden on individuals. It would bring millions *into* the tax system, when Lawson wanted to take them out.[14] And the public spending implications, as he foresaw them, would make tax reductions of any kind more difficult.

At this stage, Lawson was not alone in his opposition. Leon Brittan, the Home Secretary, was deeply uneasy. In early April he sent a paper to the studies team warning against the possible use of the electoral roll as the basis for collection of a poll tax. The Home Office was concerned that a poll tax would be seen

[14] Curiously this fundamental inconsistency attracted little debate inside the party, though it is highlighted by David Willetts in his *Modern Conservatism* (1992), 59–60.

as a tax on voting, and that there might be other civil liberties implications. Even within the Department of Environment, there were still rumblings of dissent. In mid-May Andrew Tyrie, who had just been appointed special adviser to Patrick Jenkin and was later to serve Lawson in the same capacity, sent Jenkin and Baker a highly critical minute. He warned them of the serious electoral damage the poll tax was likely to wreak, particularly among the critical group of C1 and C2—lower-middle and skilled-working class—voters who had stuck by the Tories in the previous two elections, and whose support was essential for another victory.

Jenkin and Baker listened courteously; Baker was clearly concerned. But the steam-roller proceeded unchecked. With prime-ministerial enthusiasm evident, Baker took personal charge of the project. New officials were brought in: Peter Owen had been added to strengthen the D.o.E.'s own input, and advice was sought from John Redwood and Oliver Letwin in the No. 10 Policy Unit.

While the drafting of memos and counter-memos was proceeding in Whitehall, events in Scotland were once again forcing the pace. George Younger, Lord Whitelaw, and others with Scottish concerns were preparing for the forthcoming Scottish Conservative party conference. The run-up to the Perth conference saw heated and increasingly public exchanges between Younger and Nigel Lawson about the amount of relief available to cushion the revaluation. Both Whitelaw and Lord Home, the former Prime Minister, weighed in to support Younger, securing an increase in the relief fund from £36m. to £50m. Lawson made it publicly clear that this generosity was 'exceptional'.[15] Such episodes were to become almost monthly occurrences as the poll tax progressed and ever more strident appeals for extra cash were directed at Lawson.

The conference, in the second week of May, was dominated by the rates question and polls showing Tory support north of the border down to only 22 per cent. There had been some discussion beforehand of announcing at Perth an autumn bill to

---

[15] *Guardian*, 8 and 11 May 1985.

replace the rates. Younger wanted to give as firm as possible a commitment to the conference, but even he saw that an autumn deadline was unrealistic. However, in a crucial passage of his speech cleared by No. 10 only minutes before he rose to speak, Younger made a firm commitment to produce reform plans.[16] To the consternation of his officials in the Scottish Office, who had no idea what he was about to say, Younger proclaimed: 'the *status quo* is not an option'. In her speech to the conference, Mrs Thatcher acknowledged that recent rates demands had come as a 'thunderbolt', and reiterated Younger's commitment to publish proposals so rectify the 'anomalies and unfairness that are inherent in the present system' before the end of the year.[17]

By the time the cabinet committee held its first meeting on 20 May, therefore, a public commitment had already been given to far-reaching reforms north of the border. Since the poll tax was the only proposal on the table for dealing with the existing 'anomalies and unfairness', a humiliating public climb-down would have been involved in a decision not to proceed. Had there been any doubt as to the outcome of the crucial first meeting, this might well have tilted the balance.

POLL TAX SAILS THROUGH CABINET COMMITTEE

In fact, the outcome was never in doubt on 20 May.[18] There was no attempt by Mrs Thatcher to pack the committee or curtail the discussion. It was not necessary. The meeting lasted two-and-a-half hours and was attended by every minister with a domestic brief except for the Lord Chancellor. John Gummer, the Tory party chairman, was also present. Patrick Jenkin tabled a paper which gave as options both a flat-rate and a graduated levy. A few cautionary voices were raised. Lord Gowrie said it was 'a great plunge' which should be done with 'very great care'; Leon Brittan was cool about the plans; and

[16] *Guardian* and *Scotsman*, 10 May 1985.
[17] *Financial Times*, 11 May 1985.
[18] Accounts of the meeting, on which this paragraph is partially based, are in Baker, 123–4, Thatcher, 649–50, Lawson, 575.

Nigel Lawson spoke to his dissenting memo. But everyone else was favourable, or remained silent. Mrs Thatcher dismissed Brittan and Lawson's objections sharply. The Chancellor was invited to work up his alternative rates proposals, but no one else supported them and the Baker–Waldegrave poll tax gained overwhelming support. There was next to no debate about structural reform, about changes in local government voting, or the proposed City grant. These aspects of the Chequers package were effectively dropped. Mrs Thatcher finished by expressing the hope that a definitive decision about the shape of the final proposals could be taken in September, with a view to a Green Paper in the autumn and legislation in the 1986–7 session, before the election.

A decision with important implications for the developing proposals was made early on, though it was wholly separate from discussions about the poll tax. It was decided to introduce a '20 per cent rule', whereby every household would have to pay at least 20 per cent of their local tax bill.[19] At the time three million households received full rate rebates: from April 1988 onwards, every one of them would have to pay a fifth of their rates bill. Social security payments would be increased to cover the average cost to the affected households. This decision was important, in that it showed cabinet support for the 'everyone should pay something' approach which had been adopted by the studies team and endorsed in principle by the cabinet committee.

Cabinet committee and team meetings over the summer wrestled with a range of technical and political problems. A number of studies were undertaken about the distributive impact of the move to poll tax. Some of these studies proved contradictory, and an outsider, Evan Davis from the Institute for Fiscal Studies,[20] was brought in to help. Political problems began to emerge in the shape of the 'Accrington' problem and the 'Mrs Kashoggi' issue. The former difficulty arose because people living in areas with low rateable values (and thus relatively small rates bills) would lose heavily out of the move to

[19] Cmnd. 9691, *Reform of Social Security*.
[20] Later economics correspondent of the BBC.

poll tax. Many of the heaviest losers would be in the north-west of England. Mrs Kashoggi was chosen to represent the significant minority of very wealthy individuals whose local tax bills might fall from, say, £5,000 to £150 because of the move from rates to poll tax. But, as the move to the new tax was supposed to be revenue neutral, gainers and losers were an inevitability. In the words of one team member: 'all the time we talked about the differential impact on shires and cities—which was code for Tory and Labour Voters'.

Although the basic team of ministers, civil servants, and external assessors carried on developing the new tax, changes were taking place to the *dramatis personae*. Leonard Hoffmann, author of the dissenting note before the Chequers meeting mentioned earlier, had been appointed a judge, and therefore ceased to be an assessor. More outside help was sought from academics such as Richard Jackman of the London School of Economics (who did work on the non-domestic rate) and Christine Whitehead, also of the LSE (who was asked to assess the impact of poll tax on the housing market). The Institute for Fiscal Studies assisted in developing a model which allowed the D.o.E. to test the impact of local tax reform on households and areas. Then, in September, Patrick Jenkin was replaced by Kenneth Baker as Secretary of State for the Environment. William Waldegrave stepped up from Under-Secretary to Minister of State.

Baker owed his promotion partly to his success in promoting the poll tax, but more to his skill in public relations, a com-modity in short supply in the later Thatcher cabinets.[21] His appointment had clear implications for the future of local gov-ernment finance. Had he and Waldegrave been removed to different departments, the impetus for reform might have fal-tered. At this early stage Nigel Lawson might have been able to defeat or deflect a new, less committed, set of ministers. But with the architects of the new system now at the head of the

---

[21] His demolition of Ken Livingstone in a televised debate earlier in the year weighed particularly heavily with Mrs Thatcher. N. Ridley (1991), *My Style of Government*, 36.

Department of the Environment, there was no prospect of doing so.

Beyond the world of the studies and the Chancellor's growing hatred of the poll tax, the war between central and local government continued unabated. The GLC was still in existence. The failing grant system was still in use. Senior officials at D.o.E. continued to warn ministers that a legal challenge might cause embarrassment to the government at any moment. Indeed, pressure on the rate support grant had intensified in the year following the critical Audit Commission's report, discussed earlier. First, the National Audit Office (NAO), watchdog of central goverment's own expenditure, conducted an investigation of the grant arrangements, concluding that the system of targets and penalties which had been superimposed on the block grant had 'detracted still further from the original purposes of the system, to the point of making its sophistication worthless'.[22] The NAO report went on to suggest that the government's examination of rate support grant within the review of local government finance [considered in detail above] should lead to 'a clear definition of the weight and priority to be given to its various potential objectives, all of which it may not be possible to achieve, or even to pursue, at the same time'. The NAO report was followed, as is customary, by an inquiry by the Public Accounts Committee (PAC).

This inquiry provided D.o.E. officials—Terry Heiser (by now permanent secretary) and Peter Owen (now leader of the studies team)—with another opportunity to give evidence about aspects of local government finance. In fact, their views were given to the PAC on 8 May 1985, six weeks *after* the key presentation to the Prime Minister at Chequers on 31 March 1985 (at which Heiser had been present), and, indeed, after the decision to pursue the idea of a poll tax had been taken. The full shape of the proposed new local government finance system— poll tax, national non-domestic rate, and a substantially revised grant system—was now in place, if not formally approved.

Heiser and Owen provided the PAC with a doughty defence

[22] National Audit Office, 1985, para. 38.

THE RISE AND FALL OF THE POLL TAX

of block grant, targets, and penalties. This performance showed civil servants at their best (or worst, depending on one's point of view), providing an articulate defence of a grant system which they believed to be flawed and which the Prime Minister had, to all intents and purposes, decided to abandon. Heiser stated:

the new system [block grant plus targets and penalties], with all its pressures, has concentrated minds wonderfully on financial management. Although the system is much criticised for its difficulties and complexities I do believe it has sharpened thinking about spending, about getting value for money, in a way which previous systems did not.[23]

The local government finance review was mentioned, briefly, by Heiser in his evidence:

[the studies] began towards the end of last year and are now well advanced. They are much wider than any previous study that has been undertaken by this Government . . . These studies are actually looking at every element in the equation on both sides—income and expenditure.[24]

The Permanent Secretary hinted, though only just, at the scale of the reforms which would soon emerge from the studies. It was almost the first the outside world knew of the scope of the review in progress.

By now, it remained only for the cabinet committee to approve a specific reform plan. There was, however, a last-ditch attempt by one of the three remaining assessors—Tom Wilson, the Glasgow economics professor who had opposed the scheme from the start—to remove the poll tax element of the scheme. After the Capital Hotel meeting in February, where he expressed his dissent, Wilson was effectively isolated from the review and not even shown the dissenting note of his fellow assessor Lenny Hoffmann. Over the summer he protested to Rothschild. At Rothschild's behest, a meeting was held in August, at Rothschild's bank, at which were present the 'studies team' officials, Baker, Waldegrave, and the three remaining

[23] Committee of Public Accounts, 1985, 13.   [24] Ibid. 14.

84

assessors. Everyone who spoke, including the civil servants, spoke in favour, apart from Wilson. True to form, Rothschild himself said little, but what he said was gently supportive. It was the last time the assessors were called upon.

Baker was anxious to have a rates replacement package agreed by the Tory conference in early October. (Almost every key decision in the poll tax saga was made in the immediate run up to a party conference, by ministers anxious for something to wave from the rostrum.) He just made it in time. At cabinet committee meetings on 23 September and 3 October, with thirteen ministers present, Kenneth Baker won endorsement for his worked-through plan to replace domestic rates with a resident's charge (although Nigel Lawson, 'loyally and effectively supported by my new Chief Secretary, John MacGregor', voiced his 'grave misgivings').[25] The new levy would be run in parallel with a reformed property tax, with the poll tax element of the local tax raising 70 per cent of local tax income and the property tax collecting the remaining 30 per cent. Baker was cautious about the possibility of a direct move from rates to a new tax. Nigel Lawson, who again voiced his misgivings about the poll tax, welcomed the property tax element of the proposals.[26] Lawson won an argument over capping: the Treasury wanted to retain the power to cap high-spenders. Baker and his Environment Department colleagues were unhappy about the retention of capping, as they believed that financial accountability would be undermined if councils were not seen to be wholly responsible for their own spending and taxation.

It was agreed to publish a Green Paper in the New Year, but the timing of progress thereafter was still undecided. Younger, who was opposed to any rates element in the Scottish tax, was adamant that legislation should be on the statute-book for Scotland before the election likely to be held in mid-1987. Baker, briefing journalists at the Tory conference the week after the 3 October cabinet committee, said legislation in the existing parliament had 'not been ruled out',[27] but he was clearly

---

[25] Lawson, *View from No. 11*, 576.   [26] Ibid. 576.
[27] *The Times* and *Financial Times*, 10 Oct. 1985.

disinclined to proceed that fast and rapidly decided not to introduce legislation for England and Wales before the election.

Baker's speech to the Tory conference at Blackpool was preceded by his now obligatory slide show highlighting the iniquities of the status quo. It was the first such visual spectacle to which a Conservative conference had ever been treated, but subsequent conferences were to get repeat viewings. At the Tory local government conference in March 1986 it put one of the audience 'in mind of a successful lesson in A-level British government'.[28] The slide show, and the proposal for a poll tax, gained a warm reception from the activists, who cheered the abolition of the rates to the rafters of the Winter Gardens.[29] It was received equally warmly by the Tory councillors five months later.[30]

Drafts of the Green Paper circulated around Whitehall in the autumn of 1985. The official title of the new poll tax changed once more. Out went 'resident's charge' and in came 'community charge'. The new nomenclature was important: it suggested a charge for the services provided to the local community rather than a tax. Sadly, no one remembers who thought of the fateful name. Further cabinet subcommittee meetings occurred, at which Lawson maintained his opposition. But to no effect. The continued existence of rates (or something like them) reassured the doubters. So did the D.o.E.'s projections for the size of the first poll tax bills—an average of £150, exceeding £200 in only thirty-six authorities.[31] During October and November, it became clear that the introduction of a wholly new property tax to raise just 30 per cent of local tax income would be expensive and unpopular. Instead, the team decided that rates should be kept, but with a gradual move from the existing domestic rates to the new community charge. More effort was put into working out how the proposed system would be administered, and into estimating the distributional

[28] R. Kelly, *Conservative Party Conferences* (1989), 65–6.
[29] *The Times*, *Guardian*, and *Financial Times*, 10 Oct. 1985.
[30] Kelly, *Conservative Party Conferences*, 65–6.
[31] Baker, *Turbulent Years*, 125.

effects. It was also agreed to introduce a 'safety net' to limit the transfers between north and south in the early years.

The Green Paper was approved by a cabinet subcommittee just before Christmas. On New Year's Eve Kenneth Baker went to Chequers to go through the details with the prime minister. 'I left her late in the day still, I suspect, regretting that the customary annual festivities were about to disrupt her workflow.'[32]

APPROVING THE GREEN PAPER

On 9 January 1986 the full cabinet discussed the poll tax for the first time. Approval was a formality: it had gone through exhaustive cabinet committee scrutiny over the previous seven months, and had been overwhelmingly endorsed at every stage. Ministers had before them the final draft of a Green Paper scheduled for publication almost immediately. Not even Nigel Lawson bothered to register dissent at the full cabinet. The Green Paper was approved in about fifteen minutes.

The one minister who might have raised objections in full cabinet was Michael Heseltine, who as Defence Secretary had not been party to any previous discussions. But by chance the Green Paper was on the agenda below the Westland affair, which had been rumbling throughout the Christmas and New Year break. In one of the more famous ministerial resignations of recent British history, Heseltine walked out of the meeting when he failed to get his way, provoking an on-the-spot cabinet reshuffle.

When news of the cabinet filtered back to the D.o.E., one of the senior officials involved in the studies team grinned and said: 'we've just won the next election for Labour.' However, Baker's proposals were still hedged with safeguards and opportunities to row back. Poll tax would be introduced only gradually. Domestic rates would taper off over a decade. Nothing at all would happen before 1989 or 1990. The changes agreed in January 1986 were far less radical than those finally introduced three years later. By then, the studies team was pre-history.

[32] Ibid. 125.

5

ENACTMENT, 1986–1988

The community charge goes between the Scylla of the
rates and the Charybdis of local income tax. It goes
through the middle without hitting either of those rocks.
Nicholas Ridley, House of Commons Standing
Committee, March 1988

On 28 January 1986, three weeks after cabinet approval, *Paying
for Local Government* was launched. It received an almost silent
send-off. The day was more memorable for the explosion of the
space shuttle *Challenger*, which dominated the evening news
programmes and next morning's press.

It was the fourth time that an important milestone in the poll
tax's progress had coincided with an external drama. The day
the local government finance studies were announced at the
Tory party conference in Brighton in October 1984 was followed the same night by the IRA bomb at the Grand Hotel.
The cabinet meeting in January 1986 at which the final proposals were agreed was overshadowed by Michael Heseltine's walk-
out. And the meeting of ministers and officials at the
Department of the Environment which gave the seal of
approval to the poll tax, in March 1985, ended with a tremen-
dous clap of thunder. 'We went over to the window,' recalled
Kenneth Baker, 'and watched as great flashes of lightning lit up
the whole of Westminster while the thunder continued to rum-
ble'; whereupon Baker turned to William Waldegrave and said:
'I hope the community charge won't produce such a storm.'[1] It
did.

---

[1] K. Baker, *The Turbulent Years* (1993), 122.

PAYING FOR LOCAL GOVERNMENT

Paying for Local Government was quite unlike any Green Paper that had gone before. Whereas government consultation documents had hitherto been dense and drab, not least those concerning local government finance, this one was racy and colourful. It came in large A4 format, with bright, glitzy graphs, pie-charts, and tables. Kenneth Baker's presentational hand was on every page. The very title conveyed an important message. Mrs Thatcher's distaste for local government was well known: *Paying for Local Government* conveyed the idea that councils were an irksome and undesirable burden.

The Green Paper gave three main reasons for abandoning the previous system: the malfunctioning of the grant system; the extent to which local authorities' marginal spending was funded by non-domestic ratepayers; and the mismatch between those who were entitled to vote in local elections, those who benefited from local services, and those who paid domestic rates.[2] Pie-charts provided statistical support for these points. The Green paper gave no explanation of how the previously insoluble problem of reforming the rates had, finally, been solved. What it did instead was to offer three possible ways forward, reject two of them, and then describe the advantages of the third.

The first of the possible solutions was to reform the structure of local government. This idea was rejected on the grounds that structural change would cause too much disruption, and would do nothing to resolve endemic financial weaknesses. The second option was to increase central control over local government, but such an increase was held to involve too much Whitehall intervention; it would also lead to an undesirable increase in central government staffing and duplication of effort. The third, and optimal, option was 'improving local accountability'. Such an improvement was to be achieved in three ways:

- better arrangements for the taxation of non-domestic ratepayers, so that the payments they make towards local services do

[2] Cmnd. 9714, *Paying for Local Government*, ch. 1.

not conceal from local voters the true costs of increased spending;
- a more direct and fairer link between voting and paying, with more local voters contributing towards the cost of providing local authority services; and
- clearer grant arrangements, so that the consequences of increases or reductions in spending are felt directly and straightforwardly by local domestic taxpayers.[3]

Rates, which had had their origins in the Poor Law of 1601, and which had been accepted by the 1983 White Paper as an inescapable tax, were summarily dismissed in two paragraphs. Too few people directly paid rates; revaluations were unpopular; and the tax-base was unevenly spread. Local income tax and local sales were also rejected. The first was held to be unfair, the second impractical. A community charge was the way forward, backed up by reforms to non-domestic rates and the grant system.

The government summarized its proposals thus:

Non-domestic rates should in future be set by central government, as a uniform rate in the pound. The proceeds would be pooled and redistributed to all authorities as a common amount per adult. The introduction of such a scheme would be accompanied by a revaluation of non-domestic properties.

Domestic rates should be phased out over a period of up to ten years and replaced by a flat rate community charge, payable by all adults. There would be a separate community charge register in each area.

The grant system should be radically simplified. It would consist of needs grant, which would compensate for differences in what authorities needed to spend to provide a comparable standard of service, and standard grant, which would be paid to all authorities as a common amount per adult. The formula for assessing authorities' relative spending needs should also be reviewed, with a view to making it less complex and more stable.

Distributional effects arising from the introduction of the new grant and non-domestic rate arrangements would be offset by a system of self-financing adjustments.[4]

The purpose of the new system would be 'to ensure that the

---

[3] Cmnd. 9714, *Paying for Local Government*, ch. 9.   [4] Ibid. 76.

local electors know what the costs of their services are, so that armed with this knowledge they can influence the spending decisions of their councils through the ballot-box'.[5] The new system would be introduced first in Scotland (probably in 1989) and then in England and Wales (in 1990).

The government started as it meant to go on. The tables and charts in the main part of *Paying for Local Government* showed, to the surprise of most commentators, that the proposed community charge would be more progressive than the rates. Figure 11 on page 25 (reproduced overleaf) showed that— before rebates—rates took a greater share of 'net household income' than would poll tax from households with the lowest incomes, while for middle- and higher-income levels, poll tax actually took a greater share of income. Only from the tiny numbers of households in the highest bands of income did community charge take a smaller share of income than rates.

Figure 11 was an early example of the government's efforts at presentational delusion. Carefully tucked away in Annex F was Figure F7, which showed a very different picture from the one in the main body of the Green Paper. Figure F7 showed the impact of rates and community charge *after* rebates, i.e. the actual bills to be paid. Moreover, unlike the figure on page 25, which compared households by bands of 'net household income', Figure F7 (also overleaf) looked at the comparison by 'net household income by equivalent income band'. The crucial difference, which only tax and benefit experts could detect, was that the latter chart compared *like* households. Figure 11 on page 25 was, in reality, not comparing like with like.

From Figure F7 it appeared that a majority of middle-income households would lose by the shift to poll tax, while higher-income households stood to make significant gains. So opaque was Figure F7, and the accompanying statistics, that it was not possible to devine precise figures for gainers and losers, but the overall picture was unambiguous.[6] The reality of the

[5] Ibid. p. vii.
[6] Fig. F7 gives no figures for the number of households in each of its bands of 'equivalent net weekly income'. However, the clear losers from F7 were households with adjusted net weekly income of between £75 and £150—about

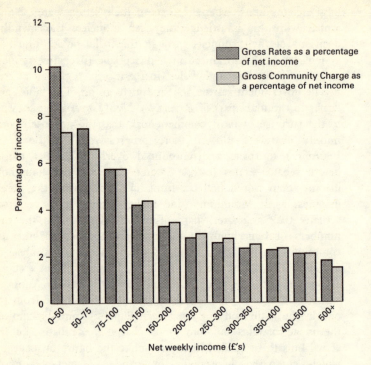

Fig. 5.1 1986 Green Paper: gainers and losers from a community charge (1986)

proposed local tax reform was revealed. <u>Poll tax would hit the not-quite-poor hard</u>. Ministers started a process of gentle self-delusion, as if they believed that by masking the impact of the new tax, no one would notice when the real bills went out, least of all those having to pay them. Such careful handling of awkward figures continued throughout the years from 1986 to 1990. Unfortunately for the government, the public eventually noticed the difference between the creative statistics in Figure 11 and the reality of Figure F7.

Kenneth Baker even deluded himself about the press reaction to the poll tax and the other proposed reforms. In his memoirs he says it was 'favourable'.[7] In fact it was almost completely hostile, the favourable bits being largely reports of his reception by Tory backbenchers. On 29 January, *The Times* thundered, under the heading 'Benefits of Rates':

Verbiage about community charge confuses its nature. A true charge gives the payer an option. A true community charge would be one which a local electorate willingly imposed upon itself, a tax for services it had chosen. The government's version is a poll tax for services which it will define and whose cost and level of provision it will closely supervise.

The leader went on to defend the rates and to attack the poll tax. (The press rarely used the long, official, title of the new tax. Government propagandists should have realized that the ease of using 'poll tax' in headlines rather than the cumbersome 'community charge' would ensure the general use of the shorter name.)

The *Financial Times* took a similar line, calling for an updated property tax. More predictably, so did the *Guardian*, while the *Daily Telegraph* and most of the tabloids had little to say one way or another. A few days after the launch *The Economist* went straight for the jugular. Its lengthy assessment concentrated on gainers and losers:

half of the population in 1985. The clear gainers were households with adjusted net weekly incomes of more than £200. Those in the income bands of £400 a week and above stood to save half or more of their rates bills.

[7] Baker, *Turbulent Years*, 122.

All tax reforms hurt somebody. Losers howl, while winners give little thanks. Slow phasing of the community charge would mean few of either in the first year. . . . The trouble is that broad-brush figures include many hard cases—and it takes only a few hard cases to produce lots of hostility. And the big losers, young singles and couples, are floating voters.[8]

It went on to warn about administrative nightmares.

The long transition while the reform is installed promises to be a gigantic mess. For years, domestic rates and community charge would run in tandem (thanks for an extra new tax, prime minister), with the balance shifting constantly and leaving voters even less clear than now about who caused what increase and why.

The criticisms voiced by *The Economist* were highly prescient. The prospect of chaos of years of dual-running for rates and poll tax proved sufficiently threatening for the government to abandon it even before the legislation was introduced. Once poll tax was to be introduced overnight, the concerns about losers would be magnified. The shape of things to come was already becoming clear, at least to observers outside the Whitehall bunker.

However, Kenneth Baker did rather better on the Tory backbenches. Just before he rose from the government front bench to make his statement to the Commons, Nigel Lawson leaned across and murmured: 'It will be her King Charles's head.'[9] But their eyes fixed on the prize of abolishing the rates, and little suspecting the problems in store, most Tory MPs gave Baker's plans a guarded welcome.[10] John Heddle (Mid-Staffordshire) pointed out that it was bound to create losers as well as winners; Robert Rhodes James (Cambridge) raised the question of students; and Michael Cockeram (Ludlow) warned Baker that he had opened a Pandora's box which would inaugurate a 'long-running period of protest beside which the Westland affair will be but a brief interlude'. But such criticism was drowned in a chorus of praise. In retrospect the most telling remarks came from Keith Hampson (Leeds North-West)

[8] *The Economist*, 1 Feb. 1986.   [9] Baker, *Turbulent Years*, 126.
[10] *HC Debs.*, 28 Jan. 1986, cols. 801–13.

and Baker himself. Hampson noted that a poll tax 'is tolerable only if it is small', and wanted it to cover far less of local authority expenditure than domestic rates; while Baker assured MPs the new tax would 'start at a low level' and 'be modest for most people'. For good measure, he added that the shift to poll tax would be 'both gradual and manageable in terms of household incomes'.

The poll tax launched, the studies team celebrated their triumph at a party at William Waldegrave's Kensington home on 12 March. Kenneth Baker, Lord Rothschild, Leonard Hoffmann, Christopher Foster, Anthony Mayer, Oliver Letwin (a member of Mrs Thatcher's policy unit, and soon to move to N. M. Rothschild), and several others attended the reunion. Some of those present could barely believe what they had achieved—or, indeed, that their ideas would finally be carried through to legislation. To encourage them, a fortnight after Waldegrave's party came the denouement of another great local government drama. The Greater London Council and the six metropolitan county councils were finally abolished. Ken Livingstone's reign was ended, to the accompaniment of fireworks over the Thames. Despite his brilliant campaign, Mrs Thatcher had prevailed. Having slain one of Tory demonology's most potent enemies, the time seemed ripe to move on to another.

'CONSULTATION'

William Waldegrave's party was more a reunion than a celebration, for by March 1986 the studies team had been disbanded and new officials had taken over the project. Anthony Mayer, the effective 'team leader', had been head-hunted by N. M. Rothschild, the merchant bank, back in October 1985—at the behest of Lord Rothschild himself.[11] Other officials returned to day-to-day jobs in the Department of the Environment. The assessors were not called upon again. Lord Rothschild died in 1990. Sir Leonard Hoffmann, appointed a High Court judge before the end of the review, hit the headlines at the end of

[11] He went on to become chief executive of the Housing Corporation in 1991.

1993 for chairing a committee which proposed that two of London's world-famous orchestras should have their government subsidies slashed. Sir Christopher Foster went on to play a similarly important back-stage role in the privatization of British Rail, and for his pains was appointed a director of Railtrack, which took over ownership of British Rail's fixed infrastructure.

From early 1986 onwards, the early stages of the preparation of legislation and implementation were put in the hands of Chris Brearley and subsequently, from 1987, Neil Summerton. As the civil servants in charge, their styles and outlook were very different from those of Heiser and the other brash officials on the studies team. Brearley, in his mid-forties, was a more traditional, reassuring, pipe-smoking type of civil servant who exuded an aura of calm competence. Crucially, he was also respected by local government. Summerton, a quiet, unassuming man in his early thirties, was also keen to work with, not against the local councils. Later in 1986, the Department of the Environment advertised for an economic adviser to assist with the reform package. David King, an academic economist from Stirling University, was appointed to work with D.o.E. officials for a year from February 1987. King had published books and papers relatively sympathetic to the idea of a poll tax.[12]

A long period of consultation had been set aside by Kenneth Baker, from January to the end of October 1986. It inaugurated a phoney war which lasted until the 1987 general election. During this time, the poll tax was virtually dead as a political issue. This is not to say there was no activity in the background. Rather, Labour made no running with it, and there was a general suspension of belief that it would actually happen. The reform was several years off; there would be a general election which the Tories might lose; the idea seemed, perhaps, too fantastic to believe.

A total of 1,217 responses were made to the Green Paper; 479 came from individuals, most of the rest from local councils or professional bodies. The individuals largely favoured the idea; the councils and professional organizations were mostly

[12] Notably *Fiscal Tiers* (1984).

hostile. It was the first time in the review process that the government had asked councils what they thought, and their response was predictable. The majority of local authorities and their associations favoured the retention of domestic rates. Half of the responses from local government favoured a local income tax as an alternative local tax. As the government's own analysis of the responses commented: 'The majority of local authorities which commented opposed the community charge on the grounds that it would be expensive and difficult to collect and operate and that, in their view, it would be regressive and unrelated to ability to pay.'[13] As for the professional organizations, CIPFA, the respected independent body for local government finance officers, criticized the poll tax on grounds of local accountability, fairness, efficiency, and administrative complexity.[14] The Institute for Fiscal Studies, a number of Oxford economists, and the Rating and Valuation Association, said much the same.[15] In December 1986, John Gibson, an economist at the University of Birmingham, published research in *Local Government Chronicle* which suggested that the redistributive effects of the new tax would be more adverse than the government had predicted in the Green Paper.[16]

The responses to the formal consultation cut no ice with ministers. More important to them was the reaction of the Tory party's back-benchers and grass-roots activists, which was generally favourable. The party's local government conference at Wembley in early March gave the plans a warm reception, aided by an informal pep talk from Mrs Thatcher to assembled councillors over lunch. At the Central Council in Felixstowe a

[13] '*Paying for Local Government*. Summary of responses to the Green Paper in England', Dept. of the Environment unpublished paper (1986).

[14] CIPFA, *Response to Paying for Local Government*, Cmnd. 9714 (1986), 2. Rita Hale, CIPFA's formidable local government expert, had started to analyse the impact of the tax the year before. See R. Hale, *Poll Tax: Some Initial Analyses* (1985).

[15] S. Smith and D. Squire, *Local Taxes and Local Government* (1987); D. Helm and S. Smith, 'Decentralisation and Local Government', *Oxford Review of Economic Policy* (1987); *Community Charge/Poll Tax: The Facts*, Rating and Valuation Association (1987).

[16] J. Gibson, *The Politics and Economics of the Poll Tax* (1990).

fortnight later—a smaller mid-year version of the annual conference—nearly all the speakers welcomed Baker's proposals: the only notable criticism, as at the Wembley conference, was from shire Tories aggrieved at their allocations from the grant system.[17]

While the formal consultation was proceeding, the government was already drafting a bill to reform local government finance in Scotland, determined from the outset that the poll tax should be the replacement for domestic rates. Within the Department of the Environment, far more significant than the consultation was the effect of ministerial reshuffles, which produced a changing of the ministerial guard as complete as the turnover of officials a few months earlier.

In May, Kenneth Baker moved from the D.o.E. to Education and Science, where he was to employ his presentational skills to the full in promoting reforms, such as the National Curriculum and the opting-out of schools, that were nearly as radical as the poll tax he left behind. He was replaced at Environment by Nicholas Ridley, the Transport Secretary. A chain-smoking Etonian contemptuous of the Tory old-guard and much of the Establishment, Ridley was a political oddball. Not lacking in private charm, and popular with his civil servants, his public manner was brusque and often offensive,[18] and he owed his position to an intellectual affinity and political friendship with the Prime Minister dating back to the 1970s. No one doubted the significance of Ridley's appointment: he brought, Mrs Thatcher recalled, 'a combination of clarity of thought, political courage and imagination to the questions surrounding the implementation of the new system'.[19] In particular, he brought a thoroughgoing hostility not just to the existing local authority system, but to the very idea of local government as an

[17] R. Kelly, *Conservative Party Conferences* (1989), 85–90.

[18] The fall summed up the man: a *Spectator* interview in July 1990, in which he described the European monetary system as 'a German racket to take over the whole of Europe . . . [Helmut Kohl] . . . will soon be trying to take over everything'. After German protests, Mrs Thatcher was forced, reluctantly, to accept Ridley's resignation.

[19] M. Thatcher, *The Downing Street Years*, 651.

autonomous political sphere. Famously, Ridley told a local authority audience as Environment Secretary that in an ideal world councils would meet just once a year, to hand out contracts to companies winning tenders to provide local services. And he meant it. 'Inside every fat and bloated local authority there is a slim one struggling to get out,' he declared in a 1988 Centre for Policy Studies pamphlet.

None the less, Ridley did not start out as an ardent fan of the poll tax. Indeed, he started off largely ignorant about the evolution of the tax, in which he had played virtually no part.[20] When Waldegrave was doing his studies, Ridley told him he liked the principle of the poll tax, but could not see it as 'a large revenue raiser'.[21] Nigel Lawson claims that initially Ridley was 'not at all comfortable' with the policy.[22] In a Channel 4 interview shortly before his death Ridley admitted as much, saying that it took a 'fairly exhaustive examination' to convince him of its virtues. But having done so 'successfully'—being resolutely opposed to the only viable alternative, a local income tax—he never looked back. Considering the options available, he quickly concluded that only the rates, local income tax, and poll tax were viable: since rates were 'unpopular and unfair', and a local income tax would give councils 'a weapon for the redistribution of income', it had to be poll tax.[23]

Four months after Ridley's appointment (September 1986), the junior ministers in the department also changed. Waldegrave was replaced by Sir Rhodes Boyson as the local government minister, and Christopher Chope was given the under-secretaryship, a position he held until July 1990. As London MPs, Boyson and Chope were strongly influenced by the 'loony-left' authorities of the metropolis, and had a strong antipathy to local government in its 1980s guise. Chope, a

---

[20] He never discovered much more. In the space of three pages in his memoirs he mistakes the date of the key Chequers meeting, delays the Scottish revaluation by a year, pleads ignorance of Lawson's dissenting memorandum, and credits Edward Heath with rates rebates introduced by Crossman 8 years earlier. N. Ridley, *My Style of Government* (1991), 121–4.

[21] Ibid. 124. [22] N. Lawson, *View from No. 11*, 577.

[23] Ridley, *My Style of Government*, 127.

one-time leader of the south London borough of Wandsworth, was far from naïve about the problems of local taxation, but he did little to question the poll tax. Rhodes Boyson concluded in late 1986 that the political priority was the coming general election, not the poll tax which might follow it.

Two small, but significant, changes were made to the poll tax in the latter months of 1986, both at Ridley's instigation. First, it was decided to cut the transition period from ten to four years. Ridley in fact argued for three, on the grounds of the bureaucracy and expense of dual running. The Treasury, represented by the Chief Secretary, John Major, pressed for five years. Four years was a compromise. Secondly, it was decided to impose a 20 per cent charge on students, despite Kenneth Baker's objections.[24] Unsurprisingly, students were to be in the vanguard of opposition to the proposed tax; the raucous campus protests stood out in contrast to the general apathetic student response to later Thatcherism. Having failed to get students excluded, Baker responded with the idea of exempting everyone under 21, but that got nowhere—and would, in any case, have shot a hole through the argument for the tax as a mechanism to improve accountability.

In retrospect, Baker regards these two decisions, together with Nigel Lawson's 'underfunding' of the introduction of the tax, as 'fatal mistakes'.[25] Fatal or not, they showed that barely months after the launch of the Green Paper, significant aspects of the tax were being redesigned on the hoof, with little or no reference to the original plan and the considerations underpinning it. It was a process which was to continue right up to the launch of the tax three years later.

Baker's concerns were not shared by either Mrs Thatcher or the vocal among grass-roots Tories. On the contrary, the annual conference in October 1986, at Bournemouth, cheered Ridley when he declared that the poll tax would be 'at the very top of our agenda' (a remark preceding Mrs Thatcher's more famous 'flagship' boast). According to one report, the conference heard a catalogue of horror stories from representatives serving on

[24] Baker, *Turbulent Years*, 127.   [25] Ibid. 127–32.

'hard-left' councils, with the London borough of Brent branded a 'fascist left-wing junta' by one prospective parliamentary candidate.[26]

SCOTLAND FIRST

Drafting the Bill to introduce the poll tax into Scotland began soon after the launch of *Paying for Local Government*, and continued in earnest through the spring and summer of 1986.

Scotland was never intended as the poll tax 'guinea-pig'. From the outset the reform was intended to apply to Great Britain as a whole, and it was only introduced into Scotland first because of George Younger's determination to have the necessary legislation on the statute-book before the general election, expected to be in 1987. As Steve Norris, Tory MP for Oxford East, put it in a Commons debate on the Scottish poll tax, 'our Scottish colleagues are trail-blazers rather than guinea-pigs'.[27]

By the time it came to trail-blazing, Younger had moved from the Scottish Office to the Ministry of Defence, replacing Heseltine. Malcolm Rifkind, a sharp-witted Edinburgh barrister, became the new Scottish Secretary. Scotland was Rifkind's first cabinet post, and he was every bit as committed to the poll tax as Younger. He, too, had a marginal seat, and regarded the poll tax as essential to holding it.[28] However, like Younger he had to confront a Scottish Office uniformly opposed to the reform. The permanent secretary, Sir William Kerr Fraser, was by 1986 one of the few front-rank survivals from the Callaghan government. Recruited to the Scottish Office in 1955, and appointed principal of Glasgow university on his retirement in 1988, Kerr Fraser was the archetypal Scots public servant: cautious, shrewd, and thorough. He warned both Younger and Rifkind about the intractable practical problems of the new tax;

[26] Kelly, *Conservative Party Conferences*, 152.

[27] *HC Debs.*, 9 Dec. 1986, col. 262.

[28] In early 1985 Rifkind's constituency association in Edinburgh issued a public statement claiming the government had been 'uncharacteristically dilatory and incompetent' in its failure to bring about rates reform.

unlike Terry Heiser at Environment, he never took a resolute 'can do' approach to ministerial whims. Ian Penman, the deputy secretary responsible for local government finance, was equally concerned. But the message they got back was unambiguous. 'You don't have to face the music on the doorstep in Scotland, so can't understand why we need this so badly,' Younger told them in so many words. They got the message. 'George was hell bent on it, and the situation was almost out of control,' recalls one of the officials involved.

Drafting the Bill none the less turned out to be 'something of a nightmare', in the words of another of those involved. The more they got into complexities, the more concerned became the Scottish Office—ministers and as much as officials—at the problems of implementation. Michael Ancram, the Scottish Office junior minister responsible for the drafting, became convinced that the requirement on students and the unwaged to pay 20 per cent would prove unworkable—'paying people to pay a tax,' as he put it. He and his officials were also deeply worried about the rolling poll tax register, believing it would prove an administrative impossibility. Ancram took his concerns to a cabinet subcommittee chaired by William Whitelaw, which included the English local government ministers. He was told to put the 20 per cent provisions back in the Bill, and got similarly short shrift with other proposed relaxations. The 'one of us' mentality had something to do with it: Ridley and Waldegrave thought Ancram had 'gone soft', and were determined not to sacrifice principles in the Scottish Bill. But the fact that the English ministers were not at this stage having to grapple with detailed legislative provisions also coloured their outlook. Scottish Office officials, in particular, were struck by the lack of support they received from D.o.E. counterparts even on procedural and administrative questions.

The Abolition of Domestic Rates (etc.) Scotland Bill was the last major measure introduced into parliament before the 1987 election, receiving its Commons second reading on 9 December 1986. As with the name 'Community Charge' the title of the Bill was a significant pointer to the government's views and prejudices. It met virtually no Tory opposition at any stage of its progress through either House. Rifkind hailed it as a 'radical reforming measure . . . to abolish a discredited and unpopular local tax'.[29] At second reading, not a single Tory MP dissented by speech or vote. Rousing support came from, among others, Michael Hirst (Strathkelvin and Bearsden), Alex Fletcher (Edinburgh Central), and Barry Henderson (Fife North-East), all of whom were to lose their seats at the subsequent election. 'It sailed through with barely a murmur,' recalls Gerry Malone, Tory whip for the Bill's committee stage, who also lost his seat.

A few English Tory MPs had serious reservations about supporting the Scottish poll tax, but were told by Younger or Rifkind that it was 'utterly vital' for the Tories' electoral prospects north of the border. They all fell into line, or, in a handful of cases, abstained. Indeed, in the Commons the most lukewarm note was struck by John Biffen, no 'wet', who as Leader of the House had to move the guillotine motion to expedite the passage of the Bill on 11 February. Although he did not remotely consider it a resigning issue, Biffen had little time for the poll tax and could bring himself to describe it only as 'a determined response to the challenge of finding an alternative to the present discredited rating system'—immediately after which *Hansard* records an intervention from the Labour MP John Home Robertson: 'Keep a straight face.'[30]

However, in response to back-bench pressure, two significant government amendments were made during the Scottish Bill's parliamentary passage. First, the implementation phase was drastically shortened. Under the Bill as introduced, the poll tax was to have been phased in over three years between April 1989 and March 1992; at the report stage in the Commons—against the advice of his officials—Michael Ancram accepted an amendment to introduce the tax in one go in 1989. Rifkind and Ancram, convinced of the electoral benefits of the poll tax, were sympathetic to calls for an end to the transitional period, while Donald Dewar, Labour's Scottish spokesman, welcomed the

---

[29] *HC Debs.*, 9 Dec. 1986, col. 200.   [30] Ibid., 11 Feb. 1987, col. 323.

change as 'sharpening the divide between the parties'.[31] It was also to be a precedent for a similar decision taken with regard to England and Wales later in the year. Scottish Office civil servants stressed to their ministers the huge gains and losses likely to be experienced by some areas in the transition from one tax to the other. As one recalls: 'under the old grant system, we used to get alarmed about areas losing up to £5 a head from one year to the next: with poll tax, we were talking about £5 a head *per week*, and told them so.' But to no avail.

The second change concerned responsibility for collecting the tax. As introduced, the Bill provided for an individual in each dwelling to be designated 'head of the household' for the purposes of collecting the tax; that person would have had responsibility for collecting the tax from the others. Under pressure from Labour and some Tory back-bench MPs concerned about the civil liberties aspect, the provision was dropped, leaving individuals liable only for their own tax. One minister believes that in retrospect this was a fatal decision. 'It meant that in the transitory world of multiple occupations, student dwellings and the like, we simply couldn't get a handle on anyone responsible for paying the tax.'

The Bill sailed through the House of Lords, under the watchful eye of Lord Whitelaw. The government lost not a single vote on the Scottish poll tax in the Upper House, and felt obliged to make only a few trifling amendments in response to criticism there.

The Bill enacted, Scotland had one last role to play in the poll tax story. It was for Scotland to demonstrate to its proponents that the poll tax could be implemented, to its opponents that it couldn't, and to both parties that the course ahead was littered with obstacles.

THE 1987 GENERAL ELECTION

When the 1987 election came, the poll tax proved to be a non-issue. In the light of the political disaster which ensued, this

---

[31] *HC Debs.*, 4 Mar. 1987, col. 934.

seems odd. Certainly, the Conservatives were not in the least defensive about the reform. The party's *Campaign Guide* claimed the community charge 'could put local government back on a really satisfactory democratic basis'.[32] It claimed that 51 per cent of households would be better off under the new tax, no more than 25 per cent would lose more than £1 per week, while 86 per cent of pensioners living alone would face lower bills. The manifesto commitment went straight for Labour:

the abuses of left-wing Labour councils have shocked the nation. The Labour Party leadership pretends that this is a problem in only a few London boroughs. The truth is that the far left control town halls in many of our cities.

The manifesto then justified the proposed flat-rate poll tax with an appeal to fairness:

Many people benefit from local services yet make little or no contribution towards them: this throws too heavy a burden on too few shoulders. There is much wrong with the present system of domestic rates. They seem unfair and arbitrary. . . . We will tackle the roots of the problem. We will reform local government finance to strengthen local democracy and accountability. Local electors must be able to decide the level of service they want and how much they are prepared to pay for it. We will legislate in the first session of Parliament to abolish the unfair domestic rating system and replace rates with a fairer Community Charge.[33]

No mention was made of any possible administrative issues raised by the reform.

The Tories' decision to home in on Labour's local government record was well judged. Peter Mandelson, Labour's key strategist, was determined to keep the 'loony left' out of the election; the last thing he or Neil Kinnock wanted was to have to defend Citizen Ken, Red Ted, nuclear-free zones, baa-baa white sheep (allegedly a Lambeth primary school nursery rhyme), or the persecution of Maureen McGoldrick by Brent.[34]

---

[32] Conservative Party, *Campaign Guide*, 1987, 334.   [33] Ibid.

[34] In August 1986 the left-wing Labour council in Brent suspended

Since debating the poll tax would inevitably bring them up, it was deliberately downplayed. Despite a torrent of policy documents about local government in the previous four years, local government merited a mere seven paragraphs in Labour's manifesto. Rate-capping would be scrapped, as would the poll tax in Scotland. Labour would 'restore the right of councils to decide their own policies and plans, which will be subject to the decisions of local people at annual local elections'.[35]

Norman Tebbit was especially effective in peddling damaging stories about Labour councils during the election. Jack Cunningham, Labour's local government spokesman, and his deputy Jack Straw, produced anti-poll-tax material for the election, but the shadow cabinet ruled that it should not be sent out—under heavy lobbying from Mandelson and Charles Clarke, Neil Kinnock's chief of staff. Nevertheless, on the two occasions when Cunningham did raise the poll tax, it excited little or no media interest. From the point of view of the Labour strategists, this was doubtless a relief, but it ensured that the community charge was barely discussed. Even the Tories were baffled by Labour's failure to run with the issue.

Conservatives found little reaction to the poll tax in England and Wales, though there was the beginning of a reaction in Scotland. The Nationalists, in particular, were effective in presenting the poll tax as something imposed on Scotland by the southern, Thatcherite, English. The Tories saw their Scottish representation more than halve in the 1987 election, falling from 21 to 10 seats. Poll tax was one of the causes, but few of the defeated Scots thought it decisive. The Nuffield study of the election makes not one reference to the poll tax as an issue in the campaign. Defence dominated the hostilities.[36] As fate would have it, the parliament returned in the election saw the

Maureen McGoldrick, a local headmistress, for alleged racist conduct. There were protracted protests, rebukes from the national Labour leadership, lawsuits, and a teachers strike before the council reluctantly withdrew the suspension.

[35] Labour Party Manifesto, 1987, 11.

[36] D. Butler and K. Kavanagh, *The British General Election of 1987* (1988), 89–113.

collapse of the Berlin Wall and the virtual eradication of defence as an issue dividing the parties, while the poll tax was to overwhelm the country for the best part of three years.

FLAGSHIP POLL TAX

The election produced a Tory landslide. Mrs Thatcher's Tories gained an overall Commons majority of 100—down from the 140 won in 1983, but still the third largest majority won by any party since 1945. In so far as a general election gives a mandate for anything, no one could doubt that the government had a mandate for the poll tax, which had been in the manifesto. To scotch any doubts as to her resolve, at a pre-recess talk to the 1922 Committee of Tory back-benchers in July 1987, Mrs Thatcher made her famous reference to poll tax as the 'flagship of the Thatcher fleet'.

None the less, the design of the flagship was still far from decided, and its passage through parliament was far from assured. So low profile had poll tax been in the election and the months before, that most Tory MPs were turning their mind to it for the first time. The more they did so, the more worried many of them became. None realized this more acutely than the admiral of the fleet. Shortly after the election Mrs Thatcher was told by the whips that there were barely 150 'clear supporters' of the poll tax, against nearly 100 'doubters' and 24 outright opponents. 'There was a real danger that over the summer recess many of the doubters would commit themselves against the [community] charge altogether,' she recalls.[37]

So the government trod warily. The Queen's Speech opening the new session of parliament revealed only that 'a Bill will be introduced to abolish domestic rates in England and Wales, and to make new arrangements for the finance of local government.'[38] In her speech in the ensuing debate on the address, Mrs Thatcher devoted precisely two sentences to the new tax. Neil Kinnock was a little more expansive, but still underplayed

---

[37] Thatcher, *Downing Street Years*, 652.
[38] *HC Debs.*, 25 June 1987, col. 39.

the issue. He concentrated his attack not on the unfairness of the new tax but on the principle of a tax on the right to vote. 'With the poll tax, the government are saying: no representation without taxation,' he said, adding (optimistically, given the out-turn): 'the vote in the British democracy is to cost an average of £205 per adult per year if the government have their way.'[39]

The government could afford to play it long. With an unusually protracted parliamentary session of sixteen months at its disposal, there was no rush; the aim was to have the legislation on its parliamentary way by January 1988. At this early stage, ministers and whips went out of their way to hint, even on occasion to state categorically, their preparedness to consider a range of options, including a graduated tax. Michael Mates, an unlikely but determined opponent, even got an undertaking from Nicholas Ridley that his officials would be put at Mates's disposal to work out the details of a banded tax: if the difficulties could be overcome, Ridley told him, the government would entertain the idea seriously. Ridley himself had no serious intention of making changes, but his junior ministers and the whips proffered olive branches not just out of concern for the smooth passage of the bill. They were anxious to avoid unnecessary blood on the carpet: poll tax was a cause to which few of them were passionately attached, and some, at least, wanted to keep escape routes open should the flagship spring dangerous leaks.

In any case, the design of the flagship was proving highly contentious within the government, where there was still no agreement on certain key features. The most important of these was the question of phasing the transfer from rates to poll tax—'dual-running', in the contemporary jargon.

Even before the 1987 election, Department of the Environment officials were urging an end to dual-running. Increasingly they came to see the administrative consequences of running the proposed new tax alongside rates as complex, controversial, and unpredictable. The Scots had already abandoned dual-running. Nicholas Ridley needed little convincing that the

[39] *HC Debs.*, 25 June 1987, cols. 49 and 56.

same should be done in England. In addition to the administrative problems, he was convinced that dual-running would be a political disaster: it would 'completely obscure' the 'accountability advantages' of the poll tax.[40] When confronted by Terry Heiser and Chris Brearley with a strong case for a clean break between rates and community charge, he was easily won over.

The 1987 election saw another change of local government minister, with Michael Howard replacing Sir Rhodes Boyson. Howard knew virtually nothing about local government finance on arrival, like virtually all the ministers entering the Department of the Environment in rapid succession after the departure of Kenneth Baker in May 1986. But an accomplished barrister, he learnt fast. At a meeting of Conservative MPs on 7 July, some 35 out of over 100 attending questioned Ridley and Howard closely for over two hours about the detailed effects of the community charge. There was general support for the principle of making everyone contribute towards the cost of local services, though some outright opposition from a small number of senior back-benchers, including Michael Heseltine and Sir George Young. Another group of MPs supported the community charge, but only in the context of transferring the costs of education from local to central government, and thus reducing the local tax burden. There was a spirited debate about whether the new tax should be introduced quickly or slowly.

On 14 July a cabinet committee considered the transitional arrangements for the period when the new tax was introduced. The idea of a longer period of transition for London, with a shorter period elsewhere was discussed.[41] A further meeting on 27 July was also devoted to the transitional arrangements. By this point, the argument about speed of introduction had boiled down to a disagreement between Ridley, who wanted fast implementation, and Nigel Lawson, who fought for the

[40] Ridley, *My Style of Government*, 124.

[41] By now, the government had decided to allow boroughs in inner London to opt out of the Inner London Education Authority. Such opt-outs would inevitably produce financial turbulence which might aggravate losses faced by some households at the point community charge was introduced. In the event, ILEA was abolished outright.

continued operation of dual-running. Although Ridley and Howard lobbied Tory back-benchers on the issue,[42] they ultimately conceded dual-running, and on 30 July the government announced that community charge would be phased in over four years, as agreed in cabinet committee some months earlier. In the first year of change, there would be a charge of £100 per adult, with a consequent reduction in the overall rates bill. Thereafter, there would be three further years of transition.

However, matters did not rest there. The Conservative party conference at Blackpool in October reopened the whole issue. During the local government debate at the conference there was overwhelming support for the new tax: only a dozen or so voted against the motion supporting the reform. A speech by Gerry Malone, one of the Scottish victims of the 1987 election, was received with particular rapture by the activists in the hall. Having lost his Aberdeen seat, Malone wanted to register a high-profile reminder (on an English topic) that he was still 'around'. Leon Brittan, whose parliamentary private secretary he had been, suggested that he speak about the community charge. This he did, calling for it to be introduced without any transitional period.

Despite repeated claims since, Malone was not put up to the job by Nicholas Ridley. Nigel Lawson baldly states that Ridley and Michael Howard 'contrived a succession of speakers from the floor . . . who called for the immediate abolition of the rates'.[43] Both Howard and Ridley have denied that Malone's speech was contrived; but their enthusiasm for the cause he was supporting was undoubted, and nothing was done—as it often is at Tory conferences—to deflect or stifle debate on an issue contrary to government policy.

Mrs Thatcher sat through the poll tax debate to gauge the mood of the activists. After the ecstatic reaction to Gerry Malone, she muttered to Ridley: 'We shall have to look at this again, Nick.'[44] Back in London after the conference, the cabinet

[42] Lawson, *View from No. 11* (1992), 579.   [43] Ibid. 579.

[44] The TV cameras picked up the incident and lip-readers were employed to decipher her remarks. Ridley later claimed she said: 'Do you want another

committee returned to the issue of transitional arrangements. Lawson and Baker argued for the retention of dual-running,[45] but the Prime Minister had shifted decisively to Ridley's position[46] and his view won through.

However, dual-running was not the only target of the ire of Tory activists and back-benchers. The Green Paper had promised that distributional effects of the new uniform business rate and community charge would be 'offset by a system of self-financing adjustments'.[47] These adjustments were colloquially known as 'safety nets'. The impact of the introduction of the new grant and business rate arrangements was, in most cases, to transfer resources from authorities with higher spending needs and lower resources—generally in the North and the Midlands—to authorities with lower spending needs and a larger resource base—predominantly in the South-East. Safety netting meant that the 'gaining' authorities in the South had to forgo their gains in order to fund the safety nets for the 'losing' authorities in the Midlands and the North. This system was seen by many Tory MPs in the South-East as grossly unfair: their constituents were, as they saw it, having to pay a surcharge in order to continue to support profligate Labour councils. The cry went up to abandon safety nets as well as dual-running.

On 17 November 1987 Nicholas Ridley announced that poll tax would be introduced in most places without dual-running and that safety netting would be changed. Dual-running would be abandoned in all areas except those which were spending more than £130 per head above the needs assessment used within the grant system. Where spending was £130 per head or more above this bench-mark, there would be a four-year transition from rates to poll tax. On this basis, dual-running would operate throughout inner London and in the outer London borough of Waltham Forest.

glass of water, Nick?', but, he adds in his memoirs: 'I don't think I was believed.' Ridley, *My Style of Government*, 125.

[45] Lawson, *View from No. 11*, 580; Baker, *Turbulent Years*, 129.

[46] Thatcher, *Downing Street Years*, 652–3.

[47] *Paying for Local Government*, 76.

The flagship constructed, the next task was to launch it in parliament.

GENTLEMANLY REBELS

Organized opposition to the poll tax got going on the Tory back-benches well before the Local Government Finance bill, the formal title of the legislation to enact it, made its first appearance in the Commons. With the grapeshot of the general election still in the air, a group of sceptics, headed by Sir George Young, began lobbying in private to get the 'flat rate' aspect of the tax modified. Young, a diffident but sharp and indefatigable Etonian baronet, knew only too well from his own constituency of Acton, a West London suburb, the likely impact of the tax; and as a former junior minister at the Department of the Environment (sacked, it is said, for his uncompromising treatment of the tobacco lobby) he had little trouble finding his way around Whitehall. He soon attracted a group of a few dozen like-minded back-benchers, the number growing as the practical problems of the poll tax became steadily more apparent.

Despite Mrs Thatcher's forebodings, by the time parliament reassembled in October the whips had got the number of rebels to well under fifty. The obvious enthusiasm of the Tory conference and constituency activists for the flagship persuaded some back on board; at least as many again were enticed by the prospect of flexibility in the consideration of amendments. As so often, the containing of the initial rebel threat also reduced the need for subsequent concessions. In the event, taking the three key Commons votes on the poll tax legislation together, the total number of Tory rebels were only 39; and the number on any single vote never exceeded 38.[48] With a majority of 100, the government was never remotely in danger.

Nicholas Ridley introduced the Local Government Finance bill into the Commons on 16 December 1987. The pressure to speak on the Bill led to the second reading being allotted two days. Ridley presented the Bill as above all a measure to abolish the rates. Declaring that to be the object of virtually everyone, including the Labour party, he challenged critics to come up with something better. In the main, they failed to do so—or, at least, they were extremely timid about doing so, talking vaguely about 'modernized' property taxes. Ministers used this as valuable ammunition. Arguments for accountability and fairness, though voiced, were secondary.

The first and most prominent Tory critic was Michael Heseltine, who spoke immediately after Jack Cunningham, shadow environment secretary, in the first day's debate. Heseltine reminded MPs that the poll tax had been rejected out of hand in his 1981 review. 'I wish I could come to the House and say that I had won the argument, but in truth there was no argument.' He denied the poll tax would do much to improve accountability. Rather, it would provoke profound discontent, with resentment building 'upon a platform of crude regression which seeks to make equal in the eyes of the tax collector the rich and the poor, the slum dweller and the landed aristocrat, the elderly pensioners living on their limited savings and the most successful of today's entrepreneurs.'

[48] See Ch. 10 below for a fuller discussion of the Tory rebels and Table 10.1 for a list of the rebels.

However, Heseltine's sharpest words were for the damage the poll tax would do to the Conservative party itself:

Responsibility for the rates is confused in the legacy of history. Responsibility for the poll tax will be targeted precisely and unavoidably at the Government who introduced that tax. That tax will be known as the Tory tax.[49]

Those themes recurred throughout the bill's passage in the Commons. They were taken up by other Tory critics, six more of whom spoke out against the second reading. But they made little impression on the Tory back-benches. Two of those speaking against, Edward Heath and Sir Ian Gilmour, were bitter and habitual opponents of Mrs Thatcher's; of the other four, three (Sir George Young, Timothy Raison, and Sir Philip Goodhart) were former ministers whose careers had notably failed to prosper in the 1980s. In the vote at the end of the second reading debate, the government's majority fell from its customary 100 to 72, with 17 Tories voting against—a comfortable margin nevertheless. Heseltine abstained. Several Tory malcontents, including Hugh Dykes and Michael Mates, a friend of Heseltine's, voted with the government at this stage, believing Ridley's assurances that amendments would be seriously considered later on. Had they rebelled, the government's majority would still have been decisive.

A Labour motion to refer the Bill to a committee of the whole house was defeated by a majority of 96 immediately after the main vote on the second reading, and the Bill proceeded to a standing committee in the normal way. It was not, however, a normal standing committee. In an adroit move to placate Tory opponents, Ridley pledged before the second reading that known Tory sceptics would be included on the committee. Since by now neither Ridley nor the whips had any intention of appeasing the rebels on matters of substance, they constructed a committee large enough to include Young and a few waverers without putting the government's majority in doubt. Accordingly, standing committee D, to which the Local Government Finance Bill was committed, had 44 members, about 20 more

[49] *HC Debs.*, 16 Dec. 1987, col. 1141.

than usual. The membership divided 26 Conservatives, 15 Labour, two Liberal Democrats, and a Welsh Nationalist.

Of the 26 Tories, only one, Young, was opposed to the poll tax root and branch. One other, Hugh Dykes, a notable 'wet' and ardent pro-European, was opposed to extending the tax to those at the bottom of the income scale, but was unwilling to press his opposition to the point where it might be damaging. On the Bill's key principle, therefore, the government had an assured majority. The committee also included one other Tory free-thinker, Sir Brandon Rhys-Williams, the long-serving member for Kensington who was ill at the time and died soon after the committee stage. Rhys-Williams, a tax expert, supported the flat-rate principle, but was concerned at the bureaucracy involved in the register for the new tax, and believed that it could only be 'safely' introduced if its average level was around £100, which he wanted to achieve by removing the funding of education, police, and fire services from local government entirely. However, even with Rhys-Williams in the opposition lobby, together with Young and Dykes, Ridley still had a bare majority. Of the other 23 Tories, four were ministers and one a whip; the remainder were up-and-coming back-benchers more or less ambitious for advancement. There were no other likely rebels; only one Tory member, Keith Raffan, appears to have indulged in so much as a deliberate abstention. Within two years of serving on the committee, five of the Tory back-benchers had been appointed junior ministers—including, such is the wheel of fate, Sir George Young himself.

Unusually for a Secretary of State, Ridley served on the standing committee. But Michael Howard, his Minister of State with responsibility for local government, took the lead in defending the bill. Howard, a combative debater with a pen-chant for the sarcastic one-liner,[50] owed his promotion to the cabinet in 1990 to his skills at the dispatch-box in the Commons, exhibited good effect in defending the two most unpopular measures of the 1987 parliament: the poll tax and

[50] A Labour MP's erudite investigations into the consequences of previous poll taxes met this retort: 'it is utterly typical of Labour members that fearful as they are to face the realities of today, they retreat into the mists of history to find arguments against the legislation.'

water privatization. On the Labour side, the honours were more evenly shared. Jack Cunningham took the lead, but was ably assisted by David Blunkett, Sheffield's former city council leader, and Jeff Rooker, a Birmingham MP, later to emerge as a leading champion of electoral reform in the party. For the Liberal Democrats, Matthew Taylor, baby of the House, cut his parliamentary teeth on the Bill.

As with most controversial government Bills, the standing committee was a futile marathon. Between mid-January and mid-March 1988, the committee held 35 sessions, sitting for a total of 120 hours. Starting at 10.30 every Tuesday and Thursday, it adjourned at 1 p.m., then reconvened at 4 p.m., often sitting until 10 or 11 p.m. at night, with a two-hour break for dinner—or, on the occasion of Nicholas Soames's fortieth birthday, a champagne reception. On one occasion, the committee kept going until 2.30 a.m. Most of the debate was between the two front benches, with only Young, Rhys-Williams, and Edward Leigh making more than the occasional interventions from the Tory back-benches. The committee's proceedings went virtually unnoticed in the press.

A colossal amount of committee time was spent on the first few clauses—again, typically for a controversial Bill—after which the government resorted to a guillotine so that most of the later clauses went through with virtually no debate. The committee spent 35 hours on the first two clauses alone; since these covered the issue of whether or not the tax should be flat rate, Labour and Liberal members filled the hours with ease. The axe fell after 70 hours and 17 of the Bill's 129 clauses, the guillotine motion allocating a mere 18 sittings to the outstanding clauses and sections—including all the arrangements for the community charge register, rebates, and administration.

The government did not lose any of the 173 votes held during the committee stage. Only three Tories (Rhys-Williams, Young and Dykes) voted against the government on any occasion. Only once, however, did all three do so together: this was on Sir Brandon's pet theme of 'nationalizing' education and fire-service spending so as to reduce the headline tax, an issue on which they gained no opposition support. For the rest,

Young and Dykes voted against the government on some amendments supported by the Labour party, but rarely together. Rhys-Williams abstained on a series of amendments (all defeated by one vote, because of other Tory absentees) constraining the powers of poll tax registration officers on the grounds that he could not support the clause as a whole; but in the vote on the inclusion of the clause as a whole, Dykes, who had voted for the amendments, either abstained or was absent, giving ministers a majority of one on that vote too. In the bill's entire passage through the Commons, only five or so minor opposition amendments were accepted, two of them changing the word 'March' to 'January'.

The committee stage was mostly a matter of posturing. There were a few honest attempts to improve the detail of the Bill: Sir Brandon Rhys-Williams was to the fore in attempts to sort out the detail of the registration system; and his proposal to 'nationalize' spending on education, police, fire, and civil defence was a brave stab at the central difficulty of the poll tax, the weight of local spending it was obliged to support. His analysis of the problem was insightful:

There is an element of artificiality in saying that education, police and other services are at local discretion . . . I believe that a personal charge of about £100 would be quite tolerable, and a range of charges from one authority to another of about £50 to £150 would meet the government's objective.[51]

But Ridley swept such pleas aside with barely an argument.

The government introduced a mass of amendments of its own to improve the mechanics of the Bill. For the rest, it was scrutiny by slogan and soundbite. Whenever the fairness issue arose, ministers and Tory back-benchers, led by the pugnacious Edward Leigh, simply attacked Labour for failing to produce an alternative, and recited a few carefully culled statistics. Their favourite point was that the top 10 per cent of households by income would pay six times as much in poll tax as the bottom 10 per cent—which highlighted the only group gaining rebates from the flat-rate charge. The absence of reliable data was

[51] Standing Committee minutes, cols. 62 and 1388.

stark: Young himself was forced to rely on sketchy research notes compiled by the House of Commons library to estimate the likely impact of the tax.

So the poll tax left the standing committee unscathed. However, the main confrontation was still to come, with the return of the Bill to the floor of the Commons for its report stage. By now, the potential cost of the poll tax was becoming clearly apparent. At the end of 1987 the government had commissioned CSL Consultants to estimate the financial implications of establishing the tax in Scotland: its report concluded that significant extra staff and computing would be needed in the period up to April 1989. On 14 April 1988, a few days before the debate on the vital Mates amendment, Michael Howard announced that £25m. would be made available to councils in England for preparation costs in 1988–9. By now, the committee battle was looking like a phoney war: George Young and his colleagues were mobilizing for the real parliamentary battle to come at the report stage on the floor of the House.

THE MATES AMENDMENT

Michael Mates describes his assault on the poll tax as 'one of the most gruelling things I've done in politics'. Once it became clear that his private concerns expressed to Ridley would bear fruit in an amendment seeking to modify the flat-rate principle, the atmosphere turned distinctly ugly. Severe pressure was brought on Mates himself both through his constituency ('though the whips backed off after one fruitless approach to one member of my East Hampshire executive'), and directly in an interview with the chief whip, David Waddington, who claimed ('as whips always do') that the government was set for defeat on his amendment, a defeat likely to undermine the Prime Minister. Mates's position as secretary of the influential 1922 Committee of Tory back-benchers was a particular cause of ministerial concern: it gave him a vantage-point and official respectability possessed by few of the other rebels. Though not invariably a loyalist—his chairmanship of the defence select

committee had led to some notable run-ins with defence ministers over the release of information—he was not an inveterate
rebel, and was not known as a 'wet'.

Mates's amendment called for a banded poll tax related to
income tax thresholds. Those not paying income tax would pay
half the 'standard' poll tax; those paying income tax at the standard rate would pay the 'standard' poll tax; and those on the
higher income tax band would pay one-and-a-half standard poll
taxes. The government criticized the banded charge on the
grounds that it was administratively cumbersome, would
require significant additional data to be collected, and would
create an earnings trap for people moving from one band to
another. Ridley and John Major, then Chief Secretary, were
particularly outspoken. Yet the scheme had its origin in discussions between Mates and Ridley before the bill was even introduced. Ridley said he would look seriously at an attempt to
relate the level of the poll tax to income, and gave Mates access
to his officials. The amendment resulted from those discussions;
at their end, Mates was assured by 'a senior under secretary'—
in a conversation he later cited on the floor of the House, to
Michael Howard's fury—that his amendment was 'perfectly
workable' and that the only obstacle was 'political'.

However, the political obstacle proved the largest hurdle of
all. Thatcher and Ridley would not hear of a banded poll tax,
beyond some minor extensions of the 20 per cent charge for
students and those on income support. As Lawson recognized
from the outset,[52] a banded poll tax would be tantamount to a
local income tax. However much the Treasury hated the poll
tax, it hated a surrogate income tax far more. As soon as
Mates's amendment surfaced, the whips went on over-drive to
ensure its defeat. At least two new MPs went to Mates 'in
tears, or pretty close to it' after interviews with David
Waddington. Convinced, by the end, that 'we simply didn't
have the troops', Mates made it easy for the tortured to 'jump

---

[52] Recall his May 1985 memo, which argued that once the real impact of
the tax was evident 'we should be forced to give so many exemptions and concessions . . . that the tax would rapidly become a surrogate income tax.' See
above p. 80; and Lawson, *View from No. 11*, 574.

ship'; indeed, so sure was he, from careful canvassing, that Ridley was home and dry, he told David Owen not to bother to return early from Russia for the vote.

The chamber was packed for the debate on 18 April. It was held 'in an atmosphere of crisis', recalls Ridley, with Mrs Thatcher 'extremely concerned' at the outcome.[53] At the urgings of the whips, who believed he had a short fuse, Mates was heckled and interrupted throughout his speech, and a string of loyal back-benchers proceeded to denounce him. As he expected, at the end of the debate the government had a comfortable majority of 25. Some 13 Tory MPs abstained and 38 voted against the government, the most significant rebellion against Mrs Thatcher before she was brought down nearly three years later but 13 short of the number of outright opponents needed to turn defeat into victory.

The next day, George Jones, the *Daily Telegraph*'s well-connected political correspondent, claimed: 'the size of the rebellion has shaken ministers and is bound to lead to an urgent review of the poll tax legislation.'[54] It led to no such review, merely relief that the revolt had been fought off. The only 'urgent review' was of the position of Mates himself: the loyalists who barracked him followed up the defeat with a successful campaign to have him thrown off the 1922 Committee and ejected from the chairmanship of the Conservative back-bench Home Affairs Committee. They failed, however, to get him out of the chair of the Defence Select Committee, a post he held until his appointment as a Minister of State at the Northern Ireland Office when John Major replaced Mrs Thatcher in November 1990. Michael Heseltine returned to office on the same day. Sir George Young had by then already returned to the government: Mrs Thatcher appointed him to the whips' office in July 1990, on the strong advice of Tim Renton, the chief whip, who wanted him—in Lyndon Johnson's graphic phrase—'pissing out, not pissing in'.

There was a private awareness that the poll tax enjoyed little support within ministerial ranks. Michael Mates received con-

[53] Ridley, *My Style of Government*, 129.
[54] *Daily Telegraph*, 19 Apr. 1988.

gratulatory letters from ministers, including one in the cabinet, after moving his banding amendment. When the bill reached the Lords, Roy Jenkins noted in the second reading debate:

I cannot discover any member of the present Cabinet, apart from the Prime Minister and the Secretary of State for the Environment himself, who is in favour of the legislation . . . The total stand-off which this measure has brought forth is something which I have never previously witnessed.[55]

But if the rebels in the Commons were fully aware of ministerial misgivings, ministerial opponents did not lift a finger to assist the rebels, apart from sending consoling notes after the event. Nigel Lawson expected his opposition to have been evident by his omission from the list of ministerial sponsors printed on the back of the bill,[56] a telling commentary on the nod-and-wink code observed by ministers under Thatcher, so subtle that no press commentators and virtually no backbenchers picked it up.

THE HOUSE OF LORDS

It was widely assumed that the poll tax would have a rough ride in the House of Lords. In the mid-1980s the peers had created something of a reputation for themselves for their supposed willingness to put spokes into Mrs Thatcher's wheels. In fact, most of the government's legislation sailed through the Upper House unscathed, but they made one notable intervention after the 1983 election, refusing to allow the government to abolish the Greater London Council until arrangements for the transfer of its responsibilities were in place. The arguments on that issue were quasi-constitutional, and it was thought that similar arguments in the case of the poll tax might make their lordships less than enamoured of the government's proposed revolution in local authority finance.

In the event, the constitutional arguments worked both ways, and on balance militated against an activist role for the Lords.

[55] *HL Debs.*, 9 May 1988, col. 840.
[56] Lawson, *View from No. 11*, 584.

The poll tax was unambiguously a financial measure. Since its defeat in the battle over Lloyd George's 'People's Budget' of 1909, the Lords has been disbarred from amending or delaying 'Money Bills'. The Local Government Finance bill was not formally a Money Bill, but as a measure of taxation, it was plausible to argue that the Lords should not tamper with its key provisions. The very rehearsal of the argument—not least by Nicholas Ridley, unabashed by his noble brother (a viscount)—made a number of cross-bench and Tory back-bench peers nervous about voting for amendments affecting the principles of the bill.

The constitutional brickbats were flying even before the poll tax reached the Upper House. Lord Jenkins and Sir William Wade, Master of Clare College, Cambridge, a leading constitutional authority, clashed with Lords Hailsham and Beloff in the letters column of *The Times* as to the right of the Upper House to tamper with the Bill at all.[57] Ironically, Jenkins, leader of the Liberal Democrat peers since his ennoblement in 1987, had made his literary name with *Mr Balfour's Poodle*, a study of the consequences of the peers' decision to reject Lloyd George's 1909 budget. His defence of the Lords' right to amend the poll tax was highly conditional and far from convincing. 'The correct role for an unelected second chamber is never an easy one to determine,' he conceded on the Bill's second reading in the Lords, continuing:

It is perhaps not a bad rule of thumb that it should act in such a way, as with enlightened self-interest, to enhance its own medium-term influence . . . I hazard a guess that if the Government were given an automatic immunity by this Chamber on the bill, a new phase might begin, and that the influence and interest which your Lordships' House has recently attracted might well begin to diminish.[58]

However, the weakness of the opposition to the poll tax in the Lords was only partly due to constitutional arguments.

[57] Wade wrote a *Times* feature arguing that the Lords 'may consider themselves entitled to "have a go" with the poll tax'. But the invitation came after a lengthy recital of the fatal consequences of earlier attempts by the peers to assert themselves in matters of finance. *The Times*, 4 May 1988.

[58] *HL Debs* 496, col. 842.

Equally important was the lack of senior Tories willing to lead and lobby discontented Tories, and the strength of the government's whipping operation in the key votes. Sir George Young and Sir Ian Gilmour tried to persuade a number of prominent Tory peers to take up their mantle, including Lords Pym and Prior, disaffected ex-Thatcher ministers who had gone to the Lords in 1987. They all refused, reluctant to turn on their former colleagues.[59] The best flagbearer the rebels could come up with was the unknown Lord Chelwood. As Sir Tufton Beamish, Chelwood had been Tory MP for Lewes from 1945 until 1974, succeeding his father in the seat. The model for the legendary Bufton-Tufton 'old-buffer' back-bencher, he rapidly became an object of ridicule, described by the *Sun* as leader of the 'Tufty club', and by his fellow Tory peers by less flattering titles. His speeches against the Bill were ineffective, and his attempts to rally support equally so.

Lord Denham, the government's long-serving chief whip in the Upper House, 'moved heaven and earth' (in the words of one close associate) to get the Tory backwoodsmen to the House. On 23 May, in one of the largest divisions ever held in the Lords, the key amendment to relate the poll tax to 'ability to pay' was crushed by 317 votes to 183. Its strongest opponent in the debate was Lord Whitelaw, rendering his last notable service for the poll tax and Mrs Thatcher from the back-benches (a stroke had forced him to resign in January). 'I went through all the discussions in government about the Bill before its introduction,' he reminded the peers. 'As a result I am convinced that the decision to abolish the existing rating system must be right.' Throwing the full weight of his authority as the former leader of the Lords behind the government, he urged Tories not to consort with Labour, appealing skilfully to their sensibilities:

I have become a passionate believer in this place as a revising chamber. I am equally certain that it will destroy its whole effectiveness in

[59] In the event, none of the senior 'wets' of Mrs Thatcher's first term in the Lords—Carrington, Pym, Prior, St John-Stevas, or Soames—took any part in the deliberations on the bill in the Lords.

that role if it seeks to confront the elected Chamber and the government in that elected Chamber.[60]

The Archbishop of Canterbury and three fellow bishops were in the minority, but that was insufficient to overcome the highest turn-out of Tory peers in living memory.[61] Only a handful of Tories voted with the opposition. Afterwards, almost everyone agreed it had been overkill on Denham's part (Whitelaw lamented the fact that it wasn't possible to do anything less); but it ensured that the Bill left the Upper House with only two amendments carried against the government: one to extend 80 per cent rebates to student nurses, and another to give more generous rebates to disabled people under high-spending councils. By contrast, the government amendments tabled in the Upper House made the tax purer still: it was at report stage in the Lords that amendments were moved giving the final *coup de grâce* to dual-running.[62]

The Local Government Finance Bill received the royal assent

[60] *HL Debs.*, 23 May 1988, col. 650.

[61] Ironically, it was to be exceeded five years later when in July 1993 the Lords crushed a bid by Baroness Thatcher to require a referendum to be held on the Maastricht Treaty by 445 votes to 176.

[62] *HC Debs.*, 30 June 1988.

on 29 July. By now, however, the battle was already moving out of parliament. In late July, 18 Labour MPs, almost all from the Campaign Group, went public on their intention to defy the party leadership. Dave Nellist and Terry Field, Militant-leaning MPs from Coventry and Liverpool, were in the van. Neil Kinnock moved swiftly to distance the Labour leadership from any whiff of non-payment, but he faced immediate problems with senior colleagues, notably Robin Cook, who had given public support to non-payment, partly because of anxiety to avoid a backlash which might further boost the SNP in Scotland. In mid-August a tortuous compromise was apparently agreed, whereby Cook agreed not to encourage non-payment, or to discuss it with the press, although he would still not pay the tax himself.[63] Moreover, Labour had still to come up with an alternative to the poll tax. On 20 July, the party's National Executive Committee finally approved a policy statement advocating a mix of local income tax, the Liberal Democrats' favoured option, with a property tax based on capital values.

Ministers were relieved that Labour was so ineffective in opposing the poll tax. But the poll tax did not need Labour: it was its own worst enemy, and its destructive potential was soon to be manifest in the demands dropping through every letter-box in the country.

---

[63] *Scotsman*, 19 Aug. 1988. In the event Cook paid his poll tax, in common with almost all the Labour MPs who had threatened non-payment.

6

IMPLEMENTATION 1988–1990

> The only objection to the poll tax as far as I can see . . .
> is that no one will pay. It'll be like jay-walking.
> And by no one I mean all the yobs, slobs, drifters,
> junkies, free-loaders, claimants, and criminals on day-
> release, who make their living by exploitation of the
> benefit system and overload local authority expenditure.
> As usual the burden will fall on the thrifty, the prudent,
> the responsible, those 'of fixed address', who patiently
> support society and the follies of the chattering class.
>
> Alan Clark, *Diaries* (1993), 25 March 1990

There is no evidence that the poll tax was ever popular. For all
the trumpeting by Kenneth Baker, William Waldegrave, and
their associates of the vital necessity for a poll tax to bring local
government into tune with popular demands, the original studies team commissioned no 'market research', and no subsequent
attempt was made by the government to find out what the electorate at large thought about it. The Tories had, of course,
been returned for a third term on a manifesto which included a
commitment 'to replace rates with a fairer community charge'.
But given the low prominence of the issue in the campaign, and
the hypothetical nature of the 'fairer community charge' on
offer, it was an unwise course for ministers to swallow their
own rhetoric and suppose that the voters had given a ringing
endorsement of the poll tax. As the Tory Prime Minister Lord
Salisbury remarked of one of his landslide election victories:
'when the Great Oracle speaks, no one is quite sure what the
Great Oracle said.'[1]

[1] *HL Debs.*, 15 Aug. 1895, col. 51.

As early as the summer of 1987, the Great Oracle seemed to be far from enamoured by the new tax it was soon to have to pay. A Gallup poll in late July showed that 54 per cent of the public opposed the new tax, with only 28 per cent in favour.[2] A similar survey in February, when the poll tax did not even exist on paper outside Scotland and its true proportions were largely unknown, showed only a slight majority in favour.[3] The early days were not promising.

EARLY DAYS

Public opinion was being fed by professional organizations, academics, and pressure groups, which were starting to predict the turmoil ahead. As early as May 1985, well before the decision was taken to introduce the poll tax, the Chartered Institute of Public Finance and Accountancy (CIPFA) published rudimentary but damning analyses of some of the distributional impacts of a poll tax.[4] Of the 1987 publications, a particularly revealing one was a study commissioned by Durham County Council,[5] which showed that very large losses would face people living in modest terraced houses. Over one in seven households would face local tax increases of more than 80 per cent, according to the study.[6]

Faced with evidence of growing public hostility, a cabinet committee on 27 July 1987 agreed that there should be a ministerial propaganda campaign during the autumn. On 8 September, the Department of the Environment announced that Michael Howard and the junior local government minister Christopher Chope would undertake a 'whistle-stop tour' of England to sell the community charge. On the same day, a political row broke out in Scotland about the need to have a personal identification number, similar to a driving licence number, for each local taxpayer. The opposition instantly argued that this made community charge the 'Big Brother tax'.

[2] *Daily Telegraph*, 27 July 1987.   [3] *The Times*, 20 Feb. 1987.
[4] R. Hale, *Poll Tax: Some Initial Analyses* (1985).
[5] See J. Gibson (1989), *The Politics and Economics of the Poll Tax*, ch. 6.
[6] Ibid. 107.

The National Council for Civil Liberties published a report in early October arguing for substantial data protection safeguards within the community charge legislation.[7] The pattern was already set for the next three years.

When the poll tax was first being discussed by the studies team in early 1985, an average full charge of £140 was envisaged to replace the rates entirely. On 1 April 1987, the government published figures suggesting an average charge of £205 in 1986–7.[8] Three months later, on 29 June, figures for 1987–8, based on actual spending, were showing an average poll tax of £324. However, when ministers discussed such figures they always stressed the charge which authorities could set if they spent at the government's approved spending level. So in 1987–8, Nicholas Ridley again and again concentrated on an average figure of £178 per adult. In reality, some authorities were already shown with charges of over £500, with Camden topping the list at a mind-boggling £782.

The Government clearly set about a massive exercise in self-delusion, or, alternatively, determined that any figures produced should fit an official propaganda line that the community charge was going to be a tax which would make most people better off. Time and again, D.o.E. officials were asked by ministers to produce analyses. The officials' efforts showed that over 50 per cent of households would gain because of the move to the poll tax. Such analysis was not difficult, because the calculations were made on the basis of a single year, say, 1988–9, and then on the simple assumption that precisely the same amount of money would be raised under community charge as had actually been collected by the domestic rates in that year. The move from a property-based tax to a people-based tax inevitably reduced the burden on households with one or two adults. Households with three or more adults would generally pay more. As there are more households—in terms of absolute numbers—with one adult than with three or more adults, there would inevitably be a majority of gaining households. But the

[7] *Daily Telegraph*, 5 Oct. 1987.
[8] 'Rate reform exemplifications.' Dept. of the Environment press notice no. 162 (1987).

number of gaining *adults* was close to 50 per cent, with 50 per cent being losers.

SCOTLAND GOES LIVE

The 1987 election, which followed immediately on the passage of the Scottish poll tax legislation, was an almost unmitigated disaster for the Conservative party in Scotland. The party lost more than half of its seats north of the border, and was reduced to a rump of ten MPs—insufficient, once ministers were appointed, even to man the Scottish Affairs select committee.

However, the shock was curiously muted. Coming on the same day as a second successive Tory landslide in England, which gave Mrs Thatcher a Commons majority of 100, the prime minister was not particularly preoccupied by the Scottish rout. Early in July word went out from her office that the 'Scottish problem' would have to be discussed by the full cabinet; but the same sources flatly ruled out policy changes, and made it clear that Malcolm Rifkind's attitude was one of 'wait and see'.[9] As for the Scottish select committee, the government simply refused to allow it to be re-established for the duration of the parliament.

Certainly, the view of Rifkind, Younger, even of the Tories who lost their seats in Scotland, was that the poll tax played only a minor role in the swing against them. One former MP thought it important in rallying the anti-Tory constituency to vote tactically, but even that was a minority view. 'We would have done worse still if we'd tried to ride the revaluation wave' is a typical view, endorsed by Rifkind, who thought it would be lunacy to go back on the reform now it was law. He also had a shrewd eye for Labour's Scottish predicament, both its general problem of appearing effective north of the border when it was powerless in London, and its particular difficulty of handling the Militants and Scottish National Party to its left on the issue of the poll tax.

For the short and medium term, Rifkind was right. The

[9] *Financial Times*, 6 July 1987.

twenty months between the election and the announcement by councils of their first poll tax figures saw the Scottish spotlight focus on Labour with barely a break. Three issues dogged the Labour leadership: what to do about those in its ranks, and to its left, campaigning for non-registration and non-payment; how to confront the Scottish National Party; and how to regain the initiative with local government finance proposals of its own. All three issues gave Neil Kinnock and Donald Dewar recurring headaches. The question of an alternative was not finally resolved until Bryan Gould's 'fair rates' plans of 1990. More pressing was the problem of non-payment and non-registration. After some initial prevarication, they threw their lot solidly against any form of illegality, and moved to expel from the party those consorting with the Militant Tendency in non-payment campaigns.

The issue came to a head at Labour's 1988 conference, when calls for an organized non-payment campaign reached a climax. Militant's slogan 'it's better to break the law than break the poor' had a wide appeal. After a strenuous debate, Donald Dewar carried the day against it with a bleak warning that to defy the poll tax would destroy Labour's electoral credibility. 'This is a party that aspires to be in government,' Dewar pleaded. 'I don't believe such a party can afford selective amnesia when it comes to the law of the land. That would be to sacrifice its credibility to the vast majority of electors.'[10] To underline the point, Kinnock ended the conference by sacking two of his Scottish front-bench spokesmen who had announced their intention not to pay the poll tax. Tony Benn, exasperated by his inability to get Kinnock to support the ill-fated Trafalgar Square rally in the spring of 1990, told his diary: 'The Labour Party is more frightened of the anti-poll tax campaign than of the poll tax itself.'[11] He was not far off the mark.

As early as the autumn of 1988, however, it was clear that Kinnock's main problem lay not inside but outside the Labour party. The number of Scots MPs refusing to register for or pay

[10] *The Times*, 5 Oct. 1988.
[11] T. Benn, *The End of an Era: Diaries* 1980–1990 (1992), 24 Jan. 1990, 585–6.

the tax was tiny. In the end it was only a handful of MPs, plus one MEP, Alec Falconer, who was fined £50 by a court for refusing to register or pay. The Militants were fairly easily dispensed with: Tommy Sheridan, Militant leader of first the Scottish, then the British anti-poll federation, was expelled in late 1989; the following March another six Scottish Militants were expelled, including Lynn Sheridan, Tommy's sister, and George McNeilage, his right-hand man. As for making non-payment respectable, the best the hard left could do was a much trumpeted 'Committee of 100' prominent non-payers, unveiled in the luxuriant foliage of Glasgow's Winter Gardens in November 1988, which featured a cast of seven Labour MPs, two clergymen, an actress, a few prominent academics, and had to make do with 'unknowns', including a retired customs officer, for the rest.[12]

By contrast, the threat posed by the Scottish National Party on Labour's left, campaigning resolutely on non-payment, was potent and immediate. It peaked in November 1988 at the Glasgow Govan by-election, which saw Jim Sillars, the charismatic former Labour MP who had moved over to the SNP after the 1979 election, overturn a Labour majority of 19,500 and increase the SNP vote fivefold, despite a fairly short campaign.

Meanwhile, the registration process was proceeding fairly smoothly. By November 1988 Rifkind was boasting in the Commons that 'more than 99 per cent' of adults in Scotland were on poll tax registers, despite the campaign against registration. However, stories abounded about the decline in the electoral register—one report, by Glasgow University's Applied Population Research Unit in May 1989, claimed that more than 26,000 people had 'disappeared' from the electoral registers of Scottish cities, largely to avoid paying the poll tax.[13] Even so, the numbers involved amounted to no more than another one per cent or so. Indeed, in May 1989 the Policy Studies Institute released part of a report—published in full in September, conveniently in the run-up to introduction of the tax in England

---

[12] *Independent* and *Daily Telegraph*, 22 Nov. 1988.
[13] *Independent*, 31 May 1989.

and Wales—showing a 'higher than expected registration rate'. Peter John, its author, went so far as to speculate that anti-poll tax protesters may have helped registration by raising public awareness of the tax and the penalties for non-registration.[14] When the PSI report was published in full in September, the *Financial Times* said it showed that the introduction of the tax in England and Wales 'should cause less difficulty than has been widely predicted'. Under the heading 'Easier Poll Tax Launch Forecast', it painted the report as 'additional welcome news for the Government with its conclusion that local authorities in Scotland managed to introduce the tax effectively and budget without cutting services'. Indeed, it stressed that the differences between Scotland and south of the border 'seem to point to an easier administrative experience for England and Wales', because of the additional time to prepare and the simpler administrative structures in England.[15] For his part, Rifkind did his best to smooth the introduction by periodic announcements of small sums for a transitional scheme or other, promising a low tax rate when the new scheme came into force in April 1989.

Late 1988 was, however, to be the turning-point for Scotland, as the debate moved from the hypothetical to the actual. Predictions were one thing; real charges levied by councils another. Equally, registration was no guarantee that the registered would actually pay.

The first grant settlement for the community charge in Scotland was set on 4 November 1988. Rifkind estimated that the tax levels for authorities in Scotland would, on the basis of 1987–8 spending figures, range from £313 per adult in Edinburgh to £84 in Orkney. Ian Lang, the Scottish local government minister, was quoted as saying that the predicted figures 'give the lie to the many absurd and misleading predictions about community charge levels that have been issued by our opponents'.[16] In reality (see Table 6.1) Rifkind's figures turned out to be well below the actual charges set in April 1989 (£392 in Edinburgh; £148 in Orkney) and were part of a pat-

---

[14] *Independent*, 27 May 1989.   [15] *Financial Times*, 14 Sept. 1989.
[16] Ibid. 5 Nov. 1988.

TABLE 6.1. Scotland's poll tax levels,
1989–1990

	Council charge (£)	Govt. estimate (£)
Borders	205	151
Central	213	166
Dumfries/Galloway	206	158
Fife	238	205
Highland	200	165
Lothian	305	247
Strathclyde	219	221
Tayside	241	193
Orkney	148	84
Shetland	114	202
Western Isles	171	126

tern of optimistically low estimates announced by ministers from time to time between 1986 and 1990.

It soon became clear that the first year's poll tax was going to be around 16 per cent higher than Rifkind had estimated and far higher in some areas. Councils had decided to spend far more than government estimates—about 13 per cent in cash terms. Indeed, they were encouraged to do so by the withdrawal of grant penalties, which previously had involved losses of the order of £2 for every £1 spent. This served as an open invitation to spend up in the first year of the new regime. The first year of the tax saw the gap between government provision and local budgets rise from 3.7 per cent to 6.5 per cent. In the previous five years it had actually fallen.[17]

As the reality dawned, mass protest began. In February 1989 a Scottish petition against the poll tax was delivered to Downing Street, containing over 300,000 signatures. In early April, as the poll tax started, around 15,000 joined a demonstration, the largest in central Edinburgh for years. Unfortunately for the

[17] A. Midwinter and C. Monaghan, *From Rates to Poll Tax* (1993), 7–8.

Tories, the blow fell just as the European election campaign was getting under way and Labour seemed to have turned the tide against the SNP. The European vote in June saw the Tories lose their last two European seats in Scotland, while in the Glasgow Central by-election, held on the same day, Labour easily saw off the SNP challenge. Worse still, a MORI poll published in the *Scotsman* shortly before the Euro-election showed 20 per cent saying they would take the poll tax into account when voting, against only 5 per cent who named the European Community.[18]

Initial SNP projections that the tax was 'unpaid by 500,000'—one in ten Scots—could be dismissed easily enough.[19] So could the 'army of poll tax protesters' who in July arrived on a Glasgow housing estate to protect Mrs Janette McGinn, widow of a celebrated Glasgow folk-singer, from the 'long arm of the debt recovery agent'.[20] (They appeared in other venues over the following weeks to thwart, variously, council officials, bailiffs, and the police.) By July, the horizon was somewhat less dismal for the government, with reports that 78 per cent of adults in Strathclyde had paid their poll tax—a figure the regional treasurer described as 'higher than expected', comparing favourably with Strathclyde's experience under the old domestic rating system. In the first three months of last year, 80 per cent of ratepayers had paid.[21]

As the months rolled on, SNP and Militant upped their claims for non-payment. By September the Anti-Poll Tax Federation had got the number of defaulters up to 900,000 of the 3.8m. eligible Scots.[22] However, the real figures coming in from treasurers were also far higher than previous projections. In early September Grampian, in the north-east, said its non-payment level stood at 15 per cent. A day later Lothian, Scotland's second largest council, disclosed that 17 per cent of those registered had still to make a contribution towards the community charge. Unofficial estimates suggested the figure might be as high as 20 per cent in Strathclyde. A *Sunday Times*

[18] *Sunday Times*, 11 June 1989.
[19] *The Times*, 31 May 1989.
[20] *Guardian*, 8 July 1989.
[21] *Independent*, 26 July 1989.
[22] *Daily Telegraph*, 2 Sept. 1989.

survey in early September showed one in six still to pay tax, with an average non-payment rate set to average 16.8 per cent across all the Scottish regions.[23]

It got worse still. In November Scottish banks told local authorities that they would be unable to cope with a large-scale programme of freezing the bank accounts of non-payers.[24] Another demonstration was held in Glasgow on 18 November, although it was not as large as that in April.[25] By December council treasurers were describing collection as a 'nightmare'. As anticipated by CIPFA and the other professional bodies long before the poll tax came in, it was not the first 75 per cent, but the last 25 per cent of the tax that was to prove hugely difficult and expensive to collect. Lothian reported that £25m. was outstanding and that it had asked sheriffs' officers to issue summary warrants to more than 76,000 people—12 per cent of its poll tax payers—who had still paid nothing. In the biggest region, Strathclyde, the picture was even worse, with an estimated 300,000 'refuseniks'—15 per cent of voters—owing an

[23] *Sunday Times*, 3 Sept. 1989.   [24] *Financial Times*, 29 Nov. 1989.
[25] *Scotsman*, 19 Nov. 1987.

estimated £60m.[26] By now Labour was confidently predicting that the tax was unworkable and would have to be scrapped.

At this point, the government floundered. Rifkind's immediate response was more schemes to exempt or relieve small numbers of poll tax payers, which only added to the confusion. In the autumn of 1989 those with degenerative illnesses were exempted. In December came a three-year package to help some of those who were faced with rises of more than £3 a week in their poll tax demands. Even then, the value of the relief was to be reduced by 25p per week in 1990–1 and by a further 25p in 1991–2. By December, it was estimated that one million people—almost one in three—were receiving rebates of some kind.

By now, a few Tory back-benchers could see the writing on the wall. As early as the summer of 1989 two former ministers, Alick Buchanan-Smith and Sir Hector Monro, were reported to be 'in open revolt'. Far from appeasing them, Mrs Thatcher's response was to make Michael Forsyth the new Scottish party chairman. Described even by *The Times* as 'right-wing and confrontational',[27] Forsyth's appointment was the move least calculated to reassure the doubters that the government appreciated the problem at hand. Forsyth's new deputy was William Hughes, chairman of Grampian Holdings and the Scottish CBI, who had apparently 'for some time now . . . been telling her [Mrs Thatcher] the sort of things she likes to hear about Scottish self-reliance and the enterprise culture'.[28] The only sign that the prime minister realized what was happening was a remark in response to an interviewer on Grampian TV in September that she was 'worried' by the apparently continuing decline in Conservative fortunes in Scotland.[29] 'It was difficult to understand why the Tory message was not getting through to the electorate north of the border,' she complained. She was soon to have as much difficulty 'getting through' to the English too.

[26] *Daily Telegraph*, 30 Nov. 1989; *Guardian*, 14 and 22 Dec. 1989.
[27] *The Times*, 17 July 1989.   [28] Ibid.
[29] *Daily Telegraph*, 8 Sept. 1989.

PREPARING FOR ENGLAND

As opposition to the real-life community charge flourished in
Scotland, Nicholas Ridley started a publicity campaign in
England to inform the public about the new tax. This was the
second such door-to-door campaign of its kind in this period:
the first had warned the populace about the dangers of AIDS.
As soon as the leaflets were issued, the London borough of
Greenwich challenged their legality on the grounds that they
were misleading. On 9 May 1989, the High Court ruled that
distribution of the leaflets which the government had intended
to send to every household in the country should be halted
pending a full court hearing. At the hearing a week later the
court rejected Greenwich's claims. The incident was typical of
the week-by-week problems which dogged the introduction of
the community charge.

During May 1989, cabinet-level discussions started about the
level of central grants to local government for 1990–1.
Decisions about the overall level of council spending and the
extent of grant support were generally announced to local
authorities in July. Such decisions were made somewhat in
advance of the rest of the public expenditure round. With
inflation low, there was at this stage no panic about the new
system. An average poll tax of about £270 was expected. But as
the summer wore on, different concerns about the new tax took
shape.

First, Conservative back-benchers became outspokenly angry
about the 'safety net' which gave local taxpayers in some—often
Labour-controlled—authorities protection from the redistribution of grants and non-domestic rates which would occur when
the community charge was introduced. This protection was
paid for by the requirement that local taxpayers in some areas—
many of them with Tory MPs—should forgo their gains from
the grant and business rate redistribution.

Second, it became clear that inflation was rising, and that the
assumptions likely to be built into the local government
financial settlement would understate inflation. Third, Central
Office and Downing Street were being provided for the first

time with detailed figures from several sources about the way in which community charge bills would redistribute local tax bills. Street-by-street analyses showed what the D.o.E.'s national statistics had always obscured: community charge would massively raise local tax bills for key marginal voters. By now, the Tories were falling significantly behind Labour in the polls for the first time since the 1987 election. They were to languish with dismal ratings until Mrs Thatcher's resignation in November 1990.

Local authorities, Tory back-benchers, and the Department of the Environment alike could see only one way out: more Treasury cash. It was just as Nigel Lawson had feared: once the true horrors of the poll tax became apparent, he would have to bail it out, threatening the integrity of his entire fiscal policy. Although Lawson and Ridley were ideological soul-mates, they had already had a serious falling-out over the poll tax. Before Lawson's radical tax-cutting budget of the previous year (1988), Ridley had urged the Chancellor not to cut the higher-rate tax-bands, because the coincidence of such a reduction with the poll tax reducing the local burden on the rich would be 'unfortunate, to say the least'.[30] As Lawson recalls:

Nick had the gall to try and persuade me to abandon my tax-cutting plans, in order to offset the regressive effects of the poll tax; going so far as to draft a mock statement in pseudo-Treasury language. He must have known there was no chance I would fall for this.[31]

Lawson was no keener to bail out the poll tax in 1989 than he had been to abandon his tax cuts in 1988. In the event, however, the pressure on him to do so was less than might have been expected. Ever sympathetic to pleas from the Prime Minister and Chancellor for public spending restraint, Ridley failed to press for the 'extra billion' the D.o.E. believed was essential to keep bills at affordable levels. At the crucial cabinet committee on 22 June, only Baker pressed for a higher sum, with no support from anyone else.[32]

In an interview with Channel 4 just before he died, Ridley

[30] N. Ridley, *My Style of Government* (1991), 133.
[31] N. Lawson, *The View from No. 11* (1992), 581.
[32] K. Baker, *The Turbulent Years* (1992), 131–2.

accepted that the Department of the Environment had not got sufficient grant for local government for 1990–1. 'You can say it was too little, but its not easy to get money out of the Treasury if you don't have their agreement.' Lawson, interviewed for the same programme said:

Nick did believe firmly in control of public expenditure and therefore, although he asked for extra money, he didn't ask for anything like the sums of extra money that Chris Patten (Ridley's successor at the D.o.E.) asked for because Chris Patten was not so concerned about controlling public expenditure.

Nevertheless, as Lawson was quick to add, the package—announced on 19 July—included additional local authority grants of more than £2 billion. To put this figure in context, the equivalent rise in Exchequer support throughout the whole period from 1980–1 to 1989–90 (the full period of Mrs Thatcher's premiership to date) had been some £2.4 billion. Thus, in the first year of the poll tax, even with Nicholas Ridley as Environment Secretary, the additional central support to local government rose by almost as much in a single year as it had over the previous decade. The capacity of the poll tax to consume vast sums of government cash was already clearly apparent.

The detail of the July settlement included further changes to the safety-net rules and a new grant for inner London authorities. Tory back-bench pressure had succeeded in convincing Ridley and Gummer that safety-netting had to be modified. Rhodes Boyson was quoted as saying: 'The community charge as it now stands is a Labour Party benevolent fund.' Under the remodified safety-netting rules, those authorities which gained because of the new grant and non-domestic rate distribution would see more of their extra funding flow through in 1990–1. Losers would find that they lost a larger amount than had previously been expected. But, to protect a number of authorities which—because of this new change of rules—would now lose very heavily in 1990, a new 'extra protection' grant would be introduced at a cost of £100 million. Councils receiving this new grant were all northern authorities with low rateable values (and thus recipients of relatively large grants in the pre-1990 system).

Separately from this new grant for authorities with very low rateable values, Ridley announced a new transitional grant for inner London boroughs. The government had decided to abolish the Inner London Education Authority (ILEA) at the end of March 1990. Thus the first day of community charge would coincide with the inner London boroughs taking over control of education for the first time. ILEA had always spent at levels way beyond what central government thought necessary, and there would inevitably have to be a period of financial adjustment for the new education authorities. The £100 million transitional grant was intended to assist, over four years, with the move to lower spending levels.

Finally, the 19 July announcement included the government's latest estimate of community charges. The average (on the basis of 1989–90 spending levels) was about £275, the figure which most MPs had in mind when they discussed the new tax. True, there were wide variations in the expected first year charge: Haringey was shown at £642 and Wandsworth at £148 per adult. But apart from scares about inner London and a number of other authorities such as Manchester (£404) and Basildon (£411), the average charge was still reasonably low. Figures for authorities in counties such as Kent, Hereford, and Worcester were well below £275. Many local taxpayers in the Home Counties, especially Buckinghamshire, would now face much lower bills because of the safety-net changes.

The 19 July settlement marked the third decisive stage in the poll tax catastrophe. The first was when, between March and July 1985, poll tax emerged as a replacement for domestic rates. The second was the 1987 Conservative party conference, when Gerry Malone articulated the conference's desire to abandon dual-running. The third occurred in July 1989 when, in a maladroit effort to stifle the political reaction to the new tax, the extra money made available was directed at the wrong places; most of the 'not-quite-poor' marginal voters were left largely unprotected from the large financial losses to come.

ENTER CHRIS PATTEN

Nicholas Ridley and John Gummer were replaced immediately after the July settlement. Chris Patten was appointed Environment Secretary and David Hunt local government minister. The poll tax had still to be introduced in England and Wales, yet Patten was the fourth Environment Secretary since the Baker Waldegrave studies launched the project in 1984, and Hunt was the fifth local government minister in the same period. Neither of them had had anything to do with the evolution of the new tax. As Minister for Overseas Development, Patten had spent the previous three years, in his words, 'travelling around Africa'. David Hunt came from the whip's office, where he had been cajoling recalcitrant back-benchers to support the poll tax as it went through the Commons.

It did not take Patten long to guess at the political nightmare which lay ahead. House-to-house surveys from key Tory marginals, given to him and Kenneth Baker (now Tory party chairman), confirmed the scale of the losers.[33] As the reality dawned on key groups of electors, Tory support plunged further: one poll, conducted by NOP for *Local Government Chronicle* in early October, found 63 per cent of the electorate opposing the community charge, compared with 54 per cent in 1988. Worse, social and economic groups C1 and C2 expected to be worst hit by the new tax. The front-line troops of the Thatcher revolution were about to be attacked by their own side, and they knew it.

It was immediately clear to Patten, as it had been to John Gummer at the time, that the level of grant to local government negotiated by Ridley for 1990–1 was too low: inflation was rising and there was no chance that an average charge of £275 would be achieved. Back-benchers were becoming restive. Alarm bells rang.

In his memoirs, Lawson expresses astonishment that Patten did not attempt to abort the poll tax at the outset, since 'he was in a strong position to do so'.[34] Patten insists that abortion was

[33] Baker *Turbulent Years*, 132.   [34] Lawson, *View from No. 11*, 581.

not an option, given the legal position and the advanced state of preparations for the new tax. In truth, the legal problems could have almost certainly have been overcome: a short Bill continuing the rating system would have been sufficient. Nor is there much to Baker's argument that 'the only person who can stop a tax is the Chancellor'.[35] Yet for such a course to have succeeded, the wholehearted support of the Prime Minister was the *sine qua non*. No minister in mid-1989 could have supposed Mrs Thatcher to be persuadable. Given her stance on the position in the leadership election a year later, and her ex-post justification in her memoirs,[36] any idea that she would have conceded is incredible.

At any rate, Patten never floated the idea of abolition. Instead, to Lawson's intense fury, the new Environment Secretary went directly to the Prime Minister to make his case for an additional £2bn. to supplement the £33bn. secured by Ridley. Following Patten's dash to Downing Street, David Hunt set to work with civil servants during the summer recess to think up a way of reducing the political flak. Richard Wilson, a senior Cabinet Office official,[37] chaired the group, whose other members included Terry Heiser, Chris Brearley, John Mills (from the Downing Street Policy Unit), and Michael Carpenter (from the Attorney-General's office). A team of civil servants was charged with thinking of solutions. The group examined a number of options, including getting the Treasury to pay for the safety net and some form of transitional relief for households which lost heavily because of the introduction of community charge.

The cost of immediately transferring the cost of the safety net to the Treasury was simply too high. Anyway, the group was convinced that, despite the protestations of Tory MPs

[35] Baker, *Turbulent Years*, 133. Lawson had, of course, attempted to stop the tax between 1985 and 1987. Baker adds that Lawson could have done so 'if necessary by threatening his resignation'. It would, however, have been perverse for Lawson to threaten resignation in 1989 over a policy he had endured in 1987.

[36] In *The Downing Street Years* (1993), 642, Mrs Thatcher sums up her belief that the tax would have worked, given time.

[37] Permanent Secretary at the D.o.E. following Heiser's retirement in 1992.

about safety netting, the problem of losing *households* was far more important than the political hue-and-cry created by Conservative authorities which were having to finance the safety net. Ironically, one of the worst-affected groups was pensioners living in low-rated properties.

When Lawson heard of Patten's demands, he refused to concede anything remotely approaching the £2bn., and summoned Patten to a dressing-down at No. 11, before an embarrassed Norman Lamont, then Chief Secretary.[38] Mrs Thatcher was unpersuaded that throwing money at the poll tax would solve anything.[39] However, with the party conference fast approaching, something had to be patched up rapidly. In a hastily prepared and ill-tempered cabinet committee in late-September, chaired (exceptionally) by Geoffrey Howe as deputy Prime Minister, Lawson agreed to fund the safety net after the end of the first year, and to pay for a £345m. package of further relief for the hardest-hit individuals. Patten had wanted £2bn. for the first year: he got £1.2bn. over three years, with most of the additional relief coming in the second and third years, i.e. well after the worst of the introductory problems had been encountered. A bitter Patten told a friend at a party afterwards: 'I've been screwed: until I came to this job I had no idea what a bastard Nigel Lawson was, nor how powerful the Treasury is.'

David Hunt announced the new package, of mind-boggling complexity, to the party conference on 11 October. The new transitional relief scheme, he told the applauding activists, would ensure that no individual or couple would lose more than £156 a year because of the introduction of community charge. In fact, that figure was based on the government's assumption of poll tax levels: since the highest-taxing authorities were well above the government targets, individuals stood to suffer far more heavily—a point lost on the activists, but soon to be fully apparent to those affected. Moreover, the relief would be phased out over a three-year period. In effect, this system reintroduced a limited form of dual-running: for households where rate bills were low and community charges would

[38] Baker, *Turbulent Years*, 133. [39] Thatcher, *Downing Street Years*, 657.

be high, there would be a gradual move from the lower to the higher bill. Similar—though crucially different—arrangements were announced for Wales. For Scotland, a form of transitional relief would be introduced retrospectively.

The changes announced at the 1989 Blackpool conference stood in a long line of efforts to make the community charge acceptable. In 1985 and 1986, these efforts were directed almost entirely at squaring interests within central government. During 1987, Gerry Malone and the party activists had to be placated. 1988 and 1989 saw Tory back-benchers and local authorities having more influence. By late 1989, the pressures on the new tax were severe and, inevitably, inconsistent. Party activists still favoured the full and immediate introduction of the community charge, yet they cheered David Hunt when he announced a transitional relief system which, in effect, reintroduced dual-running. Baker was by now keen to see the safety net abolished outright in the first year, to protect Tory-controlled councils facing elections in 1990.[40] Yet the effect of this on the inner cities could have been poll taxes close to £1,000 per person.

By any standards, bits were starting to drop off the edifice. In a characteristically acerbic attack on the poll tax immediately after the party conference, Simon Jenkins wrote in the *Sunday Times*:

Students at the Kenneth Baker school of poll tax studies will recall the first law of psepho-dynamics: 'Modern democracies cannot impose large, flat-rate personal taxes: electoral forces will distort them to destruction.' Even rates, a mildly progressive tax, involve rebates for some 20% of households. A poll tax, says our first law, implies more rebates simply because it hurts the poor more than the rich. MPs will simply refuse to deliver suicide notes with their electoral addresses. So it has proved. I estimate that more than half of those eligible will not pay a full tax for at least three years, and a third probably never. Already the cabinet has relieved lunatics, criminals, spies, nuns, soldiers and homeless persons. It has rebated students, the unemployed, the poor, pensioners and the disabled. Huge subsidies have been offered to high-spending, mostly Labour, councils under the 'safety net' scheme. These subsidies will next year come from the pockets of

[40] Baker, *Turbulent Years*, 134.

low-spending, mostly Tory councils, and for two years after that from national tax-payers. Such a bounty from Tory Gradgrinds to socialist Micawbers, after a decade of Thatcherism, will have future historians chewing the carpet in disbelief.[41]

Jenkins's article was no parody. Spies (or at least diplomats) were indeed exempt. Low-spending Tory areas were genuinely forgoing gains in order to underwrite losses in high-spending Labour authorities. Anomalies were being uncovered with regularity. The poll tax was advancing from the mere baroque to vulgar rococo, as the flailing efforts of ministers to dampen down political hostility produced an ever-moving target at which local authorities had to aim. Not only were council treasurers attempting to introduce the developed world's only poll tax, they were now doing so while the government continuously changed the rules.

In Scotland, autumn 1989 brought the first moves towards legal action against hundreds of thousands of non-payers. By mid-October, the Convention of Scottish Local Authorities estimated that 600,000 Scots—15 per cent of the total—had made no payment at all. Councils threatened to apply to take arrears of community charge directly from pay, or to undertake 'warrant sales' of goods belonging to defaulters. In December, the first community charge legal actions, in Grampian and Fife, began.

PATTEN'S 'AVERAGE £278' POLL TAX

When Chris Patten unveiled the authority-by-authority details of the 1990–1 revenue support grant (RSG) settlement (as opposed to the headline totals announced on 19 July), he offered a projected average charge of £278 for the first year of community charge. Projections varied from Haringey (£554) and Brent (£480) to Pendle (£173) and Torridge (£167). As a hostage to fortune, this forecast took some beating. Local government leaders condemned the figures as unrealistic. Labour shadow environment spokesman Bryan Gould described the

[41] *Sunday Times*, 15 Oct. 1989.

figure as 'an invention' based on misleading generalizations and false assumptions.

Gould was right. Privately Patten knew that the £278 figure was unattainable. Nicholas Ridley's original grant settlement, even when leavened by the announcement of transitional relief, fell well short of what was needed to ensure bills averaging £278. Patten had accepted that there was not enough cash from the first days of his arrival at D.o.E. in July. But he was concerned to talk down expectations. If £300 was seen as the norm, then £325 might become the reality. With a critical parliamentary vote on the revenue support grant due in the new year, Patten was anxious not to raise Tory back-bench alarm still further. Unfortunately for Mrs Thatcher, the more her ministers talked about an 'average' of £278, the more the public was shocked when the real community charges turned out to be far higher.

Just before Christmas, the government published figures for community charge registration. The law required that registers should be ready by 1 December, so that final preparations for billing could be undertaken. The D.o.E.'s figures showed, incredibly, that 99.95 per cent of the adult population had registered for the poll tax. The figure for the City of London suggested a registration rate of 145.5 per cent. The figures, reminiscent of turn-outs in some of the world's less democratic elections, were widely attacked. In fact, they looked so odd because they were compared with Office of Population Censuses and Surveys figures which, in turn, were based on the 1981 census and which were an understatement of real populations.

After Christmas, the last of the critical poll tax parliamentary confrontations took place, in the Commons vote to approve the RSG settlement, provisionally announced by Chris Patten in December. The vote on the substance of the 1990–1 RSG, on 18 January, united three different kinds of Conservative rebels. First, there were Sir George Young and Robin Squire's 'against it in principle' group, who had opposed the government throughout the passage of the Local Government Finance Act. Second, there were the MPs, unofficially led by Sir Rhodes Boyson, who disliked the safety net and who felt that the overall tax level needed to be cut drastically. Third, there were a number of Tory MPs who felt that the grant settlement was unfair to their areas. The government survived the vote, but its majority was reduced to 36, and Patten had to fend off a stream of Tories complaining about the settlements for their local councils in particular, or about the poll tax in general. David Hunt's winding-up speech, made without notes, steadied backbench nerves and is widely credited as the cause of his subsequent promotion to the Cabinet. Such are the vagaries of politics. But the most telling intervention came from Rhodes Boyson, himself a former local government minister in the formative stage of the poll tax. 'The government started out with good intentions,' he remarked. 'But ministers have passed through and civil servants have passed through, so no one guides the legislation through from beginning to end. Eventually, as the saying goes, a camel is a horse invented by a committee.'[42]

The camel lumbered into 1990 looking distinctly lame. Even in the depths of the machinery of government, the idea that something abnormal was happening was gaining strength. The Downing Street Policy Unit considered a number of large-scale schemes for alleviating the burden of the new tax which was, with horrible inevitability, about to cause so much political damage. Options included: a redistribution of government grants so as to achieve a more equitable local tax burden; more generous rebates across a much wider group of local taxpayers; taking the cost of education out of local government; or a large increase in central grants to local authorities. All four possibilities were ruled out by the Treasury Chief Secretary, John Major, on grounds of cost. Of course, as Prime Minister and almost exactly a year later, Major sanctioned precisely such a massive hike in central grants so as to buy off the poll tax.

During February, the press filled with stories of councils setting community charges well in excess of the government's guide-line figure. Not only Labour inner cities but also leafy places such as Surrey, Solihull, and Berkshire set budgets

[42] *HC Debs.*, 18 Jan. 1990, cols. 466–7.

which implied charges well above £278. Conservative-controlled councils such as Barnet (which embraced Mrs Thatcher's Finchley constituency) and Mole Valley (Kenneth Baker's seat) each set charges embarrassingly above the government's guidelines. Worse still, some Labour-run councils, such as Barking and Dagenham (unhelpfully Bryan Gould's home authority), were able to set a charge at or below the government's predicted figure. Patten let it be known that he was considering capping 50 to 100 authorities in an attempt to talk budgets down. Party chairman Kenneth Baker rang round to senior local Tories asking them to reconsider their budgets. But to no avail. By mid-February, pundits were claiming that average charges could be as high as £350 or more, well above the £278 projection which Patten had claimed.

Within the Conservative party views polarized about whom to blame for the mess. The rebels could content themselves with 'We told you so', though they generally took care to avoid doing so in public. Thatcherites had their worst suspicions about local government confirmed; it was seen as one of the remaining bastions of Tory wetness. One senior Conservative ex-minister was quoted as saying: 'if Conservative councils behave like socialists, they should be made to suffer the electoral consequences'. Such abuse was not new. Back in 1988 Nicholas Ridley caused a stir in writing in a Centre for Policy Studies pamphlet: 'Inefficiency is not, I regret to say, confined to councils run by the Terrible Trots.' The bulk of Tory MPs were simply fearful that the electorate would rebel against the party which had brought them such an unpopular and widely excoriated tax.

But the worst was yet to come. The Labour party provided a little gentle distraction during February by once again launching their property-and-income tax. Labour's alternative—dubbed the 'roof tax' by the Tories—generated widespread criticism, largely on the grounds that it was hopelessly complicated and, in all likelihood, impossible to administer. But nothing Labour could do could detract from the mess the government was now in. As Neil Kinnock put it to Labour's annual local government conference: 'The Tory party spent five years in Opposition, ten years in government, three Green Papers, two Acts and five Secretaries of State to stick together an acceptable, workable, local taxation system.' By the spring of 1990, it was patently clear that the community charge was not simply an unacceptable local tax, but a political catastrophe for the Conservative party.

By February 1990, another awkward issue had arrived on ministers' desks: the impact of the community charge on the Retail Price Index (RPI). It was agreed that the new tax should be included in the RPI, as rates had been. However, it was becoming clear within Whitehall that the burden of the community charge in 1990–1 was likely to be 25 or 30 per cent higher than the equivalent domestic rates bill in 1989–90. An average tax of £330 per adult would add a full one percentage point to the RPI, which was already rising steeply.

THE POLL TAX RIOTS

The government had a few potential allies in its attempts to deflect the growing political problems. The Trotskyite Militant Tendency, which had had some success in its efforts to encourage a 'can't pay, won't pay' campaign in urban Scotland, now turned its revolutionary sights on England. Protesters demonstrated at council meetings throughout the country, notably at Bristol, Norwich, Bradford, Maidenhead, Birmingham, Reading, Gillingham, Thamesdown, Ealing, Hackney, Hillingdon, and Haringey. As always with such events, it is impossible to tell how far Militant organized the disturbances, though clearly they were much involved in many areas. Privately, ministers hoped that the wider electorate would rally behind the government against televised scenes of civil disorder.

Labour politicians condemned the day-by-day reports of violence and destruction at council budget meetings. Neil Kinnock denounced the 'toytown revolutionaries' whom he feared might damage his party's credibility. Conservatives linked the violence with the fact that 28 Labour MPs had said that they would refuse to pay the poll tax. But, the opposition was helped in maintaining its distance from the far-left by the fact that many of the councils under attack were Labour-controlled. Moreover, many of the demonstrators were patently ordinary middle-class people who were affronted by what they saw as the unfairness of the community charge. The resignation of the majority of the ruling Conservative councillors at West Oxfordshire (within Foreign Secretary Douglas Hurd's constituency) in April 1990, in protest against the community charge and housing policy, strengthened the opposition's position.

The government received good news from two of its best-known flagship London authorities. Wandsworth set the lowest community charge in England at £148, with Westminster next lowest at £195. These figures, which Labour front-benchers insisted were achieved as a result of generous grant settlements for favoured councils, allowed ministers, particularly party chairman Kenneth Baker, to wax lyrical about the possibility of achieving low local tax bills. But every silver lining has its cloud. Many Conservative authorities that had found themselves in very different circumstances from Westminster and Wandsworth seethed silently at the apparent unfairness of it all.

By March 1990, Britain's poll tax was making international news. The civil disturbances at town and city halls were providing prime time television. The *Wall Street Journal* commented: 'Even the Thatcher government's strongest supporters do not deny that the new tax has been insufficiently and at times ineptly presented to the public.'[43] Mrs Thatcher and her entourage found themselves discussing 'the poll tax' with diplomats and foreign journalists at formal receptions and dinners. Senior United States politicians were alleged to have raised the issue privately with the Prime Minister at international meetings. Much of the questioning was in tones of polite disbelief. According to Ferdinand Mount in the *Daily Telegraph*, Paul Volcker, a Thatcher supporter and former head of the US Federal reserve, found it 'incredible' that she should have brought in such a tax.[44]

The 1990 Budget came and went. The new Chancellor, John Major, made a small change to the benefit system to reduce the

[43] *Wall Street Journal*, 9 Mar. 1990.   [44] *Daily Telegraph*, 6 Apr. 1990.

number of 'losers': the savings limit to qualify for community charge benefit was raised from £8,000 to £16,000. This meant that a larger number of 'not-quite-poor' people would qualify for benefit. However, the value of the concession was immediately dissipated by controversy over the government's failure to extend it to Scotland. In the rush to devise the concession the Treasury forgot about Scotland: another £4m. had to be found literally overnight to extend the concession to 20,000 residents north of the border. Even then, the government was engulfed in a dispute over whether or not the extra cash would come from existing Scottish budgets.[45]

Crucially, the budget resulted in no significant changes to the funding of local government. It was now apparent that the average community charge for 1990–1 would be £360 or more. This was over £80 higher than the projected figure which Chris Patten had published just three months earlier and almost tripled Kenneth Baker's earliest figures. The government had decided not to use its capping powers in the widespread way that had been threatened during February. The 1990 community charge bills would go out at levels far in excess of even their sternest critics' expectations.

In the same week as the budget, on 22 March, the Conservatives lost a by-election in Mid-Staffordshire, where a safe seat was won by Labour on a record 22 per cent swing. The unpopularity of the community charge was accepted to be a major reason for the Tories' defeat.

Then, on 31 March 1990, the community charge put Britain on news bulletins throughout the world. Anti-poll tax marches had been organized for both London and Edinburgh by the self-styled All-Britain Anti-Poll Tax Federation. The march through the capital, involving between 50,000 and 100,000 people, turned from a good-natured demonstration into a full-scale and bloody riot.[46]

The bulk of the marchers were members of the public determined to make their protest about the poll tax. But among

---

[45] *Scotsman*, 24 Mar. 1990.

[46] Most of the rest of the chapter is based on contemporary press and eye-witness accounts.

the tens of thousands of ordinary people were a hard-core of agit-prop activists, intent on mayhem. The march started at Kennington at 1 p.m. and made its way to Parliament Square and 10 Downing Street. Police stopped the demonstrators from delivering their anti-poll tax message to Mrs Thatcher's front door. A sit-in ensued at the corner of Downing Street and Whitehall. Some people climbed over the barricades at the end of Downing Street, while others attempted to remove them. The police started to pull demonstrators away and tried to move them towards Trafalgar Square. The mood turned nastier. Bottles and stones were thrown.

A quarter of a mile away in Trafalgar Square, Tony Benn started a speech to the crowd just after 3 p.m. Marchers who were being diverted away from Downing Street started to arrive in Trafalgar Square, from both Whitehall and Northumberland Avenue. Police reinforcements were sent in armoured vans to assist their colleagues who were now being badly pressed across the whole area along the south-west side of the square from The Mall to the Strand. As the police attempted to reinforce their colleagues, the crowd started to react against what many argued later was 'an unnecessary show of force'. The rally proper finished at 4.45 p.m., but about 3,000 remained behind. From here on, the commotion developed into a major riot which engulfed much of London's West End.

Shop windows were smashed and their contents looted. The City of Westminster's lurid green litter-bins were used as barricades or set alight. Parked cars were turned over. A car showroom at Leicester Square was destroyed. The rioters moved out of the Charing Cross–Leicester Square area and on to Covent Garden and even as far as the centre of Soho and the electronics shops in Tottenham Court Road. The Metropolitan Police effectively lost control, leaving shoppers and tourists to look after themselves.

Back in Trafalgar Square, scaffolding covering Grand Buildings (on the corner of Northumberland Avenue and Strand) was set alight. Rioters broke into South Africa House, amid Zulu war-cries. Bricks, bottles, scaffolding poles, oil drums, and fire-extinguishers were thrown at the police.

Officers on horseback and in full riot-gear were used in an effort to disperse the crowds. By early evening, much of Soho, Covent Garden, and Charing Cross was strewn with broken windows, burned-out cars, and devastation. The 1990 poll tax had led to serious civil unrest in virtually the same areas of London as the 1381 poll tax. By the end of the day 339 people had been arrested, 374 police officers and 86 members of the public were reported as injured. Twenty of the 40 police horses on duty were also injured, and there were 250 reports of damage to property.[47]

The following day a man rang and left a message on Tony Benn's answering machine. 'You fucking cunt. Now you've lost the next election for us,' it ran.[48] Labour did indeed lose the election; but in retrospect the riots had more impact in losing Mrs Thatcher the premiership.

---

[47] Figures from *HC Debs.*, 2 Apr. 1990, col. 893.
[48] Benn, *End of an Era*, 1 Apr. 1990.

7

COLLAPSE 1990–1994

High-minded talk of local democracy must not be allowed
to obscure the low-level politics of the people we were up
against.

Margaret Thatcher, *The Downing Street Years*

The Trafalgar Square riots transformed the poll tax controversy. Filmed against the backdrop of Nelson's column and the
'mother of Parliaments', the riots became an international sensation.[1] At home there was initial confusion. Mrs Thatcher,
back from the Tory Central Council in Cheltenham, treated the
disturbances as a repeat of the Orgreave riots of the miners'
strike of 1984–5. With Kenneth Baker and Home Secretary
David Waddington as chorus, she loudly praised the police and
condemned the 'hooligans', confidently expecting a public backlash against Labour for its association with the thugs. In a
Commons statement, Waddington deliberately linked the law-
breaking to the 28 Labour MPs who had said they would not
pay their poll tax.[2] Neil Kinnock was afraid of just such an outcome, and was almost as loud as Mrs Thatcher in his condemnation of the begetters of the riots.

In fact, opinion polls over the following two weeks showed
that the riots had had a negligible impact on public attitudes.
The poll tax remained as unpopular as ever, and Labour's lead

[1] Visiting Durban 3 years later, in the week of the assassination of Chris
Hani, the South African communist leader, one of the authors met this retort
on asking a businessman whether violent protests were to be expected: 'Don't
worry—it won't be nearly as bad as your poll tax riots.'

[2] *HC Debs.*, 2 Apr. 1990, esp. cols. 896 and 900. In response to Dave
Nellist: 'Here we go again—the same sort of weasel words as we heard at the
time of Orgreave and Wapping.'

actually increased. By the end of April, Labour's average poll lead was 23 per cent, with a Gallup poll in the *Daily Telegraph* putting Labour a staggering 26 points ahead.[3] Another poll showed only 12 per cent support for the poll tax, with one in three preferring a return to the rates.[4] The deep unpopularity of the tax evidently coloured popular attitudes to the disturbances. Fashionable academics and commentators such as Alan Ryan and Robert Harris even debated in the broadsheets the case for civil disobedience to thwart the poll tax. At any rate, the voters blamed the government squarely for introducing the tax in the first place, and the events of 31 March gave no opening for the government to rally opinion behind 'law and order' in the guise of a poll tax collection officer.

Mrs Thatcher soon realized the position. As she put it in her memoirs, the 'law-abiding, decent people' were in league with 'the mob'.[5] However, her reaction was one of exasperated bitterness, with no readiness to tackle the problem at its roots. It was, in many ways, a repeat of her reaction to the funding crisis of the previous autumn, when Chris Patten found her 'understanding about the politics, but reluctant to do anything about it'.[6] Most of the problems, she believed, were caused by the 'perversity, incompetence, and often straightforward malice of many local councils'—and the thugs supporting them.[7]

From now on, the poll tax was to become intimately bound up with increasingly bitter assaults on Mrs Thatcher's leadership style. Ever since her famous 'flagship' jibe, the tax had been associated with her personally: now it was becoming deeply unpopular, the failure to reform it was seen as a condemnation of her personally. In a sense this was unfair: her colleagues were at least as much to blame for the introduction of the poll tax. But the government's inflexibility to calls for reform or abolition in the spring and summer of 1990 was above all *her* inflexibility; and with each passing week, the blame attached ever more firmly to her personally.

---

[3] *Daily Telegraph*, 25 Apr. 1990.   [4] *The Times*, 30 Apr. 1990.
[5] M. Thatcher, *The Downing Street Years* (1993), 661.
[6] Letter to the authors, Nov. 1993.
[7] Thatcher, *Downing Street Years*, 660.

YET ANOTHER REVIEW

Four days after the Trafalgar Square disturbances, on 4 April, Chris Patten, as Environment Secretary, launched the Conservative Party's local election campaign for 1990. Under the heading 'CHRIS PATTEN SAYS COMMUNITY CHARGE IS THE FAIREST SYSTEM', a Central Office press notice quoted Mr Patten as saying:

It is only by ensuring that everyone pays something that we can ensure justice for those who are currently paying too much. Widows, single pensioners and single parent families understand that even if the Labour Party doesn't. . . . As I have travelled the country over the last few months I have found widespread acceptance of the principle of the community charge. The complaints have been about the level of the charge.

So Patten, too, was reaching instinctively for the widows and pensioners to justify the poll tax. All the more appropriate, then, that he should have been sitting next to party chairman Kenneth Baker. Almost five years after his role in the creation of the community charge, Baker was now back attempting to mitigate its political impact.

Also on 4 April, Chris Patten announced that he intended to cap twenty local authorities. Mrs Thatcher was keen to cap more; but Patten did not want to take on more councils, and there were doubts about the government's legal authority to do so.[8] Patten claimed that twenty councils had increased their budgets by 16 per cent in cash over the 1989 figures, a 'deplorable' lack of responsibility. Sixteen out of the twenty authorities were Labour-controlled; the other four were 'hung', though Labour had effective control of two through the mayor's casting vote. Bryan Gould retaliated by claiming that Patten's list was 'rigged' and that the very decision to cap authorities undermined the financial accountability which had been the main reason for introducing the community charge. The councils themselves threatened the government with legal action.

[8] Thatcher, *Downing Street Years*, 663–4.

*'Well, that's the Complete
Works of Shakespeare, now
let's think of an alternative
to the poll tax'*

Poll tax bills, which averaged £363 per adult, were by now provoking outrage and distress in equal measure. As the new bills arrived on doorsteps, some households found that they were £1,500 or more worse off. A tiny minority in London were gaining as much as £10,000 or more. On a best estimate, there were some 27 million people living in 'losing' households and just 8 million in households which gained. The heaviest losers were people living in small properties who were earning just enough to be disqualified from receiving a rebate. Many of them, ironically, were pensioners, who were not slow to take up their pens and write to their MPs. A large proportion of these heavy losers were people on modest incomes whom Mrs Thatcher had been so successful in convincing to vote Tory in 1979, 1983, and 1987.

Why were the bills so much higher than ministerial projections? According to the local authority associations, the levels of community charge or poll tax reflect a number of factors, not all under the direct control of local government, such as the amount of government grants, the level of the business rate and the 'safety net' arrangements. It is against this background that local authorities have had to balance the needs for local services against the demands of those who pay for them. . . . We again draw attention to the underlying and continuing difference of opinion between local and central government about the true cost of providing local services. . . . The consequence of government's inability to support our view is that these costs will be met exclusively by community charge payers.[9]

Even Nicholas Ridley recognized that these remarks were partially justified. As he told Channel 4 shortly before his death:

the local authorities took the opportunity [of the introduction of the poll tax] to spend up, they really rammed it on to their budgets because they thought they could blame the government for the resulting community charges. The rate support grant was not generous, that's absolutely true. The costs of setting up the computer systems was more than we had estimated and there had been a certain amount of inflation by then which we had not expected. The result of all those and probably many other factors too, was a fairly serious miscalculation about what the actual levels of charges would be.

Ridley's characteristically honest assessment of why the poll tax averaged £363 rather than £278 put the blame on both central and on local government. He was correct. On the one hand, the authorities had pushed their spending up by about 13 per cent in cash (slightly more if a build-up of reserves is taken into account), which was about 3 or 4 per cent more than anticipated inflation. On the other, the government had been working to a low inflation forecast, had greatly underestimated the start-up costs of the new tax and had set the rate support grant below the level that either Ridley or Patten would have liked.

The London boroughs of Hammersmith and Fulham led a legal challenge against Chris Patten's decision to cap their expenditure. On 24 April the authority was given leave to seek judicial review of what it argued were the 'unlawful and politi-

---

[9] Statement by local authority associations.

cally motivated criteria' used in selecting authorities for capping. The legal challenge and the possibility that the courts
would decide that Patten had behaved unlawfully helped to
slow down tax payments—and not just in the authorities concerned. If the government's capping decision were to be
upheld, new and lower community charge bills would have to
be sent out. But if the councils won, the original bills would
stand. Many local taxpayers decided to wait and see. It was not
until the end of June—well into the new financial year—that
the Court of Appeal finally upheld Patten's right to cap all the
authorities he had designated in April.

Meanwhile, in mid-April Patten started new work within
Whitehall to examine the options for amending or reforming
the poll tax. Two committees of ministers and civil servants
were created, involving both the Treasury and the Department
of the Environment. The officials involved included Richard
Wilson, a senior Cabinet Office official (who in 1992 succeeded
Terry Heiser as permanent secretary at the D.o.E.), Chris
Brearley, John Mills (from the Downing Street policy unit) and
Michael Carpenter (from the Attorney-General's office). These
groups considered several options, including universal capping;
a more generous rebate system; and the possibility of giving the
Audit Commission, the State-appointed local authority watchdog, powers to limit council spending. Figures of £2–£3bn.
were discussed, either as additional general funding for local
authorities or, alternatively, as resources which could be targeted on individuals just outside the benefit system. The
Treasury, led by the Chancellor, John Major, insisted that extra
cash would only be released if capping were used to ensure that
the full benefit of additional central funding was to be passed
on to poll tax payers.

The Whitehall committees looked at the national non-domestic rate (NNDR) as well as at the community charge. The massive publicity surrounding the poll tax eclipsed the
unpopularity of the NNDR, which was introduced on 1 April
at the same time as the community charge. Because of the combined effects of a revaluation of the rate base and the move to a
common rate of tax, many businesses found their rate bills

much higher in 1990–1 than in the previous year. Retailers and offices in the south of England were particularly hard hit. Chris Patten's Bath constituency, packed with small traders whose rates bill rocketed with the NNDR, was the focus of some of the most strident protests, as if he did not have enough problems on his hands already.

Just before the end of April, Mrs Thatcher set up a cabinet committee to work on legislative options likely to flow from the work completed by the Treasury and D.o.E.. Mrs Thatcher chaired the committee, which included Patten, Major, John MacGregor (Education Secretary), David Waddington (Home Secretary), Malcolm Rifkind (Scottish Secretary), Peter Walker (Welsh Secretary), and David Hunt, the local government minister at D.o.E..

Confusion immediately ensued. The setting up of the committee gave everyone—Tory back-benchers as much as the press—the idea that something significant would be done about the poll tax. Mark Lennox-Boyd, the Prime Minister's parliamentary private secretary, created waves by letting Tory back-benchers know that there would be a review;[10] but no sooner had he done so than other No. 10 sources were briefing Tory back-benchers and the press that no drastic changes were under consideration, not even the introduction of universal capping.[11] And on 28 April, Nicholas Ridley took the opportunity publicly to attack the notion of major reforms. Chris Patten and David Hunt, who were working on far more ambitious revisions and wanted to open a window for change, were livid—though Hunt was able to escape the heat, since within days Mrs Thatcher announced that he would soon succeed Peter Walker, who was standing down as Welsh Secretary.

The local elections, on 3 May, gave the electorate at large its first chance to pronounce on the poll tax. Elections took place in all metropolitan districts, the thirty-two London boroughs, a proportion of non-metropolitan districts, and a number of Scottish districts and islands. The Conservatives suffered heavy losses in most areas. Crucially, however, in the London bor-

[10] *Independent*, 27 Apr. 1990.
[11] *Financial Times*, *Guardian*, and *Daily Telegraph*, 28 Apr. 1990.

oughs of Wandsworth and Westminster, the Tories not only held control, but dramatically increased their majorities. Kenneth Baker had spent much of the local election campaign parading the virtues of these two Tory 'flagship' authorities, frequently being pictured on their streets. Conservative gains on the two councils gave him his cue, and he launched a highly successful media blitz presenting the vote in the two boroughs as the voice of the country at large. Baker had always excelled at such presentational hype, and he carried it off with aplomb. The media took the bait: Wandsworth and Westminster were on its collective doorstep, and both had vocal council leaders effective on television. Unfortunately for the Tories, the media were not alone in being taken in: Mrs Thatcher, whose political future had been tied up with the Conservatives' success or failure in the local elections, swallowed Baker's propaganda whole. All that was needed, she told everyone around her, was time for things to settle down: the electorate would come right in the

end, and she had no intention of caving in to public or back-bench pressure for a U-turn.[12]

What was the reality? On 12 May *The Economist* published research, carried out by Strathclyde University politics lecturer John Curtice, showing that the poll tax had indeed had an electoral impact (see Table 7.1).

TABLE 7.1. Per cent change in Conservative vote, 1986–1990

Ave. household poll tax	Con. councils		Lab. councils	
	London	Rest of Eng.	London	Rest of Eng.
Less than £610	+5.1	− 2.4	+1.3	−5.6
£610–685	+0.1	− 6.7	−5.7	−2.8
£685–775	N.A.	− 8.6	+9.0	−3.0
Over £775	N.A.	−10.1	+3.0	+2.2

The Conservatives did best in Tory-run authorities with low poll tax and in Labour-run ones with high poll tax; they did worst in high poll tax Conservative-run authorities and low poll tax Labour-run ones. *The Economist* concluded:

Judged by its first outing in England and Wales the poll tax could yet achieve the principal aim for which it was designed. . . . It does look likely that the poll tax was taken by a sizeable number of voters as a reliable guide to the efficiency and competence of the local council.[13]

That, however, was an extraordinarily partial gloss on the results. For the seats being contested in 1990 had last been fought in 1986, a calamitous year for the Tories. If the best the party could show outside London was a 2.2 per cent increase in its vote in 'loony' authorities levying poll taxes in excess of £775, its electoral future was hardly rosy.

[12] Thatcher, *Downing Street Years*, 664.
[13] *The Economist*, 12 May 1990.

HESELTINE THROWS DOWN THE GAUNTLET; THE
REVIEW CONTINUES

In any event, thanks to Wandsworth, Westminster, and Kenneth Baker, Mrs Thatcher lived to fight another day. Seven days, to be precise. For on 10 May, Michael Heseltine launched a broadside in the shape of a major article in *The Times*. Fired by the suggestion that Mrs Thatcher did not intend to make any fundamental changes to the poll tax, Heseltine returned publicly to the issue for almost the first time since his single speech in opposition to the tax in the House of Commons two years previously. Heseltine consulted a number of local government experts—including Rita Hale of CIPFA—on the speech and went much further than suggesting changes to the community charge. He argued that local authorities should face all-out elections if they proposed to spend above a centrally determined spending level. He called for more effective transitional relief for losing households; the freezing of safety-net receipts in those authorities which received them; and exemptions for elderly people living with relatives, for the physically disabled, and student nurses. When Heseltine added to all that a requirement that the community charge should be banded according to income—as in the defeated Mates amendment—the abolition of the poll tax in its existing guise was all but declared, despite his protestations to the contrary. For good measure, he wanted a longer-term review to consider a move to single-tier councils, elected paid mayors, tougher value-for-money audits, and a new grant system.

Heseltine's article could be read only one way: as the opening shot in his unannounced leadership challenge to Mrs Thatcher. Its author continued to insist that he could 'foresee no circumstances' in which he would mount such a challenge. In reality, it was the core of his manifesto—and by laying it out so explicitly before the government had barely started its own review, he skilfully crushed whatever small chance there was that the Prime Minister would adopt any of his proposals.

On 3 May, Michael Portillo had been appointed to replace David Hunt as local government minister at the D.o.E.. Young, ambitious, and capable, Portillo did not allow a single doubt to cloud his public or private advocacy of the poll tax. His job was to sell it; and whatever his innermost thoughts, he did it single-mindedly until Mrs Thatcher was politically dead. At the outset, however, there was believed to be still a faint chance that the leader might herself a signal a retreat: as May turned into June, the press filled with 'will she? won't she?' stories about the Prime Minister's intentions. The cabinet committee wrangled over its possible proposals. The idea of exempting millions of non-working wives was rejected; so was the possibility that larger rebates might be extended to the very poor. Injecting billions of pounds to produce a once-and-for-all cut in tax levels was deemed too costly. Spending departments, led by John MacGregor at Education and Science, fought hard to protect their budgets rather than see further poll tax relief.

Initially, the idea of capping all authorities was rejected as legally and administratively unworkable. Mrs Thatcher favoured it; Chris Patten opposed it, and had some support from John Major, who as a former whip was worried about getting the necessary capping legislation through the Commons. Mrs Thatcher was given a blunt warning on that score by the whips: She recalls:

A number of our own backbenchers were now in a mood not far short of outright panic and it was difficult to know how they would react to any new legislation which appeared to give them a chance—through amendments—to overturn key aspects of the community charge.[14]

That view was bolstered by legal advice that new powers might be undermined by judicial review. However, on 13 June the law officers modified their view, advising that universal capping was possible under existing legislation, provided councils were given adequate warning of what ministers deemed to be 'excessive' spending. For Mrs Thatcher, this was manna from heaven. At a further meeting on 26 June it was decided to proceed with 'general' capping for the following financial year—announcing in advance the spending level at which authorities

[14] Thatcher, *Downing Street Years*, 665–6, also the source for most of the next paragraph.

would be capped (and taking away much of their remaining fiscal autonomy in the process).

The essential conclusion—that the poll tax would remain unchanged—was now made public. Michael Portillo said as much to the Association of District Councils conference on 29 June. The Prime Minister had decided that the worst was over; like the later stages of the Westland crisis and the miners' strike, it was just a question of sitting in the Downing Street bunker and waiting for the shelling to stop.

During June the first court appearances of English non-payers took place in the Isle of Wight. Administrative difficulties were reported from councils throughout the country: poll tax payments were coming in much more slowly than they had been at the equivalent time of year for domestic rates, though only in inner cities did there appear to be a critical problem. While non-payment was running at about 50 per cent in Liverpool, Lambeth, and Hackney, it was estimated to be under 10 per cent in many non-metropolitan districts. Many local authorities were having to borrow money to make up their income shortfall.

On 27 June, the Court of Appeal upheld the government's right to cap the authorities it had targeted in early April. The judgment was a significant addition to the government's legal armoury, because it accepted that Whitehall's 'standard spending assessments'—formula-based benchmark figures of need to spend for each council—could be used as the criterion for capping. However, the only immediate relief it gave the government was the comfort of not having its earlier capping decisions overturned, with all the consequent disarray in the inner cities.

On 19 July, a year to the day after Nicholas Ridley's original announcement of the grant settlement for year one of the poll tax, Chris Patten unveiled the final conclusions of the community charge review and the outline financial details for local authority spending and grants for the following year (1991–2). Patten's objective was to keep the poll tax below the politically sensitive £400 level, by aid of more grant and vigorous capping. An additional £3.26bn. of central support was to be pumped into local authority coffers. Of this, £310m. would be targeted at households which had previously paid low rates bills, by an extension of the 'transitional relief' scheme which had been announced by David Hunt at the previous year's party conference. The projected total for council spending in 1991–2 was set at £39bn., an increase of 7 per cent over the budgets for 1990–1. By the standards of previous years, this was a generous and relatively realistic settlement, offering a reasonable prospect of containing percentage increases in the poll tax to single figures.

None the less, the 19 July announcement confirmed the continued existence of the poll tax. Transitional relief would reduce the sting for some households. There were also small concessions for some second homes, for mixed residential and business properties, and a change to more generous transitional arrangements for small businesses which were losing out because of the introduction of the national non-domestic rate. Safety nets would be withdrawn more slowly than had previously been announced. But the flat-rate poll tax, paid by all, remained intact. In reality, that was all that mattered.

Labour attacked the Patten proposals accordingly. But Labour was still under pressure to come up with definite proposals of its own. After months of havering, on 26 July, Bryan Gould launched 'fair rates', Labour's alternative. This tax was different from the property-and-income tax which had been launched previously: the anti-income tax lobby within the party—led by the shadow Chancellor, John Smith— had been at work and removed the complex income link which was a prominent feature of the earlier version of Labour's proposals. Under the new system, Labour would move immediately back to a tax based on the old rating valuations. Following the first revaluation—on the basis of a blend of capital values, rebuilding, maintenance, and repair costs—machinery for a rolling revaluation would be put in place. A more generous rebate system would ensure that the poor would not pay local tax. Non-domestic rates would be returned to local government control, thus increasing the proportion of council income coming from local sources from 30 per cent (under community charge) to over 50 per cent.

In late August the Institute of Public Finance reported that one person in five of those registered had not paid any community charge. In London, 27 per cent had yet to make a payment. No one was certain what proportion of the population had failed to register altogether. Arrears by the end of the year were projected to be £1.7bn. out of a total of £12bn. The Audit Commission, in its annual report, warned that despite the resilience of most of local government in setting up and operating the poll tax, there were 'danger signs' affecting the maintenance of the register and the collection of the charges. The courts were being flooded by local authorities applying for court summonses and for 'liability orders', which would allow the councils to collect unpaid community charge directly from individuals' incomes, from their social security benefits, or by use of bailiffs to remove goods from the homes of offenders. The Audit Commission estimated that local authorities might have to take five million non-payment cases to court.

Yet the government continued to batten down the hatches. None wielded the hammer more firmly than Michael Portillo, the enthusiastic new minister for the poll tax. In case there should be a scintilla of doubt, in his speech to the Conservative party conference at Bournemouth on October 11 he launched a full-scale defence of the poll tax and all its works. 'Before the community charge', he told the rows of somewhat sullen activists,

local government often aroused contempt amongst the well informed and apathy among the rest. When democracy is held in such low esteem, it is only a matter of time before you lose it altogether. The apathy has been ended by the Community Charge. In the pubs today they speak of little else. Just about everyone in the land knows exactly what they are paying in Community Charge—in many cases all too well. . . . The Community Charge is a courageous, fair and sensible solution. Far from being a vote loser . . . it will be a vote winner.

Indeed, they *were* speaking about little else in the pubs. That was Mrs Thatcher's problem.

MRS THATCHER'S DOWNFALL

Portillo's counter-attack against opponents of the poll tax was one of the last such speeches ever made. Political events far more exciting than the tedious struggle over local government finance were to provide the denouement to the poll tax drama.

On 18 October the government was humiliated by a by-election in the south coast resort of Eastbourne, 'that Jerusalem of the middle classes' as Edward Pearce aptly describes it.[15] The Liberal Democrats cruised to a 4,550 majority, overturning the 17,000 majority won in 1987 by Ian Gow, Mrs Thatcher's long-standing parliamentary private secretary, who had been murdered by an IRA bomb in August. 'Thatcher's poll tax' was practically the sole issue in the by-election. A fortnight later Sir Geoffrey Howe resigned from his all but meaningless post of deputy prime minister, after years of growing disaffection with the leader he had served loyally since the mid-1970s. Differences over European policy mingled with bitterness at loss of the Foreign Office in 1989, exacerbated by repeated personal humiliations at the hands of the Prime Minister and her press secretary Bernard Ingham. On 13 November came his resignation speech, perhaps the most lethal single oration the House of Commons has ever witnessed. Nominations had still to close for the annual 'election' to the leadership of the Conservative party. A day later Michael Heseltine announced that he would contest Margaret Thatcher for the post.

Heseltine immediately announced that he would initiate a 'fundamental review' of the poll tax if elected leader. Tory back-benchers knew what that meant: at the very least, a radical overhaul of the tax; very likely outright abolition. Dozens of back-benchers were bemoaning the impact of the tax on their re-election chances, and were immediately attracted to Heseltine. It was not only the poll tax *per se* which counted in the election: the government's repeated failure to make more than tinkering changes encapsulated growing back-bench anxiety about Mrs Thatcher's whole style of leadership. It was the

---

[15] Edward Pearce, *Machiavelli's Children* (1993), 62.

same with the European issue, where her rigid intransigence, and public denunciations of all things European, was visibly splitting the party. During the campaign the Prime Minister pointedly refused to offer concessions on either score. Cranley Onslow, chairman of the back-bench 1922 Committee, told her that he hoped 'something substantial' could be done about the poll tax. Her response?

I intervened to say that I could not pull rabbits out of a hat in five days . . . I could not now credibly promise a radical overhaul of the community charge, no matter how convenient it seemed.[16]

By now, it was more a matter of survival than of convenience. On 20 November Mrs Thatcher was ahead in the first ballot of the leadership contest, but by four votes fewer than required for outright victory. Under party rules there had to be another ballot unless Heseltine withdrew. He announced immediately that he would press ahead to the second ballot. In Paris for an international summit, the Prime Minister vowed to fight on. It was a lost cause. On her return from Paris on Wednesday 21 November, the day after the first ballot, a succession of cabinet ministers told her bluntly that she would lose if she carried on. At 9 a.m. on Thursday morning she announced her resignation. It is pointless to speculate whether a commitment from her to reform or abolish the poll tax would have yielded the critical four votes for victory. It was not forthcoming; and it was never likely to be.

The party election rules allowed new challengers to enter the second ballot. By the noon deadline on the Thursday Douglas Hurd, the Foreign Secretary, and John Major, the Chancellor, had put their hats in the ring alongside Heseltine. Both committed themselves to a 'fundamental review' of the poll tax. Their commitments lacked the detail or enthusiasm of Heseltine's, but their backers stressed to everyone their determination to lance the boil. As one of Major's key backers put it in a strategy meeting on Thursday morning: 'we can't let a chink of light come between us and Heseltine on the poll tax.' On 27 November, John Major was elected leader of the

[16] Thatcher, *Downing Street Years*, 848.

Conservative party. He succeeded Margaret Thatcher as Prime Minister the following day.

One of Major's first acts was to appoint Michael Heseltine as Environment Secretary. Some saw poetic justice in this appointment. Having fought Mrs Thatcher on the poll tax, he now had the job of sorting it out. He set about the task with his customary gusto. But with the Conservative party in a state approaching civil war, it was a task requiring unaccustomed delicacy.

THE FINAL REVIEW

Michael Heseltine's appointment as Environment Secretary is a rare example of a minister holding the same cabinet post twice. Many of the faces which met him on his return to Marsham Street were familiar from his first stint at the D.o.E. between 1979 and 1982. Terry Heiser, who had been a deputy secretary, was now permanent secretary. Other senior officials, such as Derek Osborn and Chris Brearley, were also still there, up the scale. He told them what he wanted: a full review. They set about it with the same dedication they had shown to the poll tax over the previous six years.

Barely a week after his appointment, on 5 December, Heseltine announced a full review of local government finance, structure, and internal management. In itself, the review was hardly a surprise; nor was his decision to lump in structural issues. These had been a key part of his *Times* package unveiled in May, and would help make the emasculation or abolition of the poll tax more palatable within the Conservative party. The surprise came in his offer, thrown out in his Commons statement, to engage the opposition parties 'fully' in the review. This was a master-stroke, all the more effective for being totally unexpected. Launched with all the bravado Heseltine could muster, it left the Labour party reeling in the House of Commons, and at one blow eliminated much of the party political capital Labour could make out of the government's tribulations. In the event the Liberal Democrats accepted and Labour refused: but by the time it came to the talks themselves, their substance was almost irrelevant.

In his Commons statement, carefully crafted to draw the sting from right as well as left, Heseltine claimed that there had been 'a broad measure of support for the simple idea that nearly everyone should make a contribution to the cost of the local services they consume'.[17] This view was taken to mean that the poll tax might continue, albeit in a highly modified form; equally, it did not rule out a property-based tax where people living in larger properties would pay more than those in smaller ones. Heseltine added that an 'argument much advanced' was that community charge would have been more readily accepted if the bills had been lower. There was only one possible interpretation: local taxation would have to be lower if it were to be acceptable. Few disagreed: it was the overwhelming verdict of a wide-ranging survey published in January 1991.[18]

Heseltine's style was typically combative, but by the standards of the previous five years there was a marked softening in the language about local councils. He told the Commons he wanted a 'proper partnership' between central government and local authorities, so as to provide a 'stable and just basis' for the development of local government.

Michael Heseltine's review of local government finance and structure could not have been conducted more differently from the 1984–5 studies. There were some superficial similarities. A 'review team' of Environment Department officials—though with no outsiders from the Treasury or elsewhere—was created, headed by Robin Young. Young, a former private secretary to Patrick Jenkin, was an ambitious under-secretary, very much in the Heiser mould of the modern, resolutely meritocratic, activist official. He had been involved in the 1984–5 studies (as a D.o.E. official, rather than as a team member), and had been present at a number of crucial meetings during the development of the poll tax. Chris Brearley, who had picked up the community charge in 1986 and seen through its implementation, first as under-secretary and then as Deputy Secretary, was Young's boss. For a number of D.o.E. civil servants, this was a

[17] *HC Deb.*, 5 Dec. 1990, cols. 315–25.
[18] A. Bloch and P. John, *Attitudes to Local Government: A Survey of Electors*, Joseph Rowntree Trust (1991).

case of conversion from midwife's assistant to undertaker within six years.

But unlike the 1984–5 studies team, Young and his team were not given the think-tank's freedom to think thoughts about the wholesale restructuring of local government. The terms of reference were limited and simple: to come up with a replacement for the poll tax. Heseltine and Major had not firmly determined that the community charge should be abolished outright. But when Heseltine recited the mantra 'nothing has been ruled in, and nothing has been ruled out', as he did almost daily, everyone knew that a continuation of the *status quo* was definitely out.

January and February 1991 saw a flurry of apparently well-informed newspaper leaks about the government's intentions, with property taxes allied to personal charges appearing in numerous shapes and sizes. It was a deliberate strategy of policy-making by 'leak and reaction'. As one cabinet minister put it: 'we were reading things in newspapers which could only have come from those sitting at review team meetings the previous day'. Again, it was in stark contrast with the 1984–5 review, when almost nothing was deliberately leaked, journalists were completely off the scent, and team members were concerned with only one external reaction—the Prime Minister's.

The reaction was not slow in coming. Nigel Lawson told all and sundry that the poll tax should be abolished, writing press articles disclosing his original hostility to the tax and his May 1985 plan for a modernized property tax. Yet apart from Lawson, Tory opponents of the poll tax were reluctant to throw their lot fully behind a revamped property rating system, while supporters of the poll tax showed no such restraint. Nicholas Ridley defended the poll tax with almost his last breath, even calling for an increase in the top rate of income tax to keep it afloat.[19] For many Tories, that simply reinforced the impression that Ridley's judgement had been entirely warped by three years fashioning the tax. But others could not be dismissed so easily. William Waldegrave, now Health

[19] N. Ridley, *My Style of Government* (1991), 134.

Secretary, speaking at a press conference during the campaign for the by-election in Ribble Valley, Lancashire, caused by David Waddington's ennoblement to be leader of the House of Lords, said that he had no regrets and no apologies to offer for the tax that he had helped to create. Norman Tebbit added his support for the beleaguered charge.

Ian Lang, the Scottish Secretary, fought harder than any cabinet member to keep the poll tax. Furious that 'sources close to Michael Heseltine' were leaking the review group's deliberations in such a way as to rule out even a shadow of the poll tax, he rallied the No Turning Back group ministers such as Michael Forsyth and Christopher Chope to insist that a per capita element could be kept. Unlike Forsyth, Lang was no ideologue: his rearguard action was motivated more by the conviction that the community charge had settled down in Scotland, and that further local tax upheaval north of the border would be disastrous.

The civil servants and ministers conducting the review trampled through very familiar territory. Terry Heiser, Chris Brearley, and Robin Young had all been involved in 1984–5 studies. Michael Heseltine had published the 1981 Green Paper *Alternatives to Domestic Rates*, with much of the work done by Heiser and his colleagues. Michael Portillo, the Minister for Local Government was, within nine months, involved in his second full review of the community charge. Portillo's position was a little difficult because he had been so much to the fore in selling the community charge during the latter months of 1990. But no one could have detected any embarrassment from his public performances.

However, they were not working alone. A further key difference with 1984–5 was the close involvement of the Treasury at every stage. Its permanent secretary Sir Terence Burns, another 'Terry', was determined not to let the D.o.E. land the Treasury in another catastrophe, and he set some of his key officials to work, armed with Nigel Lawson's earlier plan for a banded property tax. Moreover, both John Major and Norman Lamont, his campaign manager turned Chancellor, were convinced that the government's ability to survive the forthcoming election critically depended upon an early cut in the headline rate of the poll tax—in advance of any reform, which could only take effect after the election. Only the Treasury could engineer an immediate cut: and there was only one window of opportunity available for making it, the spring 1991 budget.

By late February, the media and Tory back benchers were growing restless at Major's supposed 'dithering' on the future of the poll tax. The most cutting criticism came from Major's former boss Nigel Lawson, who pointedly reminded the Commons of the French politician Mendès-France's dictum: 'to govern is to chose'. The dithering was partly deliberate: Major believed he had to 'play it long' if he was to avoid ructions on the right when the inevitable abolition of the poll tax was announced. But the delay was caused just as much by chronic indecision—in Marsham Street and the Treasury as much as No. 10—about how much of a per capita element to include in a modified property tax. The internal wrangling was cut short by the Ribble Valley by-election on 7 March. Ribble Valley was the Conservatives' thirteenth safest seat, but as a northern constituency which had previously enjoyed low rateable values, it housed precious few friends of the poll tax. The Liberal Democrats romped home to a 4,601 majority. 'The poll tax died here,' proclaimed the victorious Liberal after the declaration of the result.

In reality, the poll tax was already dead; Ribble Valley simply hurried on the funeral and the reading of the will. As Nicholas Ridley put it: 'the government had itself discredited the community charge, causing it death by a thousand cuts.'[20] Within days of starting the review the civil service team under Robin Young narrowed the possibilities down to four leading options, all familiar from earlier reviews. As presented to a cabinet committee on 14 March, they were:

(i) keep community charge but massively increase rebates;
(ii) a banded property tax with a small poll tax add-on;
(iii) a banded property tax with discounts for households with fewer than three adults;
(iv) a simple property tax.

[20] N. Ridley, *My Style of Government* (1991), 134.

The meeting hardened up support for an option involving a banded property tax with some allowance for the number of adults in the household. The concession of a link to the number of adults living in a property was just enough to appease the 'little old lady' lobby who still wanted to ensure that such people paid a lower local tax bill than a multi-earner household next door.

But before the government could publish the results of its review, Norman Lamont dropped the largest bombshell of the whole poll tax saga. In the final minutes of his budget speech on 19 March he announced an increase in value added tax from 15 per cent to 17.5 per cent to fund a £140 reduction in the poll tax paid by all adults throughout Britain. At one stroke, and a cost of £4.5bn., the 1991–2 community charge was reduced from an average £392 to £252. The opposition and media alike were stunned. No hint of this strategy had leaked before the budget, despite the heavy reporting of the review team's work. It was an undoubted coup for Major, who had worked closely with Lamont on the VAT switch for more than a month before the budget. In addition to reducing the potency of the poll tax, it largely neutralized the charge of dithering; and its almost universally favourable response significantly increased Major's leeway in dealing with the poll tax itself.

Needless to say, the decision to cut local tax bills by £140 in mid-March, a fortnight before the start of the new financial year, caused local authorities terrible problems. Their community charge bills for 1991–2 were largely printed and, in some cases, already sent out. Moreover the decision to lop £140 off all charges led the government to announce further changes later in March (at a cost of £1.2bn.) to the 'community charge reduction scheme' which gave protection to households which had lost most heavily out of the introduction of the poll tax. Sir Jack Layden, chairman of the Association of Metropolitan Authorities, complained: 'Overnight still more changes have been made . . . can you wonder if our staff have been reduced to something akin to despair?' But desperation among local authority treasurers had never been high on the list of the government's concerns.

COUNCIL TAX IS LAUNCHED

Two days after the budget, Michael Heseltine announced the abolition of the poll tax. As he put it in his Commons statement:

the public have not been persuaded that the charge is fair. We have therefore decided that from the earliest possible moment the community charge will be replaced by a new system of local taxation . . . there will be a single bill for each household comprising two essential elements, the number of adults living there and the value of the property.[21]

There were a number of ways of valuing property, which would 'require careful evaluation and extensive discussion and consultation'. The total amount collected by the new levy would reflect the £4.5bn. cut in local taxation announced by the Chancellor during his budget speech.

In addition to the new property tax, Heseltine also announced that the structure of local government would be reviewed in the non-Metropolitan areas of the country, with a presumption in favour of unitary (single-tier) authorities. A local government commission would be created to do the job. Finally, the internal management of local government, embracing such matters as the committee system and the calibre of councillors, would be reviewed.

In April the D.o.E. published a consultation paper entitled, plainly, *A New Tax for Local Government*. Compared with Kenneth Baker's fulsome, confident, and colourful Green Paper of 1986, this one was short, tentative, and black-and-white. It offered options for taking account of the numbers of adults in a household and options for the property base of the new tax. Property would be the basis of the tax, with valuation based on rental value, capital value, rebuilding costs, or banding of properties into broad categories of value. Possible bands of value were quoted in the paper, suggesting that there might be a total of seven, with the lowest value band covering homes of up to 50 per cent of the average property value and the highest

---

[21] *HC Debs.*, 21 Mar. 1991, cols. 401–5.

band being over 200 per cent of the average value.[22] Adults could be subject to a flat-rate supplement to the property tax, with or without a limit on the number of such supplementary amounts. Alternatively, it would be possible to have a system of personal discounts if there were fewer than a specified number of adults in a property. The government made it clear that it favoured a 25 per cent discount for single-adult properties.

Finally, the consultation paper conceded that households with the lowest income would receive 100 per cent rebates. There would be no minimum contribution to the new tax, in the way that there had been a 20 per cent minimum under community charge. 'Capping would be strong and effective.' There would be transitional arrangements to help households which lost significantly out of the introduction of the council tax. There would be only one bill per property. If the government had learned one thing above all from the poll tax trauma, it was the pointlessness of taxing people with little or no income.

Inevitably, poll tax zealots deplored the proposed 'council tax'. Douglas Mason, author of the 1985 Adam Smith Institute pamphlet on the poll tax, condemned it as akin to 'killing off a child when it is one year old—simply because it cannot fully walk or talk'. But the chorus was distinctly muted. Following the £140 per adult reduction of the tax in the budget and the commitment to abandon it altogether, the opinion polls showed the issue of local taxation slipping quickly out of the electorate's mind. Most Tory MPs wanted to keep it that way, and the abolition of the poll tax was the surest way of doing so.

Ironically, just as the poll tax was being buried, the Labour party started making independent political capital out of local taxation for practically the first time in the entire saga. Launching Labour's 1991 local election campaign on Radio 4's *Today* programme in April, Bryan Gould claimed that Labour's 'fair rates' would result in local tax bills being £140 per household lower than those being sent out after Norman Lamont's £140 cut in the budget. Chris Patten, on the same programme,

---

[22] *A New Tax for Local Government*, Dept. of the Environment Consultation Paper (1991), para 2.27.

could only say that he was 'gobsmacked' by the revelation. A bitter row then took place in the media about rival figures, in which Labour gained the upper hand, encouraging the government to move as fast as possible with poll tax abolition.

Consultation on the government's proposals was completed on 21 June. Although there were some concerns voiced by bodies such as the Audit Commission (about the general state of local government finance), the Chartered Institute of Public Finance and Accountancy (about the possible need to have a council tax register), and the Institute of Revenues Rating and Valuation (about the short timetable before the new tax was to be introduced on 1 April 1993), there was no concerted criticism. The opposition parties argued that single adult discounts kept alive the spirit of the poll tax, but the public seemed unconcerned. The only significant change made by Heseltine, in response to complaints that very large properties would pay the same local tax as high-value, though not super-rich ones, was the addition of an eighth band for properties valued over £320,000 (with different figures for Wales and Scotland).

Preparatory work for council tax started immediately. The valuation of properties—into the eight bands of value—had to take place as soon as possible if the new tax was to be introduced in 1993 as planned. The Local Government Finance and Valuation Bill was introduced into parliament to provide for the valuation of properties throughout Britain. It passed with little ado, and received royal assent on 25 July 1991. Revaluations took place between January and May 1992.

LAST DAYS OF THE POLL TAX

The poll tax remained in the news during the summer and autumn of 1991, but with nothing like the intensity of the previous year. There were continuing tales of woe about non-payment. On 11 July, Terry Fields, Labour MP for Liverpool Broadgreen, was sent to prison for 60 days by magistrates in Bootle for non-payment. Refusal to pay appeared to be getting worse during 1991, largely because of the delay in sending out poll tax bills which followed Norman Lamont's £140 reduction, but also, some argued, because of popular reactions to the news that poll tax was to be abolished. By the end of September, it was estimated that in Scotland 12 per cent of the tax for 1989–90 was still unpaid, plus 23 per cent of tax for 1990–1, and 77 per cent of the 1991–2 tax. However, in rural and sub-urban England, most councils reported collection rates of over 90 per cent. Chronic non-collection remained an urban prob-lem. But the scale of failure in the larger towns and cities meant that overall the tax collection rate was faltering.

The Queen's Speech in November 1991 included a reference to the Bill which would sweep away poll tax and introduce council tax. The Local Government Finance Bill, which had its second reading in the House of Commons on 11 December 1991, provided the legislative framework for the new tax. As with the community charge, much of the detail of the new tax required secondary legislation. The progress of the bill was weakly contested. During the early months of 1992, politicians were far more concerned about the impending general election. The final stages of the bill were rushed through by the govern-ment with unseemly haste by 6 March, to make sure that it reached the statute-book before the election campaign.

VALEDICTION

As in 1987, local taxation played little part in the general elec-tion of 1992. By abandoning both Mrs Thatcher and her flag-ship, the Conservative party had denied Labour and the Liberal Democrats two of their most potent weapons. Labour tried hard to pin the blame for the poll tax disaster on senior Tories who were still around, notably on Kenneth Baker, William Waldegrave, Chris Patten, and Michael Howard. In the case of Chris Patten, who lost his Bath seat, some of the mud appears to have stuck. But for the most part, John Major was able to bask in the glow of having abolished the poll tax and cut tax bills, which was of more immediate electoral concern than the fact that his predecessor had introduced the tax in the first place. The issue lacked political potency.

On 9 April 1992 the electorate returned the Conservatives

with a majority of 21. The reasons for their victory—and for Labour's fourth successive defeat—are considered elsewhere.[23] Obviously the poll tax did not cost the Tories the 1992 election. Perhaps in a paradoxical way it even won it for them. As with Suez in 1956–7, the short-term difficulties faced by the government during a crisis were largely forgotten when the next election took place, in each case under a new leader.

The costs of Britain's third poll tax were considerable. At least £1.5bn. was wasted on setting up, administering, and replacing the community charge. In other words, £1.5bn.-worth of taxpayers' money was spent on computers, staff, buildings, paper, postage, bailiffs, and all the other elements necessary to introducing and then abolishing the tax. In addition, the transfer costs to the national taxpayer had, by the end of 1993–4, totalled well over £20bn. Revenue support grant had to rise far faster after 1990 than before. The decision to cut local tax bills by £140 per adult, coupled with extra community charge reduction scheme costs, further increased the annual central grant to local government by about £6bn. Put another way, the basic rate of income tax could have been about 4p in the £ lower in 1994–5 than it actually was (or VAT some 4 percentage points lower) if the community charge had never been introduced and abandoned. The costs in terms of good public administration are discussed in more detail in Chapter 12. But it is worth noting here that the capacity of local authorities to collect revenue, which had been exceptional (99 per cent) under domestic rates, was badly damaged. When the community charge was abolished in 1993, it was estimated that £2–£2.5bn. of tax was still unpaid. Collection will continue until the end of the century. Much of the money will never be recovered. It will take years for urban areas to move back to the high levels of tax collection achieved prior to 1990. Some councils may never do so.

Electoral registration and the 1991 census were also damaged by the poll tax. Local authorities found that the numbers registered to vote fell as the electorate came to believe that their

[23] D. Butler and D. Kavanagh (1992), *The British General Election of 1992*.

appearance on the electoral register might lead to cross-checking with the community charge register. The poll tax probably caused 700,000 omissions from the 43 million expected to be entitled to vote.[24] As for the census, people clearly, if wrongly, thought that if they filled in their census form, their council might gain access to the information thus provided.

Another element in the poll tax inheritance continued to haunt the government well after the tax itself had been laid to rest. Michael Heseltine's original announcement in 1991 that poll tax would be abolished was accompanied by a commitment to set up a Local Government Commission to review local authority structure in the non-metropolitan areas of England. At the time many commentators saw this move as an attempt to generate diversionary flak to cover the poll tax retreat. By 1993 the work of the Local Government Commission (LGC) in reviewing council boundaries had itself become deeply controversial, threatening nation-wide upheaval and huge reorganization costs. The Department of the Environment issued guidance to the Commission which subsequently had to be revised. Most of the early proposals were very unpopular with the government, with Conservative back-benchers, with local authorities, and (as far as could be ascertained) with the general public. The LGC's combative chairman, Sir John Banham, was in open conflict with the Department of the Environment. In another guise, the poll tax jinx lives on. Appropriately enough, the minister left to deal with the review was John Gummer, the seventh Environment Secretary in eight years, who as Tory party chairman in 1984 strongly urged the abolition of the rates, and as local government minister between 1988 and 1989 played a role in the evolution of the poll tax.

Despite concerns about the implications of the community charge experiment for local tax collection and public administration, the council tax was introduced with little fuss—either political or administrative.[25] Compared with the first year of the

[24] I. S. McLean, 'The Poll Tax and the Electoral Register', in A. Heath (ed.), *Labour's Last Chance?* (1994)

[25] Audit Commission, *The Sooner the Better: Progress Report on the Council Tax* (1993).

poll tax in 1990, however, much was different in 1993. Michael Howard, Environment Secretary for the year after the 1992 election, ensured that, in effect, all authorities had their spending capped. In November 1992, he announced the criteria which would determine whether an authority's spending was excessive. If the council chose to exceed this figure, it risked being capped. Only three councils chose to do so, which left all the rest passively spending at or below a government-set limit. The grant settlement was sufficiently generous to ensure that when 1993-4 budgets were set during February and March 1993, the overall spending total was only about 2 per cent higher than in 1992-3. The council tax set was equivalent, overall, to a standstill in local taxation as compared with the previous year.

Despite the zero average rise in local tax, the government also introduced a system of transitional relief to assist those households which lost most heavily because of the move to the new tax. The lessons of 1990 had been well learned. There were inevitable shifts of local tax burden as a property-based tax replaced the community charge. People living in higher-valued properties would, generally, lose out, whereas those in lower-valued ones would often gain. Because there were more properties with higher values in the south of England, there would be considerable losses in many authorities in the southern regions. Transitional relief provided temporary support for losing households.

The relative ease with which the council tax was introduced must in large part be because of the abject nature of the poll tax. Arguably, it took the disaster of the poll tax to make a modernised property tax such an attractive possibility.

The net result? A local property tax continues to exist, albeit one which raises only 20 per cent of authorities' revenue income. Few seem keen to change it—certainly not in the direction of a poll tax. Local government has survived, but in so emaciated and withered a form that some doubt whether it deserves the name. The Conservatives are still in power. Several of the authors of the poll tax continue to adorn the Cabinet table. As for Mrs Thatcher, she remains defiant to the end. 'Its benefits had just started to become apparent when it was abandoned,' she insists.[26]

[26] Thatcher, *Downing Street Years*, 667.

PART II

THE POLL TAX AND BRITISH GOVERNMENT

> An observer who looks at the living reality will wonder at the contrast to the paper description.
>
> Walter Bagehot, *The English Constitution* (1867)

The story of the poll tax from 1984 to 1991 throws light on many aspects of British government. Ultimately, the efficacy of a system can be tested only when it is under strain. If, in retrospect, the poll tax initiative should be seen as a fiasco, was the government machine at fault? If individuals were culpable, surely the system must share the blame. The institutions of Westminster and Whitehall are supposed to have evolved safeguards against bad judgement by politicians or civil servants. In the case of the poll tax, one misjudgement followed another over six years and two parliaments. The safeguards manifestly failed. How, and why, did they do so?

Some of its begetters still defend the poll tax, variously believing that it could have worked if it had been persisted with, or if it had been introduced in a modified form, or if it had been backed by a little more luck and a lot more money. But, even if they are right, something must be wanting in a system that allowed a major tax reform to flounder through inadequate planning, and then to be abandoned, post-haste, by the very politicians who had spent the previous five years sponsoring it. There is, moreover, nothing in the poll tax affair that would preclude its repetition in some new policy area. Strong Prime Ministers recur; so do large parliamentary majorities; so do the electoral and social pressures generated in settling how the tax burden should be shared.

In this second section we are concerned to see what light the poll tax saga throws on the conventional wisdom about the working of British government. At the heart of any such discussion must lie the position of the Prime Minister and the cabinet, which we address first. However, the civil service put flesh on the bones of a per capita tax, the Conservative party and parliament gave the finished product their unconditional blessing, while the opposition parties and public opinion proved powerless to thwart it until it been in operation nation-wide for nearly a year (two in Scotland). Chapter 9 examines the role of the civil service, Chapter 10 that of parliament, and Chapter 11 looks at the political parties and wider public opinion, both in reflecting and influencing events. Chapter 12 seeks to weigh the impact of the poll tax on its prime victim, local government. The two final chapters draw the threads together. Chapter 13 considers the 'if onlys' of the story, and seeks to answer some basic questions. Who was to blame? Why did it fail? Could it have worked? The concluding chapter than offers a tentative verdict on the place of the poll tax in British politics and history.

8

CABINET

The community charge is generally presented as a doctri-
naire scheme forced on reluctant ministers by an authori-
tarian Prime Minister and eventually rejected by public
opinion as unworkable. Mistakes were certainly made . . .
but this picture is a tissue of nonsenses.

Margaret Thatcher, *The Downing Street Years* (1993)

'Cabinet government' is the simplest phrase to describe the
British way of running affairs. In the eyes of Lord Hailsham,
who sat at the cabinet table longer than anyone else since the
war, 'it is one of the permanent gifts conferred by British political genius on the science and art of civilised government'.[1]
From Bagehot onwards, commentators have sought to describe
the science and assess the art, aided by ministerial memoirs
which partially—in both senses of the word—illuminate life at
the top.

However, when it comes to assessing how important policies
weave their way through the executive machine, we know surprisingly little about the operation of modern cabinet government. The story of the poll tax cuts across many of the simpler
descriptions to be found in textbooks. It shows the cabinet itself,
the 'efficient secret' of Bagehot's account,[2] to be a purely formal
institution, insignificant to the evolution of policy or the taking
of decisions. However, it is equally destructive of notions of
'prime-ministerial government' which have gained wide acceptance in recent decades. It shows the cabinet structure to be
vital to the process of decision-making, however unimportant

---

[1] 'Cabinet Government', 1987 Granada Lecture.
[2] W. Bagehot, *The English Constitution* (1867), ch. 1.

the full meetings of the cabinet proper may be to the operation of modern government.

The first section of this chapter elaborates on that theme. Two other aspects of the poll tax have important ramifications for an understanding of modern cabinet government. One lies in the remarkably high rate of ministerial turnover and the other in the fact that the poll tax was adopted and implemented in defiance of the Chancellor of the Exchequer and of the Treasury, the central Whitehall department. The second and third sections examine these aspects of the affair.

PRIME-MINISTERIAL GOVERNMENT?

Over the past thirty years commentators have engaged in a passionate debate over the extent to which British government should be described as 'cabinet government' or as 'prime-ministerial government'—or even as 'presidential government'.

The view that the Prime Minister is only *primus inter pares*, propagated in the late nineteenth century by Bagehot and A. V. Dicey and still largely supported in the 1930s by Sir Ivor Jennings, has long since been abandoned. It was little more than an 'Aunt Sally' by the time Crossman made his celebrated attack on the idea in the 1963 reissue of Bagehot's *English Constitution*. Indeed, Dicey himself did not fully adhere to it. 'The sovereignty of parliament is still a fundamental doctrine of English constitutionalists,' he declared in 1885, but developed the point thus:

[this] sovereignty can be effectively exercised only by the Cabinet, which holds in its hands the guidance of the party machine. And of the cabinet which the parliamentary majority supports the Premier has become at once the legal head and, if he is a man of ability, the real leader.[3]

Dicey's contemporary, John Morley, moved from his modest description of the Premier as 'the keystone of the cabinet arch', to writing in his biography of Sir Robert Walpole that the

[3] A. V. Dicey, *Introduction to the Study of the Law of the Constitution* (8th edn., 1915), p. cii.

power of the Prime Minister was 'not inferior to that of a dictator, provided the House of Commons will stand by him'.[4] Indeed, W. E. Gladstone, the subject of Morley's more famous biography, was described as a 'dictator' by one of his colleagues, as was the other great late-Victorian Prime Minister, Lord Salisbury.[5] Gladstone, Disraeli, Salisbury, and Asquith were dismissing ministers before the First World War. They dominated the media of their day, and often took important decisions after consultations with only a few colleagues, sometimes with one or none.[6] Once the cabinet secretariat and Prime Minister's policy unit (then dubbed the 'kitchen cabinet') was established by Lloyd George in 1916, all the essentials of the modern premiership were in place.

The rise of the modern presidency, if there be such a thing, is not therefore a recent development.[7] In reality, now, as a century ago, there are some strong Prime Ministers, some weak ones. The strong are able to dominate their cabinets to a dictatorial degree; the weak are highly dependent on the consent of senior colleagues, and/or fickle parliamentary majorities, for the making of most important decisions, whatever the illusion created by modern, highly personalized television reporting. Of the last six Prime Ministers, only two (Thatcher and Heath) come unambiguously into the 'strong' camp. Three (Home, Callaghan, and Major) belong to the weak camp, with Harold Wilson oscillating between the two at different stages of his premierships. Sir Alec Douglas-Home was so weak he might truly be described as *primus inter pares*.[8]

Few would deny that in her heyday Margaret Thatcher had more complete control of affairs than any twentieth-century Prime Minister except for Lloyd George and Churchill in

---

[4] J. Morley, *Walpole* (1889), 158.

[5] Andrew Adonis, *Making Aristocracy Work* (1993), 30.

[6] J. P. Mackintosh, *The British Cabinet* (3rd edn., 1977), 298–343.

[7] *Pace* M. Foley, *The Rise of the Modern Presidency* (1993). The sources of authority cited by Foley for the 'modern presidency' were virtually all at the disposal of Lloyd George 80 years ago, and most of them available to Gladstone fifty years before that. Tellingly, Foley's analysis goes back no further than Macmillan's premiership (1957–63).

[8] A. S. King (ed.), *The British Prime Minister* (2nd edn., 1985), esp. 164–5.

wartime. Under her rule fewer and fewer matters had thorough discussion in full cabinet. According to Nicholas Ridley:

She did not see it [the cabinet] as a body to take decisions, except decisions of the gravest importance.[9] She saw it as the forum in which all important activities were brought together and reported upon. She saw it as the body to approve individual ministers' policies. She used it as a tactical group to discuss the immediate problems of the day.[10]

Despite the pressure of business, the full cabinet met for fewer hours in the 1980s than in any decade this century. Typically Mrs Thatcher held between forty and forty-five meetings a year, barely half the number under Churchill and Attlee. The number of cabinet papers circulated in the 1980s represented only a sixth of the annual tally in the late 1940s and early 1950s.[11] It was not just to cabinet committees that decisions were devolved: Mrs Thatcher tended increasingly to utilize ad hoc committees and 'bilateral' meetings with individual ministers to decide policy. As Nigel Lawson observes: 'what had started off as a justified attempt to make effective decisions in small and informal groups degenerated into increasingly complex attempts to divide and rule.'[12] He later remarked that in the 'long-drawn-out final phase, she had become reckless over Europe, reckless over the poll tax, reckless over what she said in public, and reckless over colleagues'. Douglas Hurd, her last Foreign Secretary, believes such 'divide and rule' tactics cost her the premiership:

The main reason for Margaret Thatcher's loss of the leadership was, I believe, her failure over the years to make the best of the cabinet system . . . she did not understand that colleagues too had knowledge and views, and she relied on her individual powers excessively.[13]

[9] Ridley may have had the Falklands War in mind in that aside. Mrs Thatcher was careful to engage the support of the entire cabinet before launching the task force to recapture the islands in April 1982 (Thatcher, *Downing Street Years*, 179–81). However, the decision was of unique importance, and her position highly vulnerable after the humiliation of the Argentinian invasion.

[10] N. Ridley, *My Style of Government* (1992), 28.

[11] P. Hennessy, *Cabinet* (1986), 99–100.

[12] N. Lawson, *The View from No. 11* (1992), 936.

[13] Review of Margaret Thatcher's memoirs, *Spectator*, 6 Nov. 1993.

'Twas not ever thus. Despite her famous remark in an *Observer* interview shortly before the 1979 election that she could not 'waste time having any internal arguments', in her first term Mrs Thatcher was careful to keep the Tory party's power-brokers, notably Willie Whitelaw, with her on key decisions. But as she grew senior to all her colleagues and more certain of her 'individual powers' (following her defeat of the 'wets' in 1981, of General Galtieri in 1982, and of Arthur Scargill in 1985), she relied less and less on the advice and confidence of her senior ministers and made her impatience increasingly plain. The near-disaster of the Westland affair in 1986 was followed by a brief period of caution, but after the 1987 election triumph she came to believe, as one colleague put it, that she could 'walk on water'. Her dramatic falling out with Nigel Lawson and Sir Geoffrey Howe over exchange rate and European policy between 1988 and 1990 has received blanket coverage in the memoirs and interviews of the protagonists. Mrs Thatcher was not the first Prime Minister to have highly (and publicly) strained relations with senior colleagues. 'What I have done is to surround myself with friends and to isolate Callaghan,' Harold Wilson brazenly told the cabinet of his 1966 reshuffle, moments before the Chancellor entered the room.[14] But under no other premiership since the Second World War have relations at the top broken down so spectacularly.

How does the poll tax fit into this picture? The insignificance of the full cabinet to decision-taking is well attested by the poll tax. The cabinet did not so much as discuss the proposal for the tax until January 1986, fifteen months after the initial studies team had been established and more than seven months after the key decision of principle had been taken by a cabinet committee. The full cabinet merely rubber-stamped the draft of Kenneth Baker's Green Paper *Paying for Local Government*, which had been endorsed at a cabinet committee before Christmas. Nigel Lawson, a strong opponent of the proposals at every earlier stage, did not even bother to register dissent at the full cabinet. It was not just that by now it was too late: as

---

[14] B. Pimlott, *Harold Wilson* (1993 edn.), 437.

another former Chancellor put it to us, 'the cabinet is far too public a forum for the Chancellor to announce his disagreement with the Prime Minister on a key policy—unless he wants it to be across the world's press the next day, making his or the prime minister's position untenable.'

But if the cabinet was irrelevant as a decision-taking forum, the cabinet structure, as an umbrella embracing the dozen or more key ministers and meetings between them, was fully engaged at every stage in the rise and fall of the poll tax. It is quite wrong to say that 'the heart of the problem was the erosion of some of the checks and balances of cabinet government'.[15] Nearly half of the cabinet was present at the Chequers meeting of 31 March 1985, which gave the initial impetus to the policy (not just a 'small number of cabinet ministers', as Richard Shepherd would have it).[16] More than half of the cabinet was involved in the cabinet committees which successively endorsed the principle of the scheme (May 1985), agreed the worked-up plan of the Green Paper (December 1985), and supervised the drawing up of legislation first for Scotland (summer 1986) and then for England and Wales (summer and autumn 1987). The decision to scrap the tax and replace it with a revamped rating system, taken in the spring of 1991, was also agreed by a cabinet committee comprising half the cabinet.

Only at the implementation stage, between autumn 1988 and the downfall of Mrs Thatcher in November 1990, was a smaller number of ministers involved. Key decisions about transitional funding arrangements, and the several internal reviews of the operation of the tax, were taken in small groups, some in 'bilaterals' chaired by the Prime Minister (or, in the case of the bitter dispute over funding between Chris Patten and Nigel Lawson in September 1989, by Sir Geoffrey Howe as deputy Prime Minister). But the overall policy had been endorsed by a wider group. There was no pressure among other ministers for a wider reassessment, and the speed with which many of the

[15] R. Shepherd, *The Power Brokers: The Tory Party and Its Leaders* (1991), 190.

[16] See Ch. 4.

financial decisions had to be taken made such a reassessment impractical. Indeed the most important financial change—the switch of £4.5bn. of local authority spending from the poll tax to VAT in March 1991—was made in the annual budget, which by long convention is never discussed in cabinet or cabinet committee.

Emphatically, therefore, the poll tax story gives little support for the notion of 'presidential government' in Britain. Mrs Thatcher's protestation, in the epigraph to this chapter, is supported by all the participants. 'It is quite untrue to say that her Cabinet colleagues were "bounced" into accepting it,' insists Nigel Lawson. 'Despite her profound personal commitment, she observed the proprieties of Cabinet Government throughout.'[17] Earlier chapters make it abundantly clear that apart from Lawson, all the key ministers, from across the cabinet's departmental and ideological spectrum, endorsed the poll tax. Indeed, the leaders of the supposedly 'pragmatic' wing of the cabinet, Willie Whitelaw and George Younger, were among its most earnest and insistent advocates. As one of his senior officials put it, Younger was 'hell-bent' to have the poll tax introduced into Scotland as early as possible, without any of the delay, transitional arrangements, or safeguards envisaged in the original scheme devised by Kenneth Baker.[18] The only charges that can fairly be levelled against Margaret Thatcher are that she was in the vanguard with Waldegrave, Baker, Younger, and the others; that she, as the one senior minister in the same post throughout the saga, failed to keep the reform on its original course; and that she clung to it after a critical mass in her party wanted 'something' (rarely specified) to be done about it.

In a 1993 lecture on cabinet government, John Wakeham, a senior minister who spanned the Thatcher and Major cabinets, noted that 'many commentators who bemoan what they see as the decline of the cabinet as a decision-taker fail to appreciate its significance as the cement which binds the government together.'[19] The poll tax saga supports Wakeham's thesis that the cabinet is significant as 'cement binding the government

---

[17] Lawson, *View from No. 11*, 561.   [18] See p. 85 above.

[19] *The Times*, 11 Nov. 1993.

together'; it also has something to say about the nature of the cement. In particular, it highlights the remarkable interplay of formal and informal procedures which lie at the heart of modern cabinet government.

As we have noted, the cabinet, through its committees, was fully and formally engaged in all the decisions which led to the poll tax. It would, however, be simplistic to believe that the move towards the poll tax was conducted wholly within the formal decision-making structure of the cabinet and its committees. In reality, a parallel set of informal forums played a critical role in the evolution of the policy. Some of the forums involved ministers alone and some a combination of ministers and advisers; but all were outside the regular cabinet structure, often dovetailing awkwardly with the formal structure.

The most obvious such forum was the Chequers gathering of 31 March 1985. Although not a formal meeting of a cabinet committee, it played a critical role in the evolution of the policy, and is regarded by Mrs Thatcher as the occasion on which the poll tax was truly 'born'.[20] There is nothing new in day-long meetings at Chequers to thrash out major policy departures. Wilson and Callaghan both took to holding meetings there on a fairly frequent basis.[21] Yet in the case of the poll tax—and doubtless other policies with a similar genesis—the effect of such informality was to play into the hands of those supporting the policy, and to make it harder to forestall once it gained prime-ministerial blessing. In the first place, the meeting was so informal that its significance was underrated even by those invited. Nigel Lawson was absent, 'having been assured that this was simply a preliminary discussion at which no decisions would be taken'.[22] Secondly, no papers were circulated before or at the meeting, and few of those there had any idea what a full-fledged poll tax might actually look like. The only information available to ministers on the day was that supplied by Kenneth Baker and William Waldegrave in their slide show.

[20] See Ch. 4.

[21] Cf. Pimlott, *Wilson*, 437 and 672, and Richard Crossman's *Diaries*, iii (1977), 627 and 845.

[22] Lawson, *View from No. 11*, 571.

By the time the policy began to go through the established cabinet machinery, with papers supplying details, it had already
achieved critical momentum.

It is often remarked that the power of the Prime Minister
lies in his or her ability to control the agenda of meetings. An
equally considerable power is his or her ability to control the
forum in which decisions are taken. The Chequers meeting is
but one instance of that in the poll tax saga. No less important
was the initial decision, in autumn 1984, to opt for a 'quickie'
review of the alternatives to rates. Mrs Thatcher's hostility to
royal commissions and quasi-independent committees of inquiry
was well known. But just as important was her and Patrick
Jenkin's desire to have the investigation over in a matter of
months, and their appreciation that on past form any quasi-
independent inquiry would very likely reaffirm the rates. The
Layfield report was only ten years old, and it had taken eighteen months to compile. Jenkin's 'studies' team managed to
undo its work in less than five months.

The use of informal forums—notably the studies team and
the Chequers meeting—had one other significant bearing on the
outcome of the 1984 rates review: it enabled the Department of
the Environment to keep the other departments, particularly
the Treasury, at arm's length. As a policy, the poll tax engaged
a remarkably high proportion of government departments. Four
were directly affected by the reform (Environment, Scotland,
Wales, Treasury), and it had significant ramifications for four
others (the Home Office because of the poll tax register; Trade
and Industry and Agriculture because of the provisions relating
to business rates; and Education because of the position of students). Indeed, of all the departments, only Energy and the
Foreign Office were wholly uninvolved. Yet departments
besides the D.o.E. were excluded from all forums engaged with
the detailed work of the review until it became *de facto* policy.
The original studies team was an internal D.o.E. affair;
although it included officials from outside, they were not in any
sense representatives of their departments. The first the
Scottish Office knew in any detail of what was happening was
at the Capital Hotel meeting in February 1985—a month before

the Chequers meeting. It was the same after Chequers: even at that late stage, there was no involvement of officials or ministers from the Scottish Office, the Home Office, or the Treasury, all of which were far more sceptical about the poll tax than was the D.o.E.. The exclusion of the Treasury is particularly remarkable.

In the case of the poll tax, therefore, John Wakeham's 'cement' served to bind the cabinet as a whole to a policy radically affecting the entire government, yet generated in a matter of weeks by a tiny group of enthusiasts from one department. Assent was freely given, because most ministers affected wanted a solution to a problem, and the poll tax was the only one on offer. 'Procedure', Norman St John-Stevas once said, 'is the best constitution we have.'[23] The poll tax was not an exercise in prime-ministerial autocracy, but a classic product of prime-ministerial procedure.

MINISTERIAL TURNOVER

In the eight years it took to devise, introduce, and repeal the poll tax there were seven Secretaries of State for the Environment, and under them eight ministers for local government.

The rapidity of turnover was higher than typical, though not much so. Richard Rose has shown[24] that the average tenure of cabinet ministers since 1964 has reduced only slightly, from 2.53 years in Wilson's 1964–70 government to 2.43 in the Conservative governments from 1979 until 1991. Furthermore, the heads of the big spending ministries (including the D.o.E. for its control of local government spending) have changed at an above-average rate throughout the period. Since 1974 the average tenure of transport ministers is 1.7 years, of environment ministers (or those exercising the functions of the contemporary Environment Secretary) 1.9 years, of education ministers 2.1 years, and of social security ministers also 2.1

[23] Hennessy, *Cabinet*, 7.
[24] 'The Political Economy of Cabinet Change', in Frank Vibert (ed.), *Britain's Constitutional Future* (Institute of Economic Affairs, 1991).

years. In fact, it does appear that the rate of turnover among Environment Secretaries increased in the 1980s (see Table 8.1). Over the period of the poll tax there were seven trade secretaries and five education secretaries. One has to go back to the 1950s to find a notably slower rate of ministerial turnover in the second-ranking 'spending' ministries.[25]

TABLE 8.1. Turnover among Environment Ministers[a] in post-war governments

Government	No. of cabinet ministers	Average tenure (years)
Labour 1945–1	2	2.6
Conservative 1951–63	5	2.6
Labour 1964–70	2	2.8
Conservative 1970–4	2	1.9
Labour 1974–9	2	2.6
Conservative 1979–Jan 94	9	1.6

[a] Ministry of Health 1945–51, Housing and Local Government 1951–70, Environment 1970–94.

Source: David Butler and Gareth Butler, *British Political Facts 1900–1994* (1994).

The reasons for such rapid turnover are not hard to find.[26] Prime Ministers are concerned with survival not continuity of administration: reshuffles, and the prospect of them, are important instruments of party management. Furthermore, the political skills required of a cabinet minister are at least as important—often more so—as intellectual or administrative capacity; and with the advent of television they are more

[25] During the entire 13 years of Tory rule from 1951 to 1964 there were only five ministers of housing and local government; only two (Macmillan and Brooke) ascended to one of the great offices of State: the other three (Duncan Sandys, Charles Hill, and Keith Joseph) were regarded as unlikely to make it to such eminence, yet kept in post.

[26] Rose, 'The Political Economy of Cabinet Change', in F. Vibert (ed.), *Britain's Constitutional Future.*

continuously in demand and on display than previously. If ministers are found to lack them, or if the government is going through a period of unpopularity, the pressure for change is strong. Changes of the D.o.E. between 1985 and 1993 reflect both factors. Battered by Ken Livingstone and Derek Hatton, Patrick Jenkin's demise was only a matter of time by the spring of 1985. A year later Kenneth Baker, his successor, was needed by Mrs Thatcher at the education department to give it a higher political profile. Nicholas Ridley, his successor, gave way to Chris Patten in 1989 because Patten's public relations skills were judged vital to 'selling' the poll tax. Patten, in turn, was required by John Major as party chairman after Mrs Thatcher's downfall, when Michael Heseltine was seen as the man to end the poll tax. The poll tax abolished, Michael Howard took on the implementation of the council tax until, needed at the Home Office in May 1993, he gave way to John Gummer.

Such rapid turnover gives the lie to the argument that single-party government is a guarantee of ministerial stability. Cabinet ministers in coalition governments in Austria and (west) Germany have enjoyed an average tenure of five and four years respectively since the mid 1960s.[27] It is far easier to move ministers in Britain, where the Prime Minister is leader of the only party in government, invested with the sole power to hire and fire.

Is the rate of turnover in Britain harmful to administration and policy making? Rose notes: 'a managing director of a leading company would expect to spend half a dozen years in the post, and a bishop often remains in place for a decade or more. In universities . . . each academic devotes 30 or 40 years to mastering a single field of knowledge.'[28] By contrast, a cabinet minister with responsibility for a budget running to billions is little more than passer-by—a 'tourist' in the 'Whitehall village'.[29] Ministers mostly have no more than a superficial grasp of their portfolios; even if they succeed in mastering some of the complexities, they have little or no 'institutional memory'. It is hard to dispute that such a regime has ill effects.

[27] Rose, 'The Political Economy of Cabinet Change', in F. Vibert (ed.), *Britain's Constitutional Future*, 52.

[28] Ibid.   [29] J. Bruce-Gardyne, *Ministers and Mandarins* (1986), 2.

However, the poll tax experience raises some uncomfortable questions about the nature and extent of the ill effects. On the face of it, the saga might be thought to demonstrate the consequences of continual chopping and changing at the behest of ministers new to the job. In Peter Riddell's view, 'the shambles of the Tories' policy towards local government in part reflected the succession of ministers at the Department of the Environment, each with their own ideas.'[30] In particular, the switch in May 1986 from Kenneth Baker to Nicholas Ridley brought to the D.o.E. a minister with no knowledge of the preceding work on the poll tax, who progressively discarded the safeguards and transitional arrangements integral to the original Waldegrave–Baker scheme. Baker, for one, is adamant that this was the cause of the catastrophe in 1989–90.[31] Lawson was particularly anxious to maintain a transitional period, to make it easier to 'row back' if disaster struck (as he expected).[32]

Yet the case is far from clear-cut. In the first place, the key permanent officials at the D.o.E.—particularly Sir Terence Heiser, the permanent secretary—appear to have been as keen as ministers to see the end of 'dual-running' in England and Wales. Heiser and his colleagues gave nothing but encouragement to Ridley's change of heart, believing the accountability and administrative benefits of a clean break would outweigh the shock. The shock was essentially political, and it was the job of ministers to take account of it and to tailor policy accordingly. Baker undoubtedly appreciated the political risks, and tailored his scheme to minimize them;[33] Ridley showed no such appreciation, on one occasion even citing the scale of the protests as proof that the policy was working. Nor was this an isolated failing. Almost everyone involved—including Ridley—believes in retrospect that the 1990–1 local authority grant settlement exacerbated the problems of introducing the tax, because it starved authorities of cash and drove up the first bills. Yet by the time it came to negotiate that settlement, Ridley had been in charge of the Department of the Environment for more than

---

[30] P. Riddell, *Honest Opportunism* (1993), 209.

[31] Kenneth Baker, *The Turbulent Years* (1993), 117–19.

[32] Lawson, *View from No. 11*, 576–8.   [33] See Ch. 4.

two years. Therein lies the second point to be noted. The longest-serving Environment Secretary of the period was Ridley, who was at the helm of the D.o.E. for three years and two months—far longer than the average tenure of Environment Secretaries in recent decades. Yet it was under Ridley that most of the key mistakes were made, save that of having dreamt up the tax in the first place. By contrast, his successor, Chris Patten, had been in the job barely days before he could see the political whirlwind advancing over the horizon.[34]

The only morals to be drawn, perhaps, are that ministerial longevity is not an end in itself, nor is it necessarily desirable or undesirable for ministers to be liberated from an inherited 'departmental view'. Above all, ministers need sound political judgement. In some cases that judgement will be improved by long departmental service. But long-serving cabinet ministers can and do exhibit poor judgement over a long period. In truth, the quality of decision-making by cabinet ministers depends more upon their political, intellectual, and administrative training before they reach the cabinet, than upon their departmental know-how once there. If Britain's political class has weaknesses in this wider respect, they are not new.

This discussion merits two telling footnotes. First, not one of the ministerial changes in Mrs Thatcher's government from 1984 until her fall was caused by a resignation on the issue of the poll tax. Secondly, of the twenty-two members of John Major's first government, no fewer than eleven had had direct ministerial involvement in the evolution of the poll tax. Proof, perhaps, of Norman Lamont's dictum: in politics you can recover from anything (though he didn't).[35]

THE TREASURY AND NO. 10

If the poll tax casts an odd light on claims of prime-ministerial autocracy, it casts a still stranger shade over another axiom of modern British government—the pre-eminence of the Treasury among departments.

---

[34] See Ch. 6.   [35] *Independent*, 30 Nov. 1993.

That pre-eminence is not a recent phenomenon. In the nineteenth century the Prime Minister often combined the post with that of Chancellor of the Exchequer, and since then the chancellorship has almost invariably gone to a close political associate of the Premier, often the 'number two' figure in the government. The doctrine of 'Treasury control', also dating back to the nineteenth century, is generally believed to give the Treasury a stranglehold over virtually all areas of policy with spending implications. And as a department, the Treasury has the cream of Whitehall officials. 'Their overall ability is very high, and they rightly dominate central government,' claims Bernard Donoughue. 'Their intellectual dominance is assisted by a shrewd policy of territorial colonisation across Whitehall. Able Treasury men are often placed into senior positions in other Whitehall departments.'[36]

Nigel Lawson certainly believed the Treasury's supremacy to be undiminished under his chancellorship in the 1980s. 'The Chancellor', he writes in his memoirs,

has his finger in pretty well every pie in government. This follows partly from his responsibility for government spending, and partly from tradition. As a result, he can exert a significant influence on policies which are announced by other ministers and which the public does not associate with the Treasury at all. The Chancellor, if he proceeds with care and caution, can affect the content and not merely the cost of other ministers' policies.[37]

Yet Lawson was able to affect neither the content nor the cost of the poll tax, a major tax change and one of the most important 'pies' on the table of the third Thatcher term. How does this failure square with the doctrine of Treasury supremacy?

It may be that Lawson did not proceed with sufficient 'care

[36] B. Donoughue, in A. S. King, *The British Prime Minister* (2nd edn., 1985), 48–9. Equally telling is the remark of Sir Leo Pliatzky, second permanent secretary to the Treasury in the early Thatcher years, on the officials of another department: 'My impression is that many of the senior officials there were well up to the Treasury level, but it was a bigger department and the talent was more thinly spread'. L. Pliatzky, *The Treasury under Mrs Thatcher* (1989), 161.

[37] Lawson, *View from No. 11*, 273.

and caution'. Certainly, his absence from the vital March 1985 Chequers meeting was 'foolish', in his own admission.[38] But more significant factors were at play, which in all likelihood would have outweighed Lawson's presence at Chequers on the fateful Sunday. In the first place, even senior ministers can afford sustained tension in their relationship with the Prime Minister only a small number of issues at any one time: Lawson had tension enough on the question of exchange-rate policy, and was unprepared to allow the poll tax to wreck his working relationship with Mrs Thatcher. Secondly, however extensive the Treasury's web, it has never penetrated into the minutiae of local authority finance, disabling it from taking an activist role in the evolution of the poll tax. Thirdly, even in the greatest offices of State, departmental weight and the assistance of brilliant officials only counts for so much: the political weight of the minister himself is at least as important to success in intra-governmental battles. Taken together, these three factors weaken the notion that on the home front the Treasury is invariably a government within the government.

In a roundabout way, Lawson himself concedes all three points. It is evident from his memoirs—and our interviews—that the Treasury was dependent upon D.o.E. statistics and information throughout the poll tax affair. Only when it came to the council tax in 1991 did the Treasury play anything other than a marginal role in the design of the successive local taxes of the period. This is a cautionary note for those who see 'centralization' as a long-running, almost inevitable feature of modern British government. On the contrary, throughout the modern period local authorities have been largely unconstrained by the Treasury shackles imposed on central government, except in so far as they have been dependent on government grants (a large but far from absolute caveat). In so far as they have been subject to central control in their own fiscal sphere, it has been exercised by the Department of the Environment and its predecessor ministries, i.e. the departments that have seen their main role as acting as the voice of local government

---

[38] Lawson, *View from No. 11*, 571.

in Whitehall. In the 1980s, the vehemence of the Tory hostility to local spending, indeed to the very idea of local government, infected even the D.o.E.—directly through some of the ministers appointed to head it (notably Ridley), and indirectly through the readiness of civil servants to do their masters' bidding. A host of new controls were imposed, most of them still in force. But, significantly, there has been no extension of 'Treasury control' to local government. Come a governing party without the *a priori* hostility to local autonomy and spending characteristic of post-1979 governments, and local authorities might find it fairly easy to regain their fiscal autonomy, in league with the Department of the Environment.

On the question of political 'weight', Lawson recognizes in his memoirs that for all his weight in government, his personal following on the Tory back-benches was always small, and that he made little attempt to cultivate it. At no stage was he a serious challenger to succeed Mrs Thatcher. That fact helps account for the strength of the partnership in Lawson's first five years at the Treasury. But his independent power-base for thwarting determined prime-ministerial designs was correspondingly limited, for all the resources of the Treasury. 'Cabinet colleagues', he recalls,

were too ready to assume that I was always voicing an official Treasury view . . . When I argued that the poll tax would be a political disaster, one of the reasons—although not the main one—why this cut so little ice was that colleagues were too ready to assume that my real objection was a Treasury fear that the poll tax would lead to increased public spending.[39]

Having failed to carry his point in cabinet committee, Lawson made no attempt to wreck the policy by surreptitious briefing or leaking. The press cuttings of 1987, 1988, and 1989 are surprisingly free from anti-poll-tax stories which have any appearance of a ministerial origin. Lawson appears to have expected people to divine his lack of enthusiasm from the mere fact that his name did not appear as a sponsor on the printed Bill presented to the House of Commons.[40]

[39] Ibid. 251.   [40] Ibid. 584.

At the time, that blend of strength and weakness was poorly understood; even in retrospect, many commentators believe Lawson could have thwarted the poll tax if he had exerted himself. In the light of the chancellorship of Norman Lamont (1990–3), who exhibited neither intellectual nor political weight in the job, and never looked better than vulnerable, it is easier to appreciate Lawson's position.

Given the Treasury's distance from local government, and the fact that Lawson's political position was insufficiently strong to thwart the poll tax in cabinet, the Chancellor could probably have destroyed it only by intimating to Mrs Thatcher that he regarded it as a resigning issue. Yet he was never prepared to go that far, and Mrs Thatcher knew it. One close to events remarked: 'she believed she had seen off Nigel, and that he was content to keep quiet on the issue.' Or as Lawson puts it:

Senior ministerial resignations are few and far between—I was the first chancellor to resign for more than thirty years—and there are good reasons for this. If Cabinet ministers resign whenever they disagree with a policy being pursued, Cabinet Government would be impossible. You certainly fight your own corner, but you can never expect to win every battle. In this case what was at issue was a proposal that did not lie within my own range of ministerial responsibilities, and which was not a matter of high principle but simply a grotesque political blunder. When I did resign, it was because a situation had arisen which made it impossible for me to carry out my job successfully. Whatever other troubles the Poll Tax may have caused, it did not do this.[41]

In other words, it was not his bailiwick, so he was prepared to let alone provided he was left alone. That takes us full circle, to the debate about cabinet versus prime-ministerial government. Ultimately cabinet government only works as collective government if a strong desire exists to act collectively, and if the Prime Minister sets much store by collective decision-making. In her later years Mrs Thatcher set no store by the latter; and her ministers, anxious to curry her favour in their own spheres, had little desire for the former. In essence, decision-

---

[41] Lawson, *View from No. 11*, 583.

making required agreement between a departmental minister and the Prime Minister: the views of colleagues were important only to the extent that they influenced either the one or the other. That was certainly the case with the poll tax. 'Stone walls do not a prison make.' No more do a dozen ministers sitting around a table constitute cabinet government.

9

CIVIL SERVICE

> The soul of our service is the loyalty with which we execute ordained error.
>
> Lord Vansittart,
> former permanent secretary at the Foreign Office.[1]

'In my view,' wrote Nicholas Ridley in his account of the Thatcher government, 'a good cabinet minister can always get the best out of the civil service.'[2] The poll tax demonstrates the truth, and full significance, of that remark.

No one could accuse the Department of the Environment's senior officials of 'avoiding the last ounce of commitment', which a highly placed mandarin once hailed as the hallmark of the 'good civil servant'.[3] Sir Terence Heiser, the department's permanent secretary, was instrumental in the launch of the 'studies' which created the poll tax. He put his best brains on the studies team. Their work, conducted at breakneck speed, enabled William Waldegrave and Kenneth Baker to believe that a per capita tax would remedy the failings of local government and could indeed be made to work. The D.o.E.'s senior officials then facilitated the introduction of the poll tax. As its enormities grew, they devised ever more complex and ingenious schemes to keep it afloat. Without flinching, less than a year after the introduction of the poll tax they set to work on its replacement, and had the council tax in operation within two years.

The introduction of the poll tax would not have been

---

[1] Quoted in P. Hennessy, *Whitehall* (1989), 483.
[2] N. Ridley, *My Style of Government* (1991), 41.
[3] Quoted in N. Lawson, *View from No. 11* (1992), 247.

remotely possible without the total engagement of Heiser and his colleagues. A refusal to obstruct was not enough: their unswerving loyalty and commitment were essential. In her memoirs, Mrs Thatcher likens the poll tax to the nineteenth-century Schleswig-Holstein question, which, as Lord Palmerston once remarked, only three people understood—one was dead, one was mad, and the third, himself, had forgotten it.[4] In mid-1980s Whitehall, only a handful of people—not many more than three—had a thorough mastery of local government finance. All were civil servants: no minister ever came close to that category. As Lord Armstrong, Cabinet Secretary at the early stages of the poll tax saga, put it:

Anything to do with local government finance is rebarbatively complicated. The eyes of ministers and civil servants whose departments are not directly involved tend to glaze over when the subject comes up because the detail takes a long time to master, and the devil is in the detail.[5]

Of the twenty-odd ministers closely involved in the rise and fall of the poll tax, William Waldegrave probably had the best grasp of the complexities involved, from his work on the studies team. Yet Waldegrave arrived in the Department of the Environment after the 1983 election, less than a year before the 'studies' started, and he gave up responsibility for local government before the poll tax legislation was even introduced into parliament. As for the rest, former barristers such as Michael Howard and Malcolm Rifkind were able to 'mug up' detail for a Commons debate or to resolve particular issues, but they never had a firm grasp of the complexities underlying them.

Books on the civil service give great prominence to the debate on civil service 'obstruction': in particular, to how far determined civil servants, articulating a 'departmental view', can frustrate a radical government.[6] It is an issue about which

---

[4] M. Thatcher, *The Downing Street Years* (1993), 643.

[5] Letter to the authors, Nov. 1993.

[6] See G. Fry, *The Changing Civil Service* (1985), ch. 2; Hennessy, *Whitehall*, esp. part 2 and ch. 15 ('The Thatcher Effect'); G. Drewry and T. Butcher, *The Civil Service Today* (2nd edn., 1991), esp. chs. 8 and 11; P. Kellner and N. Crowther-Hunt, *The Civil Servants: An Enquiry into Britain's Ruling Class*

civil servants and ministers are themselves highly sensitive.[7] The poll tax story makes it appear a somewhat artificial concern. The main question arising from our study is whether 'activist' civil servants were too closely involved in the evolution—as distinct from implementation—of a highly contentious policy, and whether they should have done more to alert ministers to the repercussions likely to follow from such a hazardous initiative.

Most of the officials involved insist that ministers were determined upon the policy from an early stage, and that any ritualistic wringing of hands by them would have been a pointless, even unprofessional, endeavour. We do not dissent from that view. Professional etiquette dictated that only one of the key officials involved from an early stage was in a position to issue anything approaching a formal warning—Sir Terence Heiser, as permanent secretary. He did not do so.

(1980); and H. Young and A. Sloman, *No Minister: An Inquiry into the Civil Service* (1982).

[7] In their diaries, Richard Crossman and Tony Benn are obsessive about the subject. For a 1980s Tory disquisition on the theme, see Jock Bruce-Gardyne, *Ministers and Mandarins* (1986).

However, the formal relationship between officials and ministers is only one part of the picture. Heiser and some of his colleagues appear, by all accounts, to have been enthusiasts for the poll tax, and to have underestimated its effects almost as seriously as did ministers. Why so? The answer, we believe, is to be found in three sources. First, it is embedded in the professionalism of the modern civil service, which far from seeking to place a drag on controversial or apparently unworkable policies, places a premium on giving effect to them—once it is clear that they are the will of the government as a whole, and not (as with many of Tony Benn's projects) the whim of a single minister. Secondly, it has much to do with the isolation of Whitehall, an isolation especially pronounced in the case of the Department of the Environment, which is physically removed from the local authorities it is charged with overseeing. Thirdly, it has to be seen in the context of a breakdown in relations between central and local government in the mid-1980s, a breakdown as serious at the 'official' as at the 'political' level.

The third theme is closely related to the second, since Whitehall's isolation contributed to the breakdown. Accordingly, the rest of the chapter assesses the 'new professionalism' and 'Whitehall isolation' against the backdrop of the poll tax.

THE NEW PROFESSIONALISM

Since the implementation of the Northcote–Trevelyan Report in the 1870s, the tradition that ministers can rely on professional and non-partisan support from a career civil service has been firmly established. Governments change; officials remain. Ministers can count on the problems facing them being exhaustively analysed, with a clear statement of alternatives being presented to them by their officials. Somewhere there seems to be a vision of a perfect world in which advisers advise and ministers decide. Civil servants offer an objective summary of the full range of possible policies, and, when ministers opt for a particular line of action, they implement the decision as efficiently as possible, whatever their private misgivings.

The world may not be quite like that, but the formal

doctrines assume that it is. At the heart of British government there lie two similar-sounding but quite distinct principles. The first, discussed in the previous chapter, is the doctrine of collective ministerial responsibility ('We all hang together lest we hang separately'; 'a minister must resign before disagreeing openly with cabinet policy'). The second involves individual ministerial responsibility—the formal rule that, for every action of a servant of the Crown, a minister must be ready to answer to parliament. It is a doctrine policed by the Clerks at the Table in the House of Commons; they decide whether a parliamentary question deals with a matter for which a particular minister is answerable. Legitimate concerns arise about the impact of the *Next Steps* agencies for this practice, but no Whitehall agency was involved in the evolution or implementation of the poll tax, so it need not concern us here.

The doctrine of ministerial responsibility implies a contract between ministers and civil servants. Ministers get the praise or the blame for anything done in the name of the government; civil servants get power but anonymity; they do not, in an individual way, have to accept responsibility for the policies they have recommended. After all, they may not approve: like barristers, they are doing the best they can for a client, while in no way giving their personal endorsement to his or her actions. It is for civil servants to tell ministers how best to implement their policies, however misguided they may consider them to be.

The poll tax illustrates this well. The story in the media was of Heseltine, Baker, Waldegrave, Ridley, Patten, and, above all, Thatcher. The public did not hear of Sir Terence Heiser, let alone his subordinates as they worked, not just on the detail, but on the overall viability of the project.

The relationship between ministers and their permanent secretaries has been dubbed the 'vital joint in Whitehall'.[8] But while its importance is undoubted, its nature is less easy to determine, since permanent secretaries are an anonymous breed. The best known in history, by a considerable margin, is TV's

[8] Anthony Sampson, quoted by Drewry and Butcher, *Civil Service Today*, 150.

Sir Humphrey Appleby, yet the imaginative memoirs of his 'boss' Jim Hacker are a suspect guide to his profession.[9] Of the pithy sketches, the best is perhaps that of Lord Beveridge, who likened the relationship between a permanent secretary and minister to that of husband and wife in a Victorian household.[10] The minister is head of the household, formally taking all important decisions, but doing so on advice which he usually finds 'very uncomfortable to disregard'. Like the Victorian wife, the permanent secretary 'has no public life; is quite unknown outside the house; and wields power by influence rather than directly'. Tellingly, Beveridge's memoirs are entitled *Power and Influence*.

In the poll tax saga, the influence of the permanent secretary is imprinted in every chapter. Sir Terence—'Terry'—Heiser's term at the helm of the Department of the Environment, from February 1985 to May 1992, exactly covers the birth, life, and death of the poll tax. Many of those to whom we spoke praised or blamed him for what happened. No one close to events in the D.o.E. excluded him from their account.

A tough East Ender who rose through the ranks on a reputation of grit and competence, Heiser was the antithesis of the Sir Humphrey 'suave, public school, Oxbridge' persona. Mrs Thatcher held him in high regard as the archetypal 'can do' civil servant: as she famously said of Lord Young, 'he comes up with solutions, not problems'. Yet Heiser was neither an avowed nor a closet Thatcherite. On the contrary, he had a similarly 'gritty but effective' standing with Labour ministers in the 1970s, owing his rapid ascent to a successful stint as Tony Crosland's private secretary in the mid-1970s.[11] Above all,

[9] J. Lynn and A. Jay, *The Complete Yes Prime Minister: The memoirs of Sir James Hacker* (1986).

[10] Drewry and Butcher, *Civil Service Today*, 150.

[11] Susan Crosland, *Tony Crosland* (1983 edn.), 288. Crosland told Sir Ian Bancroft, his permanent secretary, that he wanted as his private secretary someone 'with sharp edges—not only intellectually, but who could stand their ground'. He got Heiser. Bancroft rose to be head of the home civil service, but Mrs Thatcher did not regard him as sufficiently 'can do' and he retired early. In 1986 Bancroft told an interviewer: 'the grovel count amongst ministers in this administration and, I think necessarily, therefore, in some officials has been much higher than normal.' Hennessy, *Whitehall*, 623, 625.

Heiser was a highly competent technician, long schooled in the supervision of local government in general and in the minutiae of local authority finance policy in particular. He had served in the Ministry of Housing and Local Government (as was) since the 1950s. After his private office term he spent three years in the D.o.E.'s housing directorate, dealing with local authorities at every turn; from there he went to the D.o.E.'s local government finance directorate for two years, then on to a four-year stint as deputy secretary responsible for local government (1981–5) before appointment as permanent secretary.

Most of the other officials involved in the design and implementation of the poll tax had similar qualifications of impeccable professional 'neutrality' and technical competence. None of the officials engaged on the 1984–6 'studies team' that produced the poll tax was an avowed Thatcherite. One was, privately, a Labour supporter; another had been a Liberal at university; a key adviser brought in from outside after the Chequers meeting had until recently been a member of the SDP. As for experience, Anthony Mayer, the first civil service leader of the 'studies' team, had served on successive local government desks since 1967; Peter Owen, who became the lead official on the team after Mayer's departure to N. M. Rothschild in 1985, had been a private secretary to D.o.E. ministers in the early 1970s, and spent three years in the department's local government finance directorate in the late-1970s. Most of the other D.o.E. officials involved also had impressive track records handling local government policy.

Emphatically, then, the poll tax was not drawn up or implemented by officials who were politically motivated or ignorant of the complexities of local taxation policy. Indeed, the episode makes a telling commentary on the themes, much rehearsed by the Fulton enquiry in the 1960s and persisting still, that the higher civil service suffers from a 'generalist' tradition and ethos. 'The permanent secretary is, almost by definition, the generalist *par excellence*,' proclaims one recent text.[12] That, assuredly, is true of most permanent secretaries on most areas

---

[12] Drewry and Butcher, *Civil Service Today*, 46.

of their responsibility. In the case of the poll tax, however, the permanent secretary and other senior officials involved were all *specialists*. It is true that Heiser and his colleagues were not local government practitioners, and, in drawing up the poll tax, they failed sufficiently to remedy this weakness by consulting with those who were. But they were as expert on the subject in hand as it was possible to be, short of having 'done time' in a local authority or studied for a degree in local government finance—'a dull paper in any university politics course, one taken only by people with a touch of tedium or serious ambition'.[13] A more exciting paper, perhaps, would ask the student to speculate on the likelihood of *generalist* senior officials, approaching the issue in a more detached fashion, developing any enthusiasm for the poll tax. Certainly, Sir George Moseley, Heiser's predecessor, who was far less expert on local government finance than his successor, never had any truck with the idea; nor did Sir William Kerr Fraser, permanent secretary at the Scottish Office until 1988, who strongly cautioned his ministers against the proposal. Ministers require objectivity from their senior officials; and objectivity often requires a certain measure of detachment.

By itself, technical mastery hardly counts as a key component of the 'new professionalism' in the civil service. Senior officials in the 1970s and 1980s may have been more committed to their briefs than their predecessors, but if so, it was a marginal change of degree, not of kind. More significant was the readiness of senior officials in the 1980s to dispense with traditional structures and ways of 'doing things'. The managerial revolution in the civil service has been well documented—particularly its chief fruit, the *Next Steps* programme launched in 1988, which has already shifted two-thirds of all civil servants into quasi-autonomous executive agencies and could ultimately leave a core of only 10 per cent of the service (about 50,000 civil servants) in the central Whitehall departments.[14] However, the

[13] E. Pearce, *Machiavelli's Children* (1993), 46.

[14] For the debate about civil service reform see, in particular, A. Davies and J. Willman, *What Next: Agencies, Departments and the Civil Service* (Institute for Public Policy Research, 1991) and Sir Peter Kemp, *Beyond Next*

revolution has also had a marked, if less determinate and there-fore less appreciated, impact on the policy-making 'core' who were not directly affected by *Next Steps*. One aspect of it is an enthusiasm on the part of key officials for turning policy into 'projects', with 'teams' and 'managers' designated to 'see it through'.

Termed the 'activist mentality' by one senior official we encountered, the approach is well illustrated by Terry Heiser's attitude to the poll tax. Once it was clear that Patrick Jenkin wanted to revisit local taxation, Heiser reassured him that another review need not be as sterile as the previous two. He set up a special team dedicated to the job of finding a replacement for the rates, and seconded his ablest officials to it. Variously reconstituted, the group saw the poll tax through its evolutionary stage, until it came to drawing up legislation after the 1987 election. When the tax, as introduced, ran into problems, an interdepartmental review team was set up to examine options. And when the flagship finally ran aground in early 1991, a third team, under Robin Young, who had played a part alongside the first team back in 1984, was set up to find a replacement.

There is, of course, nothing novel in the establishment of committees of officials to study problems or issues sent to them by ministers. The innovative feature of the poll tax 'teams' was the close association of such groups with the process of policy-making at ministerial level. When the 1984 review was established, D.o.E. ministers had not decided upon a per capita tax: they wanted to explore options systematically. By the time it finished, they were committed to the poll tax. In the intervening four months, William Waldegrave, in particular, turned the review team into a close approximation of a think-tank, a term used by more than one of our interviewees. The divide between 'advising' and 'deciding' is always blurred: in the case of the poll tax, it is more than usually difficult to disentangle the two, because they took place so closely in tandem and in a remarkably informal atmosphere. As we recorded in Chapter 3,

Steps (Social Market Foundation, 1993). The government's objectives are laid out in its Dec. 1993 White Paper, *Next Steps Agencies in Government*, Cmnd. 2430.

Waldegrave and his officials started the project by mutual brainstorming, and would break off late at night for a game of bridge or a take-away meal.[15] In this context, it is worth noting how minor a role the D.o.E.'s political advisers played in the process. The justification for political advisers, introduced by Harold Wilson in the 1970s, was that they relieve officials from having to deal too closely with political exigencies. Yet neither of the D.o.E.'s two political advisers of the day was on the initial studies team, nor did political advisers play any appreciable role at any later stage.

In other words, ministers and officials devised the poll tax together. In this respect the poll tax was not a case apart, but typical of first-order policy departures in the mid- and late 1980s. To take two comparable cases, the mid-1980s Fowler social security reforms, and the late-1980s reorganization of the health service, were both devised by dedicated project teams working closely with ministers. In each case, ministers took responsibility; without them, the reforms would never have happened. But ministers did not 'decide' first, and then ask their officials to 'implement' after.

That, inevitably, brings us face to face with the question of civil service neutrality. According to John Ward, former general secretary of the First Division Association of senior civil servants, the duty of the civil servant is to ask three questions: will it work? is it fair? and will it lead to extra work or cost? 'A good civil servant will go further and make positive recommendations, even if these are contrary to the views of ministers.'[16] As the official statement of *Duties and Responsibilities of Civil Servants in Relation to Ministers*, issued in 1987, puts it: 'it is the duty of the civil servants . . . to give to the Minister honest and impartial advice, without fear or favour, and whether the advice accords with the Minister's view or not.'[17]

With the poll tax there is reason to believe that key officials became infected with their masters' zeal. Senior officials talked

[15] See pp. 50 to 61 above.
[16] Drewry and Butcher, *Civil Service Today*, 160.
[17] *Duties and Responsibilities of Civil Servants in Relation to Ministers*, Dec. 1987, para. 7.

openly about the damage 'loony left' councils were doing to local government. At the crucial Capital Hotel meeting on 3 February 1985, a sceptical adviser was surprised that the voice of dissent was so completely missing. At vital moments, the detailed figures that would show up local anomalies and injustices (and more particularly the implications for the 'not quite poor' who were to be worst affected by the change) seem not to have been thrust before ministers. Detailed research on the impact of the new tax was commissioned from the Institute for Fiscal Studies *after* the Chequers meeting of March 1985, but how much was done before is a matter of dispute. One official on the review team assured us that detailed appraisals were made of the local impact, but were downplayed for political reasons. By contrast, ministers closely involved insist that they never saw such figures; nor, indeed, did they even appear to be conscious of the later work done by the IFS. Whatever the position on that score, it is clear that no early warning was given of the likely degree of non-payment. It was only after the Chequers meeting that the Home Office sounded a warning on the issue of the register and the implications for civil liberties. Civil servants, moreover, must take part of the blame for the belated realization of how high the level of poll tax would be. The drift from an acceptable £178 per head in 1987 to an intolerable £363 in 1990 was something about which officials might well have given earlier notice. They would have realized the implications of a less than generous grant settlement for 1990–1, coupled with the facts that all marginal spending would fall on the community charge and that inflation was rising faster than forecast. They also had long experience of the spending policies of local authorities: for instance, it was noted in Chapter 2 that the radical change in local authority structure in 1974, following the Redcliffe-Maud report, was accompanied by rates increases of about 30 per cent in the first year of the new authorities.[18] Even the Scottish experience of poll tax bills in year one of the new system should have been enough to raise the alarm in the D.o.E.[19]

[18] See pp. 21–2.
[19] Spending by Scottish authorities rose by about 13% above inflation in the first year of the poll tax.

One missed opportunity undoubtedly lies in the failure suffi-ciently to exploit the administrative resources of the State. Federal systems gain from their pluralism; a policy innovation is often tried and polished in one region before being generally adopted nation-wide. The United Kingdom is not a federation, but many things are done differently north and south of the border. Over the years England has probably been too slow to learn from Scottish experience in fields such as legal adminis-tration and policies on education, liquor licensing, and shop hours. In the case of the poll tax, there was no attempt to pilot the innovation, although it was decided from an early stage that the reform would be carried through first in Scotland. In the event, the poll tax was introduced in England only a year after its launch in Scotland, with ministers adamant that the Scots were not being treated as guinea-pigs. In retrospect, it would have been a good thing if Scotland had been so treated, and the lessons learnt before the poll tax was extended to England and Wales.

Any decision to pilot the tax would have been the responsi-bility of ministers, not officials; all that can be said against the latter is that they do not appear even to have suggested the idea. But in defence of 'activist' D.o.E. officials, another impor-tant consideration needs to be highlighted. By the time of the studies in 1984, the Conservatives had already been in office for five years, and were planning their programme for their next term. By force of circumstance, policy changes were taking place *in office*, not in opposition. It was not a question of a new set of ministers coming into office and presenting their 'policy' to Whitehall: Mrs Thatcher and her colleagues were already there, trying to formulate policy to respond to their own per-ceived failures. Since the government had deliberately turned its back on royal commissions, departmental committees, and other forums for engaging outsiders in the process of policy formulation, the civil service had to do the job instead. In the case of the poll tax, there were four outside advisers, but their role was limited and, with one exception, their advice appears to have been ignored.

In a letter to *The Times* in 1993, Lord Armstrong and Sir

Frank Cooper rejected any idea that officials might become unduly politicized by close association with ministers from a party continuously in office over a protracted period. They claimed it would take twenty-five years, throughout which the party in power had 'followed a sustained and evident policy of preferring those who were known to support them politically in making their senior civil service appointments', for such a danger to arise.[20] The civil servants behind the poll tax were not remotely 'Thatcherites' by affiliation, but the experience shows that the 'new professionalism' of the civil service made 'undue politicization' a real danger within five years.

WHITEHALL ISOLATION

In the chronological account, it was noted how incredulous overseas observers were at the very notion of a poll tax. At the time, many UK commentators, and some officials, were similarly aghast at the idea of Britain proceeding with a system of taxation untried or rejected by the rest of the developed world. Andrew Tyrie, a special adviser who worked first for Patrick Jenkin at the D.o.E. and then for Nigel Lawson at the Treasury, and opposed the poll tax throughout, was fond of pointing out that he could find only two overseas bedfellows for the new impost—one in Guinea-Bissau, and the other in Papua New Guinea, where opposition had forced its reform into a hut tax.

No serious international studies were made before the poll tax was adopted. The studies team which devised the tax never travelled abroad; nor did it undertake systematic analysis of any overseas system of local government taxation or finance. The attitude of ministers and officials alike was summed up by the approach taken in the 1986 Green Paper *Paying for Local Government*, where 'international comparisons' occupy the concluding four pages of the 133-page document, buried in the last of ten annexes.[21] The last table in the annexe[22] compares local

---

[20] *Times*, 7 Jan. 1993. Lord Armstrong was Secretary to the Cabinet between 1979 and 1987; Sir Frank Cooper permanent secretary at the Ministry of Defence, 1976–82.

[21] Annexe K, 130–3.   [22] Fig. K3, 132.

tax systems in the twenty-three developed countries belonging to the Organization for Economic Co-Operation and Development. It shows that all but four of the OECD states had a local property tax; and more than half had a local income or profits tax, in most cases as well as a property tax. None had a per capita tax. Yet the conclusion drawn was this:

The information set out (in the annexe) can only show a snapshot of the situation at a particular time. It cannot reflect issues of current concern which may lead to a change in institutional or financial arrangements. One such issue is the growth of local government within the national economy.[23]

The annexe concluded by mentioning that a conference would soon be held by the Council of Europe, at which one of the principal themes would be local government finance.

It is hard to know what to make of those words. Two implications might have been drawn: first, that the absence of a poll tax elsewhere in the OECD was irrelevant, because 'issues of current concern' in the UK overrode the experience of other developed countries; second, that the rest of the OECD was also suffering from excessive local spending, and would have to adopt similarly drastic solutions. Yet no evidence was cited that financial pressures were leading other countries to adopt a poll tax, or anything like one. So unless ministers were seriously expecting to be able to make converts at the Council of Europe, the conclusion must be that the government was consciously turning its back on the wisdom of the rest of the OECD without so much as examining it.

However, it was hardly necessary to look across the Channel to see the enormous social and administrative problems likely to be involved in introducing a per capita tax. Local authority treasurers could have told the D.o.E. at the outset: indeed, as we have seen, local authorities, and expert bodies closely linked with local authority finance officers, did so.[24] Yet they played no part whatever in the 'studies team' that devised the poll tax. In her memoirs, Mrs Thatcher says she dismissed alternatives to the poll tax—local income tax and sales tax—partly because

---

[23] Cmnd. 9714. *Paying for Local Government*, 133.   [24] See Ch. 5.

they 'would have been highly bureaucratic'.[25] Any council treasurer could have told her that a poll tax was far worse than either on that score.

There was, of course, consultation *after* the publication of the Green Paper in January 1986, when most of the local authorities responding pointed out the significant problems in store. This, presumably, is what William Waldegrave had in mind when in a 1993 lecture he referred to the 'enormous consultation' there had been over the poll tax.[26] Yet the criticisms made virtually no impact: indeed, once the Green Paper was published, the only significant change to the design of the tax made in response to outside pressure was the abolition of dual-running, a change made at the behest of the 1987 Conservative party conference, but already supported by Nicholas Ridley, then Environment Secretary.

The specific question as to why no local government finance practitioner was engaged in the 1984–6 studies is tied up in the party politics of the time. Yet two important general points arise. There is, first, the ignorance of the D.o.E. on questions of local authority administration, resulting from the almost complete separation of central and local administration in the UK; and second, the stark contrast between the D.o.E.'s formulation of the poll tax, from which local authority experts were excluded at every stage, and the formulations of tax changes by the Treasury, where the responsible administrative bodies are engaged from the outset.

The separation of local and national administration in the UK dates back to the development of the modern system of public administration in the late nineteenth century. Whitehall and the town halls have always recruited their staff separately. While civil servants are servants of the Crown, employed on a common basis, local authority officials are servants of their local authority, governed by terms and conditions laid down by their particular council. Periodically since the war, particularly after the Fulton inquiry of the 1960s, initiatives have been launched

[25] Thatcher, *Downing Street Years*, 649.
[26] Speech to Social Market Foundation conference on 'Reforming the Role of Government', Dec. 1993, 7.

to break down the particularism of individual departments and the barriers to promotion between 'clerical' and 'administrative' grades; in the 1980s, there was an equally pronounced drive to erode the barriers between Whitehall and the private sector.[27] But little attempt has ever been made to break down the barriers between local and national administration. Whereas in France and Germany, interchange between local, regional, and national administration is common, in Britain it virtually never occurs. No senior official in the D.o.E. responsible for the poll tax had ever worked in local government. Since the poll tax, the government has launched a scheme to encourage short-term exchanges of senior officials between central and local between town halls. As yet, however, little appears to have come of it.

As for the contrast between D.o.E. and Treasury practice in the evolution of tax policy, it is necessary only to contrast the poll tax with one of the Treasury's major tax reforms of the 1980s: the introduction of independent taxation for married couples, which came into effect on the same day as the poll tax in 1990. The Inland Revenue was engaged in plans for independent taxation from the outset: every aspect of the reform was devised by the Treasury after exhaustive consultation with the Revenue, and the reform as introduced bore the Revenue's imprint in crucial respects. In particular, it was introduced with scrupulous attention to winners and losers, with special reliefs to minimize the number of losers.[28] The Treasury was appalled at what one official called the 'cavalier' attitude taken by the Department of the Environment to the impact of 'their' poll tax.

Customs and Excise and the Inland Revenue have always played a key role in the reform of national taxation.[29] Institutional machinery exists to ensure regular consultation. Both Inland Revenue and Customs and Excise have policy planning

[27] In addition, policies of hiving off front-line civil servants into quasi-autonomous agencies, local management of schools and hospitals, and compulsory competitive tendering of local government services, were intended to introduce a more market-orientated ethos into the public sector.

[28] *Financial Times*, 21 Mar. 1990.

[29] See. A. Robinson and C. Sandford, *Tax Policy-Making in the United Kingdom: A Study of Rationality, Ideology and Politics* (1983), esp. 87–95.

units responsible for studying taxation changes, advising the Treasury as needed.[30] 'Local government' has no comparable unit. The nearest equivalent is the Consultative Council for Local Government Finance, established by Tony Crosland in 1975, which continued to meet throughout the 1980s.[31] But its role is simply to survey spending requirements and amendments to the grant system for the forthcoming year. It consists of regular but unwieldy meetings at which ministers and local authority leaders exchange 'views'—or, more typically in the 1980s, insults. It rarely attempts to take a 'long view'.

Thus, in the run-up to the poll tax the only national body with a brief to examine the local taxation system was the Department of the Environment's own local authority finance directorate. The directorate was concerned not just with policy, but also with the execution of the D.o.E.'s administrative duties with regard to local finance. The latter duty is important. The directorate was not a 'pure policy' body: it had to administer the grant system, and make sense of the increasingly cumbersome system of 'targets' and 'penalties' devised in desperate bids by ministers in the early 1980s to constrain local spending within the existing regime. By 1984 Terry Heiser and his colleagues were convinced that the system was unsustainable: a large part of the attraction of the poll tax to them was that it offered the prospect of freedom from their own local finance incubus in one bound. It is not hard to see why D.o.E. officials put their own administrative ease above that of local government itself, particularly when local government was not at the 'table' devising the reforms.

'NOTHING TO DO WITH THE CIVIL SERVICE'?

In a 1993 lecture, William Waldegrave went out of his way to exculpate the civil service for any blame for the poll tax. It had, he said, 'nothing to do with the civil service and the outside experts who had performed exactly what their democratically

[30] A. Robinson and C. Sandford, *Tax Policy-Making in the United Kingdom: A Study of Rationality, Ideology and Politics* (1983), 95.

[31] Tony Travers, *The Politics of Local Government Finance* (1987), 42–3.

elected masters has asked of them.'[32] Put like that, he was undoubtedly right. The 'political masters' did indeed wish to see a per capita tax in place, and key ministers in the D.o.E. made their own decision in favour of the poll tax early on in the work of the studies team. The civil service was facilitator, not brainchild.

Nevertheless, the role of the modern, non-partisan civil service is not just to execute ministerial wishes, but also to advise and to warn. In the case of the Department of the Environment and the poll tax, its warnings were ineffective and its advice poor.

[32] Waldegrave, 'Reforming the Role of Government', (Social Market Foundation lecture), 7.

10

PARLIAMENT

> The main task of Parliament is still what it was when first summoned, not to legislate or govern, but to secure full discussion and ventilation of all matters.
>
> L. S. Amery, *Thoughts on the Constitution* (1947)

Why did the poll tax sail through parliament unscathed? Could or should it have been stopped—or, at the very least, have been amended to make it more workable and less manifestly unjust?

To the partisan these questions might seem loaded, and to the academic naïve. Yet to most contemporaries including a fair proportion of Tory MPs, the community charge as enacted was a profoundly misguided project. As for naïvety, only the insular British approach to the study of legislatures, exemplified by L. S. Amery in the epigraph, gives credence to the notion that, in parliamentary democracies with disciplined parties, parliament is necessarily no more than a talking-shop. In most parliamentary democracies, legislative–executive relations play a role, often a significant one, in the evolution of public policy and the enactment of legislation. Why parliament is so weak in Britain, and why it had virtually no impact at all on the poll tax, are serious questions requiring serious analysis.

The questions are of particular significance because the community charge was both a major new tax and a major constitutional innovation. As such, it combined the two characteristics which, historically and comparatively, might be expected to have guaranteed it special parliamentary attention. Historically, the role of parliament was to scrutinize requests from the Crown for taxation. Nor is that a predemocratic role: until well into this century, tax policy was a central and often fraught aspect of the relationship between governments and parliament. Equally, in most Western parliamentary democracies, constitutional innovation is a field in which the legislature retains wide-ranging powers to check initiatives by the executive—even an executive which has a secure parliamentary majority for the purposes of taxation and ordinary legislation.

The extent of Britain's peculiarity in these respects is highlighted by the Dutch political scientist, Arend Lijphart, in an influential 1984 work comparing democratic systems.[1] Based on his study of the operation of twenty-one democracies, Lijphart notes nine defining characteristics of 'majoritarian' systems:

(1) the concentration of executive power in the hands of one party;
(2) the fusion of executive and legislature;
(3) the weighting of power heavily in favour of one house or parliamentary chamber ('asymmetric bicameralism');
(4) a two-party system;
(5) the alignment of parties on the basis of one broad set of issues (a 'one-dimensional party system');
(6) a first-past-the-post electoral system;
(7) a unitary and centralized government;
(8) an unwritten Constitution, conferring sovereignty on parliament;
(9) an exclusively representative democracy, with no role for referendums.[2]

Using these nine characteristics to align his twenty-one democracies from the most 'consensual' on the left to the most majoritarian on the right, Lijphart placed the United Kingdom on the far right. Only New Zealand, which inherited the 'Westminster model' from its colonial parent in an unusually pure form, was placed in a more extreme position.[3] Since New Zealand is a far smaller (3m. population) and more socially homogeneous country than Britain, its status as a more

[1] A. Lijphart, *Democracies: Patterns of Majoritarian and Consensus Government in Twenty-one Countries* (1984).
[2] Ibid. 6–9, 23–30.
[3] Ibid. 215–22.

majoritarian regime than Britain was questionable even in 1984. However, in two successive referendums in 1992 and 1993 New Zealanders voted decisively to change their electoral system from first-past-the-post to proportional representation, in the teeth of opposition from both of their major parties. Britain is now isolated on the extreme.

Lijphart's nine characteristics are a useful point of departure for a discussion of parliament in general and its role with regard to the poll tax in particular, since seven of them involve the role of the legislature within the political system, and all seven more or less account for the enactment of the poll tax. Given the prevailing levels of popular support for the three main parties in the late-1980s, and their respective policies for local taxation, it is inconceivable that a proportional voting system could have yielded a government able to carry through the poll tax, whether it was a coalition or not. In all probability a written Constitution, conferring an assured constitutional status on local government within the United Kingdom, would have made a poll tax enacted against the strenuous opposition of local authorities an impossibility. A strong second chamber, directly or indirectly elected, might have thwarted the plan. The institutionalization of local referendums to decide local tax controversies, as seriously considered by the government in 1981, might have averted the move to poll tax as a device to improve 'accountability'. And irrespective of all the foregoing, an executive less dominant within the legislature than Britain's would almost certainly not have introduced the poll tax—nor been able to implement it. Without the full exertions of the whips, backed up by a bloated pay-roll vote embracing more than a third of all Tory MPs, the Mates amendment for a banded poll tax would probably have been carried; and that would have gone far towards transforming the poll tax into a local income tax.[4]

[4] A point made forcefully by Professor Tom Wilson, one of the assessors on the initial review team, who believed the poll tax was bound to be a transitional tax, probably resulting in a local income tax unless it was scrapped in its entirety (as happened). See his essay in S. Bailey, and R. Paddison, *The Reform of Local Government Finance in Britain* (1988), esp. 103–4.

The rest of the chapter looks in more detail at the component weaknesses in parliament's scrutiny of the poll tax. It starts with the deafening silence of the select committees. The scrutiny of the legislation by the Commons and Lords is then examined, the section on the Commons addressing the issue of the representativeness of the poll tax for an assessment of the role of parliament, given the size of the Thatcher government's Commons majority. By way of conclusion, we discuss an important aspect of the affair which might be thought to mitigate, even redeem, the verdict of parliamentary failure: the fact that the parliament which enacted the poll tax also repealed it. Does the rise and fall of the poll tax in fact exhibit the operation of a parliamentary self-correcting mechanism, acting to purge deeply unpopular and unworkable legislation?

THE SILENCE OF THE SELECT COMMITTEES

The package of measures enacted in the Local Government Finance Act 1988—poll tax, uniform business rate, new grant and capping arrangements—constitute the most far-reaching reform of local authority finance this century. Taken together with compulsory competitive tendering of local authority services, an obligation imposed on councils by the 1988 Local Government Act, which passed through parliament in the same session as the poll tax and its associated reforms, it represented a radical redefinition by parliament of the political and constitutional role of local government. Yet the revolution took place without a single inquiry by a select committee of either House of Parliament.

The only parliamentary scrutiny of the issues at stake took place when the government presented its legislation. By then, of course, ministers had determined their policy in all essentials. The opportunities afforded by the legislative process for investigation of the underlying principles of the bills, or of the problems they were intended to tackle, were slight. House of Commons standing committees, responsible for scrutinizing government bills, have rightly been termed 'debating committees' representing 'the House in miniature',[5] rather than scrutiny committees representing the House as an investigative forum. The standing committee on the Local Government Finance Bill was no exception.[6]

Select committees exist for MPs and peers to address broad issues of public policy apart from the legislative process, and to do without the government's whip hand dominating proceedings. Reforms of the select committee system in both Houses in the 1970s were intended to systematize and improve their operation. Following a 1978 report by the Commons Procedure Committee, and an initiative the following year by Norman St John-Stevas, Mrs Thatcher's first Leader of the House of Commons, a system of departmental select committees was established, one shadowing the work of each government department.[7] An Environment Committee was among the new select committees, with a remit that included local government. Select committees for Scottish and Welsh affairs were also set up, able to examine local government in their respective spheres. By the time of the Stevas reforms, the House of Lords had already revised its committee structure, acting on similar impulses. The peers established permanent select committees to cover the European Communities and science and technology policy, with provision for *ad hoc* select committees to deal with other important public policy issues.[8]

At no stage in the 1980s did any select committee of the House of Lords address the question of local government, except indirectly through enquiries by the European Communities Committee that had ramifications for local councils. In the whole decade the Lords established only two *ad hoc* select committees: to address the questions of overseas trade and the mandatory life sentence for murder. In most bicameral systems, the second chamber takes a special interest in constitutional

[5] J. A. G. Griffith and Michael Ryle, *Parliament: Functions, Practice and Procedures* (1989), 270.

[6] See Ch. 5 for an account of the Bill's committee stage.

[7] See Priscilla Baines, 'History and Rationale of the 1979 Reforms', in G. Drewry (ed.), *The New Select Committees* (2nd edn., 1989), 13–34.

[8] See A. Adonis, *Parliament Today* (2nd edn., 1993), 222–5.

questions. Apologists for the House of Lords often claim that it does in fact do so—pointing, for instance, to its action in rejecting the War Crimes Bill (1989) and in forcing the government in 1984 to abandon its plans to abolish the Greater London Council before the post-abolition arrangements had been set in place. Yet, if the Upper House was a conscientious guardian of the Constitution, it might have been expected to take a special interest in relations between central and local government, particularly at a time when they were under unprecedented strain. It did not do so.

More remarkable, however, was the silence of the House of Commons select committees. Since 1979 the Welsh and Scottish committees have never addressed the question of local government. Indeed, for the central years of our study the Scottish committee was not even in existence: the government refused to allow it to be reappointed for the 1987 parliament, because the Tory rout in Scotland in the 1987 election left the government with too few Scottish back-benchers to ensure a reliable Tory majority.

As for the Environment committee, after its foundation in 1980, it addressed local government finance only once as a subject in its own right—in its 1982 inquiry into the issues raised by Michael Heseltine's 1981 Green Paper *Alternatives to Domestic Rates*.

Thereafter, the Environment committee paid attention to most major policy fields in its departmental remit—except local government, which in terms of expenditure and domestic salience was the most important. While the studies team was engaged in the 1984–5 review, the committee was investigating the British Board of Agrément, the operation and effectiveness of Part II of the Wildlife and Countryside Act, and the problems in the management of urban renewal—the latter report being the closest it came to the questions of local government finance and central–local relations in the period covered by this book. In the nine months after the publication of *Paying for Local Government*, the committee addressed itself to the Sports Council, to planning appeals and public enquiries, and to radioactive waste. When the Bill to introduce the poll tax into

Scotland was presented in the autumn of 1986, the committee decided to look at historic buildings and ancient monuments, and the Property Services Agency. When the turn of England and Wales came a year later, it focused its attention on air pollution. In 1989, year one of the poll tax in Scotland, it reported on the British Waterways Board, toxic waste, and the disposal of low-level radioactive waste at Drigg. True to form, in 1990, year one of the poll tax in England and Wales, it gave priority to contaminated land, pollution of beaches, and EC environmental policy. Unsurprisingly, the collapse of the poll tax, the subsequent Heseltine review, the decision to return to a property tax, and the enactment and introduction of the council tax, all occurred while the Environment committee had other preoccupations.

Many of the inquiries listed above were on 'green' issues of national and international significance. Given the vast scope of the Environment committee's remit, weighing the competing claims of different policy areas was bound to be problematic. But it is hard to see how any objective assessment would have given the Sports Council and the Wildlife and Countryside Act priority over the crisis in local government finance in the late 1980s.

The committee's neglect of local government was deliberate. Its chairman from 1983 to 1992 was the Tory MP Sir Hugh Rossi, formerly a junior minister at the Department of the Environment and well acquainted with local government issues. In 1985 Rossi explained his committee's policy on investigations to the Liaison committee, the body responsible for monitoring all the departmental select committees. 'We decided', he wrote:

as an act of conscious policy, not to become involved in topics which are the subject of major political controversy or which are likely to be debated fully on the floor of the House in any event. Instead we decided to identify and concentrate on areas of public concern where the political parties had not defined their attitudes and in which it appeared that ministers had not much time to investigate in depth for themselves. In this way we would enhance our prospects of producing unanimous all-party reports which would thereby carry conviction and influence the decision-making process.[9]

[9] Cited in Drewry, *New Select Committees*, 406.

In Rossi's view, those principles precluded any inquiry into local government—finance, structure, or functions. Hence the committee's decision to opt for major 'green' issues, where political controversy was slight and partisan divisions few. As a natural loyalist and a recent member of Mrs Thatcher's government, Rossi may also have felt a commitment to shielding the government from potentially embarrassing reports. But most other members of the committee, Labour as well as Tory, appear to have endorsed his outlook. Indeed, the decision, prior to Rossi's chairmanship, to hold an inquiry into the 1981 Green Paper split the committee down the middle, with the Labour members strongly opposed.[10]

The work of the Environment committee in the 'green' sphere is not to be denigrated. A recent study of its reports in the area supports the view that the government is more likely to follow a committee's recommendations when the issue involved is technical and scientific and not controversial between the parties.[11] Yet the implication of the 'Rossi doctrine' is stark: that the job of select committees is essentially supplementary to the government's own research, so their efforts should concentrate on relatively uncontroversial issues. The committees hope that officials will then take some notice of their reports when they come to prepare legislation or develop policy. The extreme limitations of this doctrine should be noted. Select committees are not only to restrict themselves to issues on which they can act with unanimity: they must also not seek to duplicate any policy formulation being done in government departments. A third aspect of the Rossi doctrine also stands out: the assumption that debating an issue 'fully' on the floor of the Commons is an adequate substitute for a select committee investigation.

In short, the Rossi doctrine consigns the select committees to the political car-park. They are to keep clear of all moving 'policy' traffic; they are not to seek to intrude when anyone else— parties, ministers, or officials—is already in motion; and their

[10] Ibid. 155.
[11] D. Hawes, *Power on the Back Benches? The Growth of Select Committee Influence* (School of Advanced Urban Studies, Bristol, 1993).

only strategy is to attract the attention of ambling ministers on their way to their cars. Moreover, the doctrine is concerned merely with reports and ignores the processes of parliamentary inquiries or with the effect they can have on providing MPs with policy advice, bringing them in touch with outside opinion, and informing them of the likely impact of different approaches, even when it is not possible to secure complete consensus. The doctrine also excludes the select committees from considering issues of political controversy even where, as with the poll tax in the mid-1980s, the government had still to announce a policy, and political divisions were evidently as much within as between the parties.

Not all the select committees have taken so restrictive a view of their role as the Environment committee. Other committees have not been afraid to tackle issues of partisan controversy, particularly since the slashing of the Major government's parliamentary majority in the 1992 election. In the coal controversy of 1992–3, not only did the Trade and Industry committee decide to hold an inquiry into the closure of pits, but the government itself co-operated with the inquiry once its parliamentary majority appeared to be endangered by a serious back-bench revolt.[12]

It must be recognized that even the more activist committees have had a distinctly limited role in the policy-making process. By any policy test, the Trade and Industry committee failed in its bid to redirect government energy policy: unable to influence the fundamental pressures created by the structure of electricity privatization in 1990, or to sustain popular momentum behind a 'save the pits' campaign, the policy of closures proceeded in 1993 almost exactly as planned by the government at the outset. Without a fundamental rebalancing of the relationship between executive and legislature, select committees will rarely, if ever, play a significant role in shaping policy; and the select committees themselves are far too weak to play more than an incidental part in engineering any such rebalancing. As Drewry puts it, the committees 'are, and realistically can only aspire to be, in the business of scrutiny and exposure, not of government'.[13]

[12] Adonis, *Parliament Today*, 145–7 and 174–5.
[13] Drewry, *New Select Committees*, 426.

It must, of course, be doubtful whether any select committee inquiry would have had much effect on *Paying for Local Government*, either before or after its publication; though since the Environment committee did nothing, we cannot be sure. Yet there can be no doubt that the failure of MPs and peers to gather any detailed, independent assessments of the likely impact of a poll tax helps to explain why they proved so impotent to scrutinize the tax against the critical yardsticks of its efficiency as a tax, its collectability, and its ramifications for the administration and effectiveness of local authorities. Apart from the government's own statistics and opinions, legislators had nothing to draw on besides a few notes prepared by researchers in the House of Commons library, and the odd briefing by local authority associations and bodies like CIPFA. They just had to take the government's word for everything, a poor principle of action for parliamentarians in any respectable democracy.

THE HOUSE OF COMMONS: 'SOUND AND FURY SIGNIFYING NOTHING'

Whatever charges can be laid against parliament for enacting the poll tax, insufficient debate is not one of them. The Local Government Finance Bill took more than seven months to pass through the two Houses. Between December 1987 and July 1988 it dominated the parliamentary timetable, consuming more than two hundred hours of debate spread over some forty parliamentary days. Around a third of all MPs, and more than a hundred peers, took part in the proceedings at some stage. Sheafs of amendments were tabled and every clause was scrutinized (albeit many of them only in the Lords). So great was the pressure that during the Bill's committee stage in the Commons, the parliamentary printers could not keep up with the deluge and special arrangements had to be made.

Nor were the critics of the poll tax mute. In the Commons Sir George Young kept up a vigorous critique of the tax, predicting almost all of the faults that in due course were to undermine it. With the Mates amendment, debated at report stage in the Commons, Young and his supporters made an all-out bit to overturn the flat-rate principle, and they appeared at the time to have a sporting chance of success. Certainly, Mrs Thatcher thought they might succeed. Before the bill started on its passage she was alarmed at the lack of support for the poll tax on the back-benches,[14] and the tactics used by the whips to ensure the defeat of the Mates amendment verged on the desperate.[15] Yet it was sound and fury signifying nothing. In the event, the government never came close to defeat, and the number of rebels never exceeded 38 on a critical vote.

Why did Tory opponents fail to make any significant changes to the poll tax, despite the fact that the whips could identify only 150 of 375 Tory MPs as 'clear supporters' at the outset?[16]

The size of the government's majority provides part of the explanation. With a majority of a hundred, at least fifty malcontents would have been needed to carry any amendments against the government—or to sustain a standing committee or Lords' amendment carried against ministers. Significantly, the same assessment by the Tory whips which found only 150 'clear supporters' for the tax also identified only 24 'outright opponents'. Apathy and ambition are a government's chief allies in shoring up its majority. Of the 100 Tory back-benchers initially identified as sceptical or non-committal, virtually all were susceptible to the blandishments of the whips. They almost invariably are. The main job of a government back-bencher is to support the government; and the main ambition of a government back-bencher is to become a minister—or, at least, to gain some of the loaves and fishes at the government's disposal. Only an exceptional degree of resolve or antipathy to a particular measure is likely to provoke sustained dissent.

Table 10.1 gives a more detailed picture of the Tory poll tax rebels. Only 39 Tory MPs voted against the government on one or more of the 3 critical votes on the poll tax legislation (the second and third readings and the Mates amendment). Tellingly, of those 39, all but 8 were either former ministers (resigned, sacked, or never offered office by Mrs Thatcher) or

---

[14] M. Thatcher, *The Downing Street Years* (1993), 652.   [15] See Ch. 5.
[16] As reported by Mrs Thatcher, *Downing Street Years*, 652.

back-benchers of more than ten years' standing (i.e. with little prospect of climbing up the ministerial tree). For the most part, the list of rebels is a litany of bitter opponents of Mrs Thatcher (Edward Heath, Sir Ian Gilmour, *et al.*) and long-established free spirits (Anthony Beaumont-Dark, Sir Peter Tapsell, *et al.*). Of the 8 rebels elected in 1979 or after, it is notable that 4 sat for highly marginal seats, and were probably more concerned about immediate electoral survival than ministerial promotion. The pattern was the same in the fourth and final critical division affecting the poll tax—the vote on the 1990–1 rate support grant settlement, a focus of widespread back-bench discontent because by now the size of the first year's poll tax bills was becoming apparent. All but 5 of the 29 rebels were either former ministers or long-time back-benchers.

What if the government's majority had been smaller? Given the number of rebels, and the vote on the Mates amendment (which reduced the government's majority from 100 to 25), it might be supposed that the government would then have been obliged to give way, either in whole or part. After all, if 13 Tory MPs had voted the other way the Mates amendment would have been carried. If the government's majority had been about 20 fewer, the same might have happened; if it had been 60 fewer— i.e. 40 rather than 100—then the 17 rebels who voted against the second reading might even have warned the government off introducing the bill in the first place.

A government with a smaller majority, and less arrogant in its assumption of power than was Mrs Thatcher's by 1987, might indeed have pulled back from the poll tax, or at least modified it. But the argument is somewhat simplistic, for MPs rebel far more readily when they know that their defection will not defeat the government. As Michael Mates himself put it:

we were never remotely close to winning. Ignore the final vote: when the majority goes down, the pressure on individuals goes up. I always knew we were going to lose. With a smaller majority, the pressure would have been still more intense.[17]

---

[17] Interview with the authors.

TABLE 10.1. Conservative poll tax rebels

	Second reading 17 Dec. 1987	Mates amendment 18 Apr. 1988	Third reading 25 Apr. 1988	Rate support grant 18 Jan. 1990
R. Adley†		X	X	
J. Aitken†		X		
R. Allason				X
A. Beaumont-Dark†	X	X	X	
A. Buchanan Smith*		X		
W. Benyon†	X	X	X	X
J. Biffen*		X	X	
Sir N. Bonsor†				X
R. Boyson*				X
I. Bruce				X
Sir. A. Buck*		X		
P. Cormack†	X	X	X	
J. Critchley†	X	X		
H. Dykes†		X		X
C. Gill				X
Sir I. Gilmour*	X		X	X
Sir P. Goodhart*	X	X	X	X
J. Gorst†		X		
H. Greenway†				X
K. Hampson†		X		
K. Hargreaves	X	X	X	X
Sir B. Hayhoe*	X	X	X	X
A. Hazelhurst†		X		
Sir E. Heath*	X	X		
M. Heseltine*		X		
R. Hicks†		X		X
R. Howell†				X
M. Irvine	X	X	X	
Sir G. Johnson-Smith*		X		
D. Knox†	X	X	X	X
J. Lee*				X
J. Lester*	X	X		X
M. Mates†		X		X
R. Maxwell-Hyslop†				X
Sir A. Meyer†	X	X	X	
Sir C. Morrison†	X	X	X	X
J. Pawsey*				X
Mrs E. Peacock		X		
Sir T. Raison*		X		
T. Rathbone		X	X	X
G. Riddick		X		
R. Shepherd			X	X
Sir D. Smith*				X

	Second reading 17 Dec. 1987	Mates amendment 18 Apr. 1988	Third reading 25 Apr. 1988	Rate support grant 18 Jan. 1990
R. Squire	X	X	X	X
Sir P. Tapsell†		X		
P. Temple-Morris†	X	X		X
C. Townsend†		X		
B. Wells		X		X
Sir J. Wiggin*				X
T. Yeo		X		
Sir G. Young*	X	X	X	X
Rebel Con. Total	17	38	17	29

† Backbencher for at least 10 years.
* Former minister.

"ONE MORE STEP – AND I'LL BLOW YOUR BRAINS OUT!"

The truth of Mates's remarks was graphically demonstrated by the passage of the Maastricht Treaty[18] through the House of Commons in 1992–3. Maastricht caused far greater dissension among Conservative back-benchers than had the Bill to enact

[18] i.e. the European Communities (Amendment) Bill, which enacted those parts of the Maastricht Treaty requiring parliamentary approval.

the poll tax. The number of irreconcilables was higher (over 30), the passion with which they propagated their views was greater, and the government's overall Commons majority was a mere 21. Yet on the critical votes which could, potentially, have wrecked the Bill, the whips invariably reduced the number of rebels to single figures and staved off defeat. In the event, the government lost only two votes: one on a minor issue not affecting the Treaty as such, and the other on a resolution to 'note' the government's policy of opting-out of the social chapter of the treaty. In a classic exhibition of the ultimate power of the executive over the Commons, John Major responded to the latter vote by tabling an immediate motion of confidence. He won by a comfortable margin, with all the rebels back on board. It might be objected that the Maastricht Treaty was somewhat unusual in enjoying conditional Labour support for the principle of ratification (though not for the procedural and some substantive issues which could still have wrecked the bill). Yet a similar tale could be recounted of the passage in 1993 of the railway privatization legislation, fiercely opposed by Labour, and of the nationalization and trade union legislation of the last Labour government, enacted in 1975-6 by a government which no longer had a clear majority.[19]

Furthermore, it is misleading to dwell on the exceptional nature of large parliamentary majorities in Britain, an explicit or implicit assumption of much of the literature on Thatcherism. Of the fourteen general elections held since 1945, precisely half have yielded majorities of more than 40—i.e. sufficiently large to carry through virtually any prime-ministerial ambition mentioned, however loosely, in the party's election manifesto. Five of the elections produced landslide majorities of 90 or more. And those figures understate the sway of large majorities, since no parliament starting with a government majority of 40 or

[19] The 1974-9 Labour government suffered 42 defeats on the floor of the Commons, and Philip Norton has used the period as a case-study in the rise of parliamentary dissension (*Dissension in the House of Commons 1974-79* [1980]). However, until the government lost its majority in 1976 it was able to get all its Bills through the Commons, including radical provisions in the nationalization and trade union bills fiercely opposed by some of its backbenchers.

fewer has lasted for less than four years—most of its legal term. Taken together, the seven parliaments since 1945 with government majorities of 40 or more have lasted nearly twice as long (31 years against 17) as the seven parliaments with government majorities of less than 40. Large majorities are the norm in Britain, not the exception.

The passage of the poll tax legislation through the Commons exhibits another important facet of the government's dominance over parliament: its control of procedure. J. A. G. Griffith long ago pointed up the fact that the executive's sway 'is such that Members accept ministerial decisions concerned not only with Government policy, but with the procedures which Governments follow'.[20] The poll tax legislation conferred sweeping 'Henry VIII clauses' empowering ministers to make regulations covering key aspects of the bill; indeed, on the crucial question of capping powers, even the government was surprised to discover from its law officers how unlimited were the powers granted by the legislation. In the event, the Local Government Finance Act enabled the Environment Secretary to cap the spending of every local authority in the country, directly contrary to assurances given by ministers during its passage through parliament.

The procedure of the Commons itself was carefully manipulated by the government to ensure that the poll tax legislation emerged unscathed. Having given assurances that Sir George Young and other malcontents would be allowed on the standing committee to examine the bill, the committee was deliberately enlarged to preserve the government's majority over any conceivable coalition of opposition plus rebels. Standing committees normally have between 18 and 25 members.[21] The committees on the 1988 Housing and Education Reform bills were enlarged to 31 members, because of their controversial nature. The committee on the Local Government Finance Bill had 44 members.

The progress of the poll tax through the Commons highlights another theme of significance to the parliamentary politics of the 1980s. It was one of the last stands of the so-called

[20] J. A. G. Griffith, *Parliamentary Scrutiny of Government Bills* (1974), 255.
[21] Griffith and Ryle, *Parliament*, 271.

'wets', the liberal, consensus-minded, anti-Thatcher grouping within the Conservative parliamentary party. Between 20 and 30 'wets' continued sniping at Mrs Thatcher throughout the 1980s. They were not a cohesive, still less a set group: some, like Sir George Young and Michael Heseltine, were in government for more of the Thatcher years than they were out of it, and were far from consistent back-bench opponents. Yet the stance of the 'wets' was fairly consistent throughout the 1980s, and the poll tax rebellion constituted their last effective stand against a piece of legislation, though they were also to play a role in Mrs Thatcher's downfall two years after its enactment. With Mrs Thatcher's departure, the 'left–right' divide within the Conservative parliamentary party took on a fundamentally different aspect: the right, not the left, felt itself out in the cold under John Major, and the 'caves' were populated by those who had been most intimate with the former leader.[22]

The poll tax was not only a last stand of the 'wets': it typified their whole mode of operation during a decade of fitful activity. Sir George Young's rebellion was an essentially gentlemanly affair, with little organization and less passion. Within the Conservative parliamentary party, the poll tax had enemies aplenty and few true friends; but there were no back-bench guerrillas prepared to lay siege to the Bill and put themselves beyond the pale in the process. The poll tax was no Maastricht; no Tory was prepared to die in the ditch to try to prevent it going through, a telling commentary not only on the 'wets' but on the 'inevitability of Thatcherism' by the late 1980s and on how dulled Tory sensibilities had become to issues of distribution.

The parliamentary passage of the poll tax was strictly orderly. Sir George Young, an impeccable Etonian, never wavered in his hostility to the poll tax; but at heart a loyalist, he appeared almost embarrassed at rocking the boat and stuck to polite, reasoned arguments. It was entirely in character that within two years of the passage of the bill he should have

[22] For a study of the role of the 'wets' see Nicol Rae, 'Moderates Lost and Found', in A. Adonis, and T. Hames (eds.), *A Conservative Revolution? The Thatcher–Reagan Decade in Perspective* (1994).

accepted appointment as number three in the Tory whips' office. Michael Mates, a bluff, determined colonel, was a friend of Heseltine's, and was later to organize his 1990 challenge to Mrs Thatcher with military precision. But as he remarks: 'we were doing a number of things together at the time, but this was not one of them.' He was anxious not to be seen as Heseltine's side-kick, still less as a 'poll tax bore'. As soon as his attack failed, he withdrew from the field. In that respect, he was following Heseltine's own example. Having made his counterblast against the 'Tory tax' in the first day's debate, Hestletine made no further speeches on the bill. His eyes on the succession to Mrs Thatcher, and anxious not to be branded a bitter irreconcilable in the Edward Heath mould, he gave no further support to Young and his snipers beyond back-stage encouragement and a vote in favour of the Mates amendment.

Furthermore, co-operation between, and resolution among, the rebels was poor. On the Commons standing committee considering the bill, only once did the three malcontents vote together; and not once did they do so on an occasion when the government could have been defeated.[23] Nor was there much co-ordination with rebels in the Lords. Young tried to find a Tory heavyweight to lead the opposition in the Lords, but failed. He had to make do with Lord Chelwood, a somewhat ridiculous figure with no appeal to Tory or cross-bench peers.

THE HOUSE OF LORDS: NO REAL BOLDNESS

Whereas in most federal Constitutions, and some others, the second chamber has a special role to play in reforms with constitutional implications, particularly those affecting subnational government, in Britain the House of Lords is incapacitated from playing any meaningful role.

On all post-war evidence, any idea that the Lords acts as a constitutional long-stop is fanciful. With the exception of Bills to extend the life of parliament, the constitution recognizes no such thing as a constitutional Bill. In so far as the Lords has

[23] See Ch. 5 above.

any special claim to protect the Constitution, it is accordingly nebulous, and amounts to no concrete power in practice; and with constitutional reforms that have tax implications, it is barred from playing any role at all. For the purposes of most constitutional reforms, the UK has a unicameral parliament. The poll tax experience makes that crystal clear.

The poll tax was not presented as part of the annual budget, nor was it enacted by the vehicle of the annual Finance Bill, so the Lords was not barred by statute or convention from seeking to amend it. The peers debated the Local Government Finance Bill, and amendments to it, like any ordinary Bill. But public arguments as to the constitutional incapacity of the Lords to challenge the poll tax, because it was a tax,[24] weighed heavily with Tory and cross-bench peers, and would probably have been sufficient to guarantee an easy Lords passage for the legislation even without the exertion of the Tory whips.

Contrary to expectations, when it came to the votes, the poll tax aroused remarkably little Tory dissent in the Lords. Not just the principles, but most of the details, went through with only a handful of Tory peers voting against. Taking together all 33 votes on the Local Government Finance Bill in the Lords, most of which were on issues of minor import, the average vote was 115 to 79 in the government's favour, giving the government an average of 59 per cent of the votes. On the key amendment proposing to relate the tax to ability to pay, the vote was 317 to 183 in the government's favour, a pro-government vote of 63 per cent. Only two of the 33 votes in the Lords on proposed amendments to the tax were lost by the government, both on trifling issues. Evidently, therefore, the government was safe without its hereditary backwoodsmen. The cross-benchers sided disproportionately with the government throughout, and the number of regular Tory rebels was tiny.

In all these respects, the Lords was acting true to form. Despite the claims of some academic and journalistic commentators, the Lords is not an independent-minded assembly. For most purposes, the Conservative party has an assured majority;

[24] See above, p. 122.

and the incidence of cross-party voting is no more pronounced in the Lords than the Commons. Ironically, the life peerage, brought into being in 1958 to increase the pitiful non-Tory representation in the Upper House, is now a bastion of the Conservative party. Of the 189 peers created by Mrs Thatcher during her eleven years in Downing Street, 92 (49 per cent) took the Tory whip, while only 45 (24 per cent) and 10 (5 per cent) took the Labour and Liberal Democrat whips respectively.[25] As for the cross-benchers, all analyses of their voting behaviour in the Lords have shown them to be a strongly pro-Conservative force, typically dividing two-to-one in the Tories' favour in the division lobbies.[26]

The passage of the poll tax thus underlines the verdict of Donald Shell's comprehensive study of the Lords at work during the 1985-6 session, in which he concludes that most of the Lords' work 'may fairly be described as minor, technical and drafting amendments to bills'.[27] The Lords is 'reasonably diligent and generally dull, with a whiff of expertise but no real boldness, with conscience but not too much credibility, with a little public profile but no actual power'.[28]

'THE MISLEADING IMAGE OF CABINET OMNIPOTENCE'?

The parliament elected in 1987 had a Conservative majority of 100. Yet it turned out to be anything but Mrs Thatcher's poodle. Two years into its life the first rumblings of dissent began on the Tory back-benches. A year later, perhaps the most devastating parliamentary assault ever made on a sitting Prime Minister was launched on the floor of the Commons by Sir Geoffrey Howe in his resignation speech. It was followed swiftly by the dismissal of Mrs Thatcher by the Tory majority; and within months of that by the repeal of the poll tax, the 'flagship' of her final term.

---

[25] Adonis, *Parliament Today*, 197. The 10 for the Liberal Democrats includes Liberal and SDP creations.

[26] Ibid. 234-6.

[27] D. Shell (ed.), *The House of Lords at Work* (1993), 332.   [28] Ibid. 334.

Those events must weigh in any account of the docility of parliament in its treatment of the poll tax legislation between 1986 and 1988. They highlight not just the instinct for survival among MPs, but also the extraordinary flexibility of British parliamentary practice in the face of a crisis. On the eve of the critical leadership ballot of Conservative MPs in November 1990, Lord St John of Fawsley, the Bagehot scholar and (as Norman St John-Stevas) Mrs Thatcher's first Leader of the House of Commons, declared the election to be a 'constitutional monstrosity'. Mrs Thatcher was 'constitutionally unassailable', he declared, because 'reigning prime ministers cannot be removed from office against their will save by one thing: the carrying of a vote of no confidence on the floor of the Commons'.[29] But in Britain, once makes a precedent. Since the removal of Mrs Thatcher, the Tory leadership election rules have been retained with only minor modifications, making a similar coup perfectly possible in future.

However, there is nothing new in MPs afraid of electoral oblivion reaching for any weapon to hand to boost their re-election chances. Students of legislative behaviour in the US have long given the phenomenon a central place in their explanatory models.[30] The repeal of the poll tax took place when most Tory MPs were convinced it was a serious vote-loser. When, by contrast, two years earlier most of them had regarded it in a more neutral light, there was no similar check on the 'elective dictatorship'. Indeed, if anything the experience of the enactment of the poll tax shows the majoritarian characteristics of the British system to be less constrained even than allowed for by Lijphart. In his comparative study, Lijphart qualifies his verdict as to Britain's relative position by noting that 'strong informal customs restrain the majority': 'although majoritarian,' he continues, such customs had to be set against 'the misleading image of cabinet omnipotence'.[31] Evidence of the increasing vulnerability of governments on the floor of the House of Commons, the revival of the House of Lords, and the

[29] Adonis, *Parliament Today*, 250.
[30] D. Mayhew, *Congress: The Electoral Connection* (1974).
[31] Lijphart, *Democracies*, 10.

Nationalist revival in Scotland and Wales are all cited in support.[32]

Lijphart was writing in the early 1980s. The experience of the Thatcher government reveals the 'image of cabinet omnipotence' to be anything but 'misleading'. For as long as the Conservative party felt itself to be electorally invulnerable, its parliamentary majority was at the Prime Minister's beck-and-call; indeed, it was so even in periods of vulnerability, until the extreme trough of 1990 coincided, fortuitously, with a leadership election, a plausible challenger, and a credible alternative policy. But then, the 'elective dictatorship' was always that—an autocracy conferred and removable by election. There is no reason to suppose that a future election could not yield a captain bent on sailing a flagship as misguided as the poll tax. Nor to doubt that it would sail through parliament unscathed, with a fair wind.

[32] Ibid., 10–16.

11

PUBLIC OPINION

Deep in their instinct people find what I am saying and
doing right. . . . I sort of regard myself as a very normal,
ordinary person, with all the right instinctive antennae.

Margaret Thatcher, August 1980

Much of the poll tax story lies in Westminster and in
Whitehall. Much, too, lies in the halls of local government. But
it was also an issue which, more than any other in recent
British politics, involved outside groups and a mass audience.
The Conservative party's local activists played an important
role in the evolution of the policy. So did the party's conferences, an underrated influence on Tory policy-making. And the
crisis over the tax as implemented was dominated by the wider
voice of public opinion, as manifested by opinion polls and
popular protest in a myriad of forms.

Parties lie at the heart of modern government. In Britain
they are largely unknown to the law, and the relationship of
parties to parliament and government is regulated entirely by
custom and convention. The story told in these pages is primarily about the Conservative party, many of whose most
important activities take place behind a veil. But oddly the
Labour party was a prime cause for the tax being introduced.
The excesses of some councils, almost all Labour-controlled,
led to progressively greater central interference with local government finance. The 'targets' introduced in 1981–2, as well as
the rate-capping announced in 1983, proved clumsy and unpopular instruments from which politicians and bureaucrats wished
to escape. The 'studies' of 1984–5 offered the poll tax as an
ingenious and comprehensive solution to perform that task and

to bring councils to heel at the same time. It was seen as a weapon that would restrain the Liverpools and the Lambeths, since angry taxpayers would seek to punish their profligate councillors at the polls. The attraction of accountability, of 'everyone pays', was strong. The idea appealed to believers in market forces and public choice. It also appealed to many who would be among the gainers from the abolition of property-based rates—and these were mainly Conservative voters.

The first two sections of this chapter therefore focus on the Conservative party and the opposition parties respectively, in particular on their role in the evolution and enactment of the poll tax. The third section addresses the wider organs of 'public opinion', concentrating on the later stages of the saga.

TORY DEMOCRACY

The Conservative party is, arguably, Britain's most important yet least understood political institution. Tory governments have been the rule since the advent of the mass electorate in the 1880s. The Tories have won thirteen of the twenty-one elections since the First World War; and they have held office, with or without allies (usually without), for all but twenty-eight years of this century. Yet even informed commentators believe the party to be little more than an electoral machine to sustain an omnipotent leadership—omnipotent, that is, until it loses an election or appears to do so, when the power is abruptly transferred to other hands.

Such a picture is a distortion of the real locus of power in the Tory party, and the relationship between the leadership and the 'grass roots', even for the days of Disraeli, Salisbury, and Baldwin. It is still more offbeat as a description of the modern Conservative party. Its curious survival owes something to the perennial unfashionability of the right as a subject of academic study, but more still to the absence of formal processes of internal democracy in the Conservative party. Whereas for most parties in liberal democracies (including Britain's Labour and Liberal Democrat parties) internal elections, and the faction-fighting organized around them, are the stuff of intra-party machinations, they are largely incidental to Tory politics. For the Conservative party represents the British Constitution in microcosm: it is an idiosyncratic blend of custom, practice, and a few new or codified rules, assembled over several centuries. Rules do exist, and some of them are critically important, notably in the arrangements for selecting parliamentary candidates, and the provisions for leadership elections introduced in 1965 and modified in 1975 and 1991. But for the most part, opinion flows through the party informally, not formally. Tories have traditionally been contemptuous of the very idea of internal democracy, with its images of caucuses, deselections, bitter infighting, and the humiliation of leaders by activists at party conferences. Lord Hailsham used to delight in likening the party to a Quaker meeting in which consensus emerges spontaneously. Conservative disputes mostly go on behind closed doors, with constant efforts to build and maintain consensus within the party at all levels.

As a result, the internal processes of the Conservative party have been underestimated as an influence on policy-making. This is particularly true of the Conservative party conference, which is typically dismissed with Balfour's celebrated quip that he would rather take advice from his valet than from a party conference. As Robert McKenzie put it in his classic study of British political parties, the annual Tory conference is 'primarily . . . a demonstration of party solidarity and of enthusiasm for its own leaders'.[1] McKenzie conceded that even Balfour could not ignore his followers entirely,[2] but his drift was clear enough. One of the most popular current textbooks on the policy-making process in Britain gives less than a page to the Tory conference, citing first Balfour, then McKenzie, with a brief note that live television coverage gives the Tory conference 'a greater prominence in the policy-making of the party than was once allowed'.[3]

---

[1] R. T. McKenzie, *British Political Parties* (1963 edn.), 189.

[2] Ibid. 82.

[3] A. G. Jordan, and J. Richardson, *British Politics and the Policy Process* (1987), 108. The brief section comes after 7 pages on the Labour party conference.

Tory conferences appear at every turn in this account of the rise and fall of the poll tax. They feature not as 'demonstrations of party solidarity', but as powerful organs of grass-roots sentiment and discontent, and, at key stages, as driving forces behind the evolution of the policy. The account gives strong backing to a recent but little-noticed book by Richard Kelly, who argues, on the basis of a study of six Tory conferences in 1986, that the 'Conservative conference system'—that is, all eight or so conferences each year, not just the *Oktoberfest* of the party as a whole—has been 'seriously undervalued' and has a 'considerable influence' on policy.[4] Successive conferences played a role in the evolution of the poll tax. Two stand out in particular. The 1985 Scottish Conservative party conference at Perth, held in the wake of the disastrous 1984–5 rates revaluation north of the border, was a powerful stimulus to the quest for a new tax to replace the rates; it also precipitated George Younger's seminal announcement, before the cabinet committee on rates reform had even met, that the government would publish reform proposals before the end of the year, 'with the status quo not an option'. Two years later, in October 1987, the annual Conservative conference at Blackpool reopened the vexed question of phasing in the poll tax. 'We'll have to look at this again, Nick,' said Mrs Thatcher, after Gerry Malone's rapturously received speech calling for immediate abolition of the rates. The result was an end to so-called 'dual-running' of the poll tax with rates for a four-year transitional period. Malone's speech is in danger of being lumped together with the 1950 Tory conference demand for 300,000 houses as one of the only two post-war examples of a Tory conference appearing to change a specific policy. It is far more useful to view it as part of a continuum which embraced all the Tory conferences from 1984 to 1990. Each one acted as a focus for decisions and announcements about the poll tax, pressurizing the process of design and implementation from start to finish.[5]

Kelly believes there is a 'strong case' for attributing the poll

[4] R. Kelly, *Conservative Party Conferences: The Hidden System* (1989), esp. 178 and 184.

[5] For accounts of these conferences, see Chs. 4, 5, and 6.

tax wholly to the 1985 Perth conference.[6] That would be going too far. Rather, the interplay between conferences and other forces needs to be appreciated. Three other forces, in particular: pressure from constituency party activists, the predispositions of the party élite and the ambition of individual ministers. The constituency pressure preceding the 1985 Perth conference is documented in Chapter 3. Mrs Thatcher, George Younger, and William Whitelaw were agitated about the degree of grass-roots hostility to the 1984–5 rates revaluation months before the Perth conference: the main impact of the conference was to concentrate their minds on producing a replacement before further outbursts of activist and electoral anger. But they were, in any case, disposed to make such a reform, and work on the project had been started a few months before the outcome of the Scottish revaluation was known. The recommendations of the Waldegrave–Baker 'studies' team were presented to, and endorsed by, the Chequers meeting six weeks before the Perth conference. Mention of the 'studies team' also raises the issue of the interplay between successive conferences, for the studies team was itself established in part to minimize protests against the rating system expected at the 1984 Brighton conference.[7]

Then comes the ambition of individual ministers, and its manifestation at Tory conferences. The days when Tory leaders treated party conferences with disdain are long past. However, it is not votes but popularity which the ambitious court: since at least the 1960s reputations have been won and lost by conference speeches, particularly—but not exclusively—at the annual conference. Reginald Maudling failed to win the Tory leadership, some think, through his inability to concoct populist perorations. Michael Heseltine, Kenneth Baker, and Peter Lilley stand out as recent 'conference darlings'. Transitory as such popularity may prove, several Tory leadership contenders, or flagbearers for a section of the party, will at any one time be craving for adulation among the party faithful, while every senior figure in the party dreads a poor reception on the conference floor. Nigel Lawson, no rabble-rouser on the best of days,

---

[6] Kelly, *Conservative Conferences*, 185.   [7] See pp. 44–5 above.

charted his popularity in the party during his Chancellorship by the reception given to his conference speeches:

I started with the usual honeymoon from my appointment in June 1983 to the summer recess . . . Then came a poor, though not disastrous patch, from my rather indifferent 1983 Party Conference speech until my rapturously received first Budget in 1984. But the glow lasted only a few months after which there was a very lean period, including my 1984 Conference speech (the least well received of the series) the nadir of which was probably the sterling crisis of early 1985, to my first enthusiastically received Conference speech, that of 1985. This triggered a steady climb back, leading to my really strong and supposedly 'unassailable' phase, which lasted from the 1986 Budget to the summer recess of 1988.[8]

In the case of Patrick Jenkin at Brighton in 1984 and George Younger at Perth in 1985, determination to have 'something to offer' a conference on the question of rates reform was a significant motivation in their support for an alternative to rates. In similar vein, Kenneth Baker was determined to have a concrete reform scheme to wave at the 1985 conference, while Chris Patten hastily put together a new poll tax relief scheme to provide a sop to throw from the conference platform in 1989.

Personal as much as party considerations therefore give Tory conferences appreciable influence. It has almost nothing to do with formal votes, almost everything to do with 'mood' and 'reception'. It is very much a two-way dialogue. In the conclusion to his study, Kelly tentatively puts his finger on an important factor for explaining the increased influence of the conference. He notes a 'new self-confidence' and 'populism' among Tory conference representatives, partly the result of electoral success but also deriving from 'a growing belief among Tory activists that social trends are at last on their side'.[9] That belief is not misplaced. The past thirty years has seen the 'salariat' vie with the manual working-class for electoral dominance, with the skilled working-class increasingly identifying, in lifestyle and voting behaviour, with the former not the latter.[10]

[8] N. Lawson, *The View from No. 11* (1992), 271.

[9] Kelly, *Conservative Conferences*, 193.

[10] A. Heath *et al.*, *Understanding Political Change* (1991), ch. 5. See also A. Heath *et al.*, *Labour's Last Chance?* (1994), 283.

As those trends have advanced, Tory activists have become progressively more representative of society at large; and that, in turn, has increasingly led the party's leadership to treat the party conference as a barometer of national opinion—or, at least, of that swathe of it essential to winning general elections. That certainly holds true for the poll tax. Speeches against the rates had been the stuff of Tory conferences since the foundation of the National Union in 1870. But at no stage before the 1980s were the activists swept away by the virtues of a per capita tax weighing most harshly on Labour voters; nor would the leadership, alive to electoral exigencies, have paid much attention to them if they had been. Yet by the mid-1980s typical Tory activists and conference-goers genuinely saw themselves as the voice of 'middle opinion'; and their leaders came to view them in the same light.

Moreover, the party's élite—its MPs and leaders—came in the 1980s to adopt much of the same 'self-confidence' and 'populism' as its activists, based in part on the same social shift and feeling of close identity with 'middle opinion'.[11] None exhibited those facets more powerfully than Margaret Thatcher, daughter of a respectable Grantham grocer and MP for the north London suburb of Finchley. 'Deep in their instincts people find what I am saying and doing right,' the Prime Minister told one interviewer. 'And I know it is because it is the way I was brought up. I'm eternally grateful for the way I was brought up in a small town. We knew everyone, we knew what people thought. I sort of regard myself as a very normal, ordinary person with all the right instinctive antennae.'[12] If there was one sentiment that every home-owner in Grantham and Finchley shared, it was hatred of the rates, and resentment of the 'millions' that did not pay them and sponged off those who did. Mrs Thatcher knew it; she had heard it at Tory meetings and conferences year after year; and she shared the conviction passionately. It is not difficult to see why she was so easily per-

[11] See A. Adonis, 'The Transformation of the Conservative Party in the 1980s', in A. Adonis and T. Hames (eds.), *A Conservative Revolution? The Thatcher–Reagan Decade in Perspective* (1994).

[12] Quoted in H. Young, *One of Us* (1991 edn.), 208.

suaded about the virtues of the poll tax; nor why she stuck to it even as it delved the depths of opinion-poll unpopularity and popular protest.

In the event, the poll tax hit hardest the 'very normal, ordinary' people—in particular, households of two or more people in low-rated areas like Grantham who faced significant hikes in their local tax bills. It was Mrs Thatcher's failure to appreciate this which was a large part of her undoing. Possibly, the fact that her constituency was Finchley, an outer London suburb whose home-owners emerged relatively well from the switch to poll tax, distorted her judgement. (Michael Portillo, the archetypal 'new Tory' who served as local government minister in the final months of her premiership, represented nearby Enfield and gained a similarly unrepresentative view from his political base.) It was not just that Mrs Thatcher did nothing; she gave no appearance of understanding the problem. For once, her 'instinctive antennae' deserted her. At any rate, Tory backbenchers from the areas hit, whether old-style paternalists or new-breed populists, lost no time in venting their spleen. And when it came to the leadership election on 20 November 1990, the one unambiguously modern, democratic instrument in the Tory party's constitution, it undoubtedly influenced the verdict they pronounced in the privacy of a voting-booth in committee room no. 10 of the House of Commons.

By that vote, Mrs Thatcher joined a long line of Tory leaders more or less forcibly removed from office. But there was a certain symmetry to her demise: the most democratic penalty inflicted on the most populist a leader in the Tory party's history. Certainly, no less populist Tory leader would have dared risk a poll tax, let alone make it a flagship of his or her government.

THE 'OPPOSITION'

In a perfect world, where parties reflected public opinion faithfully, there would have been no poll tax. The Tories would never have committed themselves to it in the first place. And had they done so, the vehemence of the opposition of the other parties, reflecting public opinion more faithfully, would have put them off the idea. In the classic electoral world of Anthony Downs, where parties in a two- or three-party system are after the median voter, no majority party with pretensions to government would have dared put itself out on a limb on a front-rank issue, for fear of dire electoral consequences.[13] In a sense, of course, Downs came right in the end: the vehemence of opposition, combined with the Tories' desire to stay in government, did scupper the poll tax. But why did it not do so before the tax was enacted? Or before it was implemented in England and Wales in 1990, by when the full extent of its unpopularity was apparent?

The conviction of Mrs Thatcher and her soul-mates that, 'deep inside' the median voter did support the poll tax, or at least the principles underpinning the tax, provides much of the explanation. The qualification is important. By 1990 it was hard for even the most ardent Thatcherite to pretend that the poll tax was popular. Rather, to the bitter end the tax's supporters clung to the belief, fortified by polls, that widespread support existed for the idea that everyone should make a contribution towards local government services. All that was needed was to get the mechanism right. Three years after she left office Mrs Thatcher still believed it would have proved acceptable 'given time'.[14]

Yet that is only one part of the picture. For opinion to have flowed through parties on the Downs model, the other parties—in particular Labour, the main electoral challenger to the Tories—had a critical part to play. They had to be the loud, siren voice of public opposition to the poll tax from the beginning. It was a part they proved unable to fill, with Labour most conspicuously inadequate to the task.

There are three distinct aspects to the inadequacy of the opposition parties. First, the stark divisions between them on both the tactics of opposition and the policy which should have been pursued instead. Secondly, the determination of the Labour party not to give salience to the issue, in part because

[13] A. Downs, *An Economic Theory of Democracy* (1957).
[14] M. Thatcher, *The Downing Street Years* (1993), 667.

of a serious underestimation of popular opposition to the poll tax. And third, controversies internal to the opposition parties which distracted them from the task of opposition, and weakened them when they turned their mind to it.

Taking the third factor first, the internal distractions were most evident in the centre parties. The Liberal-SDP Alliance had taken nearly a quarter of the vote in the 1987 election. It was the main challenger to the Tories in non-metropolitan southern England. As the 'Alliance' it sent shivers down Tory spines in the mid-1980s as it won stunning local and by-election victories, particularly in the 1985 county council elections. As the Liberal Democrats, formed from the union of the SDP and the Liberal party in 1988, the 'centre force' was to cause the Tories equal distress in the early and mid-1990s.[15] By 1991 it was clear that the Liberal Democrats could continue to command at least a fifth of the vote, concentrated in the south and south-east. When their vote rose significantly above that level, as it did in the mid-term in the 1979, 1983, and 1992 parliaments, Tory alarm at the electoral consequences became serious.[16]

However, there was no mid-term centre-party revival in the 1987 parliament. In the years taken up with the enactment and introduction of the poll tax, the SDP and the Liberal party were engaged in a civil war over the future of their alliance, in particular the plan to form a new united party favoured by most Liberals and a majority of Social Democrats, but not their leader, David Owen. The tale is familiar and needs no recital. It suffices to note that the memoirs of the participants contain reams on the civil war, but virtually nothing on the poll tax. The Social and Liberal Democrats (one of the four successive titles adopted by the erstwhile 'Alliance' during the 1987 parliament) sank to 5 per cent in the 1989 European elections, three

[15] See Ch. 7 for the Eastbourne and Ribble Valley by-elections.

[16] See J. Curtice and M. Steed, App. 2 to D. Butler and D. Kavanagh, *The British General Election of 1992* (1992), esp. 332–7, for an analysis of the party's success in consolidating and building strength in its (mainly southern) heartland. Although the 'centre' vote fell from 25.4% in 1983 to 17.8% in 1992, its vote fell only from 31.5% to 29.5% in those seats in which it took second place in 1992.

months after the introduction of the poll tax in Scotland. They were pushed to fourth place behind the Greens, who soared up to take 15 per cent of the vote, and more still in the Alliance's southern heartlands. The Liberal Democrats were running only marginally higher in the opinion polls when the poll tax was extended to England in April 1990. Significantly, the subsequent Liberal Democrat revival, in the tail-end of the 1987 parliament, coincided with the depths of the poll tax crisis and gave a dramatic edge to Tory unpopularity. The loss to the Liberal Democrats of the Eastbourne by-election in October 1990, fought almost exclusively on the poll tax, exacerbated back-bench Tory jitters; while the still more dramatic defeat in Ribble Valley (March 1991) underlined the seeming impossibility of regaining popularity while the tax was on the statute-book.

By then, Labour was already trouncing the Tories in by-elections and opinion polls. In March 1990 Labour won the Mid-Staffordshire by-election on a record swing, and the party surged briefly to a 20 per cent lead in the opinion polls. Neil Kinnock's 'new model' Labour party exhibited none of the centre parties' internal divisions at the national level. But for the purposes of the party's opposition to the poll tax, Labour's remaining and gaping internal divide—between the leadership and the radical left in several of its inner-city bastions—could not have been more harmful. Until the extent of popular protest was manifest in the reaction to poll tax bills, Labour gave no special prominence to the poll tax as an issue.

Neil Kinnock consistently sought to dissociate himself from his local councillors—although only a small proportion of them served in Lambeth, Brent, and Liverpool, the three authorities which generated most of the adverse media coverage. As was made plain in our earlier chapters, this led him consistently to downplay the poll tax as an issue dividing the parties. It was deliberately marginalized in the 1987 campaign by Kinnock and Peter Mandelson, his chief strategist. Even in the spring of 1990, Kinnock and his closest advisers were as concerned about the effect on 'middle opinion' of any hint of association with the poll tax rioters as they had been about stirring up popular protest in the first place. Kinnock's fears about Labour's local government image distorted the party's judgement on the relative popularity of the rates and the poll tax, since the highest-rated areas, producing the most vociferous anti-rates agitation, were to be found in inner-city Labour-dominated areas. While the bill to enact the poll tax was under preparation, Labour leaders concentrated their fire on the civil liberties aspect ('a tax on the right to vote', etc.) not on the distributional impact. Indeed, they were largely ignorant about the impact. There is no evidence from the parliamentary debates that Labour spokespeople appreciated the scale of losses for middle-income earners implicit in the appendices to the 1986 Green Paper. Their attack focused on the poor, not the middling-income households, i.e. the voters who, in effect, sank the tax, and whose opposition was always likely to be critical to its defeat. In part this was a question of misjudgement: it was also a question of inadequate information. Labour devoted almost no resources to modelling the effects of the tax and thus gauging the likely public outcry. It might be objected that the opposition has few resources for the task: it has at its disposal nothing like the research arm of Congress, or the personal staffs of congressmen. Yet with more than £1 million a year available in the mid-1980s in so-called 'Short money' to aid it in its work as the official opposition, Labour did have resources. But it chose—as all opposition parties choose—to devote them to research assistants for individual shadow cabinet ministers, enabling them to score points better across the chamber of the House of Commons and in press releases, and not to any research unit which could have undertaken the type of work necessary to appreciate the full implications of front-rank policies like the poll tax.

In any case, the government was only marginally the more significant of Labour's opponents on the poll tax issue. The Scottish Nationalists were a close second; and with almost a quarter of the Labour parliamentary party sitting for Scottish seats after the 1987 election, the post-1988 SNP revival on the back of a fierce anti-poll tax campaign, including non-payment, was uppermost in the mind of many Labour leaders. The loss of the Glasgow Govan by-election to the SNP in November 1988 caused particular *Angst*. It led to protracted and bitter internal disputes about the legitimacy of non-payment, embracing the party's local government, regional, and national conferences in 1989 and 1990. It diverted the party's campaigning resources. And it bolstered Neil Kinnock and most Labour leaders in London in their inclination to downplay the poll tax as an issue.

However, the Labour–SNP conflict was merely one aspect of the wider failure of the opposition to come together in the 1987 parliament—or, indeed, in the parliaments before and after. The poll tax had enormous potential as an issue around which to build a national, single-issue crusade against the government embracing everyone from the opposition parties to non-aligned interest groups, professional associations, and the media. In France, Germany, and Italy such alliances are common, and often vital to the building of opposition coalitions able to challenge sitting governments. In France, even the issue of state funding of schools, intrinsically less substantial material than the poll tax, has regularly produced broad opposition coalitions, and demonstrations of hundreds of thousands of 'respectable' citizens on the streets of Paris.[17] In Britain, by contrast, no attempt was made by the opposition parties to forge such an alliance. Labour and the Liberal Democrats, separated by an ideological hair's breadth in their approach to taxation, made no attempt even to agree on an alternative policy. The Liberal Democrats opposed the poll tax with a local income tax; Labour havered between various options, tentatively opting for a combined income/property tax at the outset and moving towards a purer property tax at the end. But anxious not to offend the losers, it launched no campaign on either. Significantly, the only national campaign against the poll tax was that launched by the fringe ultra-left groups, including

---

[17] In January 1994 300,000 demonstrators took to the streets of Paris to oppose the Balladur government's proposed extension of financial privileges to Catholic schools. The government had conceded most of the demonstrators' demands before the demonstration even took place. *Financial Times*, 17 Jan. 1994.

Militant and the Socialist Workers, which came together in 1989 in the British Anti-Poll Tax Federation. Its success in mobilizing crowds and popular antipathy—notably in the March 1990 Trafalgar Square demonstrations—is a telling commentary on the opportunity available to the established opposition parties had they made any efforts to come together.

Even in the light of the internal and external divisions discussed so far, it still appears remarkable that no such efforts were made. Ultimately, it was not particular divisions and preoccupations which explain the void. It was the British 'way of doing things', a set of ingrained political principles with a long history, usually dignified with the word 'culture'. Chief among those principles are single-party government, fear of coalitions even if the parties composing them share common ideas and policies, and a belief that extra parliamentary agitation is to be controlled not stimulated. The poll tax exhibited all three principles in practice. The effect was to build walls between the parties and public opinion, without which the introduction of the poll tax would have been far more problematic.

PUBLIC OPINION

Opinion polls from 1988 onwards showed not only the growing unpopularity of the government but also, more specifically, of the poll tax. In MORI surveys between 1987 and 1990 the number approving of the poll tax stayed steadily around 25 per cent. But the proportion positively disapproving rose from 45 per cent to 73 per cent. Table 11.1 shows the findings of NOP polls, sponsored by the *Local Government Chronicle* in the 50 most marginal seats in England and Wales each April from 1988 to 1990. Of those who in 1990 said they had switched from the Conservatives, 56 per cent gave the poll tax as the main reason. It is significant that in 1988 39 per cent blamed their local council and only 33 per cent the government for their high rates but by 1990 the poll tax was overwhelmingly blamed on the government (56 per cent) rather than the local council (18 per cent).

The British election survey, conducted after the 1992 general

TABLE 11.1 Polls on fairness of poll tax

'Do you consider [the local poll tax] fair or too high?

	1988	1989	1990
'Fair'	43	39	25
'Too high'	46	52	71

election found that 49 per cent of their nation-wide sample thought that the poll tax had been 'important' or 'very important' in deciding votes. Looking back only 7 per cent regretted the ending of the poll tax, although 28 per cent thought it had been a good idea but that the government was right to give it up. Partisanship plainly coloured these judgements as Table 11.2 shows.

TABLE 11.2 Verdicts on poll tax

	Good idea and should have gone on	Good idea but right to end it	Bad idea and right to end it
Con.	13	47	39
Lab.	1	8	90
Lib. Dem.	4	24	71
Overall	7	28	64

In retrospect 90 per cent of Labour supporters and 71 per cent of Liberal Democrats saw no virtue in the poll tax but only 39 per cent of Conservatives were unequivocally hostile.

The Conservative party's private market research tried to look for comfort for the government but the findings of a survey in mid-May 1990 contained ample warning of the trouble ahead. Offered the proposition: 'Leaving aside the level of the Community Charge it is a good idea in principle that everyone should pay something towards the local government services they use', 78 per cent of respondents agreed and just 17 per cent disagreed. But only 48 per cent thought that 'the new Community Charge will make local authorities more careful about how they spend money': 37 per cent disagreed. When it came to the question of the level of tax, 31 per cent thought it was fair and 62 per cent thought it was unfair; responses were significantly affected by the local level of tax—where it was under £300 the verdict was favourable 48–45 per cent but where it was over £400 the division changed to 15–71 per cent. People knew that rebates were available and 36 per cent thought they were eligible (77 per cent of these had already applied). On the question whether rates or the community charge was fairer, rates won 54 to 30 per cent. In the light of such findings, it was hard to suggest that the 'flagship' would be a winner in any electoral battle.

Local government elections underlined the trouble the poll tax was causing. The eighteen Conservative councillors in West Oxfordshire who left the party *en masse* had few imitators. But in the May 1990 elections the Conservatives fared disastrously, being left with fewer councillors that at any time since the war. However, the 1990 elections offered a deceptive comfort to the Conservatives. They did well in most of London; Westminster and Wandsworth stood notably out against the tide. In these two boroughs the poll tax was very low and there was a swing against Labour that was in sharp contrast to the rest of the country; perhaps it was possible to argue that the promised logic of accountability really did work (even though it had not worked in Bradford, the Conservatives' other flagship borough).[18]

The goal of accountability was confused by the need to decide whom to blame. In a high poll tax Labour area, should one vote against the Conservative government which had introduced the tax, or against the Labour councillors who were responsible for its level locally?

[18] See C. Rallings and M. Thrasher, 'The Electoral Impact of the Poll Tax: Evidence from the 1990 Elections', in I. Crewe *et al.*, *British Politics and Elections Year Book 1992* (1993). See also J. Gibson and J. Stewart (1992), 'Poll Tax Rates and Local Elections', *Political Studies*, 40/3: 20.

The poll tax never intruded into constituency politics in the way that the European issue has done over the years. No candidate seems to have owed selection or deselection to it—unless we count Terry Fields, the Liverpool MP who was sent to prison for refusing to pay the tax; the Labour party later expelled him for his association with Militant.

It was an issue that lent itself to pressure-group politics. Think-tanks played a part. The idea had been floated by the Adam Smith Institute. It was tested and criticized by the Institute for Fiscal Studies and by many academics.[19] The Low Pay Unit and the Child Poverty Action Group were energetic in opposition. Naturally the local authority associations, as the next chapter shows, were the most active of the lobbyists.

In an organized and an unorganized way the mass public became involved. The poll tax provides a rare example of an issue which galvanized not only the Militant Tendency and extreme left, but with it substantial numbers of the wider less politicized public. 'Can't pay, won't pay' campaigns were started in many inner-city areas. As in 1381, the new tax became a lightning-conductor for a range of dissatisfactions with the government. It was a widely based movement, even embracing many Conservatives. The high point of public pressure came with the demonstration in London on Saturday 31 March 1990. Over 300 police were injured and over 300 arrests were made.[20]

The poll tax failed to win public approval. The cause must lie mainly in the substance of what was proposed and in its clumsy implementation, but a contribution may have been made by its presentation in the media. The government invested a lot of effort in selling the poll tax but its coverage, even in Conservative-orientated newspapers, was generally hostile, while the neutral television networks had to reflect the stories available to them which were hostile.

The government's own publicity department, the Central

[19] See Ch. 5.

[20] Ironically the police themselves were angry over the poll tax because, exempt from rates in the past, they were now to have to pay the poll tax; the *Police Record* published a cartoon of an injured policeman hobbling home to be greeted by a poll tax demand.

Office of Information, put out several leaflets explaining the poll tax and D.o.E. ministers, most notably Michael Howard and Christopher Chope, made special efforts to explain the tax to newspaper editors, national and local. The Party chairman instructed all Cabinet ministers to make at least one pro-poll-tax speech. Nigel Lawson alone refused, although Geoffrey Howe spoke only reluctantly and in a very lukewarm way.

The opposition criticized the three leaflets issued by the Central Office of Information: *Paying for Local Government* (October 1987); *You and the Community Charge* (January 1989); and *The Community Charge (the so-called Poll Tax): How it will Work for You* (May 1989). They were said to go beyond the legitimate exposition of administrative change. Ogilvy and Mather, the advertising agency enlisted to help the COI, protested that the material contained no slogans, no gimmicks, and no logos. A Court challenge was rejected.[21]

It is striking that such limited coverage was allotted to the poll tax from 1986 onwards. In a useful study of media behaviour, Deacon and Golding show how little space was given to the subject in the 1987 election and indeed in 1988 when the legislation was going through parliament and how it suddenly rose to enormous prominence in the spring of 1990.[22] Figure 11.1 (overleaf) is taken from their work. The way in which the issue subsided in prominence during the summer of 1990 is almost as striking as its sudden upsurge that spring.

The content of the coverage, too, is significant. There was a focus on how the poll tax was damaging for Conservative prospects but there was a failure, even in the serious press, to cover either the broad rationale for the tax or the technical details of its operation. The government's case was damaged by the number of Conservative dissidents. Michael Mates and Sir

[21] On 9 May 1989 the borough of Greenwich secured an interim injunction against the D.o.E., forbidding the distribution of a leaflet, because it was 'misleading'. On 16 May this was overruled by two judges sitting together in the High Court, on the ground that, at the worst, the leaflet was only 'misleading by omission'.

[22] D. Deacon and P. Golding, 'When Ideology Fails: The Flagship of Thatcherism and the Local and National Media', *European Journal of Communications*, 6 (1991), 291–303.

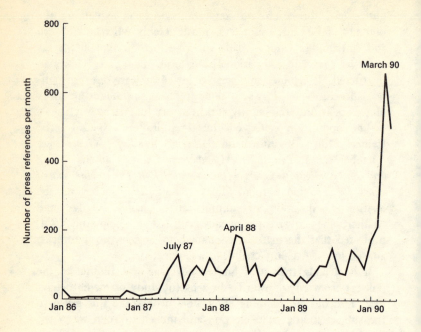

Fig. 11.1 National Newspapers' Poll Tax Coverage
(January 1986–April 1990)

George Young may have made limited impact on the House of
Commons but they, like the resigning councillors in West
Oxfordshire, helped to advertise Conservative disunity. Local
authorities, particularly the large ones, which were Labour-
controlled and possessed of substantial public relations departments, were able to present a very negative picture of what the
poll tax was doing to local administration and to social justice.

The poll tax was a public relations disaster. But the problem
was inherent in the policy. It was not primarily a matter of presentation.

12

LOCAL
GOVERNMENT

> Margaret did not have much time for local councils,
> which she expected to be the agents of central govern-
> ment. She said to me once with a resigned sigh, 'I sup-
> pose we need them.' However, many local activists in the
> constituencies were councillors, and some MPs had also
> served as councillors, as I had done . . . In addition the
> party made great efforts in all local government elections
> to win control of councils. So there was something schizo-
> phrenic in our attitude to local government.
>
> Kenneth Baker, *The Turbulent Years* (1993)

At the time, it was an open question whether local government
would survive the poll tax. The burden of collecting the tax
precipitated a virtual collapse in the finances of some city
authorities. The nationalization of the business rate halved the
local tax-base at a stroke. Near-universal capping of expenditure, together with other expedients that were introduced by
the government in a desperate bid to keep tax bills down for
the second year, drastically reduced local fiscal discretion. Then
the demise of the tax, in early 1991, raised the serious possibility that all local taxation would be abolished outright, rendering
local authorities explicitly the agents of Whitehall.

It is a tribute to the idea of local government in Britain, and
to the professionalism of most local authority treasurers, that
the worst forebodings were not realized. Indeed, the idea of
local government proved surprisingly robust: even Mrs
Thatcher shrank from repudiating it *in toto*, as the epigraph
confirms. The most ardent proponents of the poll tax claimed it

as a device to revive and restore local government, not to undermine it. In Nicholas Ridley's words, the community charge was 'a logical step towards greater local authority freedom: it should allow us to stand much further back from local government because the electors will stand much closer'.[1] For many on the Tory right, such language was a thin, unsubtle mask to cover bitter hostility to a local government system largely controlled by the enemies of Thatcherism. But it is significant how rarely it was stated in those terms. Only in the chaotic, embittered final months of Mrs Thatcher's premiership did the mask slip.

Yet even within the Conservative party, traditions of respect for local government died hard. None represented them more than Michael Heseltine, who never ceased to trumpet a constructive role for local authorities, however ardent his attacks on wasteful council expenditure. A determined foe of the municipal left, Heseltine never subscribed to the poll tax; and on returning to office as Environment Secretary after Mrs Thatcher's fall in 1990, he at once set about trying to rebuild central–local relations. As he put it to the Commons in his first major speech back in government:

There is I believe a chance for a new, constructive phase in the development of local government. In all my consideration of these difficult issues, I cannot escape the fact that some of the greatest moments in British history have coincided with the times of resolve, civic pride and municipal initiative in our great towns and cities . . . The country wishes us to try to identify a stable and just basis for the future development of local government and the provision of local services.[2]

Accordingly, the first part of this chapter relates the poll tax to the idea of local government in Britain. The second part considers local government's experience of the poll tax, and leads to a broader, stocktaking third section which discusses the state of local government after the turbulent years.

---

[1] N. Ridley, *The Local Right: Enabling not Providing*, Centre for Policy Studies, Policy Study 92 (1988), 15.

[2] *HC Debs.*, 5 Dec. 1990, cols. 315–25.

THE POLL TAX AND THE IDEA OF LOCAL GOVERNMENT

One of the most serious fault-lines in contemporary British government is the chronic tension between powerful traditions of local rule and of central rule—between the idea of local government and the idea of parliamentary sovereignty.

Both traditions have long histories and sound pedigrees. Britain, minus Ireland, has been a unitary state, with a single, legally sovereign parliament, since the union with Scotland in 1707. England has been ruled as a unitary state for several centuries more. Yet the principle of local autonomy is of longer standing. A national system of local government with wide discretionary powers has been in existence since time immemorial, albeit regulated by statute since the Middle Ages. James II's attempt to revoke and rewrite local charters in the mid-1680s was one of the issues precipitating the Glorious Revolution of 1688. For fewer than 150 years since the Glorious Revolution—the period between the Act of Union with Ireland (1800) and the Irish settlement of 1922, and the two decades since the abolition of Northern Ireland's Stormont parliament in 1972—has the existing territory of the United Kingdom been legally subject to a single parliament. One might even quibble with the period since 1972, given Britain's accession to the European Community in 1973.

In retrospect, the Victorian era was the high point of the sovereignty of parliament as a legal and practical reality. Yet the briefest survey of Victoria's reign highlights the ambiguity of that 'reality'. While the Victorian constitutionalist A. V. Dicey famously lauded parliamentary sovereignty as 'the dominant characteristic of our political institutions',[3] J. S. Mill, the Victorian theorist of representative government, heralded local government as a cornerstone of liberty and effective rule. 'It is', he declared, 'but a small portion of the public business of a country which can be well done, or safely attempted, by the

---

[3] A. V. Dicey, *Introduction to the Study of the Law of the Constitution* (10th edn., 1959), 39.

central authorities.'[4] The two views were not incompatible: Dicey himself gave constitutional conventions—which made up the 'constitutional morality of modern England'[5]—a status equal to that of the sovereignty of parliament, and local government was one such convention. Successive Victorian governments crafted the fabric of Britain's modern local government system, through the great statutes of 1835 (municipal corporations), 1888 (county councils), 1894 (parish councils), and 1899 (metropolitan boroughs). Local government played a critical role in the evolution of urban and social policy—as Michael Heseltine recognized in his December 1990 speech. Municipal leaders such as Joseph Chamberlain in Birmingham exploited to the full the legal and fiscal resources at their disposal.

There was thus plenty of scope for tension between governments in London and local authorities beyond. Late-Victorian and Edwardian municipal radicals fought a running battle with Tory governments suspicious of their pretensions and determined to prevent excessive local spending.[6] Even in Victorian Westminster, however, the doctrine of parliamentary sovereignty was not held inviolate. The issue of full-scale devolution dominated late-Victorian politics. Gladstone, the great Liberal Prime Minister, came close to setting Britain on the road to federalism with his Irish Home Rule Bills of 1886 and 1893.[7] The first draft of Asquith's Home Rule Bill of 1912—ultimately thwarted by the outbreak of the First World War—proposed the creation of parliaments for England, Scotland, and Wales as well as Ireland.[8]

In terms of size, local government was transformed between the eras of Joseph Chamberlain and Margaret Thatcher. By 1979 local authorities were consuming 25 per cent of public spending and 10 per cent of GDP. Table 12.1 shows the change in their financing as the century advanced. Yet in terms

[4] J. S. Mill, *Representative Government* (1861), 266.

[5] Dicey, *Law of the Constitution*, 418.

[6] See K. Young, *Local Politics and the Rise of the Party: The London Municipal Society and Conservative Intervention in Local Elections 1894–1963* (1975); and A. Offer, *Property and Politics 1870–1914: Landownership, Law, Ideology and Urban Development in England* (1981).

[7] V. Bogdanor, *Devolution* (1979), 10–41.   [8] Ibid. 35.

TABLE 12.1 Local government finance and manpower, 1900–1980

	Total expenditure	Govt. grant	Grant as %	Total employed
1900	£101m.	£12m.	12	555 000
1930	£424m.	£108m.	26	541 000
1960	£1 866m.	£706m.	38	639 000
1980	£18 669m.	£11 846m.	63	931 000

of constitutional status, the Victorian ambiguity survived intact into the 1980s. The intervening decades saw several devolution schemes come and go, the last—for Scotland and Wales—failing in referendums only months before the 1979 election. They also saw Ireland divided, and home rule for the six north-easterly counties remaining within the UK first instituted and then, in 1972, abandoned. The debate on the status of subnational government was still essentially the same; and it appealed to traditions and realities of power which were largely unchanged. In his influential study of central–local relations in modern Britain, Jim Bulpitt describes the period from 1926 until the early 1960s as one of a 'dual polity'—'a state of affairs in which national and local *politics* were largely divorced from each other'.[9] In retrospect, the dual polity was an exceptional state, the product of exceptional circumstances—notably the rapid accretion of state welfare responsibilities at a time when the central government was overwhelmed (almost literally) by overseas and imperial responsibilities.

Bulpitt's thesis that the 1980s represented 'a new and important phase in the development of United Kingdom territorial politics'[10] needs qualification, therefore. It was new and important in so far as it represented a significant shift from the *status quo ante*. But it was far from new in terms of the fundamental

[9] J. Bulpitt, *Territory and Power in the United Kingdom: An Interpretation* (1983), 235.
[10] Ibid. 236.

exigencies of territorial politics, from which perspective it is more properly viewed as a reversion to an earlier pattern of central–local relations. Characteristically, the Thatcherite with the shrewdest grasp of the fundamentals was Nigel Lawson. As he put it to the Treasury and Civil Service Select Committee of the House of Commons in January 1985, with the poll tax advancing across the horizon:

We suffer from an unfortunate constitutional set-up in this country as a result of our consistent pursuit in every way of the middle way. There are countries like West Germany and the United States which have a genuinely federal constitution and where local authorities . . . are genuinely held to account. They are independent authorities and the electorate understands the responsibilities that these authorities have for managing their own affairs. That does not work too badly. You also have the opposite. The French, very logically, have a unitary constitution and carry it to the extreme where nearly every decision is dictated from the centre—Paris—and the head of the *Département*, the *préfet*, is appointed from the centre. That works out not too badly. We have a curious mixture because our constitution is midway between the two: we have a unitary constitution but nevertheless the local authorities have considerable autonomy.[11]

In fact, Lawson was out of date with regard to France. Elected regional councils had been established by Mitterrand's socialists in 1982, somewhat weakening the direct control of Paris in local affairs and inflicting on France the 'curious mixture' Lawson so disliked in Britain. The 1980s saw Italy and Spain go down the same road—neither of them embracing full-fledged federalism, yet both devolving significant functions and spending power to elected regional governments. By the late-1980s the UK was the only one of the larger European Union states to have rejected regional devolution—even though there was strong pressure for it, particularly from Scotland.[12] Mrs Thatcher's government was adamantly opposed to regional devolution or any strengthening of local government.

Given that no Tories—and few others in the 1980s—believed

[11] N. Lawson, *The View from No. 11* (1992), 562–3.
[12] See V. Wright and Y. Meny (eds.), *Centre/Periphery Relations in Western Europe* (1985).

federalism to be an option for the UK, the implication of
Lawson's disquisition is crystal clear: the 'unfortunate' part of
Britain's constitutional set-up was the 'considerable local autonomy' accorded to local councils, and the sooner and further it
was curbed the better. It is important to understand this mind-
set, for it is impossible to make sense of the poll tax apart from
the Thatcher government's unbending determination to curb
local autonomy. The poll tax was not presented in that guise:
on the contrary, as remarked above, the language was that of
local freedom and accountability. But the reality was starkly
evident from the plethora of local government reforms enacted
immediately after the 1987 election—not just the poll tax, but
the nationalization of the business rate, draconian powers to cap
local authority spending, compulsory competitive tendering of
local authority services, the removal of polytechnics from local
authority supervision, and the introduction of 'grant-
maintained' schools independent of local education authorities
and funded directly from Whitehall. Lawson's opposition was
not to the curbing of local autonomy, but to the poll tax as a
viable means to that end. Significantly, although he opposed the
poll tax, Lawson supported all the other reforms.[13] Indeed, he
wanted to go further than Kenneth Baker's incremental 'opting-
out' scheme for state schools, by removing education—by far
the largest local government responsibility—from council control in one fell swoop. 'The wresting of the schools from the
so-called local education authorities' was, he argued, 'the essential basis for educational reform.'[14]

For Thatcherites, much of the appeal of the poll tax lay in
the conviction that it would reduce local spending. It would, it
was hoped, prove unpopular for councils to seek to levy a poll
tax at a high level; and because it was a nominal, not a percentage, tax it would neither benefit from 'fiscal drag' (as did
income tax), nor would it prove easy for councils to increase
year on year. To appreciate the point, one need only recall the
reasons why its proponents dismissed a local income tax out of
hand. In Kenneth Baker's words, a local income tax would give

[13] Lawson, *View from No. 11*, 572 and ch. 43 ('Reforming Education').
[14] Ibid. 609.

councils 'immense power . . . establishing a Labour Chancellor of the Exchequer in town halls'.[15] In any case, if the poll tax alone did not contain local spending, there was always capping. The original Baker–Waldegrave plan envisaged an end to capping once the poll tax was in place. Any such external restraint on councils' freedom of action represented a hole in the heart of the government's formal case for the poll tax. The basic premiss of the poll tax was that it would restore local accountability and responsibility. Yet Lawson and the Treasury would not let go; nor would Mrs Thatcher; and nor, in their heart of hearts, would Kenneth Baker and Nicholas Ridley, who as successive environment secretaries put up next to no resistance to capping accompanying the poll tax.

Why was the Thatcher government so set on centralization? At the time, ministers were wont to insist that local government had broken a post-war understanding about its role. In reality, however, even at the low point of central–local relations in 1984–5 only a tiny number of councils were flouting the law or breaching conventional understandings as to their powers. The Widdicombe Committee, set up by Patrick Jenkin in April 1985 to consider the state of local government and improvements to its workings, concluded that 'real problems' and abuse of power had occurred in only a 'very small number' of authorities.[16] Ironically, Widdicombe reported in June 1986, midway through the consultation period for the *Paying for Local Government* Green Paper. The Widdicombe report, based on detailed research and survey data, refuted or qualified many of the bald assertions in the Green Paper. It showed that local election turn-out had not dropped significantly in recent years: in England it had remained consistently at about 40 per cent since the early 1970s.[17] As for accountability, a survey for the Committee found that nearly a third of electors could name correctly at least one of their councillors, while 20 per cent of

---

[15] K. Baker, *The Turbulent Years* (1993), 118.

[16] *Reports of the Committee of Enquiry into the Conduct of Local Authority Business* (chaired by David Widdicombe), Cmnd. 9797, i. 63. (All references below are to vol. i.)

[17] Widdicombe, 38.

the electorate had had some contact with their councillor, two-thirds of whom were satisfied with the response.[18] Contrary to pervading myths, only 4 per cent of serving councillors in the mid-1980s were found to be unemployed, while a third were in the public sector—the same proportion as in the population at large.[19] More than three-quarters of respondents were satisfied with the service provided by their local council, a higher proportion than were satisfied with central government.[20]

Widdicombe clashed swords directly with Baker's poll tax Green Paper on the critical issue of the relationship between local voters and taxpayers. Noting the Green Paper's claim that a 'poor linkage' existed between the two, with only 18m. of 35m. local electors paying rates and 3m. of the 18m. receiving full rates relief, Widdicombe countered that 'the linkage might not be quite as poor' as those figures suggested. Its own survey of public attitudes found 94 per cent of electors claiming that their households paid rates. 'This indicates two things,' Widdicombe argued. 'First, most electors who do not themselves pay rates are members of a household that does. Second, many electors perceive of themselves (or their households) as 'ratepayers' even when their rates are partially or wholly rebated.'[21]

In other words, neither the problem of local irresponsibility nor that of unaccountability were as serious as the government alleged. In explaining the government's determination to curb local government one is tempted, therefore, to resort to Sidney Low's celebrated dictum about the British Constitution—that 'we live under a system of tacit understandings, but the understandings themselves are not always understood'.[22] That, however, would be fundamentally to misunderstand the government's motivation. Nigel Lawson, the brains behind the governing philosophy (if not always the precise measures) of mid-term Thatcherism, did not *misunderstand* the conventional position of

---

[18] Ibid. 41. [19] Ibid. 27.

[20] Ibid. 40. Cf. the 1991 Rowntree survey on public attitudes to national government showing only one in three broadly satisfied with the *status quo*.

[21] Ibid. [22] S. Low, *The Governance of England* (1904), 12.

local government. As we have just seen he understood it perfectly, but he wanted to change it radically. In his memoirs he is quite open as to why: because he believed local authorities to be poor providers of services—particularly education—and because accountability for services provided locally was too weak.[23] Lawson, for one, did not spend much time attacking local government as a whole for being in the grip of the 'loony left': in his view, its failure extended across the board.

Another force was at play: the politicization of local government. The research carried out for the Widdicombe Committee starkly exposed this development, but its report fails to appreciate its full significance. The research revealed a sharp rise in the role of political parties in local government over the twenty years prior to the mid-1980s. In 1965, only 50 per cent of councils were controlled by a party or a coalition of parties; by 1985 that figure had risen to 84 per cent.[24] And with parties came polarization and ideology. Widdicombe's survey of the attitudes of councillors found 63 per cent agreeing with the proposition that 'the first concern of the elected member is to implement the party manifesto'.[25]

The importance of this politicization cannot be overstated. For the first time, it meant that local government across the country—not just, as previously, in the cities and some of the larger towns—had become part of the battleground between the parties. Local elections are characteristically mid-term elections; by the mid-1980s the opposition parties were routing the Tories in local elections across the country—not excluding the 'true blue' Home Counties, where in a dozen or so counties coalitions of the Labour party and SDP/Liberal Alliance took control after the 1985 county elections. It did not matter that most councils were not 'extreme': all that mattered was that they were a focus for political activity by opposition parties to a degree never before witnessed. As Nicholas Ridley put it, Tories could not abide 'the use of local government as a plat-

---

[23] Lawson, *View from No. 11*, esp. ch. 43.
[24] Maud Committee on the Management of Local Government (1967), v. 97; Widdicombe, 30.
[25] Ibid. 33.

form to conduct political warfare against central government rather than as the means to provide efficient local services'.[26]

Note the 'rather than'. In reality, as Widdicombe reported, most local authorities *were* providing reasonably efficient local services. They were also unashamedly partisan, just as Tory authorities had been in opposition to the Labour governments of the 1960s and 1970s. The battles over grammar schools and comprehensives come instantly to mind. But in the mind of a Tory élite which, by 1985, was firmly entrenched in government and power, fierce resentment at the success of the opposition parties in colonizing local government naturally fed the belief that local councils were inefficient and needed to be emasculated. Therein lies a large part of the explanation for the poll tax.

LOCAL GOVERNMENT AND THE POLL TAX

The replacement of the domestic rating system by the poll tax was, by any standards, revolutionary for local government. It abolished a tax which could be traced back in a recognizable form to the Poor Law of 1601, and, in various rudimentary forms, to the thirteenth century. Local government in Britain had developed on the basis of income derived from the rates. Other Anglo-Saxon countries, notably the USA, Canada, Australia, and New Zealand, had followed the British example and funded their local government systems using property taxes.

There has never been a shortage of schemes to replace the rates. In Chapter 2 we described the efforts to reform local government finance in the post-war period. Yet rates seemed to be an inescapable fact of life. Even Mrs Thatcher, who in 1974 had committed the Conservative party to abolish domestic rates, was not convinced that the policy could be carried through until early 1985. Rates may have been criticized, but the alternatives seemed even worse.

When it came, the poll tax was introduced in defiance of local government. Councils and councillors were not consulted

---

[26] Ridley, *The Local Right*, 31.

before the reform was introduced; nor were council officers, who were near-universally hostile to it. From the time of the earliest newspaper leaks about the possibility of a poll tax, civil servants and local authority officers discussed the implications of such a policy. Professional bodies representing local authority finance and revenue officers soon took a keen interest in the development of the new tax. The Chartered Institute of Public Finance and Accountancy (CIPFA) and the Institute of Revenues, Rating and Valuation (IRRV) were the leading bodies contributing to the debate. The Audit Commission, a government-appointed watchdog, also published papers on the administrative consequences and costs of the community charge.

Once local authorities and the professional bodies were involved, the negative aspects of poll tax gained greater prominence. For instance, in August 1986 Howard Longden, Chief Executive of Hove district council and a leading member of the IRRV, wrote an article in CIPFA's house journal spelling out, in stark terms, the extra costs and losses of revenue which would come about if the community charge were introduced.[27] CIPFA's official response to the Green Paper was straightforwardly hostile. It argued that a community charge would be 'much more complex and much more expensive to administer than rates. . . . the proposals do not represent a practical basis for raising local revenue. . . . Whatever the merits of the community charge proposals they fail totally when matched against attendant administrative consequences and costs.'[28] CIPFA was not once consulted by the government before the publication of the 1986 Green Paper.

In retrospect this may seem remarkable, but it is fully explained by the politics of the process outlined in Chapters 3 and 4. Up to the point when the Green Paper was published in January 1986, Kenneth Baker and William Waldegrave, the ministers steering the policy, were primarily concerned with generating a sufficient consensus behind the poll tax within the government. This meant making the scheme convincing in

[27] H. Longden, 'Counting the Cost of Collection', *Public Finance and Accountancy*, 22 Aug. 1986.
[28] CIPFA, *Response to Paying for Local Government* (1986).

principle and plausible in outline. The intricacies of making it capable of administration barely entered into the long debates of late 1984 and 1985.

The front-line relationship between government and local authorities in England can be seen at the regular meetings of the Consultative Council on Local Government Finance (CCLGF) in London. This body brings the Department of the Environment and all other departments involved with local government together with the local authority associations: ministers, councillors, civil servants, and local government officers all attend these meetings. The five local authority associations represent the county councils, district councils, metropolitan authorities, and London boroughs. Similar arrangements exist in Wales and Scotland. The CCLGF has a number of officer subgroups which undertake work on statistics, local tax administration, the grant system, capital expenditure and other matters. These groups meet more frequently than the Consultative Council itself. The earliest official discussions between the government and local authorities about the community charge took place at the CCLGF and its subgroups during 1986 and 1987.

Notwithstanding the official views of the associations and professional bodies, civil servants and their local authority counterparts started preparations for implementation as soon as it was clear that the poll tax would go ahead. Concrete preparations were limited before the 1987 general election, partly because there was still a possibility that the Conservatives would lose office, and partly because as far as England and Wales were concerned, there was no legislation. D.o.E. officials, however, had to start drafting legislation early in 1987. In order to know what shape the legislation should take, it was necessary to talk with local authority officers and Scottish civil servants who were preparing for community charge in 1989.

The implementation of the poll tax is a testament to the professionalism and dedication of senior local authority finance officials. Regardless of their personal or institutional opposition to the concept of a poll tax, professional finance and revenue officers took the view from the start that there was no alternative but to make the best of a bad job. If the community charge

*'Specialist subject: local
government finance,
March 18–21, 1991'*

became law, professional officers had no choice but to implement it. Unless the money was collected successfully, local government could lose its source of tax income. Like it or not, the
community charge had to be made to work.

The Department of the Environment commissioned consultants Price Waterhouse to examine the costs of implementing
the new tax. As there were no poll taxes operating elsewhere in
the developed world, there were no comparative situations upon
which to base any estimates of costs. The consultants estimated
that some £270–300m. (revenue and capital) would have to be
spent in 1988, 1989, and 1990 in preparation for the new tax,
followed by an additional £200m. or so in each year thereafter
because of higher running-costs. An extra 19,000 full-time staff
would be required permanently to administer the community

charge.[29] This report implicitly pointed to the bonanza that lay ahead for computer companies, envelope manufacturers, public sector administrators, and bailiffs.

If local authority officers were prepared glumly to implement a new system of local taxation that many of them considered unworkable and unacceptable, the reaction of their political masters was more varied. A minority of Conservative councillors strongly supported the community charge. Rather more were suspicious of the administrative and redistributive consequences that would flow from it. A few Tory councillors expressed their outright opposition. Labour and the Liberal Democrats were agreed on their hatred of the proposed tax, but their unity was blurred by the small minority of Labour councillors who broke away from their party's official line and encouraged non-payment campaigns and by the few Labour councils which said that they would not implement the community charge.

Non-implementation campaigns were, in reality, doomed from the start. Mrs Thatcher's government was used to coping with recalcitrant councils. Legislation was now drafted to be watertight and, if possible, judge-proof. The Local Government Finance Act 1988 gave local authorities legal obligations which they could not avoid. Preparations had to be made and paid for. Senior officers prepared reports for committees, including costings, which paved the way for the community charge. Members were faced with the choice of voting down such reports (and thus risking legal action against themselves) or passing them and allowing the officers to start preparations. Despite the currency of allegations that several inner-city Labour leaderships were explicitly encouraging non-payment, every council in the country did, eventually, make available the resources necessary to collect the new tax. A number of Labour councils came up with bright ideas which would damage the tax, though in lawful ways. Some councils wanted community charge bills to be sent out without any reference to the local council at all: the bill might be headed 'Government Poll Tax Demand' and an

[29] Price Waterhouse, *Implementation and Collection of the Community Charge, 1: Forecast of Costs* (1988).

address given which wholly disguised the council. A number of councils toyed with the idea of naming their community charge headquarters 'Margaret Thatcher House' or something similar. In the end, the government produced regulations which precisely determined what was printed on community charge bills.

During 1988 and 1989, each local authority responsible for the administration of the community charge (London boroughs, metropolitan districts, non-metropolitan districts, and Scottish regions) set up a team of officers to plan the new tax. In most cases, a senior officer from the finance department would be charged with determining what would be necessary, in terms of officers and resources. Outside organizations, notably consultancies such as Capita and CSL Ltd, created their own consultancy divisions to assist authorities with the task ahead. Computer companies, whose machinery and software would be so important in making it possible to undertake such a vast administrative task, put on seminars and exhibitions. A small industry grew up arranging conferences about the community charge.

In the spring of 1988, the Department of the Environment, the Welsh Office, the Department of Social Security, and the local authority associations agreed jointly to produce practice notes about the community charge. The first was published in May. These joint publications included interpretations (in non-legalistic language) of the legislation and regulations under which the community charge was to operate. Between May 1988 and July 1990, practice notes were produced at the rate of about one a month, covering all aspects of the tax.

Public information about the community charge was to come from three sources: the media, the government, and local authorities themselves. The newspapers and television have massive coverage to the alarums and excursions which accompanied the passage of the Local Government Finance Bill through parliament. But the intricacies of how the community charge would actually operate had been blurred by relentless debate about the treatment of student nurses, the severely mentally handicapped, and the armed forces. In May 1989, the government distributed a leaflet to every household in the country about the new tax, offering other and more detailed leaflets to anyone who asked for them. Local authorities, particularly those which opposed the new tax on principle, were faced with a dilemma. If they failed to publicize the community charge and did not encourage people to pay it, their income (and thus spending) would be reduced. Registration for the charge started in the spring of 1989, which meant that authorities had to explain to every household why they were being asked to fill in a form. Most councils followed up registration (which was completed by 1 December 1989) with further local publicity to maximize the numbers registered and also to ensure that as many people as possible who qualified would receive benefit. Even those authorities most strongly opposed had to generate positive publicity for the community charge during the winter of 1989–90.

Authorities had to think creatively about how to extract as much of the poll tax as possible from an unwilling populace. Massive efforts were made to encourage people to use direct debit arrangements to pay. The Post Office was signed up to handle payments. Councils introduced new, user-friendly, offices (including mobile ones) to facilitate payment. Much inventiveness went into thinking of ways of making payment easier. Billing was on time in the overwhelming majority of authorities. The media focused attention on the vast bureaucratic efforts needed to maintain the register, to print 40 million bills, and to send them out in late March or early April 1990. Changes in regulations had made a difficult task worse. Apart from a few city authorities which started preparations late, and a number of councils which suffered from teething troubles with their computers, there were remarkably few hiccups.

During 1990, almost all of the predictions made at the outset by CIPFA and the local authority associations came true. The public, as represented in opinion polls, loathed the new tax. Although initial registration had proved relatively easy, its maintenance proved a nightmare. Collection levels fell well behind the comparable figures for domestic rates.[30] Horrible

[30] Audit Commission, *The Administration of the Community Charge* (1990), para. 81.10.

difficulties arose in dealing with the very poor, who now had to pay 20 per cent of their local tax bill. The courts clogged up, and dealt with cases differently from one area to another.

Between 1991 and 1993, the same officer teams had to prepare for Michael Heseltine's council tax. The time available to set up the council tax was just half of the four years given to preparing for the community charge. Yet in the period between March 1991 and April 1993, local authorities did manage to maintain payments of the fatally wounded poll tax while setting up local government's third tax within 1,100 days. Council tax implementation followed a similar pattern to its predecessor. Legislation was passed, joint central/local officer groups were set up, practice notes were published, publicity campaigns were mounted. Professional organizations published guides.[31] But the atmosphere was very different from the earlier poll tax implementation. The government was desperately keen that the council tax should avoid the pitfalls of the community charge. Local authorities knew that council tax was the last chance for local taxation, and they supported the form of the tax itself, which was broadly progressive.[32] This strength of purpose in both Whitehall and the town halls made for an excellent working relationship. Every effort was made to achieve consensus. In stark contrast to the poll tax, the Department of the Environment was widely praised within local government for its openness and care.

THE STATE OF LOCAL GOVERNMENT

Where did the poll tax leave local government? The first thing to note is that council spending went up, not down. In 1990–1 and the years since, local government has maintained its long-term share of GDP and public spending, notwithstanding some transfers of responsibilities to and from central government. Emphatically, the poll tax did not achieve the government's

[31] e.g. C. Farrington and M. Lee, *Council Tax: Your Guide* (Institute of Rating, Revenues and Valuation, 1992).
[32] Cf. J. Hills and H. Sutherland, *Banding, Tilting, Gearing, Gaining and Losing: An Anatomy of the Proposed Council Tax* (Suntory-Toyota International Centre for Economics and Related Disciplines, LSE, 1991).

avowed objectives of freeing local authorities to provide the levels of service desired by their electors with minimal interference from Whitehall. But equally, central control has not enabled Whitehall to bear down on local spending to anything like the extent that many in government hoped it would.

What about public perceptions of local government? In 1990, the first year of the operation of the poll tax in England and Wales, there can be little doubt that it sharply raised the public's interest in local taxation. Turn-out in the May 1990 local elections was up on the long-term average.[33] Opinion polling showed that the majority of the public believed that the government was responsible for the new tax. However, research suggested that different levels of local tax had an impact on electoral performance by incumbent councils in London. Overall, there can be little doubt that because of the vast publicity which attended its introduction, and also because of the large increase in the number of local taxpayers, the community charge raised public perceptions of local taxation, and to that extent enhanced accountability. But it was a narrowly one-dimensional view of accountability, presupposing on the one hand that the level of local taxation was the only, or at least the prime, factor in influencing local voting behaviour, and on the other hand that accountability could not be promoted between elections by mechanisms other than elections. Both presuppositions were deeply flawed.

Ironically, the sponsors of the poll tax themselves lost faith in the efficacy of the electoral process as a means of promoting accountability and efficient local government. In an important but little-noticed speech to CIPFA in July 1993, William Waldegrave, the poll tax's chief architect, all but disowned its key principle—the linkage between voting and taxpaying. Addressing the question of a supposed 'democratic deficit' making public bodies unresponsive—something the poll tax was specifically designed to tackle—Waldegrave had this to say:

there is no guarantee—indeed there may not even be a sporting chance—that by periodically expressing his or her decision at the

---

[33] Cf. *The Economist*, 12 May 1990; J. Gibson and J. Stewart, 'Poll Tax, Rates and Local Elections', in *Political Studies* (1992).

ballot box the citizen (by the use of that sovereign power) will necessarily obtain on a continuous basis efficient, properly accountable, responsive public services. You don't have to go far back in history to see that. The key point in this argument is not whether those who run our public services are elected, but whether they are producer-responsive or consumer-responsive. Services are not necessarily made to respond to the public simply by giving citizens a democratic voice, and a distant and diffuse one at that, in their make-up.[34]

Presumably Waldegrave had the poll tax experience in mind when looking 'back in history'. At any rate, it explains the government's emphasis since the demise of the poll tax on 'citizen's charters', contracting out, and the like.

It is hard to object to that emphasis as one strand in policy for service provision, whether by local or central government. The separation between setting standards and funding services on the one hand, and actually providing them on the other, has without question enhanced the average level of efficiency of service provision. Few would wish to return to the world before compulsory competitive tendering for council services; and though there are legitimate questions about the impact of frequent tendering on employee rights and motivation, and about the administrative burden of organizing contracting out for minor services, the vision of the local authority as regulator and funder, not direct provider, is gaining general acceptance.

It is important, however, to recognize the limitations in the new doctrine as it applies to the idea of local government. It is one thing to institute mechanisms improving the efficiency and effectiveness of service provision. It is quite another to suppose that those mechanisms can or should take the place of local democratic processes in deciding the services to be provided in the first place. Yet that is precisely what the government has done, by remorselessly constraining the scope for local authorities to regulate and fund services at the same time as requiring them to cease providing services directly.

As we have seen, the remorseless attack on the autonomy of local authorities predated the poll tax. But the poll tax acceler-

[34] *The Reality of Reform and Accountability in Today's Public Service*, Lecture to Public Finance Foundation, 5 July 1993, 13.

ated it, and it has continued unabated since the repeal of the poll tax. The transfer of non-domestic rates to central control, a major part of the 1990 reform package, meant that the proportion of local government spending funded out of local taxation fell from 56 per cent to about 30 per cent. Table 12.1 shows the trends.

The £140 cut in community charge in Norman Lamont's 1991 budget further reduced the locally raised proportion to about 20 per cent. As central funding rose, capping was extended in a way which effectively controlled the spending of every authority in England. By the time that council tax was introduced in 1993, the expenditure total of every local authority in the country was, in effect, dictated by Whitehall. Locally determined taxation now raises the relatively modest annual sum of about £10bn., net of social security and other reliefs; another 4 per cent on VAT, or 5p on the basic rate of income tax, could comfortably replace it. Centrally appointed quangos have proliferated to an unprecedented degree, steadily eating away at the functions of local authorities.

The Widdicombe report brilliantly highlights the current predicament of local government in Britain.

If local government is strong on the delivery of services but weak in the extent to which it provides for local democratic self-expression, it ceases to be sufficiently distinct from local administration. If on the other hand it is strong on democratic self-expression, but weak on service delivery, the danger is that it will in the long term become only a means of democratic expression, and that services will be administered by other means. These are the Scylla and Charybdis between which local government must steer if it is to continue to be viable.[35]

Local government averted complete shipwreck on the shoals of the poll tax. But it has a hard navigation ahead if it is to avoid becoming little more than the local agent of the central government—the local *préfet* which Lawson so admired across the Channel.

[35] Widdicombe, 58.

13

QUESTIONS

> Has there ever in recent political history been a greater act of folly than the poll tax? What a botch up. What a bloomer. What a gaffe, bungle, goof, fluff, fiasco, boner, clanger, howler and flop. What a fatheaded, boneheaded, dunderheaded, blunderheaded, muttonheaded, knuckle-headed, chuckleheaded, puddingheaded, jobernowled wash-out of a cock-up.
>
> Robert Harris, *Sunday Times*, 24 February 1991

In our pursuit of the poll tax, we found that many of those involved still argued over responsibility for the policy, many of whom said 'If only . . .'. We ourselves debated long about responsibility for the débâcle, and about the key moments and the missed opportunities, either of stopping the tax or of making it work. It seems right to explore some of the basic questions and hypothetical scenarios that were put to us.

WHO WAS TO BLAME?

Responsibility for the decision to replace property rates with a poll tax lies unambiguously with Conservative ministers in office between 1984 and 1987. Often the genesis of policies gets lost in the mists of time, with tinkering, successive reviews, and Whitehall toing-and-froing. Not so with the poll tax. No respectable Whitehall or official body supported the idea when the Waldegrave–Baker review team started work in 1984. Even the Adam Smith Institute had floated the idea only in the bold-est of outlines, and was not to publish a blueprint until after the team had reached its conclusions. Moreover, those involved accept the responsibility. William Waldegrave, the policy's chief architect, accepted in a 1994 interview that it was a 'mistake' and that 'John Major was right to repeal the legislation'.[1]

Waldegrave and Kenneth Baker, the ministers in charge of the 1984—5 studies team, were the prime initiators. Without them, the poll tax would never have got off the ground. Yet many ambitious policies are floated by ministers, only to be scotched in the cabinet system. The poll tax was elevated from 'bold idea' to 'government policy', in the space of barely three months, because of the enthusiastic backing of the Prime Minister and key colleagues. Mrs Thatcher was converted at the Chequers meeting on 31 March 1985, and never looked back. George Younger and William Whitelaw, facing a political storm over revaluation in Scotland, were desperate for a plausible alternative to the rates, and seized on the Baker–Waldegrave plan with barely a query. The strong support of Lord Whitelaw, Mrs Thatcher's deputy and an enormously respected and reassuring figure within the Cabinet and Tory party, was utterly vital. For at the time the policy was strenuously opposed by the Chancellor of the Exchequer (Nigel Lawson), and was regarded sceptically by the Home Secretary (Leon Brittan). Had Whitelaw come down firmly against the poll tax, and made his opposition plain to Mrs Thatcher privately at an early stage, it might never have got anywhere. At this stage in her premiership Mrs Thatcher was still careful to gauge the balance of opinion in her cabinet and party before embarking on radical initiatives. With the balance strongly opposed, it is unlikely that she would have put herself out on a limb by adopting the poll tax. But once the Prime Minister was committed, only a resignation threat by Nigel Lawson, or quasi-public efforts by him to discredit the idea in the spring of 1985, could have tipped the balance against.

In his only reasoned public statement on the genesis of the poll tax, William Waldegrave explained in a 1993 lecture:

In the way the policy was originated, formulated and carried through it was almost a model of how . . . modern policy should be formulated. There was a project team. There were outsiders. There was published

[1] *Walden*, 16 Jan. 1994.

analysis and enormous consultation. There was modelling of outcomes using the latest technologies. What there wasn't (it is now generally alleged) was a correct political judgement by the Cabinet of the day. That was nothing to do with the civil service and the outside experts who had performed exactly what their democratically elected masters had asked of them. . . . In the end there is no magic wand which can ensure that human decision-makers avoid mistakes.[2]

The 'magic wand' theme is taken up in the conclusion. For the rest, however, Waldegrave's apologia sits uneasily with our account. The project team was entirely an internal Whitehall affair: outsiders, in the shape of the Institute for Fiscal Studies, were not brought in for advice until after the poll tax had been adopted by a cabinet committee. If by 'outsiders' Waldegrave meant the four 'assessors' who were asked to give their views on the project team's work, then the remark is odder still, for two of the four assessors strongly opposed the proposal for a poll tax and made their opposition plain, while a third (Lord Rothschild) gave the idea no more than lukewarm support.

As for the 'published' analysis and 'enormous' consultation, nothing was published before the Green Paper *Paying for Local Government* appeared in January 1986, and none of the criticism made in the subsequent consultations was taken on board. Even inside the government no papers were available until a late stage. The critical decision at the Chequers meeting in March 1985 was taken on the basis of a slide show and oral presentation, with no documents circulated. The first document available to senior ministers was a 'specification report' for the new tax prepared after the Chequers meeting: on the basis of that, Nigel Lawson composed his devastating critique of the tax, which anticipated virtually all the key weaknesses, including the serious distributional impact the tax was likely to have. Nor was there any consultation of any kind with local authority experts at this early stage.

Like the causes of the First World War, the origins of the poll tax can be broadened to include almost everything in Britain's modern political system and history. The civil service,

[2] Speech to Social Market Foundation Conference on 'Reforming the Role of Government', 1 Dec. 1993, official text, p. 7.

parliament, the party system, and not least local government itself, all played a part in generating the poll tax. None of them comes out of the experience with much credit. But responsibility for initiating and pushing through the policy can be attributed narrowly.

WHY DID IT FAIL?

The poll tax failed for three reasons. First, it proved impossible to collect a large proportion of the tax in many inner-city areas, where mobility, hostility, and tacit evasion defeated the administrative resources of local authorities which were themselves opposed to the levy. Secondly, the level of tax was too high, and the increase in taxation for a majority of the electorate too great, which both increased the non-collection rate and raised popular hostility to fever pitch across the country. Thirdly, the tax increases for those affected were too visible and too abrupt, with the same repercussions.

In our view, these factors would have made effective abolition of the poll tax unavoidable, even had the Major government not adopted that course as early as it did. In her memoirs, Mrs Thatcher expresses the belief that 'given time, it would have been seen as one of the most far-reaching and beneficial reforms ever made in the working of local government'.[3] Yet time was the one commodity which the poll tax did not have. Although the bitter discontent of the spring of 1990 had reduced somewhat by the autumn, huge public hostility would have been an annual event at budget-setting time had the poll tax remained in force. Even if ruthless capping had kept large annual increases at bay, levels of non-payment in inner-city areas approaching 20 per cent would in all probability have continued. So would the hundreds of thousands of prosecutions annually. And so would the strong underlying hostility and perception of unfairness which ultimately made continuation in any form a political non-starter. Had Mrs Thatcher remained in office in November 1990, she would doubtless have

[3] M. Thatcher, *The Downing Street Years* (1993), 642.

attempted to keep the 'poll tax' in being. How long she would have succeeded in doing so is a matter of conjecture. But one can be fairly certain from the concessions made even before her fall—notably the £2.5bn.-worth of reliefs announced in the previous year—that on the most optimistic view of her prospects, the tax would have been radically overhauled.

That leaves the three hypothetical scenarios put to us by many of those involved: that the poll tax might have worked if those on lower incomes had been exempted, and/or had it been introduced at a far lower level, and/or had it been phased in. Kenneth Baker is to the fore on all three fronts. His original proposal was for a phased tax; he argues that the poll tax was sabotaged by the decisions to end phasing, not to exempt any of those without independent incomes from paying the 20 per cent, and not to cushion the introduction with sizeable Treasury grants.[4]

Obviously one cannot give a definitive verdict either way. If a large swathe of those on lower incomes had been exempted, and another large swathe of those on below-average incomes and/or members of households suffering huge losses from the transition from rates had been given a lower rate, then the poll tax might have proved sufficiently collectable to survive. And if it had been introduced at, say, half of the average £363 of the first year, with those safeguards, then it might have proved sufficiently acceptable to survive. There is, however, an uncomfortable circularity to both arguments, since both proposals were considered and rejected by the Thatcher government, on more than one occasion, on the grounds that they would undermine the principles upon which the whole reform was based. Exemptions and banding would, it was argued, obscure the tax and reduce 'accountability', while a prime objective of the reform was to reduce, not to increase the burden of local government on the national Exchequer. At the time this view was summed up by the former Tory minister George Walden, who wrote that he had been 'seduced' by the tax as a means of 'revitalising local government'; however, 'when the charge turned

---

[4] K. Baker, *The Turbulent Years* (1993), 127–31.

out to be roughly double what was expected, the whole system of thought on which it was based became unsustainable'.[5]

The option of exempting completely those required to pay 20 per cent was deliberately rejected during the drawing up of the Scottish Bill. Baker's later proposal to exempt students—only a small proportion of the 20 per cent payers—was also rejected. Mrs Thatcher risked her most serious Commons defeat of the 1987 parliament to scotch the widely supported Mates amendment to band the poll tax according to income tax thresholds. Moreover, the tax could only have been markedly lower had another tax (i.e. the rates) been kept alongside it, or had there been a significant switch to national taxation at the time of introduction. The first option was abandoned at cabinet committee stage; the original proposal would in any case only have retained rates to cover 30 per cent of locally raised taxation. The option of switching expensive local services to national taxation was also rejected at that stage. Throughout the evolution of the policy, Lawson trumpeted his opposition and warned that the Treasury would not bail out the new tax; so his failure to do so in the event should not have surprised his colleagues, least of all Kenneth Baker, who knew Lawson's views from the outset.

What about phasing? It is self-evidently true that had the introduction of the tax been phased, its initial impact would have been lessened, and the opportunities to iron out anomalies and injustices, or even to recast the whole tax, would have been greater. But the main difficulty with phasing lay in the undoubted expense and complication of dual-running. The poll tax cost twice as much as the rates to collect. In the early stages of phasing, many payers would only be liable for very small sums. The costs of putting them on the register and, even more, of chasing up non-payers was constant, regardless of the sums collected: it would have infuriated town halls and might have led to the whole scheme being killed by ridicule. The establishment of the tax would necessarily be interrupted by a general election and the sponsors of the tax would be condemning themselves to years of niggling controversy. It is a paradox

[5] *Sunday Telegraph*, 'Muddling through to the right answer at last', 22 Mar. 1991.

that dual-running was left in place, only to be abandoned at a late stage, in a handful of authorities—all but one in inner London—which in the event had the highest charges.[6]

It therefore appears to us that the poll tax was bound to end in catastrophe once the cabinet committee took the key decisions of principle on 20 May 1985, given that Mrs Thatcher and an overwhelming majority of her ministers were determined and able to proceed at every subsequent stage. However, that still leaves the question which intrigued us throughout our investigations. Why were ministers not able to see the disaster looming? In particular, why was it not clear to them from an early stage that if there were no change to the overall amount collected in local taxation, then households of two or more adults living in low-rated properties—a significant proportion of the electorate, concentrated in marginal seats—would lose, in some cases heavily? Our investigations suggest three reasons for the fatal oversight, each of them a telling commentary on the wider politics of the affair.

First is the failure of officials most closely concerned with the poll tax, notably Sir Terence Heiser, the D.o.E.'s permanent secretary, to sound alarm bells at any stage. Chapter 9 has dealt at length with the issue of the civil service's role in the poll tax saga: suffice it to note here that the key officials responsible at the early stage were determined to give swift effect to ministerial wishes, and felt a strong personal commitment to the reforms.

Secondly, the turnover of ministers ensured that at each key stage, those responsible had not been engaged in the previous stage. Ridley and his colleagues, responsible for drafting and carrying the legislation, had not been involved in the review team; Chris Patten and his colleagues, charged with its implementation, had played no part in either the studies or the legislation. In short, there was no ministerial memory. As we noted in Chapter 8, in itself rapid ministerial turnover does not explain the catastrophe: the key errors were made at the outset; and the serious compounding of them at the implementation

---

[6] Thatcher, *The Downing Street Years*, 653.

stage was at the behest of Nicholas Ridley, the longest-serving Environment Secretary of the 1980s. It does, however, go some way to accounting for Ridley's extraordinary insouciance at the prospect of millions of large-scale losers from the new tax. He had neither seen, nor been a party to, the work on the distributional impact of the new tax carried out by the review team and the Institute for Fiscal Studies in the summer and autumn of 1985. That work had alarmed Baker at the time[7] and persuaded him to proceed with a lengthy transitional period.

Thirdly, ministers made the extraordinary mistake of confusing the feebleness of the opposition to the poll tax inside parliament with the strength of resistance likely to be encountered outside. Almost all the ministers to whom we spoke emphasized the lacklustre nature of Labour's opposition: 'they were a walk-over', 'all the problems came from our side, not theirs', were typical comments. Earlier chapters have highlighted Labour's weakness.[8] Anxious to deflect attention from left-wing Labour authorities and nervous about the unpopularity of rates with property-owners, Neil Kinnock and his strategists deliberately downplayed the issue. Labour's research on the likely impact of the poll tax was virtually non-existent: had it been otherwise, the party's opposition might have been more forthright and effective. Either way, ministers committed a fundamental error in believing that from the front-bench in the Commons they were looking at the real opposition to the tax.

DID THE POLL TAX BRING DOWN MRS THATCHER?

On 20 November 1990, if only two Conservative MPs had switched their votes Margaret Thatcher would have remained Prime Minister, at least for the time being. It was a desperately close-run thing and Mrs Thatcher probably lost the vital two votes through the incompetence of her campaign managers. But the extent of the support for Michael Heseltine reflected a deep disillusion that would not have evaporated had he attracted two

---

[7] See pp. 78–9 above.

[8] See, in particular, pp. 105–7 for the 1987 election; and p. 257 for the absence of any research by Labour on the likely impact of the tax.

votes fewer. Ever since the triumphalism celebrating her tenth anniversary in office on 4 May 1989, Mrs Thatcher's stock had been going down. The prime cause was, undoubtedly, the state of the economy. Her style of operation, the handbagging immortalized in Sir Geoffrey Howe's resignation speech, must come next as a factor. But the arrival of poll tax bills and the repeated news stories about non-payment and about the troubles of local government, in Conservative as well as in Labour areas, added substantially to the anti-Conservative tide, so notably demonstrated in the Eastbourne by-election on 21 October 1990. Heseltine put an 'immediate and fundamental review' of the poll tax at the top of his brief leadership manifesto. Other factors might have brought her down later but it seems almost certain that, if she had resisted the deceptive lure of the poll tax five years earlier, she would not have fallen when she did.

One senior minister to whom we spoke contests the popular
view that Mrs Thatcher would have won the leadership contest
if she had stayed in England on 19 November instead of going
to the Paris Summit. He argued that, had she busied herself
canvassing ministers and MPs, she would not have gained but
lost votes because of her continued private emphasis on the
virtues of the poll tax. That certainly accords with one theme
which comes clearly from our interviews with Tory MPs: that
the poll tax was important not just for its own sake, but for its
characterization of the prime-ministerial style of Margaret
Thatcher. It is a point picked up by Peter Riddell in his study
of the Thatcher government:

all it [the poll tax] showed was her hostility to local government and
demonstrated those personal attributes which her colleagues and voters
liked least about her—her determination to push through policies
regardless of other views and her lack of concern for those adversely
affected.[9]

Given the genesis of the poll tax, this may have been an
unfair characterization. But life has never been fair at the top of
Disraeli's greasy pole.

WAS THERE AN ALTERNATIVE?

The poll tax was adopted because to its authors all the alternatives were worse. It was decision by elimination. A local sales
tax would be disastrous in a small, highly mobile country. A
local income tax would install a Chancellor of the Exchequer in
each of Britain's four hundred local authorities when the
Conservatives were wedded to lower income tax. Continuation
of the rates required periodic revaluations of property which, as
the Scottish revaluation of 1984–5 demonstrated, was politically
perilous. Indeed, George Younger strongly urged his English
colleagues to proceed with their long-postponed revaluation in
1985, believing it would put the poll tax in its proper perspective.

The poll tax should have been eliminated too, given its

[9] P. Riddell, *The Thatcher Era* (1993), 221.

downside. Had it been, what was the alternative? At the time, one alternative, seriously considered by Nigel Lawson, was the abolition of local taxation and the funding of all local government centrally. Such a course would have avoided the poll tax débâcle; it would also have involved the abolition of local government worth the name, and had little support even among the most centrally minded of 1980s Tories.

Writing in 1994, nearly a year after the smooth and relatively uncontroversial introduction of the property-based council tax, it is easy to see the alternative. But one does not require hindsight for the task. Nigel Lawson proposed a tax tantamount to the council tax—i.e. a banded property tax—in his memorandum opposing the poll tax. The crucial lesson—long appreciated by the Treasury but neglected by both the Scottish Office in its 1984–5 revaluation and by the Department of the Environment in the poll tax—is that any tax reform, to be electorally palatable, must pay scrupulous attention both to the number of losers, and to the scale of their losses year-by-year. A modernized property tax backed by a deep cushion was the answer.

However, the authors of the tax believed at the time it failed to answer two questions—namely how to provide effective protection for the better-off under Labour councils, and how to enhance accountability. Ruthless capping was the answer to the first, as the government discovered late in the poll tax saga. As for accountability, an effective answer has still to be found. But it almost certainly lies in improved mechanisms of democracy, not in more onerous and resented taxes. Ironically, the government's first truly radical idea for improving accountability, the local referendum—floated but abandoned in 1981—would probably have served its ideal more faithfully than the poll tax.[10] It might yet do so.

COULD THE POLL TAX HAVE BEEN STOPPED?

In the initial discussions? Among the four external advisers to the Waldegrave–Baker 'studies' of 1984–5 there are regrets at the

[10] See p. 27 above.

failure to express scepticism still more forcibly. It is difficult, however, to see what more they could have done, short of publishing their views in the press. One of the assessors, Leonard Hoffmann, wrote a paper well before the critical meeting cogently setting out the case against the poll tax, and doing so from the 'friendly' perspective of accepting Waldegrave's premisses with regard to 'accountability' and the grant system. It was not even circulated to all those involved in the studies team. The pro-poll tax consensus among ministers and civil servants was too strong for any such fringe objections to block the idea. Once the proposal got to Chequers, and received prime-ministerial blessing, it acquired a momentum that made it unstoppable in Whitehall and the cabinet—unless, perhaps, Nigel Lawson had been prepared to make the question a resigning issue.

In parliament? The Conservatives won the 1987 election with a majority of 100. Fifty rebels were needed to block the measure—either by voting against it or, the more likely course, by making their readiness to do so plain to the whips. Yet the number of rebels never approached that number. Only 17 voted against the principle of the bill on second reading; the Mates amendment, for a banded poll tax, pushed the number up to 38, but left the government with a comfortable majority. A smaller majority might have scuppered the project; or it might have enabled the whips to exert still greater pressure on the weaker of the dissentients. Given the number of die-hard opponents with secure seats, it would probably have taken a majority of less than 40 to have made the poll tax 'unpassable'. As a financial measure with broad Tory support, there was never any prospect of it coming to grief in the House of Lords.

By mass agitation? The Trafalgar Square demonstration of 31 March 1990, and anti-poll tax rallies across the country, probably constitute the biggest mass agitation since the war. Although given only lukewarm support by the Labour and Liberal Democrat parties, it embraced groups from the extreme left to the respectable middle class. On its own, the demonstrations did little to thwart the poll tax: indeed, in the short-term they strengthened the government's resolve to stand up to 'lawlessness'. But by increasing the sense of crisis engulfing the poll tax, and giving popular opposition to the tax far greater prominence than it would otherwise have achieved, the agitation probably strengthened the resolve of leading Tory opponents of the tax to see it abolished outright, however loath they might have been to put it in such terms.

By non-payment? Non-payment as a campaign by the Anti-Poll Tax Federation and others was but one aspect of the mass agitation, and on its own played a fairly insignificant role in the downfall of the tax. A Glaswegian who stood from gaol as a non-payer in Pollok in the 1992 election polled 20 per cent of the vote, but such isolated demonstrations were more than outweighed by the enfeeblement of the Labour leadership produced by having to wrestle with the issue of non-payment among party activists. However, if non-payment as a campaign was of limited consequence, non-payment as a fact in inner-city areas undoubtedly helped undermine the poll tax. A first principle of taxation is that taxes should be collectable with broad consent. Ultimately the poll tax was not. That sealed its fate.

By critics from professional bodies? Such critics were ignored throughout. Indeed, since they were largely in ignorance of what was going on in Whitehall, their capacity to criticize was limited until the publication of the 1986 Green Paper, by when the government's mind was entirely set.

By the media or by the opposition? The media was unusually ignorant about the internal debate in Whitehall in the course of 1984 and 1985. In part this was because broad unanimity reduces leaks, while Nigel Lawson, the one prominent dissentient, kept clear of lobby journalists. But in part it was the very complexity of the subject (or, as Peter Riddell put it, the 'tedium'), which reduced interest in the issue even after publication of the Green Paper in January 1986. Fortuitously the Westland crisis occupied the political world and the media throughout the later months of 1985 and early 1986, when the key decisions about the poll tax were made and published. Westland was far more exciting for journalists and editors than details of gainers and losers from a tax not due to be introduced in England for another four years. The same applied to

the Labour leadership, which was in any case anxious to steer clear of local government as an issue, for fear of its vote-losing potential with the English middle-classes, fed for the previous five years on a media diet of 'loony-left' scandals in Britain's cities. More public debate could not have done other than make the fate of the poll tax more problematic.

DID THE POLL TAX DESTROY LOCAL GOVERNMENT?

The passage of time has radically altered our perspective on this important question. In the heat of the moment, local government appeared irreversibly, even fatally harmed by the poll tax. Its finances were in chaos. Its capacity to devote itself to anything but crisis-management and survival was minimal. And as the poll tax collapsed, one widely canvassed alternative was to nationalize all local spending, turning local authorities into little more than administrative agents of Whitehall. Had that happened, the prospect of reintroducing a system of local taxation would have been minimal. Even when the decision was taken to opt for a replacement property tax (the council tax) in early 1991, it was presented as a 'last chance'; and it was widely believed that the effect of introducing and managing three local taxes in as many years would cripple the remnants of local government for good.

In the event, such gloomy forebodings were misplaced. The transition to council tax was smooth,[11] and the net effect was to give local government a modernized property tax without the controversy that would inevitably have accompanied the reform had it been introduced as anything other than as a replacement for the poll tax. Furthermore, the Major government has gone some way to mending its fences with local authorities, aided by the final demise of the 'hard left' in the inner cities. At first the *rapprochement* was purely rhetorical, accompanied by a further erosion of local authority powers and a further strengthening of the 'new magistracy' of quangos and appointed bodies.[12] But there are already indications that the late-1980s should be seen as the low-point of local authority influence in recent decades, from which a revival—albeit modest under the present government—is occurring. The government's retreat over some of the centralizing provisions of the 1994 Police and Magistrates' Court Bill, notably the proposal to give the Home Secretary unfettered powers to appoint the chairmen and a third of the members of police authorities in England, is a clear pointer.

In retrospect, the long-term harm done to local government by the poll tax saga lies not in the poll tax itself, but in the raft

[11] See pp. 176–83 above.

[12] See Howard Davis and John Stewart, *The Growth of Government by Appointment: Implications for Local Democracy* (Local Government Management Board, 1993).

of measures which accompanied its rise and fall. Three stand out in particular: the nationalization of the business rate, the enforcement of universal capping of councils' spending, and the establishment of the Local Government Commission. The first reduced by half the proportion of local spending raised locally. The second virtually eliminated local authority discretion over total spending: in the 1994–5 financial year, virtually all councils were spending at their capping 'ceiling', with no legal discretion to increase total spending. As for the Local Government Commission, support for a move to single-tier authorities in the larger cities, and a restructuring of councils in counties with little history or sense of loyalty (notably Humberside and Avon) was desirable, but the decision to opt for wholesale restructuring has lit a fuse of region-by-region controversy likely to take years to burn out.

DID THE POLL TAX DECIDE THE 1992 ELECTION?

In a paradoxical way John Major, although he bore full collective ministerial responsibility for the poll tax, won electoral credit for being the man who got rid of the poll tax. It is also clear that the poll tax evaders who kept themselves off the electoral register were mostly people who would have voted Labour. As we showed in Chapter 11 a responsible estimate suggests that the Conservative majority in 1992 might have been 3 not 21, if this deregistration had not taken place. In the words of the nursery rhyme,

> Out of evil cometh good,
> So don't do everything you should.

14

CONCLUSION

> In the end there is no magic wand which can ensure that
> human decision-makers avoid mistakes.
>
> William Waldegrave in defence of the poll tax, 1993.

William Waldegrave's plea in mitigation for his role in the poll
tax[1] is a fitting challenge for the conclusion. Almost everyone
involved in the design and implementation of the poll tax now
recognises it as a public policy failure of the first magnitude.
But should we follow Waldegrave in consigning it to human
error—the kind of thing that could have happened in any
advanced democracy facing complex problems? Or should we
look for some more fundamental failure?

Manifestly there was human error. No one person was totally
to blame: individual ministers were partly responsible; but so
were groups, such as the initial studies team and successive
cabinet committees. So was the Conservative party as a whole,
which enthusiastically endorsed the poll tax at every opportunity. One might even extend the blame to the Labour party,
whose extreme councils did so much to discredit local government in the early 1980s. Earlier chapters catalogue, in painful
detail, the errors made by individuals, groups and parties, and
in Chapter 13 we reached some tentative verdicts. But we are,
fortunately, not responsible for compiling a definitive list of the
guilty. Readers can make their own judgements.

Yet it appears to us incontrovertible that system failure was
also to blame. The fundamental weakness stares out from the
analytical chapters in the second half of the book: namely, the

---

[1] His full defence, in a 1993 speech to the Social Market Foundation, is
quoted in full on pp. 287–8 above.

'elective dictatorship' which gave the government an almost completely free rein to carry through its poll tax plans.

Two aspects to the 'elective dictatorship' are evident from our study. The first is the absence of checks and balances faced by a government with a secure hold on the Commons. It is a commonly observed weakness.[2] In the case of the poll tax, ministers acted after cursory investigations and virtually no consultation with interested parties. Civil servants at the Department of the Environment developed the policy with barely a word of warning to ministers. Parliament was a rubber stamp. Opposition parties and outside interest groups counted for nothing. Local government, the creature of statute, was powerless to withstand a radical reconstitution of its powers and tax base. We saw in Chapter 8 that claims that the poll tax was forced through the government by Mrs Thatcher and a few cronies are wide of the mark. But the distribution of power *within* the government, however broad, is quite distinct from the existence of external checks on the actions *of* the government. While Mrs Thatcher was Prime Minister it was fashionable to argue—as Michael Heseltine did in his dramatic 1986 resignation—that the replacement of a supposed prime-ministerial autocracy with traditional 'cabinet government' would restore the constitution's checks and balances. It is not that simple.

The second aspect of the 'elective dictatorship' exposed by the poll tax saga is the freedom of a government with a subservient parliament to rewrite the Constitution at will. It might be thought that this is but one dimension of the lack of checks and balances just described. That, however, is not unambiguously the case, for traditional understandings of the Constitution—following Dicey—include the doctrine of the rule of law and an acceptance of established conventions. If conventions did indeed have constitutional force, they might have constrained a government from redefining the role of local government without any semblance of its consent. Certainly, Nigel Lawson, for one, was fully conscious that the government was embarking on radical constitutional reform in its post-1987 local

[2] The most elegant and compelling of recent disquisitions on the theme is Ferdinand Mount, *The British Constitution Now* (1992).

government legislation, which included not only the poll tax but also the abolition of the non-domestic rate, universal capping, compulsory competitive tendering, and a steady erosion in the role of local education authorities. As we saw in Chapter 12, Lawson, the brains behind mid-term Thatcherism, recognised the conventions and was utterly determined to breach them.

Constitutions are not made for all time. They need to be flexible to survive and to meet the needs of modern societies for stable, just administration and democratic self-government. For most of its modern life, Britain's unwritten constitution has proved sufficiently flexible for the job. In many respects it remains serviceable still. But the weakness of checks and balances is an undoubted cancer. Constitutional limitations on government are not 'magic wands', but if carefully constructed they can help to 'ensure that human decision-makers avoid mistakes'. The poll tax makes a powerful case for constructing—in many cases re-constructing—them with urgency.

Where does that leave local government, the recent vicissitudes of which have been central to this study? Local government has a dual role. It should be one of the foremost constitutional checks and balances; and it ought to be a prime organ of democratic self-government in its own right. It currently plays neither role effectively in Britain. Enjoying no guaranteed status, it is liable to be endlessly chopped and changed by central government—particularly governments entrenched in power and determined to brook no opposition from other spheres of political power. And it lacks sufficient autonomy and legitimacy to act as an agent of democratic self-government beyond an increasingly narrow sphere of service-provision.

The poll tax both reflected and exacerbated local government's weakness. Reflected it, because a more robust structure could probably have repelled the poll tax in the first place; and exacerbated it, because the poll tax experience further reduced local fiscal and legal autonomy, bringing local authorities close to the status of local administrations for central government. To reverse the trend, a new relationship will have to be built between local councils and the plethora of quangos—the 'New Magistracy'—established in recent years to take over local functions. The local tax base will also need to be strengthened—most obviously by restoring to local government the non-domestic rate.

Those and a host of other specific measures might be proposed to reinvigorate local government.[3] At best, however, they are a partial remedy. For they do not address the key problem of the role of elected local authorities in modern British government. In Chapter 12 we discussed the fundamental tension in Britain between notions of parliamentary sovereignty and local autonomy. With local authorities ever more emaciated, and about to endure the trauma of a third major reorganization in twenty years, it is coming to be less an ambiguity, and more a resolution in favour of central direction and control. If centralization is to be reversed, it has to be on the basis of a clear vision for the local state—a vision that extends beyond a conception of councils as mere service-providers charged with securing maximum value-for-money for council tax payers.

The absence of such a vision today is not restricted to the governing Conservative party. In a recent Fabian Society paper,[4] one of Labour's more pragmatic council leaders of the 1980s complains that Labour has no over-arching vision of a modernized state in which local councils would have an important role to play. Labour's overriding objective is to win power on the existing terms, and to wield it on those terms—albeit repealing some of the more restrictive pieces of recent local government legislation. For local government to be worth the name, it must be about more than simply providing services: it must be an alternative focus of power to national government, with substantial autonomy buttressed by an independent tax base sufficient to meet a large part of its spending needs. One of the legacies of Thatcherism is that, in its constricted sphere,

[3] For a recent prospectus see Michael Clarke, *The New Local Governance* (European Policy Forum, 1994).

[4] Margaret Hodge and Wendy Thompson, *Beyond the Town Hall: Reinventing Local Government* (Fabian Society Pamphlet 561, 1994).

local government has become a more effective provider of services than at any time since the war. Whether it can also become the means for the community to govern itself is a key test for the next generation.

APPENDIX 1: CHRONOLOGY

1974

12 September: Conservative manifesto pledges to abolish the domestic rating system and replace it by taxes more broadly based and related to people's ability to pay.

1975

9 May: Tony Crosland tells council leaders 'The party's over'.

1976

14 May: Layfield Report on local government finance advocates local income tax and a larger local tax revenue.

1977

30 January: Peter Shore's response to Layfield rejects its dichotomy between centralism and localism in favour of a middle way.

1979

9 April: Tory manifesto makes no mention of replacing rates.

1981

2 June: Heseltine announces targets and penalties to reinforce block grant incentives.

19 October: Madsen Pirie of ASI writes article in *Daily Mail* calling for poll tax.

16 December: Green Paper *Alternatives to Domestic Rates* comes out against poll tax.

1982

30 June: Commons Environment committee rejects poll tax, advocating capital-value-based rates.

1983

9 June: Tories re-elected on manifesto proposing abolition of GLC and metropolitan counties, but retaining rates for foreseeable future.

10 June: Jenkin replaces Heseltine as Environment Secretary.

7 October: White Paper on GLC abolition.

21 December: Rate-capping bill introduced (royal assent 26 June 1984).

1984

24 July: First rate-capping announced.

5 September: First tentative steps towards poll tax. Jenkin gains permission to set up inquiries into alternatives to rates; announced to Tory conference in October.

1985

12 February: New Scottish rateable values announced. Tory disquiet grows.

14 February: Poll tax discussed at Capital Hotel.

31 March: Chequers meeting to discuss poll tax as replacement for rates.

9 April: Adam Smith Institute publishes *Revising the Rating System* by Douglas Mason, advocating poll tax, possibly starting first in Scotland.

2 May: Local elections produce 24 hung councils out of 39 English counties.

9–11 May: Scottish Tory conference determines Younger and Whitelaw to press for poll tax for Scotland; press leaks suggest that poll tax is coming out top in local government finance.

20 May: Cabinet committee begins considering poll tax.

2 September: Jenkin replaced by Baker in reshuffle.

1 October: Kinnock denounces Militant and Liverpool City Council at Labour conference.

3 October: Cabinet committee endorses poll tax.

1986

9 January: Heseltine resigns; Cabinet endorses poll tax.

28 January: *Paying for Local Government* published.

21 February: 121 local authorities rate-capped.

12 March: Waldegrave celebration dinner.

1 April: GLC and Metropolitan counties abolished.

8 May: Liberals win Ryedale; Tories lose 700 seats in local elections.

21 May: Ridley replaces Baker.

9 October: Tory conference endorses poll tax.

25 November: Derek Hatton expelled from Labour party.

26 November: Introduction of poll tax bill for Scotland.

1987

26 February: Rifkind announces Scottish poll tax start on 1 April 1989.

7 May: Local elections.

15 May: Scottish poll tax bill gets royal assent.

11 June: General Election; Tory majority 101; manifesto commitment to poll tax.

6 October: Tory conference revolts against dual-runing and votes for immediate replacement of rates by poll tax; a month later cabinet committee decides to back this.

4 December: Local Government Finance Bill published.

17 December: Local Government Finance Bill, 2nd reading; 17 Tories rebel.

1988

18 April: Mates amendment rejected by 25 votes.

25 April: 3rd reading in Commons; 17 Tories rebel.

5 May: Local elections; Labour net gain of 104 seats.

9 May: 2nd reading of poll tax bill in Lords.

23 May: Lords' vote on banding; key amendment rejected 317 to 183.

27 June: Concessions to exempt a further 25,000 from poll tax announced.

13 July: Bill passes Lords.

29 July: Royal assent for bill.

1989

23 February: Conservative vote drops 24 per cent in Richmond by-election.

1 April: Introduction of poll tax in Scotland.

5 May: Conservatives lose Vale of Glamorgan by-election.

21 July: Kinnock announces Labour review of policy on local government tax.

24 July: Howe removed from Foreign Office in reshuffle. Chris Patten replaces Ridley as Environment Secretary.

7 September: Mrs Thatcher admits troubles with phasing of the tax.

15 September: Figures show 15 per cent of Scots not paying the tax.

11 October: David Hunt (local govt. minister) announces £1.3bn. of relief to cushion poll tax over next two years in speech to Tory conference.

26 October: Nigel Lawson resigns from Treasury.

6 November: Patten claims that average poll tax will be £278 for England if councils spend to government targets.

28 November: Sir A. Meyer stands against Mrs Thatcher for Tory leadership.

5 December: Thatcher re-elected 314–33, 24 spoilt papers.

1990

17 January: CIPFA says poll tax likely to be at least £60 more than the government's estimate of £278.

1 February: Labour launch scheme to replace poll tax.

15 February: Councils given an extra £21m. to administer transitional relief.

16 February: NOP poll shows 73 per cent disagree with poll tax and 64 per cent think it will make them worse off.

28 February: 14 West Oxfordshire Tory councillors, including leader, resign from party over poll tax.

2 March: Wandsworth sets lowest poll tax in England.

5 March: Four Haringey left-wing councillors resign in protest at poll tax of £573.

6 March: Demonstrations against poll tax across Britain.

20 March: Budget gives poll tax rebate to 250,000 pensioners.

22 March: Mid-Staffordshire by-election lost to Labour in 21 per cent swing.

30 March: Trafalgar Square anti-poll tax demonstration turns into a riot; 300 injured, 308 arrested.

1 April: Introduction of poll tax.

3 April: Patten announces 20 authorities to be charge-capped (Lambeth later added).

11 April: ICM poll shows 24 per cent Labour lead, increased despite Trafalgar Sq. riots.

29 April: Thatcher sets up cabinet committee to review poll tax.

3 May: Local elections: Baker presents Tory success in Wandsworth and Westminster as vindication of poll tax.

4 May: Michael Portillo appointed poll tax minister with job of selling the tax to the public.

17 May: Mrs Thatcher chairs first meeting of poll tax review group.

23 June: High Court rules charge-capping lawful; so does Court of Appeal 27 June.

29 June: Portillo rules out major changes in poll tax in speech to ADC.

8 July: Bow Group magazine condemns poll tax as financial and political disaster.

19 July: Patten announces £3.26bn. of extra transitional relief for 1991–2, aimed at ensuring average poll tax of £379, and new capping criteria.

25 July: Labour launches fair rates.

6 August: Start of Gulf crisis.

14 August: Institute of Public Finance survey shows 1 in 5 have still not paid any poll tax.

7 September: Lord Sanderson replaces Michael Forsyth as Tory party chairman in Scotland.

20 September: More violent demonstrations in London.

24 September: High Court rules against government, holding Lambeth's £521 poll tax lawful (Patten had ordered them to reduce it to £493).

18 October: Liberal Democrats win Eastbourne by-election.

31 October: Patten announces £1.9bn. package to keep poll tax down and stiffer capping criteria.

1 November: Howe resigns.

13 November: Howe's resignation speech.

14 November: Heseltine launches leadership bid.

27 November: Major elected Tory leader.

28 November: Heseltine replaces Patten as Environment Secretary.

5 December: Heseltine announces review of local government finance and organization.

1991

6 January: Major says total abolition of poll tax not on the agenda.

11 January: Audit Commission warns that poll tax may need an identity card scheme to survive.

7 March: Liberal Democrats win Ribble Valley by-election.

17 March: MORI survey shows councils in England and Wales recruited an extra 11,600 staff to administer poll tax, at estimated cost of £232m. a year.

19 March: Lamont announces £140 cut in poll tax.

21 March: Heseltine announces draft results of poll tax review.

26 March: Bill to switch funding from poll tax to VAT voted through Commons in one day.

3 April: 14 councils (3 Tory) charge-capped.

20 April: Labour launches revised 'fair-rates' policy.

16 April: Liberal Democrats launch local income tax.

23 April: Government announces abolition of poll tax and replacement by council tax.

2 May: Local elections.

16 May: Conservatives lose Monmouth by-election.

21 May: Announcement of emergency legislation to allow tighter capping.

19 June: Liverpool Council votes to privatize refuse collection service.

7 July: Labour MP Terry Fields imprisoned for refusing to pay poll tax.

22 July: Major launches Citizens' Charter.

23 July: 8th band added to council tax.

30 July: Green Paper on local government organization floats idea of directly elected local mayors.

1 November: Council tax bill introduced.

26 November: Tougher capping rules announced, with ceilings on spending of all councils.

1992

Jan–May: Valuations for poll tax bands carried out.

9 April: General Election: Conservative majority 21.

11 April: Howard replaces Heseltine as Environment Secretary.

7 May: Local elections; strong Tory showing.

12 November: Howard announces tough capping rules for all councils.

1993

1 April: Introduction of council tax.

APPENDIX 2

APPENDIX 2: KEY PEOPLE AND EVENTS 1984–1992

	Secretary of State	Minister	Permanent Secretary	Deputy Secretary	Under Secretary	Key Events
Sept. 1984	P. Jenkin (June 1983)	K. Baker (Sept. 1984)	Sir G. Moseley (1981)	T. Heiser (1981)	P. Owen (1984)	'Studies' start (Sept. 1984)
1985	K. Baker Sept. 1985	W. Waldegrave Sept. 1985	(Sir) T. Heiser Feb. 1985	K. Ennals Feb. 1985	C. Brearley March 1985	Chequers Meeting March 1985
1986	N. Ridley May 1986	R. Boyson Sept. 1986				Green Paper Jan. 1986 / Scots Bill Nov. 1986
1987		M. Howard June 1987			D. Osborn Nov. 1987	Gen. Election June 1987 / E&W Bill Nov. 1987
1988		J. S. Gummer July 1988			N. Summerton Aug. 1988	Act passed July 1988
1989	C. Patten July 1989	D. Hunt July 1989				Scot tax starts April 1989
1990	M. Heseltine Nov. 1990	M. Portillo May 1990		C. Brearley Jan. 1990		Riots; Tax starts April 1990 / Thatcher falls Nov. 1990
1991					P. Britton	Council tax May 1991
1992	M. Howard April 1992	J. Redwood April 1992	R. Wilson Sept. 1992			Gen. election April 1992

APPENDIX 3

GAINS AND LOSSES BY HOUSEHOLD TYPE AND INCOME LEVEL
(from 1981 Heseltine Green Paper)
Gain or loss as percentage of net household income

HOUSEHOLD TYPE

	1 Single adult earner			2 Two adults, one earner			3 Two adults, both earners			4 Two adults, 1–2 children, one earner		
	% average	Average	1½ average	% average	Average	1½ average	% average	Average	1½ average	% average	Average	1½ average
LONDON & SOUTH EAST												
Local sales tax	4.0%*	1.6%	-0.1%	3.5%*	1.8%	0.6%	1.4%	-0.1%	-1.3%		1.4%	0.0%
Local income tax	2.0%	-0.9%	-3.0%	2.0%	-0.6%	-2.5%	1.0%	-1.5%	-3.4%		-0.8%	-2.5%
Polltax	3.0%*	2.3%	1.7%	0.9%*	.0%	1.0%	0.6%	0.5%	0.5%		0.9%	1.0%
Gross household income	£85	£127	£190	£114	£171	£256	£148	£222	£333		£179	£269
Net household income	£61	£87	£126	£83	£119	£176	£112	£159	£228		£135	£196
REST OF ENGLAND												
Local sales tax	3.7%*	1.3%	-0.5%	2.5%*	1.0%	-0.2%	0.5%	-1.3%	-1.5%		0.7%	-0.6%
Local income tax	1.8%*	-0.9%	-2.9%	1.7%*	-0.9%	-2.7%	0.9%	-2.2%	-3.4%		-0.8%	-2.8%
Poll tax	1.7%	1.4%	1.1%	-1.4%	-0.7%	-0.2%	-0.7%	-1.0%	-0.1%		-0.2%	0.0%
Gross household income	£72	£108	£162	£92	£137	£206	£129	£193	£290		£153	£229
Net household income	£53	£75	£109	£69	£98	£141	£100	£141	£201		£118	£168
SCOTLAND												
Local sales tax	1.9%*	0.4%$	-0.6%	1.9%*	1.1%	0.4%	0.3%	-0.8%	-1.6%		0.6%	-0.2%
Local income tax	0.5%*	-2.0%	-3.9%	0.3%*	-1.9%	-3.4%	0.2%	-2.1%	-3.9%		-2.1%	-3.5%
Poll tax	1.2%	1.1%	1.0%	-0.9%	-0.1%	0.4%	-0.7%	-0.2%	0.2%		0.3%	0.7%
Gross household income	£74	£111	£166	£106	£159	£239	£132	£198	£297		£182	£273
Net household income	£54	£77	£111	£78	£112	£164	£103	£144	£205		£136	£199
WALES												
Local sales tax	3.0%*	1.0%	-0.4%	1.7%*	0.1%	-1.0%	-0.4%	-0.9%	-1.3%		0.4%	-0.6%
Local income tax	0.3%*	-1.8%	-3.3%	0.1%*	-1.8%	-3.3%	-0.2%	-2.1%	-3.6%		-1.6%	-3.0%
Poll tax	1.1%	1.0%	0.8%	-0.9%	-0.4%	-0.1%	-0.6%	-0.3%	-0.1%		0.1%	0.2%
Gross household income	£69	£103	£155	£92	£138	£207	£125	£188	£282		£150	£225
Net household income	£51	£72	£104	£70	£98	£142	£98	£137	£196		£116	£165

GAINS AND LOSSES BY HOUSEHOLD TYPE AND INCOME LEVEL (continued)

Gain or loss as percentage of net household income

HOUSEHOLD TYPE

	5 Two adults, 1–2 children, two earners			6 Two adults, 3+ children, one earner			7 Two adults, 3+ children, two earners			8 Three or more adults, two earners			9 Three or more adults, three or more earners		
	½ average	Average	1½ average	½ average	Average	1½ average	½ average	Average	1½ average	½ average	Average	1½ average	½ average	Average	1½ average
LONDON & SOUTH EAST															
Local sales tax	1.8%*	0.5%	-0.4%	2.6%*	1.1%	-0.1%	1.7%	0.8%	0.0%	1.2%*	-1.8%	-0.8%	0.3%	-0.9%	-1.6%
Local income tax	1.5%*	-0.8%	-2.6%	1.2%	-1.0%	-2.6%	1.6%*	-0.5%	-2.4%	0.1%	-2.1%	-3.6%	-0.2%	-2.3%	-4.0%
Polltax	0.8%*	0.9%	0.9%	1.0%*	1.0%	1.0%*	0.9%	1.0%	1.0%	-0.8%	-0.2%	0.3%	-0.7%	-0.3%	0.0%
Gross household income	£141	£212	£318	£127	£191	£287	£129	£210	£316	£136	£278	£418	£216	£334	£487
Net household income	£107	£163	£229	£113	£152	£219	£123	£172	£238	£194	£223	£282	£163	£230	£331
REST OF ENGLAND															
Local sales tax	1.0%*	-0.2%	-1.1%	1.6%*	0.6%	-0.1%	0.8%	-0.2%	-0.9%	0.4%	-0.7%	-1.6%	-0.5%	-1.5%	-2.2%
Local income tax	1.3%*	-0.9%	-2.8%	0.6%*	-1.2%	-2.6%	0.9%*	-1.1%	-2.9%	0.1%	-2.3%	-4.0%	-0.7%	-2.6%	-4.2%
Poll tax	-0.4%*	-0.1%	0.1%	-0.6%*	-0.1%	0.3%	-0.3%	-0.1%	0.1%	-2.7%*	-1.8%	-1.2%	-1.9%	-1.2%	-0.7%
Gross household income	£123	£185	£277	£109	£164	£246	£131	£196	£295	£149	£223	£334	£197	£295	£443
Net household income	£107	£146	£203	£101	£135	£190	£123	£164	£225	£113	£159	£228	£151	£212	£304
SCOTLAND															
Local sales tax	1.3%*	-0.1%	-1.2%	2.3%*	0.7%	-0.7%	1.8%	0.4%	-0.7%	1.3%	-0.5%	-1.8%	0.0%	-1.4%	-2.3%
Local income tax	0.9%*	-1.6%	-3.6%	0.7%*	-1.6%	-3.3%	-1.7%	-0.7%	-2.8%	-0.4%	-2.8%	-4.7%	-0.8%	-3.0%	-4.8%
Poll tax	0.1%*	0.2%	0.2%	0.7%*	0.9%*	0.7%	0.7%*	0.7%	0.7%	-1.5%	-1.0%	-0.6%	-1.1%	-0.9%	-0.4%
Gross household income	£133	£200	£299	£123	£185	£277	£127	£190	£285	£167	£250	£375	£207	£310	£466
Net household income	£114	£155	£217	£110	£148	£212	£120	£166	£219	£124	£176	£254	£157	£221	£318
WALES															
Local sales tax	0.2%	-0.5%	-0.9%	0.9%*	-0.1%	-0.9%	0.0%*	-0.6%	-1.0%	0.0%*	-1.0%	-1.6%	-0.7%	-1.4%	-1.8%
Local income tax	-0.3%*	-1.7%	-3.0%	-0.1%*	-1.8%	-3.0%	-0.2%*	-1.6%	-2.8%	-1.4%	-2.9%	-4.1%	-1.3%	-2.8%	-4.0%
Poll tax	-0.4%	0.1%	0.5%	0.0%*	0.1%	0.3%	-0.3%	0.2%	0.5%	-1.6%	-0.9%	-0.5%	-1.1%	-0.6%	-0.3%
Gross household income	£130	£195	£293	£110	£164	£247	£132	£198	£296	£162	£243	£364	£198	£297	£446
Net household income	£112	£152	£213	£102	£136	£190	£123	£164	£226	£121	£172	£247	£152	£213	£306

*Indicates households eligible for rate rebates. If they were claimed, gains would be lower and losses higher.

BIBLIOGRAPHY

Adeney, M., and Lloyd, J. (1986), *The Miners' Strike 1984–5*. Routledge & Kegan Paul.

Adonis, A. (1993), *Parliament Today*. Manchester University Press.

—— (1993), *Making Aristocracy Work: The Peerage and the Political System in Britain 1884–1914*. Clarendon.

—— and Hames, T. (1994), *A Conservative Revolution: The Thatcher–Reagan Decade in Perspective*. Manchester University Press.

Alexander, A. (1985), 'Structure, Centralization and the Position of Local Government', in M. Loughlin, M. D. Gelfand, and K. Young (eds.), *Half a Century of Municipal Decline 1935–1985*.

Audit Commission (1984), *The Impact on Local Authorities Economy, Efficiency and Effectiveness of the Block Grant Distribution System*.

—— (1993), *The Sooner the Better: Progress Report on the Council Tax*.

Bagehot, W. (1867), *The English Constitution* (but see Fontana edition (1963) for R. H. S. Crossman's new preface. See also the World's Classics edn. 1928 for A. J. Balfour's preface).

Baker, K. (1993), *The Turbulent Years*. Faber.

Bailey, S., and Paddison, R. (1988), *The Reform of Local Government Finance in Britain*. Routledge.

Benn, T. (1992), *The End of an Era: Diaries 1980–1990*. Hutchinson.

Blackstone, T., and Plowden, W. (1990), *Inside the Think Tank: Advising the Cabinet 1971–1983*. Heinemann.

Bloch, A. (1990), *The Community Charge in England*. York: Joseph Rowntree Foundation.

—— and John, P. (1991), *Attitudes to Local Government: A Survey of Electors*.

Bogdanor, V. (1979), *Devolution*. Oxford University Press.

Bruce-Gardyne, J. (1986), *Ministers and Mandarins*.

Bulpitt, J. (1983), *Territory and Power in the United Kingdom: An Interpretation*.

Burns, D. (1992), *Poll Tax Rebellion*. Stirling: AK Press.

Butcher, H., Law, I., Leach, E., and Mullard, M. (1990), *Local Government and Thatcherism*. Routledge.

Butler, D., and Butler, G. (1994), *British Political Facts 1900–1994*. Macmillan.

Butler, D., and Kavanagh, D. (1988), *The British General Election of 1987*. Macmillan.
—— —— (1992), *The British General Election of 1992*. Macmillan.
Byrne, T. (1992), *Local Government in Britain*. Penguin.
Cannan, E. (1912), *History of Local Rates in England*. London: PS King.
Carvel, J. (1984), *Citizen Ken*, Chatto & Windus.
Centre for Community Studies (1991), *The Poll-Tax: Proposals for Reform*.
Central Policy Review Staff (1977), *Relations between Central Government and Local Authorities*.
Chartered Institute of Public Finance and Accountancy (1986), *Response to 'Paying for Local Government' (Cmnd. 9714)*, CIPFA.
—— (1993), *A Councillor's Guide to Local Government Finance*, CIPFA.
Clarke, A. (1993), *Diaries*. Weidenfield & Nicolson.
Clarke, M. (1994), *The New Local Governance* (European Policy Forum).
Committee of Public Accounts (1985), *Operation of the Rate Support Grant System*, HC47 1985–6.
Conservative Party (1979), *The Conservative Manifesto 1979*.
—— (1987), *Campaign Guide 1987*.
—— (1989), *Community Charge: The Fair Way to Pay*.
—— (1992), *The Next Moves Forward: The Conservative Manifesto*.
Crick, M, and Van Klaveren, A. (1991), 'Poll Tax: Mrs Thatcher's Greatest Blunder', *Contemporary Record*, 5/3 (1991).
Crosland, S. (1982), *Tony Crosland*. Coronet.
Crossman, R. (1975), *The Diaries of a Cabinet Minister*, Cape/Hamish Hamilton.
Davies, A., and Willman, J. (1991), *What Next: Agencies, Departments and the Civil Service*.
Davis, H., and Stewart, J. (1993), *The Growth of Government by Appointment: Implications for Local Democracy*. (Local Government Management Board).
Deacon, D., and Golding, P. (1991) 'When Ideology Fails: The Flagship of Thatcherism and the Local and National Media', *European Journal of Communications*, 6 (1991), 291–303.
Dept. of the Environment (1971), *The Future Shape of Local Government Finance*, Cmnd. 4741,
—— (1977), *Local Government Finance*, Cmnd. 6813.
—— (1981), *Alternatives to Domestic Rates*, Cmnd. 8449.

Dept. of the Environment (1983), *Rates*, Cmnd. 9008.

—— (1986*a*), *Paying for Local Government*, Cmnd. 9714.

—— (1986*b*), '*Paying for Local Government: Summary of responses to the Green Paper in England*,' Dept. of the Environment unpublished paper.

—— (1987), 'Rate Reform Exemplifications', Press Notice No. 162, Dept. of the Environment.

—— (1991), *A New Tax for Local Government: A Consultation Paper*, Dept. of the Environment.

Dept. of Health and Social Security (1985), *Reform of Social Security: Programme for Action*, Cmnd. 9691.

Dicey, A. V. (8th edn. 1915), *Introduction to the Study of the Law of the Constitution*. Macmillan.

Downs, A. (1957), *An Economic Theory of Democracy*. New York: Harper & Row.

Drewry, G. (ed.) (1989), *The New Select Committees*. Clarendon.

—— and Butcher, T. (1991), *The Civil Service Today*, 2nd edn. Blackwell.

Dunleavy, P. (1991), *Urban Political Analysis*. Macmillan.

Dunn, D. (1990), *Poll Tax and the Fiscal Fake*. Chatto & Windus.

Dyer, C. (1984), 'The Social and Economic Background to the Rural Revolt of 1381', in R. H. Hilton and T. H. Aston (eds), *The English Rising of 1381*, Cambridge University Press.

Economist, The (1985), 'How the Tories Muffed Reform', 16 Mar. 1985.

Environment Committee (1982), *Enquiry into Methods of Financing Local Government in the Context of the Government Green Paper (Cmnd. 8449)*, i–iii, House of Commons Papers 217.

Esam, P. (1992), *Ability to Pay?* Assoc. of Metro Auths, CPAG, LGIU.

Fletcher, M. (1992), *Poll Tax: A Short Sharp History*. Reading: Seventy Press.

Foley, M. *The Rise of the Modern Presidency*. Manchester University Press.

Forsyth, M. (1985), *The Case for a Poll Tax*, Conservative Political Centre.

Foster, C. D. (1977), 'Central Government's Response to the Layfield Committee', Paper given at the 1977 Conference of the Chartered Institute of Public Finance and Accountancy, Centre for Environmental Studies.

—— and Jackman, R. (1982), 'Accountability and Control of Local Spending', *Public Money*, 2/2.

—— —— and Perlman, M. (1980), *Local Government Finance in a Unitary State*. Allen & Unwin.

Fry, G. (1985), *The Changing Civil Service*. Allen & Unwin.

Gibb, K. (1988), *The Community Charge and Local Government.* Glasgow: University of Glasgow Centre for Housing Research.

Gibson, J. (1990), *The Politics and Economics of the Poll Tax: Mrs Thatcher's Downfall.* Warley: EMAS.

—— and Stewart, J. (1992) 'Poll tax, Rates and Local Elections', *Political Studies*, 40/3: 20.

Gordon, J. (1989), *The Poll Tax as a Rate-Payers' Revolt.* London: Suntory–Toyota International Centre for Economics and Related Disciplines.

Grant, M. (1984), *Rate Capping and the Law*, Association of Metropolitan Authorities.

Griffith, J. A. G. (1974), *Parliamentary Scrutiny of Government Bills.* Allen & Unwin.

—— and Ryle, M. (1989), *Parliament: Functions, Practices and Procedures.* ALDN: Sweet & Maxwell.

Gyford, J. (1984), *Local Politics in Britain.* Croom Helm.

Hale, R. (1985), *Poll Tax: Some Initial Analyses* (CIPFA).

Hawes, D. (1993), *Power on the Back-Benches: The Growth of Select Committee Influence.* Bristol: SAUS.

Heath, A. *et al.* (1991), *Understanding Political Change.* Pergamon.

—— (1994), *Labour's Last Chance? The 1992 Election and Beyond.* Dartmouth.

Heclo, H., and Wildavsky, A. (1974), *The Private Government of Public Money.* Macmillan.

Heddle, J. (1980), *The Great Rate Debate.*

Helm, D., and Smith, S. (1987), 'Decentralization and Local Government', *Oxford Review of Economic Policy*, Oxford University Press.

Hennessy, P. (1986), *Cabinet.* Blackwell.

—— (1989), *Whitehall.* Fontana.

Hepworth, N. P. (1976), *The Finance of Local Government*, Allen & Unwin.

Heseltine, M. (1990), *Where There's a Will.* Hutchinson.

Hills. J., and Sutherland, H. (1991), *Banding, Tilting, Gearing, Gaining and Losing: An Anatomy of the Proposed Council Tax.* (Suntory–Toyota International Centre for Economics).

Hilton, R., and Aston, T. (eds.) (1984), *The English Rising of 1381.* Cambridge University Press.

Jackman, R. (1985), 'Local Government Finance', in Martin Loughlin, M. David Gelfand and Ken Young (eds.), *Half a Century of Municipal Decline 1935–1985.*

Hodge, M., and Thompson, W. (1994), *Beyond the Town Hall: Reinventing Local Government* (Fabian Society Pamphlet 561).

Jenkins, Simon (1989), 'Ring-a-ring of taxes . . . all fall down', *Sunday Times*, 15 Oct. 1989.

Jones, G. W., and Stewart, J. D. (1983), *The Case for Local Government*. Allen & Unwin.

Jordan, A. G., and Richardson, J. (1987), *British Politics and the Policy Process*. Unwin Hyman.

Keith-Lucas, B., and Richards, P. G. (1980), *A History of Local Government in the Twentieth Century*. Allen & Unwin.

Kellner, P., and Crowther-Hunt, N. (1980), *The Civil Servants: An Enquiry into Britain's Ruling Class*. Macdonald.

Kelly, R. (1989), *Conservative Party Conferences: The Hidden System*. Manchester University Press.

Kemp, P. (1993), *Beyond Next Steps*. Social Market Foundation Paper 17.

Kennedy, A. L. (1953), *Salisbury*. London: John Murray.

King, A. S., (1985), *The British Prime Minister*, 2nd edn. Macmillan.

King, D. (1984), *Fiscal Tiers*. Allen & Unwin.

Labour Party (1987), *Britain Will Win*, Labour Manifesto.

Lawson, N. (1992), *The View from No. 11: Memoirs of a Tory Radical*. Bantam.

Layfield, F. (1976), *Local Government Finance*. Report of the Committee of Enquiry, Cmnd. 6453.

Lijphart, A. (1984) *Democracies: Patterns of Majoritarian and Consensual Government in Thirty-One Countries*. Yale University Press.

Loughlin, M., Gelfand, M. D., and Young, K. (1985), *Half a Century of Municipal Decline, 1885–1935*. Allen & Unwin.

Lynn, J., and Jay, A. (1985), *The Complete Yes Prime Minister: The Diaries of Sir James Hacker*. BBC.

MacGregor, S. (1988), *The Poll Tax and the Enterprise Culture*. Manchester: Centre for Local Economic Strategies.

—— (1991), *The Poll Tax: Flagship of Folly*.

McKenzie, R. T. (1963), *British Political Parties*. Heinemann.

Mackintosh, J. P. (1977), *The British Cabinet*. Stevens.

McKisack, M. (1959), *The Fourteenth Century*. Oxford University Press.

McLean, I. (1994), 'The Poll Tax and the Electoral Register', ch. 13 in Heath, A. *et al.* (1994).

Mason, D. (1985), *Revising the Rating System*, Adam Smith Institute.

Mayhew, D. (1974), *Congress: The Electoral Connection*. Yale University Press.

Midwinter, A. and Monaghan, C. (1993), *From Rates to the Poll Tax*.

Mill, J. S. (1861), *Representative Government*. Dent.

Miller, W. (1988), *Irrelevant Elections? The Quality of Local Democracy in Britain*. Clarendon.

Minister of Housing and Local Government (1966), *Local Government Finance England and Wales*, Cmnd. 2923.

Morley, J. (1889), *Walpole*. Macmillan.

Mount, F. (1990), 'Band-aid: Adding a Moral Dimension to the Poll Tax', *Daily Telegraph*, 6 Apr. 1990.

—— (1992), *The British Constitution Now*.

National Audit Office (1985), Dept. of the Environment: *Operation of the Rate Support Grant System*, HC 313, Session 1985–6.

Norton, P. (1980), *Dissension in the House of Commons 1974–79*. Clarendon.

Offer, A. (1981), *Property and Politics, 1870–1914: Landownership, Law, Ideology and Urban Development in England*. Cambridge University Press.

Oman, C. (1906), *The Great Revolt of 1381*. Clarendon.

Pearce, E. (1993), *Machiavelli's Children*. Gollancz.

Pimlott, B. (1991), *Harold Wilson*. Harper Collins.

Pliatzky, L. (1989), *The Treasury under Mrs Thatcher*. Blackwell.

Rallings, C., and Thrasher, M. (1991), The Impact of the Community Charge on Electoral Behaviour? *Parliamentary Affairs* 172–84.

—— —— (1993), in I. Crewe *et al. British Parties and Elections Year Book*.

Rating and Valuation Association (1987), *Community Charge/Poll Tax: The Facts*.

Redcliffe-Maud, Lord (Chairman) (1969), *Report of the Royal Commission on Local Government in England*, Cmnd. 4040.

Rhodes, R. A. W. (1986), *The National World of Local Government*. Allen & Unwin.

Riddell, P. (1993), *The Thatcher Era and its Legacy*. Blackwell,

—— (1993), *Honest Opportunism: The Rise of the Career Politician*. Hamish Hamilton.

Ridley, N. (1988), *The Local Right: Enabling not Providing* (Policy Study No. 92, Centre for Policy Studies).

—— (1991), 'No Room for Much Review', *Guardian*, 8 Mar.

—— (1991), *My Style of Government*. Fontana.

Robinson, A., and Sandford, C. (1983), *Tax Policy-Making in the United Kingdom*.

Roots, G. (1990), *Ryde on Rating and the Community Charge*. Butterworths.

Rose, R. (1991), 'The Political Economy of Cabinet Change', in F. Vibert (ed.), *Britain's Constitutional Future*. Inst. of Economic Affairs, IEA Reading 36.

Russell, C. (1987), 'England's Last Poll Tax', *History Today*, 37.

—— (1991), *The Fall of the British Monarchies 1637–1642*. Clarendon.

Sage, L. (1990), *Paying to be Poor*.

Sampson, A. (1992), *The Union Response to the Poll Tax*.

Secretary of State for Scotland and Minister of Housing and Local Government (1965), *Committee of Inquiry into the Impact of Rates on Households*, Cmnd. 2582.

Shell, D. (1993), *The House of Lords at Work*, 2nd edn. Harvester Wheatsheaf.

Shepherd, R. (1991), *The Power-Brokers*. Hutchinson.

Smith, J. (1993), 'The UK Poll Tax and the Declining Electorate.'

Smith, S., and Squire, D. (1987), *Local Taxes and Local Government*, Institute for Fiscal Studies.

Stewart, J. G. (1986), *The New Management of Local Government*. Allen & Unwin for Inlogov.

—— and Stoker, G. (1989), *The Future of Local Government*. Macmillan Education.

Stoker, G. (1991), *The Politics of Local Government*. Macmillan Education.

Thatcher, M. (1993), *The Downing Street Years*. Harper Collins.

Travers, T. (1986), *The Politics of Local Government Finance*. Allen & Unwin.

Tuck, J. A. (1984), 'Nobles, Commons and the Great Revolt of 1381', in R. H. Hilton and T. H. Aston (eds.), *The English Rising of 1381*. Cambridge University Press.

Waldegrave, W. (1978), *Binding Leviathan*. Hamish Hamilton.

—— (1993), *The Reality of Reform and Accountability in Today's Public Service* (Public Finance Foundation Lecture).

—— (1993), *Reforming the Role of Government* (Social Market Foundation Lecture).

Ward, M. (1990), *Guide to the Community Charge*. CPAG/ Institute of Housing.

Widdicombe, D. (1986), *The Conduct of Local Authority Business* Cmnd. 9797.

Willetts, D. (1992), *Modern Conservatism*.

Wright, V., and Meny, Y. (eds.) (1985) *Centre/ Periphery Relations in Western Europe*. Allen & Unwin.

Young, H. *One of Us* (2nd ed. 1991). Macmillan.
—— and Sloman, A. (1985), *No, Minister.* BBC.
Young, K. (1975), *Local Politics and the Rise of Party: The London Municipal Society and Conservative Intervention in Local Elections 1894–1963.* Leicester University Press.
—— (ed.) (1989), *New Directions for County Government.*
—— (1989), *The Conduct of Local Authority Business since Widdicombe,* Joseph Rowntree Memorial Trust.

INDEX

Abolition of Domestic Rates (etc.)
  Scotland Bill (1986) 102–3, 104,
  229–30, 291
accountability 51, 67, 97, 109, 199, 276,
  290, 297
  aim of increasing 50, 56, 58–9, 113,
    247, 261, 283, 296
  electorate's contact with councillors
    272–3
  financial 156
  improving 89, 100, 226; radical idea
    for 296
  recommendation to improve 73
  strengthened 66, 105
'Accrington' problem 81
Acton 112
Adam Smith Institute 71, 72, 177, 262,
  286
Adley, R. 236
administrative arguments/problems 56,
  94, 97, 109, 219, 276, 279, 280
Aitken, J. 236
Alexander, A. 22 n.
All Souls, Oxford 48, 50
Allason, R. 236
Allen Committee report (1965) 17, 18
Amery, L. S. 224
Ancram, Michael 59, 63, 70, 74, 102,
  103–4
anti-poll tax campaigns 130
  All-Britain Anti-Poll Tax Federation
    151
  Anti-Poll Tax Federation 134, 298
  British Anti-Poll Tax Federation
    131, 259
  'Can't pay, won't pay' 262
  non-implementation 279
  rallies 297
  see also non-payment; demonstrations
Armstrong, Sir Robert (Lord) 68, 207,
  217–18
Asquith, H. H. 189, 268

Association for the Protection of
  Property Owners 15
Association of District Councils 165
Association of Metropolitan Authorities
  175
Attlee, Clement (Earl) 5, 190
Audit Commission 159, 167, 178, 182 n.,
  276, 281 n.
  reports on block grants system 42,
    51, 83

back-benchers, see Tory back-bench
  MPs
Bagehot, Walter 185, 187, 188, 244
bailiffs 134, 167, 279
Baker, Kenneth 27 n., 28–9, 42, 52–6
  passim, 58, 59, 63 n., 66 n., 68, 70,
    74 n., 78, 84, 86, 96, 109, 126,
    138, 142, 143 n., 148, 150, 151,
    154, 156, 194, 206, 210, 251, 265,
    271, 290
  alarmed by work on distributional
    impact of poll tax 293
  blame for poll tax disaster from
    Labour 179
  enthusiasm 5
  exposition of inadequacies of existing
    system of local government finance
    72–3
  fight for dual-running 111
  flair for presentation 60
  Jenkin replaced at Environment by 82
  keen to see safety net abolished 144
  move from D.o.E to Education 98,
    198
  next to no resistance to capping 272
  parading the virtues of 'flagship'
    authorities 161
  proposal to exempt students 291
  'conference darling' 250
  safeguards envisaged in original
    scheme 193

Baker, Kenneth (cont.):
  Thatcher convinced by the work of
    76
  Tyrie's critical minute to 79
  Waldegrave–Baker Studies 46–50, 77,
    81, 84, 95, 99, 126, 141, 199, 206,
    250, 272, 286–7, 296–7;
  see also Green Papers (1986)
Baldwin, Stanley, Earl 247
Balfour, Arthur, Earl 248
Balladur, Edouard 258 n.
Bancroft, Sir Ian 211 n.
banding, see poll tax; property tax
Banham, Sir John 42, 181
Basildon 140
Bath 160, 179
Beamish, Sir Tufton, see Chelwood
Beaumont-Dark, Anthony 39, 235, 236
Beloff, Lord 122
benefit system 151
Benn, Tony 130, 152, 153, 208 n., 209
Benyon, William 39, 236
Berkshire 148
Beveridge, Lord 211
bicameral systems 225, 228–9
Biffen, John 45, 103, 236
Birmingham 149, 268
bishops 124, 198
Blackpool conferences:
  (1985) 85, 86
  (1987) 110, 113, 140, 220, 249
  (1989) 144
block grants 27, 42, 51, 83, 84
Blunkett, David 116
Bonsor, Sir Nicholas 236
Bournemouth 100, 167
Boyson, Sir Rhodes 99, 100, 109, 139,
    146–7, 236
Bradford 149, 261
Brearley, Chris 96, 109, 142, 159, 170,
    171, 173
Brent 101, 106, 145, 256
Brereton, Don 47
Bright, Roger 47, 50, 59, 173
Brighton conference (1984) 45, 46, 88,
    250, 251
Bristol 149
British Board of Agrément 229
British Constitution 3, 7, 229, 242, 248,
    271, 273

checks and balances 303, 304
British Rail 96
British Telecom 49
British Waterways Board 230
Brittan, Sir Leon 70, 75, 78, 80–1, 110,
    287
  pressure on D.o.E to bring down
    local authority expenditure 37, 38
Brixton 32
Brooke, Henry (Lord) 197 n.
Bruce, I. 236
Bruce-Gardyne, Jock, Lord 198 n.,
    208 n.
Buchanan-Smith, Alick 136, 236
Buck, Sir Antony 236
Buckinghamshire 140
Bulpitt, James 8 n., 269
Burns, Sir Terence 173
by-elections:
  Eastbourne 168, 256, 294
  Glasgow: Central 134; Govan 131,
    257–58
  Mid-Staffordshire 151, 256
  Ribble Valley 173, 174, 255 n., 256

Cabinet 187–205, 287, 288, 292, 303
  misleading image of omnipotence
    243–5
Callaghan, James (Lord) 101, 189, 191,
    194
Camden 28, 43, 65, 128
Cannan, Edwin 17–18
Capita (consultancy) 280
capping, see rate-capping
Carpenter, Michael 142, 159
Carrington, Lord 61, 123 n.
Carvel, J. 28 n.
Catholic Schools 258 n.
CBI (Confederation of British
    Industries) 42
  Scottish 136
CCLGF (Consultative Council for
    Local Government Finance) 222,
    277
Central Office of Information 263
centralization 202, 272
Centre for Environmental Studies 49
Centre for Policy Studies 99, 148
Chamberlain, Joseph 268
Chamberlain, Neville 6

Chapman, Sydney 29
Charles I, King 13
Cheltenham 154
Chelwood, Lord (Sir Tufton Beamish) 123, 241
Chequers meetings:
  (1984) 45
  (1985) 65, 70–7, 81, 82, 87, 99n., 192, 194–6 passim, 202, 212, 216, 250, 287, 288, 297
Child Poverty Action Group 262
Chope, Christopher 99, 100, 127, 173, 263
Church of England 7
Churchill, Sir Winston 1, 189, 190
CIPFA (Chartered Institute of Public Finance and Accountancy) 97, 127, 135, 163, 178, 233, 276, 281, 283
civil disobedience 11, 155
civil liberties 75, 79, 104, 216
civil service 174, 206–23, 270
  Scottish 277
Clare College, Cambridge 122
Clark, Alan 126
Clarke, Charles 106
coalitions 258, 259, 274
Cockeram, Michael 94
collective ministerial responsibility 210, 301
Committee of Public Accounts 84 n.
computer companies 279, 280
concessions 166, 169
Conservative Party:
  British Constitution in microcosm 248
  Campaign Guide (1987) 105
  Central Office 137, 156
  democracy within 247–53
  election losses: by-elections 29, 151, 256; local 28; metropolitan county and district 160
  élite firmly entrenched in government and power 275
  Late-Victorian 14
  leadership elections 142, 168, 169, 248, 253, 293–4, 295
  life peerage a bastion of 243
  local activists played role in the evolution of poll tax policy 246

local election campaign (1990) 156
lower-middle and skilled-working class support for 79
manifestos 76, 274; (1974) 22; (1979) 25, 75; (1983) 38, 75–6; (1987) 105, 126
'No Turning Back' group 173
private market research 260
Scottish 62, 129, 229
unpopularity 256
'wets' 115, 240
see also rebels; Tory back-bench MPs
Conservative Party conferences 18, 143, 166, 246, 248, 252
  (1983) 251
  (1984) 45, 46, 88, 250, 251
  (1985) 79–80, 85, 86, 249, 250, 251
  (1986) 100
  (1987) 110, 113, 140, 220, 249
  (1989) 144
  (1990) 167
constitutions:
  federal 241, 270
  unitary 270
  unwritten 3, 7, 225, 304
  written 226
  see also British Constitution
Convention of Scottish Local Authorities 145
Cook, Robin 125
Cooper, Sir Frank 217–18
Coopers and Lybrand 49
Cormack, Patrick 27, 236
Council of Europe 219
council tax 179, 182, 206, 282
  enactment and introduction 230
  launched 176–78
  property-based 296
  transition to 300
  valuation of properties 178
  value-for-money for payers 305
County Council Act (1888) 14
Court of Appeal 159, 165
courts 165, 167, 282
Coventry 27, 125
CPRS (Central Policy Review Staff) 48, 49, 58, 59
Critchley, J. 236
Cromwell, Oliver 14
Crosland, Anthony 22, 24, 211

Crossman, Richard 18, 99 n., 188, 194 n., 208 n.
CSL Consultants Ltd 118, 280
Culpin, Robert 37
Cunningham, Jack 106, 113, 116
Curtice, John 162
Customs and Excise 221
Cutler, Sir Horace 28

Dagenham 148
Daily Mail 32
Daily Telegraph 94, 120, 150, 155
data protection safeguards 128
Davis, Evan 81
Deacon, D. 263
Delors, Jacques 6
democracies 225
demonstrations 133, 135, 262, 297, 298
  see also Trafalgar Square
Denham, Lord 123, 124
Department of Education and Science 37, 98, 164, 195, 198
Department of the Environment 36, 37, 38, 44–6 *passim*, 49, 58, 72, 75, 77, 79, 82, 83, 97, 109, 112, 128, 138–9, 160, 170–2 *passim*, 195, 196, 198–200 *passim*, 202–3, 212, 216, 219, 223, 263, 277–78, 282, 296, 303
  activist officials 217
  consultation paper, *A New Tax for Local Government* 176
  contrast between Treasury practice and 221
  effect of ministerial reshuffles 98
  Heseltine appointed to shake up 26
  introduction of poll tax and council tax 206
  joint agreement to produce notes about community charge 280
  keeping the Treasury at arm's length 195
  LGC chairman in conflict with 181
  local government finance directorate 212
  national statistics 138
  Patten's arrival 146
  political advisers 215
  Portillo appointed to 163
  projections for the size of the first poll tax bills 86

urging an end to dual-running 108
Waldegrave's arrival 207
  see also under Green Papers; Heiser
Department of Health and Social Security 47, 58
Department of Social Security 280
Department of Trade and Industry 195, 232
deregistration 301
devolution 270
Dewar, Donald 104, 130
Dicey, A. V. 188, 267, 268, 303
dictators 189
  see also 'elective dictatorship'
Diggle, Paula 35
discounts 177, 178
Disraeli, Benjamin 189, 247, 295
distributional effects 91, 111
  estimating 86–7
domestic rates 95, 105, 128, 134, 165, 180
  abolition of 22–5, 29, 75, 105, 107
  phasing out 88; gradual move from 86; tapering off over a decade 87
  replacement for 98, 128, 140, 275; average poll tax necessary 73; political difficulties 39; sales tax 25; worked-through plan 85
  unfairness of 35–6
Donoughue, Bernard 201
Douglas-Home, Sir Alec (Lord Home) 79, 189
Downing Street Policy Unit 79, 142, 147
Downs, Anthony 254
Drigg 230
dual-running 100, 109, 110, 111, 112, 125, 140, 143–4, 220, 249, 291
Durham County Council 127
Dyer, C. 12 n.
Dykes, Hugh 114, 115, 117, 236

Ealing 149
East Anglia 12
Eastbourne 168, 256, 294
EC (European Community) 134, 228, 267
  elections (1989) 134, 255
  environmental policy 230
  monetary schemes 98 n.

333

rejection of regional devolution 270
Economist, The 41, 94, 162
Edinburgh 101 n., 132, 133, 151
  Barnton 62–3
  Morningside 63
education funding 78
Edwards, Nicholas 70
'elective dictatorship' 244, 245, 303
electoral systems:
  first-past-the-post 225, 226
  majoritarian 225
  proportional representation 226
  three-party 254
  two-party 225, 254
Elizabeth I, Queen 14
Elizabeth II, Queen 3
Enfield 253
England 61, 129, 137–40, 268, 274, 300
  amount available for preparation costs 118
  attempts to levy a flat-rate poll tax 11
  capping of authorities 43
  collection rates 179
  dual-running 109
  local election turnout 272
  Midlands 111
  North 111
  poll tax figure (1990) 74
  properties with higher values in the south 182
  proposal for reduction in number of councils 19
  rate-capping controlled the spending of every authority 285
  reforms (1989–90) 34
  revaluations 17, 21–2
  riots 149
  South-East 111, 314, 315
  too slow to learn from Scottish experience 217
England and Wales 104, 192, 217, 230, 254, 277
  Bill to abolish domestic rates 107
  deferring revaluation sine die 61
  introduction of poll tax: 4, 91, 162, 180 n.; first year of operation 283; little reaction to 106; run-up to 131–2
  structural reforms (1974) 21

Essex 13, 36
European practice 3
executive power 225
exemptions from poll tax 136, 164, 290, 291

Fabian Society 304
Falconer, Alex 131
Falklands War (1982) 2, 5, 37, 190 n.
federal systems/federalism 217, 268, 270, 271
Felixstowe 98
Fields, Terry 125, 178, 262
Fife 145
Financial Times 31, 69, 93, 132
Finchley 64, 148, 252, 253
First Division Association 215
First World War 268, 288
'flagship' *Poll Tax* 101, 107–12, 113, 155, 161, 179, 243, 245, 253, 261
flat-rate poll tax 78, 112, 115, 118, 166, 234
Fletcher, Alex 103
floating voters 94
Foreign Office 168, 195
Forsyth, Michael 72, 136, 173
Foster, Sir Christopher 32, 57, 58, 66, 77, 95, 96
  'Accountability and Control of Local Spending' (with Jackman, 1982) 54–5, 59, 73
  Local Government Finance in a Unitary State (with Jackman and Perlman) 30–1, 36–7, 49
Fowler, Sir Norman 215
France 221, 258, 270
Franks, Lord 2
Fraser, Sir Hugh 29
Fraser, Sir William Kerr 101–2, 213
Fulton inquiry (1960s) 212, 220

gainers 82, 92, 93, 94, 128, 247
Gallup polls 127, 155
Galtieri, Gen. Leopoldo 191
General Elections 101
  (1974) 22
  (1979) 25 n.
  (1983) 5, 38
  (1987) 104–7, 129, 191
  (1992) 179–80, 301

General Strike (1926) 1
Germany 98 n., 198, 221, 258, 270
Gill, C. 236
Gillingham 149
Gilmour, Sir Ian 114, 123, 235, 236
Gladstone, W. E. 3, 189, 268
Glasgow 135
  Bearsden 64, 69
  Central by-election 134
  Govan by-election 131, 257–8
  Pollok 298
Glasgow University 48, 84, 102
  Applied Population Research Unit
  131
GLC (Greater London Council) 28–9,
  43, 46, 83
  abolition 7, 37, 38, 47, 121, 229
  'Say No to No Say' campaign to save
  41, 44, 95
Glorious Revolution (1688) 267
Golding, P. 263
Goodhart, Sir Philip 114, 236
Goold, Sir James 63–4
Gorst, J. 236
Gould, Bryan 130, 145–6, 148, 156,
  166, 177
government:
  presidential 188, 189, 193
  prime-ministerial 187, 188–96, 200
  unitary and centralized 225
Gow, Ian 168
Gowrie, Lord 80
Grampian TV 136
Grant, M. 43 n.
grants 27, 43, 44, 51, 90, 98, 104, 111,
  137, 141, 163, 297
  block 27, 42, 51, 83, 84
  central 18, 73, 137, 180
  City 73, 81
  cuts in 28, 78
  extra protection 139
  failing system 83, 89
  government 202
  more transparent system 59
  new 139, 140, 227
  reforms to system 65, 90
  settlements 147, 150, 216
  support 26, 137; rate 27, 83, 235,
    236–7; revenue 145, 146, 180
  Treasury 4, 290

see also penalties; targets
Grantham 252, 253
Green Papers:
  (1971) The Future Shape of Local
    Government 20–1, 23, 29, 40, 52
  (1977) Local Government Finance 24,
    25, 27, 40
  (1981) Alternatives to Domestic Rates
    29, 30, 31, 32–5, 39, 40, 45, 49,
    52, 56, 173, 229
  (1986) Paying for Local Government 2,
    81, 85, 86, 87, 88, 89–95, 100, 101,
    111, 176, 191, 192, 218, 220, 229,
    233, 257, 272, 273, 276, 288, 298
Green Party 256
Greenway, H. 236 n.
Greenwich 137, 263 n.
Griffith, J. A. G. 228 n., 239
Grugeon, Sir John 25, 31, 32
Guardian, the 76, 80 n., 86 n., 93,
  134 n., 136 n., 160 n.
Guinea-Bissau 218
Gummer, John 45, 70, 80, 139, 141,
  181, 198

Hackney 149, 165
Hailsham, Lord 122, 187, 248
Hale, Rita 163
Hammersmith and Fulham 158–9
Hampson, Keith 95, 236 n.
Hargreaves, K. 236
Haringey 140, 145, 149
Harris, Robert 155, 286
Hart, Barry 71
Hatton, Derek 7, 44, 198
Havers, Sir Michael 38
Hayhoe, Sir Barney 236
Hazelhurst, A. 236
Heath, Sir Edward 22, 39, 48, 50, 75,
  99 n., 189, 236
  bitter opponent of Thatcher 114,
    235, 241
  funding review (1971) 20
  U-turn 5
Heddle, John 30, 94
Heigham, David 37
Heiser, Sir Terence 31, 35–8 passim,
  42–3, 47, 49, 50, 58, 59, 70–1, 96,
  102, 109, 142, 170, 173, 208–14
  passim

convinced local finance system
  unsustainable 222
defence of block grant, targets and
  penalties 83–4
failure to sound alarm bells at any
  stage 292
keen to see end of 'dual-running' 199
poll tax not possible without total
  engagement of 206–7
succeeded by Wilson 159
Henderson, Barry 103
Hereford and Worcester 140
Heseltine, Michael 62, 101, 120, 210,
  240, 241
abolition of poll tax 176, 181, 198
against rate-capping 38
and Audit Commission 42
combative style 171
council tax 176, 178, 282
defers revaluation in England and
  Wales 61
leadership contest 168, 169, 293–4
opposition to poll tax 5, 30, 109,
  113–14, 170, 236
recent 'conference darling' 250
respect for local government 266, 268
reviews 72, 163–7, 168–73 passim,
  230, 294
Thatcher's remark on draft of 1981
  Green Paper 35
warning to local authorities 26–7
see also Green Papers (1981);
  Westland
Hicks, R. 236
High Court 137, 263 n.
Hillingdon 149
Hirst, Michael 103
Hoffmann, Sir Leonard 48–9, 50, 59,
  60, 65, 97
detailed opinion of poll tax 66–68,
  82, 84, 297
Home Office 78–9, 195, 196, 198, 216
House of Commons:
Clerks at the Table 210
Environment Committee 35, 36, 37,
  228, 233
library 118, 233
Procedure Committee 228
Select Committees 129, 227–33, 270
Standing Committees 88, 114, 115,

117 n., 118, 227–8, 234, 239, 241
see also Parliament
House of Lords 104, 121–5, 173,
  241–3, 297
and abolition of GLC 41, 44
guardian of the Constitution 229
revised committee structure 228
revival of 244–5
Housing and Education Reform bills
  (1988) 239
Hove district council 276
Howard, Michael 110, 118, 119, 207
blame for poll tax disaster from
  Labour 179
capping of authorities 182
council tax implementation 198
defence of unpopular measures
  115–16
efforts to sell community charge 127,
  263
replaced Boyson at D.o.E 109
Howell, R. 236
Howe, Sir Geoffrey (Lord) 39, 143,
  191, 192, 263
resignation speech 168, 243, 294
Hughes, William 136
Humberside 301
Hunt, David 141–4 passim, 147, 160,
  163, 166
Hurd, Douglas 70, 150, 169, 190

ILEA (Inner London Education
  Authority) 32, 140
abolished outright 109 n.
IMF (International Monetary Fund) 5
Incomes 34, 95, 118
bands 91, 93
below-average 290
low 177, 290
modest 157
income tax 25, 55, 72, 78, 119, 180,
  285, 295
banded poll tax related to thresholds
  119
basic rate 55
Independent, the 131 n., 132 n., 134 n.,
  160 n., 200 n.
inflation 21, 137, 141, 158
Ingham, Sir Bernard 168
Inland Revenue 71, 221

inner-city areas 257, 262, 289, 298
Institute of Economic Affairs 262
Institute for Fiscal Studies 81, 82, 97,
    216, 262, 288, 293
Institute of Public Finance 167
IRA (Irish Republican Army) 46, 88,
    168
Ireland 3, 269
    Act of Union (1800) 267
    Home Rule Bills 3, 268
    Northern, Stormont parliament 267
    settlement (1922) 267
IRRV (Institute of Revenues Rating and
    Valuation) 178, 276
Irvine, M. 236
Isle of Wight 165
Italy 258, 270

Jackman, Richard 18 n., 54, 55, 59, 73,
    82
    *Local Government Finance in a
    Unitary State* (with Foster and
    Perlman) 30–1, 36–7, 49
James II, King 267
Jameson, Richard 37
Jenkin, Patrick (Lord) 38–9, 41–7
    passim, 58, 59, 70, 74–6 *passim*, 80,
    171, 195, 214, 218, 251
    and the Hoffman paper 68
    replaced at Environment by Baker
    82, 198
    Tyrie's critical minute to 79
    see also Widdicombe Committee
Jenkins, Roy (Lord) 121, 122
Jenkins, Simon 144–5
Jennings, Sir Ivor 188
Johnson, Lyndon 121
Johnson-Smith, Sir Geoffrey 236
Jones, G. 37 n.
Jones, George 120
Jordan, A. G. 248 n.
Joseph, Sir Keith 197 n.

Kashoggi issue 81, 82
Kennington 152
Kent 12, 140
    County Council 25, 31
King, A. S. 189 n., 201 n.
King, David 96
King, Tom 35, 38
Kinnock, Neil 105–6, 148–9, 256–7

condemnation of begetters of riots
    154
problems with colleagues over non-
    payment 125, 130
underplaying poll tax issue 108, 293
Kirkcaldy 32
Knight, Ted (Red Ted) 7, 65, 106
Knox, D. 236

Labour-controlled authorities 28, 55,
    62, 64, 137, 148, 156, 296
    coalitions 274
    excesses of some 246
    extreme 302
    hatred of proposed tax 279
    high-spending 144, 145
    inner-city areas 52
    leading councillors called for illegal
        action to thwart capping 43
    left-wing 106 n., 293; abuses of 105;
        hard 41, 101
    offering a choice between more
        services or lower rates 27
    profligate 111
    under attack 150
Labour-dominated associations 71
Labour Party 44, 106, 113, 116, 117,
    136, 166, 170, 179, 247, 304
    back-bench MPs 104
    by-election successes 134, 151, 256
    Campaign Group MPs 125
    community charge a 'benevolent
        fund' for 139
    encouraging government to move
        quickly to abolish poll tax 178
    fourth successive defeat 180
    Glasgow 64
    governments 17, 18–19, 24–5, 238,
        275
    Kinnock's new model 256
    leadership 105, 125, 299; enfeeble-
        ment of 298; issues that dogged
        130
    left-wing 131; 'loony' 100, 162, 274,
        299
    local election campaign (1991) 177
    local government image 257
    lukewarm support for anti-poll tax
        rallies 297
    made no running with poll tax as an
        issue 96, 254–5

MPs who had said they would not pay poll tax 154

National Executive Committee 125

poll lead (1990) 154–5

prime cause for the tax being introduced 246

property and income tax 148

Scottish predicament 129, 130

SNP conflict 258

supporters 260

swing against 261

Tories falling significantly behind in polls 138

trade union legislation 238

whips 243

Lambeth 7, 65, 106, 165, 247, 256

Lamont, Norman 143, 173, 200, 204
budget (1991) 24, 175, 177, 178, 285

Lang, Ian 132, 173

Lawson, Nigel (Lord) 4, 38, 49, 70, 71, 82–3, 87, 94, 119, 139, 174, 194, 201–4 *passim*, 206 n., 218, 272–4 *passim*, 285, 297, 298, 303–4
abolition of local taxation 296
anxious to maintain transitional period 199
banded property tax plan 173
brains behind mid-term Thatcherism 273, 304
conference speeches 250–1
criticism of Thatcher 190
dispute with Patten 141, 142, 143, 192
fall-out with Thatcher over exchange rate and European policy 191
fight for dual-running 110, 111
fiscal policy threatened 138
Foster tries to persuade, on virtues of poll tax 66 n.
opposition to poll tax 5, 76–80, 81, 85, 86, 99, 121, 172, 191, 287, 288, 291
privatization and public opinion 57–8
refusal to make pro-poll tax speech 263
'underfunding' 100
view of constitutional set-up 270, 271

Layden, Sir Jack 175

Layfield, Sir Frank (Layfield

Committee report, 1976) 22–3, 24, 25, 29, 50–1, 52, 195

leaks 172, 298

Lee, J. 236

left-wing groups 106 n., 131, 293
extreme 262, 297
hard 41, 101
'loony' 100, 105, 162, 274, 299
militant 43
ultra- 258–9
see also Militant Tendency

legal actions 145, 279

Legge, John 12

legislatures 225, 226

Leigh, Edward 116, 117

Lennox-Boyd, Mark 160

Lester, J. 236

Letwin, Oliver 79, 95

Lewis, David 47

Liaison committee 230

Liberal Democrat Party 116, 122, 170, 179, 247
by-election successes 168, 174
favoured option to poll tax 125, 258
lukewarm support for anti-poll tax rallies 297
opposition to poll tax 258, 260, 279
whips 243

Liberal–SDP Alliance 255, 256, 274

life peerages 243

Lilley, Peter 250

LIT (local income tax) 72, 125, 258, 271–2, 295
banded poll tax tantamount to 119
clear that it was a dead duck 55
dismissed by Thatcher 219–20
favoured by local government 97
Green Paper (1981) consideration 29, 30, 32
rejected 90
transforming the poll tax into 226

Liverpool 43, 65, 247, 256
non-payment percentage 165
Toxteth riots (1981) 26
victory for Militant-dominated council 41
see also Fields; Hatton

Livingstone, Ken 7, 28–9, 46, 82, 198
'Say No to No Say' campaign 41, 44, 95

Lloyd George, David 189, 122
local authorities/government 35, 147,
   167, 246, 265–85, 294, 299–306
   passim
  abolition of 296
  action against 26–7, 29
  associations 43, 145, 157–8
  'autonomy' a persistent irritant 7–8
  burden of 290
  central government and 8, 83, 209
  changes in voting 81
  conferences 26, 86, 98, 148–9
  discredited 302
  dual role 304
  elections 261, 274, 283
  emaciated 183
  growing anarchy 52
  growth of 22
  inner city 55
  intention to cap 156
  Labour's image 257
  means of revitalizing 290
  Militant-dominated 41
  policy documents about 106
  politicization of 274
  reform 47
  shambles of Tories' policy towards
     199
  spending 24, 54, 74, 95; controlled
     by capping, every authority in
     England 285; foolproof system of
     limiting 38; high 54, 76, 78, 85,
     124–5, 144, 145; low, mostly Tory
     145; Scottish 216 n.; penalized 54;
     Thatcher government determined
     to reduce 25–6
  stable and just basis for development
     of 171
  strongly in favour of retention of
     rates 35
  structure 46, 176; two-tier 51
  supervision of 212
  taxation 24
  Thatcher's distaste for/hostility to
     89, 295
  Tories' decision to home in on
     Labour's record 105
  Tory-controlled 143, 144, 148,
     161
  Tory hostility to very idea 203

  voice of, in Whitehall 202–3
  wholesale restructuring 172
  see also accountability; CCLGF;
     GLC; Labour-controlled
     authorities; local government
     finance
local education authorities 304
Local Government Chronicle 97, 141,
   259
Local Government Commission 42,
   181, 301
local government finance 82, 89, 151,
   178, 207, 220, 229, 296
  central interference with 246
  definitive analysis of problems 22–3
  draft bill to reform 98
  grants 26, 28, 73, 137, 139, 141, 180
  growth of, within the national
     economy 219
  inadequacies of the existing system
     72–3
  new arrangements for 107–9
  review of 76, 84, 88
  rise in central support 139
Local Government Finance Act (1988)
   146, 227, 239, 279
Local Government Finance Bill (1987)
   112, 113, 115, 122, 125, 179, 228,
   233, 239, 242, 280
Local Government Finance and
   Valuation Bill (1991) 178
*Local Government Finance in a Unitary
   State* (Foster, Jackman, and
   Perlman) 30–1, 36–7, 49
local taxation 39, 176–9 *passim*, 202,
   214, 219, 282, 285
  abolition 265, 296
  bills 138, 253
  burden 24, 73, 109, 283
  complexities 212
  controversies 226
  reform 21, 33
  share of 23
  see also council tax; LIT; property
     tax; sales tax
London 12, 15, 34, 56, 61, 160–1, 167,
   258, 280
  anti-poll tax marches 151
  Capital Hotel, Knightsbridge 59, 60,
     65, 66, 73, 84, 196, 216

City registration rate 146
electoral performance by incumbent councils 283
gains and losses 157, 314, 315
inner 292; dual-running 112; high-spending authorities 78; new grants for authorities 139, 140
Labour powerless in 129
leading Labour councillors called for illegal action to thwart capping 43
longer period of transition for 109
'loony' authorities 162
Metropolitan Police 152
see also GLC; ILEA; Trafalgar Square; also under various borough names
Long Parliament 13
Longden, Howard 276
'loony left' 100, 105, 162, 274, 299
losers/losses 82, 92–4 passim, 127, 139, 140, 143, 145, 157, 296
change to benefit system to reduce number of 151
household type and income level 314, 315
relief to minimize the number of 163, 182, 221
scale of 141, 257, 290, 293
Low, Sidney 273
Low Pay Unit 262
LSE (London School of Economics) 30, 49, 82

Maastricht Treaty (1991) 124 n., 237–38
McGinn, Janette 134
McGoldrick, Maureen 106
MacGregor, John 85, 160, 164
MacIntosh, Andrew 28
McKinsey's 42
Macmillan, Harold (Lord Stockton) 17, 197 n.
McNeilage, George 131
Maidenhead 149
Major, John 2, 100, 119, 120, 147, 150–1, 172–4 passim, 193, 198, 200, 240, 287, 300
capping issue 159, 164
credit for having got rid of poll tax 175, 179, 301

elected leader of Conservative party 169–70
Maastricht treaty 238
'weak' camp of Prime Ministers 189
Malone, Gerry 103, 110–11, 140, 144, 249
Manchester 140
Mandelson, Peter 105, 106, 256
marginal voters/seats 140, 259
'marginality' 60
Mason, Douglas 32, 72, 177
Mates, Michael 108, 114, 236, 237, 241, 264
poll tax amendment 118–21, 163, 226, 233–4, 235, 291, 297
Maud Committee on the Management of Local Government (1976) 274 n.
Maudling, Reginald 250
Maxwell-Hyslop, R. 236
Mayer, Sir Anthony 47–50 passim, 59, 71, 74, 95, 212, 236
Mendès-France, Pierre 174
Merseyside 26
metropolitan counties/districts 38, 280
Mid-Staffordshire 30, 151, 256
Militant Tendency 129, 130, 134, 149, 259, 262
council dominated by 41
MPs leaning towards 125
Scottish 131
Mill, J. S. 267–8
Mills, John 142, 159
ministerial turnover 196–200, 292
Ministry of Agriculture 195
Ministry of Housing and Local Government 212
Miscampbell, Norman 36
Mitterrand, François 270
Mole Valley 148
'Money Bills' 122
Monro, Sir Hector 136
Montgomery, Fergus 36
MORI polls 134, 259
Morley, John 188–9
Morrison, Sir Charles 25, 236
Moseley, Sir George 59, 213
Mount, Ferdinand 150, 303 n.

NAO (National Audit Office) 83
National Council for Civil Liberties 128

National Curriculum 98
National Union (1870) 252
Nationalists 106, 245
  see also SNP; Wales
Nellist, Dave 125, 154 n.
new professionalism 209–18
New Zealand 225–6, 275
Next Steps programme (1988) 210, 213,
  214
non-domestic rates 73, 305
  abolition 304
  contributions 54
  distribution 14
  national (NNDR) 159–60, 166
  nationalization 77, 285
  redistribution 137
  reforms 59, 90, 285
non-metropolitan areas 176, 280
non-payment 125, 130–1, 135, 145,
  178, 262, 298
  campaigns 279
  cases to court 167
  chasing up 291
  English, first court appearances 165
  internal disputes about the legitimacy
    of 258
  repeated news stories about 294
NOP polls 141, 259, 260
Norris, Steven 101
Northcote–Trevelyan Report 209
Northumberland, Earl of 14
Norwich 149

Observer, the 191
Office of Population Censuses and
  Surveys 146
Ogilvy and Mather 263
Onslow, Cranley 169
opinion polls 154–5, 259, 281
  Labour trouncing the Tories in
    256
  unpopularity 253
opposition parties 253–9, 274, 298–9,
  303
  feebleness of, to the poll tax 293
  see also Labour Party; Liberal
    Democrat Party; SNP
Orgreave riots (1984–5) 154
Orkney 132
Osborn, Derek 170

Owen, David (Lord) 120, 255
Owen, Peter 47, 50, 58, 59, 79, 83–4,
  212

Palmerston, Lord 207
Papua New Guinea 218
Paris 258, 270
  Summit (1990) 169, 295
Parliament 224–5
  House of Commons 233–41
  rubber stamp 303
  sovereignty of 188, 267, 268, 305
  see also House of Commons; House
    of Lords
Patten, Chris 139, 141–4, 151, 155,
  166, 177–9, 210, 292
  average £278 poll tax 145–9
  capping issues 158–9, 164
  constituency protests 160
  dispute over funding between
    Lawson and 192
  local election campaign (1990) 156
  objective to keep poll tax below £400
    level 165
  on unpopularity of the poll tax 1, 4
  public relations skills 198
  relief scheme 251
Pawsey, James 29, 236
Peacock, Elizabeth 236
Pearce, Edward 41, 168, 213 n.
Peasants' Revolt (1381) 11, 12–13
penalties 27, 28, 54, 133
  cumbersome system 38, 42, 222
  defence of 83–4
  discussions about future of 43
  hope to end crisis over 58
Pendle 145
Penman, Ian 102
pensioners 54, 114, 144, 156, 157
  aggrieved 53
  couples 77
  living in low-rated properties 143
  old ladies 52, 63, 64, 175
  single 53, 78
Perlman, Morris:
  *Local Government Finance in a
    Unitary State* (with Foster and
    Jackman) 30–1, 36–7, 49
'personal charge' 66
personal identification numbers 127

Perth conference (1985) 79–80, 249, 250, 251
Pirie, Madsen 32
Police and Criminal Evidence Bill (1984) 301
Police Record 262 n.
Policy Studies Institute 131–2
poll tax 11–69
  abolition 142, 163, 176, 177, 180, 198; last days 178–9; outright 168; unavoidable 289
  banded 119, 226, 290, 297
  bills 12 n., 157–8, 178
  birth of 70–87, 211
  blame for 179, 286–9
  collapse 154–83, 211, 230; reasons for 289
  collection 78, 179, 181, 182, 281, 289
  costs of 180
  enactment 12 n., 88–125
  evolution 202, 208, 214, 249
  implementation 103, 126–53, 249, 262, 278, 292–3; impact on Retail Price Index 149; per cent of the electorate opposing 141; riots 149–54
  redistributive consequences 279
  reviews 156–7, 168, 169, 170–5, 230
Poor Law (1601) 90, 275
Portillo, Michael 163–4, 165, 173, 253
  counter-attack against poll tax opponents 167, 168
Post Office 281
Price Waterhouse 278–9
privatization 49, 57–8
Property Services Agency 230
property tax 55, 60, 85, 93, 113, 125, 174, 219, 258
  allied to personal charges 172
  banded 173, 174, 175, 176–7, 178, 296
  decision to return to 230
  flat-rate supplement to 178
  Green Paper (1981) consideration 29, 30
  modernized 73, 86, 300
proportional representation 226
Public Accounts Committee 83
public opinion 246–64
Pym, Lord 123

quangos 285, 305

racist conduct 106 n.
Raffan, Keith 115
Raison, Sir Timothy 114, 236
rate-capping 38, 39, 41, 44–5, 54, 76, 106, 151, 156, 158–60, 177, 227, 246, 296
  all authorities 164–5
  controlled the spending of every authority in England 85, 285
  end to 272
  illegal action to thwart 43
  universal 301, 304
rate support grant 27, 83, 235, 236–7
rateable values:
  highest 257
  low 81, 140, 143, 253
  Scottish households 62
ratepayers 52
rates/rating system 72, 75, 91, 99, 142, 291
  abolition 52, 86, 110, 123, 181; immediate 249; impossibility of 76; no commitment to 76; promise 74
  alternatives to 57, 72, 81, 103; quickie review of 195; plausible 287; workable 40
  bills 159–60; huge relative increases 62–3; large 53; low 166
  business, nationalization of 301
  discontent 14–20, 252, 293
  Labour's alternative ('fair rates plans', 1990) 130, 166, 177
  limitation 37–8
  local authorities strongly in favour of retention 35
  marginal shifts in the burden 62
  origins 90
  perceived unfairness 52
  property-based, abolition of 247
  reform 20–2, 34, 78; failure to bring about 101 n.; problem of 89
  replacing 79–80, 126, 286; new tax 249; schemes 275
  see also domestic rates; dual-running; non-domestic rates; rebates; revaluations; uniform business rate
Rates Act (1984) 40

Rathbone, T. 236
Rating and Valuation Association 31, 97
Rating System (Abolition) Bill (1981) 29
rebates 52, 53, 91, 119, 136, 147, 157,
    159, 164, 261, 273
  disabled people 124
  full 81, 177, 273
  pensioners unable to claim 54
  poor people 74
  students 144; nursing 124
rebels (Tory) 121, 146, 148, 236–7,
    239, 240, 297
  bitter opponents of Thatcher 235
  co-operation between and resolution
    among 241
  gentlemanly 112–18
recession 28
Redcliffe-Maud Commission (1969)
    19–20, 21, 216
redistribution 12, 61, 63, 137, 279
Redwood, John 79
Rees, Peter 70, 71, 75, 76, 77
referendums 27, 46, 124 n., 225, 226,
    296
'refuseniks' 135–42
registration 75, 131, 146, 181, 281
  non- 130, 132, 167
relief 164, 221, 251
  see also transitional relief
Renton, Timothy 121
'resident's charge' 66
revaluations 17, 21–2, 60, 159–60, 166
  Scotland (1984–5) 59, 61, 74, 129;
    degree of grassroots hostility to
    250; disastrous 249; political storm
    over 287; politically perilous 295
Rhodes James, Robert 94
Rhys-Williams, Sir Brandon 115,
    116–17
Ribble Valley, Lancashire 173, 174,
    255 n., 256
Richard II, King 11
Riddell, Peter 5 n., 69, 199, 295, 298
Riddick, G. 236
Ridley, Nicholas (Lord) 4, 45, 82 n.,
    88, 98–101, 108–15 passim; 117,
    122, 128, 138–42 passim, 146, 158,
    160, 165, 174, 190, 198–200 passim,
    203, 206, 210, 220, 249, 266, 275,
    292–3

Centre for Policy Studies pamphlet
    99, 148
  defence of poll tax 172
  Mates amendment 118, 119, 120
  next to no resistance to capping 272
  publicity campaign for the poll tax
    137
Rifkind, Malcolm 101–3 passim, 129,
    131–3 passim, 136, 207
right-wing pressure groups 72
  see also think-tanks
Rippon, Geoffrey (Lord) 39
Robertson, John Home 103
Rooker, Jeff 116
Rose, Richard 196
Rossi, Sir Hugh 230–1
Rothschild, Lord 48–50 passim, 57, 59,
    66–8, 70, 84–5, 95–6, 288
Rothschild (N. M.) 95, 212
RPI (Retail Price Index) 149
Russell, Earl 12 n.
Russia 120
Rutter, Jill 47, 50, 59, 71
Ryan, Alan 155

safety-net scheme 111, 137, 142–4, 147,
    158, 166
  freezing of receipts 163
  introduction 87
  rules 139
St Andrews University 32, 72
sales tax 55, 90, 295
  Green Paper (1981) consideration
    29–30, 32
  supported then dismissed by
    Thatcher 25, 30, 56, 72, 75, 219–20
Salisbury, Lord 14–15, 126, 189, 247
Sandys, Duncan 197 n.
Scarborough 26
Scargill, Arthur 5, 44, 191
Scotland 85, 91, 106, 127, 129–36, 178,
    186, 192, 195, 217, 256, 277
  Bill (1986) to introduce poll tax
    102–3, 104, 229–30, 291
  'can't pay, won't pay' campaign 149
  Conservative party 62, 129, 229
  decline in Conservative fortunes in 136
  devolution 269, 270
  draft bill to reform local government
    finance 98, 101

dual-running abandoned 109
English union with (1707) 3, 267
financial implications of establishing
    poll tax 118
gains and losses by household type
    and income level 216, 314, 315
government's failure to extend
    concession 151
Labour's predicament 129, 130
legal action against non-payers 145
Nationalist revival 245
poll tax levels 132, 133
rating revaluation (1984–5) 39, 46,
    61–5, 99 n., 250, 287, 295, 296
reforms (1989–90) 34
regions 280; districts and islands
    160; Grampian 134, 145; Lothian
    134, 135; Strathclyde 64, 134,
    135–6
structural reforms (1975) 21
Thatcher's ignorance of 61–2
Tories' last two European seats 134
Tory rout in 1987 election 129, 229
unpaid poll tax 179
see also Aberdeen; Edinburgh;
    Forsyth; Glasgow; Lang; Malone;
    Rifkind; Scottish Office; SNP;
    Whitelaw; Younger
Scotsman, The 63 n., 80 n., 125 n.,
    134 n., 135 n., 151 n.
Scottish Office 195–6, 213
    see also Ancram; Younger
SDP (Social Democratic Party) 212,
    243 n.
    Liberal Alliance 255, 256, 274
Second World War 1
Select Committees 227–33
    Civil Service 270
    Scottish affairs 129, 228, 229
    Welsh affairs 228, 229
Shepherd, Richard 192, 236
Sheridan, Tommy and Lynn 131
sheriffs' officers 135
Shore, Peter 24, 27
Sillars, Jim 131
single adults 177, 178
Smith, Adam 11
Smith, Sir Dudley 236
Smith, John (D.o.E. official) 47
Smith, John (shadow Chancellor/later

Labour leader) 166
Smith, Thomas 14
SNP (Scottish National Party) 125,
    129, 130, 131, 134
    Labour's loss of Govan by-election to
    257–8
Soames, Nicholas 116, 123 n.
Social and Liberal Democrats 255
social security 81, 167
Socialist Worker 259
Speed, Keith 25, 31
Sports Council 229, 230
Squire, Robin 36, 146, 237
Standing Committees 89, 114, 115,
    117 n., 118, 227–8, 234, 239, 241
Stevas, Norman St John (Lord St John
    of Fawsley) 123 n., 196, 228, 244
Stewart, Allan 72
Stirling University 96
Strathclyde University 162
Straw, Jack 106
students 94, 119
    nursing 163
subsidies 144–5
Suez 180
Summerton, Neil 96
Sun 123
Sunday Times 76, 134–5, 144, 286
supplements 56, 57, 177
Surrey 56, 148

Tapsell, Sir Peter 235, 237
targets 27, 38, 42, 43, 54, 222, 246
    defence of 83–4
    hope to end crisis over 58
taxes/taxation 14, 117, 221–2, 224–5
    banded 108
    desire to avoid 13
    mixed option 66
    per capita 32, 60, 206, 219, 222, 252
    personal 78
    phased 290, 291
    property-based 171, 182, 296
    reform of 20, 78
    roof 148
    untried or rejected 218
    see also income tax; local taxation
Taylor, Matthew 116
Taylor, Sir Teddy 29
Tebbit, Norman (Lord) 106, 173

Temple-Morris, Peter 29, 237
Thamesdown 149
Thatcher, Margaret (Baroness) 4, 5, 11,
14, 46, 48, 53, 54, 58, 63–4, 68,
69, 80, 100, 114, 123, 143, 146,
152, 157, 167, 183, 187, 191, 198,
200–7 passim, 210, 217, 220 n.,
228, 231, 234, 235, 241, 249, 265,
268, 270, 279, 289–92 passim, 303
abolition of GLC 7, 38, 95
agitated at hostility to Scottish
revaluation 250
capping of local authorities 156, 164
commitment to abolish rates 22, 275
condemnation of begetters of riots
154
confronting militant left and miners
43–4
conviction that the median voter
supported poll tax 254
convinced by the work of Baker,
Waldegrave, and their quasi-think-
tank 76
council referendum plans 27
dedicated to cutting income tax 55
determined government 8
distaste for/hostility to local government 89, 271, 295
'divide and rule' tactics 190
downfall 1, 168–70, 192, 266; role of
'wets' in 240
Finchley constituency 64, 148, 252,
253
hostility to royal commissions and
quasi-independent committees of
inquiry 195
ignorance of Scottish policies 61–2
informal pep talk to councillors 98
'instinctive antennae' 246, 253
Lawson's criticism of 190
leadership contest (1990) 142, 163,
168, 169, 293–4, 295; 'constitutionally unassailable' 244; reasons for
loss 153, 190
local income tax dismissed 219–20
Maastricht Treaty referendum 124 n.
most significant rebellion against
120
no intention of caving into pressure
for a U-turn 162

nod-and-wink code of ministers
under 121
observed proprieties of Cabinet
Government 193
persuaded about virtues of the poll
tax 252–3
proposal to move to single-tier
authorities rejected 74
regard for Heiser 211
remark on draft of 1981 Green Paper
35
resignation 138, 169, 170
sales tax supported and dismissed 25,
30, 56, 72, 75, 219–20
self-styled radical administration 40
strained relations with senior
colleagues 191
style of leadership 155, 168, 189, 295
wanted a foolproof system of limiting
local authority spending 38
'worried' by declining Conservative
fortunes in Scotland 136
would not hear of a banded poll tax
119
see also 'flagship' Poll Tax
Thatcherism 1, 6, 7, 145
enemies of 266
later 100
mid-term 273, 304
one of the legacies of 305–6
third wave of 5
think-tanks 31–2, 48, 49, 58, 76, 172,
262
Times, The 93, 122, 136, 163, 170,
217–18
Tory back-bench MPs 97, 104, 110,
117–18, 120, 138, 144, 160, 235,
253
anxiety about Thatcher's style of
leadership 168, 256
dissent 243
Home Affairs Committee 120
Lawson's personal following 203
1922 Committee 107, 119, 120, 169
opposition to poll tax 112–13, 114,
164, 234, 237–8; 'in open revolt'
136; outright, from senior
members 109
pressure from 35
recalcitrant 141

Townsend, C. 237
Trafalgar Square demonstrations (1990)
 130, 152–3, 154, 156, 259, 262, 297
transitional period 104, 290, 293
 arrangements 109–10, 111, 192, 193,
 199
 relief scheme 132, 142–4, 163, 166,
 182
 see also dual-running
Treasury 55, 138, 139, 142–3, 159, 160,
 173–4, 195, 196
 chronic indecision 174
 contrast between D.o.E in evolution
 of tax policy 221
 Customs and Excise and 222
 formulations of tax changes by 220
 grants 4, 290
 involvement in Waldegrave–Baker
 studies 47, 58
 Number Ten and 200–5
 poll tax adopted and implemented in
 defiance of 188
 rush to devise concession, forgetting
 Scotland 151
 see also Brittan; Burns; Lawson;
 Major; Turnbull
Turnbull, Frank 17
twenty per cent rule 20, 81, 290, 291
Tyler, Wat 12
Tyrie, Andrew 79, 218

unemployment 28, 55
uniform business rate 111, 227
United States 150, 244, 270, 275
U-turns 5, 162

Vansittart, Lord 206
VAT (value-added tax) 24, 175, 180,
 193, 285
Victorian era 267, 268, 269
Volcker, Paul 150

Waddington, David (Lord) 118, 120,
 154, 160, 173
Wade, Sir William 122
Wakeham, John (Lord) 193–4, 196
Waldegrave, Sir Richard 13
Waldegrave, William 5, 52, 58, 59, 64,
 68, 70, 73–8 passim, 82, 88, 193,
 194, 210, 214, 220, 276, 283–4

acceptance (1994) that the poll tax
 was a 'mistake'/apologia 172–3,
 287–8, 302
blame for poll tax disaster from
 Labour 179
brainstorming sessions 51, 215
capacity to think the unthinkable 57
chief instigator of poll tax 13, 66
exculpation of civil service for any
 blame 223–4
grasp of complexities 207
Waldegrave–Baker Studies 46–8, 77,
 81, 84, 99, 126, 141, 199, 206, 272,
 286–7, 296–7; recommendations
 250; reunion celebration 95
Walden, George 290–1
Wales 144, 178, 195, 269, 277
 creation of parliament 268
 gains and losses by household type
 and income level 314, 315
 Nationalist revival 245
 reforms (1989–90) 34
 see also England and Wales; Welsh
 Office
Walker, Peter 20, 29, 160
Wall Street Journal 150
Walpole, Sir Robert 188
Wandsworth 100, 140, 150, 161, 163,
 261
War Crimes Bill (1989) 229
Ward, John 215
warrants 135
Wells, B. 237
Welsh Office 74, 280
Wembley 98
West Oxfordshire 150, 261, 264
Westland affair (1986) 95, 165, 191, 298
 Heseltine's resignation 87, 88, 303
Westminster (borough) 150, 152, 161,
 163, 261
'wets' 48, 115, 119, 240
White Papers:
 (1983) Rates 36, 38, 45, 90
 (1993) Next Steps Agencies in
 Government 214 n.
Whitehead, Christine 82
Whitelaw, William, Lord 68–9, 70, 72,
 79, 102, 104, 123, 124
 agitated at hostility to Scottish
 revaluation 64, 250, 287

Whitelaw, William, Lord (*cont.*):
  among the most insistent advocates of
    the poll tax 193
  desperate for plausible alternative to
    rates 287
  Scottish furore heightened by
    Glasgow visit 64
  Thatcher careful to conciliate, on key
    decisions 191
Widdicombe Committee (1985) 272,
  273, 274, 275, 285
widows 52, 53, 156
Wiggin, Sir J. 237
Wildlife and Countryside Act 1981 229,
  230
Willetts, David 78
Wilson, Harold (Lord) 17, 22, 191,
  194, 196, 215
Wilson, Richard 142, 159
Wilson, Tom 48, 50, 59, 60, 66, 67–8,
  84, 226 n.

Winchester 61
worst-affected groups 143, 216

Yeo, T. 237
Young, Sir George 120–1
  opposition to poll tax 109, 112,
    114–18 *passim*, 123, 146, 233–4,
    237, 239, 240, 242, 264
Young, Lord 70, 211
Young, Robin 171–2, 173, 174, 214
Younger, George 59, 61–2, 64, 70, 72,
  74, 79, 80, 85, 101–4 *passim*, 129,
  249, 251, 295
  agitated at hostility to Scottish
    revaluation 250, 287
  blamed for effects of redistribution
    63
  'hell-bent' to have the poll tax
    introduced into Scotland as early
    as possible 193
  support for local income tax 55